Truth's Bright Embrace

Essays and Poems in Honor of Arthur O. Roberts

TRUTH'S BRIGHT EMBRACE

Essays and Poems in Honor of Arthur O. Roberts

*To a wonderful friend
and wise historian!*

edited by
Paul N. Anderson
and Howard R. Macy

*To Lee Nash,
with great appreciation
and affection.*

𝓕

George Fox University Press
Newberg, Oregon

e.media, inc., and George Fox University Press are pleased to produce *Truth's Bright Embrace* using on demand manufacturing methods. The cover was composed in Macromedia Freehand and was produced on an Indigo E-Print 1000 Digital Offset Color press. The text is set in Adobe Janson, composed in Adobe Framemaker and produced on a Xerox DocuTech. Special thanks to Darren Gilroy.

For more information on these book production methods contact:

e.media, inc.
906 N.W. 14th Avenue
Portland, OR 97209
(503) 223-5226

e.media, inc.

Truth's bright embrace : essays and poems in honor of Arthur O.
   Roberts / edited by Paul N. Anderson and Howard R. Macy.
      p. cm.
      Includes bibliographical references.
      ISBN 0-9653474-0-0 (hardcover)
      ISBN 0-9653474-1-9 (paperback)

   1. Society of Friends--History. 2. Society of Friends--
Doctrines. 3. Society of Friends--Poetry. 4. Society of Friends--
Influence. 5. Roberts, Arthur O.   I. Roberts, Arthur O. II.
Anderson, Paul (Paul Norman) III. Macy, Howard R. IV. Title:
Essays and poems in honor of Arthur O. Roberts.

BX7615.T78 1996   289.6
                                             QBI96-40121

Library of Congress Catalog Card Number: 96-77537

Contents

WORD AND WORLD

THE PUBLIC ARENA

Preface

This festschrift volume's title, *Truth's Bright Embrace*, echoes Arthur Roberts' Quaker heritage and, more importantly, his life. In personal integrity and public witness, Arthur has embraced and been embraced by truth. He has also, as he reports, been "drawn by the Light" and felt showered by its brilliance. The Light streams through the prism of Arthur's life, and its splendor draws us, as well.

The variety of topics and forms in this collection witness to Arthur's own wide range of interests and contributions. Trained in church history, his teaching responsibilities and personal interests drew him also into biblical studies, philosophy, Quaker history and interpretation, and much more. His contributions have come in books, articles, lectures, poems, sermons, musicals, and art, especially in wood. This volume's cover design draws on a portion of Arthur's black walnut sculpture on display in the Religious Studies Department at George Fox University. He describes this sculpture in *Drawn by the Light* as "depicting seed and flame, symbolic of birth by the Spirit" (p. 171).

We thank each the twenty-four contributors for their splendid work here. They are all former students of and/or colleagues with Arthur in various enterprises—the church, the academic community, the Quaker community, and public service. Their eagerness to collaborate in this work testifies again to Arthur's faithful service. The list of contributors at the end of the book contains personal reflections that say more of his work and influence.

Thanks is due as well to several individuals who helped bring this volume to completion. Katie Bartlett, Sandy Maurer, and Shannon Smith each helped in numerous ways, especially to bring order to the flow of manuscripts and electronic files. Darwin Melnyk of e.media, inc. generously guided us through all stages of production, including his designing the book cover. His experience and creativity in publishing have been invaluable.

We are also grateful to Edward F. Stevens, President of George Fox University, who supported this collection of essays as the inaugural volume from George Fox University Press. His appreciation of Arthur Roberts, his confidence in this project, and his vision for the potential of George Fox University Press have made this work possible.

As editors and contributors, this collection is a way of thanking Arthur and celebrating what he means to us. We hope you as a reader will join us in that. We also hope you will enjoy the contribution these essays and poems make to our common life.

Paul N. Anderson
Howard R. Macy

"Thank You, Arthur!"

You have led us by example,
you have encouraged us with timely words and deeds,
you have taught us in and outside the classroom
to be seekers of Truth and minders of the Light.
Thank you for your faithfulness.
Thank you for your courage.
The work of Christ is furthered through your endeavors,
and ministries of the Holy Spirit are carried out
through your energies.
From you we learn to be seekers of peace—as well as of holiness,
to be stewards of creation—
as well as builders of the new Gospel Order,
to be comforters of the disturbed—
as well as disturbers of the comfortable.
From you we learn to attend, discern and do the work of God.

We thank you, Arthur, as we thank God,
for your exemplary service and steadfast witness.
They inspire us to be stewards of the Truth ourselves,
and to offer our lives in service to humanity as a spiritual vocation.
We have written and gathered these essays
as a small way of saying "thank you"
in some of the same coin with which you have enriched our lives
—the written word—
and yet the real mark of gratitude
always comes into being through more incarnated ways,

which these essays represent, and we hope effect.
They reflect our embracing truth
inspired by the bright radiance of your witness,
and their writing and reading alike declare in polyphonic unison:
"Thank you, Arthur!"

As his readable and inspiring autobiography explains,[1] Arthur Roberts was raised in the Quaker community of Greenleaf, Idaho and received his formal education at Greenleaf Friends Academy, Pacific (George Fox) College, Nazarene Theological Seminary, and Harvard and Boston Universities. Arthur served as pastor of Everett and Kansas City Friends Churches, helped to start the Friends Church in Tigard, Oregon and has given much support as an elder or a pastoral team member to North Valley, Reedwood, Newberg and other Friends Churches along the way.

He also has contributed significantly to Northwest Yearly Meeting, serving on or clerking many of its boards, including participation on the Board of Elders, always providing directional guidance at crucial times. From 1985-1987 he helped the yearly meeting rewrite its Discipline (coinciding with the centenary anniversary of the Richmond Declaration of Faith), producing one of the finest expressions of evangelical Quaker faith and practice available today. He edited *Concern* magazine, the journal of the Association of Evangelical Friends,[2] participated in the Faith and Life movement during the 1970's and now serves ably as Editor of *Quaker Religious Thought*. Arthur has written many articles and books, and these are listed in the bibliography below.

Most of us associate Arthur Roberts, however, with George Fox College—the place he taught and wrote for nearly half a century.[3] While Pacific College had many fine instructors, Arthur helped the college raise its standards academically, and he prepared his students to be effective in service

---

1. *Drawn by the Light: Autobiographical Reflections of Arthur O. Roberts*, Newberg: Barclay Press, 1993. Far more is contained in that book than can included in this brief introduction to Arthur's life and service, and the reader is highly encouraged to read it.

2. Arthur was the editor of *Concern* magazine during the duration of the existence of the Association of Evangelical Friends (1947-1970) and wrote its history in *The Association of Evangelical Friends: A Story of Quaker Renewal in the Twentieth Century*, Newberg: Barclay Press, 1975.

3. Arthur began teaching at George Fox College immediately after completing his Ph.D. program at Boston University in 1953. While he retired from regular teaching in 1988, he continues as Professor at Large, visiting the campus several times a semester, speaking for Quaker Heritage Week and providing guidance and encouragement as needed. From 1968-1972 he served as Academic Dean, and for most of his tenure he chaired the Department of Religious Studies. Ralph Beebe comments on Arthur's coming to GFC, "A brilliant scholar who became an internationally heralded Quaker thinker, Roberts provided stability and a deep Friends conscience." (*A Heritage to Honor, a Future to Fulfill: George Fox College 1891-1991*, Newberg: Barclay Press, 1991, p.71).

and to attend the finest graduate schools in the land. Arthur was also instrumental in suggesting the name George Fox College when a name change
was considered in the late 1940's. By pointing to the founder of the Quaker
movement this new name for the college became the hallmark of a new
institutional identity, signaling commitments to spiritual renewal and social
impact commensurate with Friends' rich heritage.

On personal levels, Arthur encouraged students individually, helping
each to develop gifts of thought and expression. Such well-known Quaker
writers and leaders as Richard Foster, Howard Macy, Chuck Mylander,
Ralph Beebe, Lon Fendall, Nancy Thomas, Daniel Smith-Christopher and
many others have been mentored by Arthur personally. He and his wife
Fern held Bible studies for students in their home for many years. Arthur
founded "Samuel School" —a way of encouraging young Friends leaders
(pre-high school) to listen as did young Samuel for the divine voice calling
them into the service of God. He has inspired us all to communicate effectively, think clearly, pray fervently and live prophetically.

Arthur has helped us see that every significant and enduring movement
must be understood on a foundational, philosophic level. Not the sort of
thing a typical undergraduate student would warm to ahead of time, but
absolutely the stuff of enduring leadership once it is grasped. Because of
Arthur's combined interests in philosophy, church history, Quaker faith and
practice, personal righteousness and social justice, these important fields
become seared on the hearts and minds of all those who know him and are
taught by him. In all of this Arthur's life has been characterized by seeking,
discerning and minding Truth. The following essays group themselves
accordingly, but so does his life.

1. *Truth Revealed in Scripture:* As a teacher of Bible and as a public
speaker, Arthur has interpreted the Scriptures dynamically. He insists the
interpreter stay true to the text, and at the same time helps us apply biblical
meanings to our existence. As a philosopher and theologian, Arthur invites
us consider what it means for Christ to be the *Logos:* the Word of God made
flesh (John 1:1-18). He even presented a paper to philosophers in the Soviet
Union on the theme that Christ the *Logos* should be considered the center
of moral ideology, pointing a way forward in an era threatened by moral rel-
ativism and nuclear holocaust.[4] On another occasion Lee Nash recalls
Arthur at the very beginning of his teaching career standing and challenging

---

4. Having attended the 1985 St. Louis meeting of International Philosophers for the
Prevention of Nuclear War, Arthur also met with Russian philosophers in Moscow during June
1989 and again presented a paper. His essay, "Good and Evil in a World Threatened by
Nuclear Omnicide," developed the thesis that, "every culture and ideology has a moral center,
which for the Christian word is the *logos*, the revealed 'word' from God, and that these moral
centers can be appealed to in finding mutual peace." (*Drawn by the Light*, p.210; cf. pp.185-186
and 207-212). This paper illustrates the way Arthur's interpretation of Scripture and his spiritual convictions transcend personal issues to include global ones as well.

one of the Northwest's leading holiness figures on the pivotal text from Hebrews 12:14: "Pursue peace with all men, and holiness, without which no man shall see the Lord."[5] This speaker had emphasized the personal aspects of holiness but had failed to even acknowledge the clear emphasis on peace within the biblical text he was using. Likewise, Arthur never let his students escape the Sermon on the Mount and its implications for Christian living, or the message of the Old Testament prophets. He often said things like, "It is not only we who examine the Scriptures, but the Scriptures also 'examine' our lives and convict us toward the righteousness of God."

   2. *Truth Displayed in History:* As a historian, Arthur embodies the conviction that the genuine renewal of any movement hinges upon recovering the best from its earliest chapters and applying it meaningfully in later settings. The water is always purest at its source. For Christians this means taking the teachings and leadership of Jesus Christ seriously. For Friends it implies taking a good look at Fox, Barclay, Pennington and Penn, among others, and asking how their discoveries and convictions ought to be applied today. Arthur's first book[6] carried with it not only a narration of historical events in the life and experience of Fox, but it also made connections for the present reader designed to lead him or her into the same quality of transforming experience as those of the Quaker founder. In 1973 Arthur Roberts and Hugh Barbour published a highly significant collection entitled *Early Quaker Writings.*[7] This collection and many essays written for *Quaker Religious Thought*, the Faith and Life movement, and other settings have made Arthur's contribution to Quaker historiography one of the most significant in America—certainly among evangelical Friends. One of his most notable (and overlooked) historical contributions is the narrative history of the Quaker movement among Alaskan Eskimos.[8] In this book one detects Arthur's great sensitivity to nuance and his creative ability to identify the workings of Christ across cultures as well as time.

   3. *Truth Interpreted Among Friends:* Sound historiography leads to sound interpretation. A significant result of Arthur's work on George Fox was to

---

   5. Lee Nash (interview, March 1996) recalls that while the speaker rebuked Arthur for bringing "sectarian" interests into the discussion of holiness, Arthur defended the plain meaning of the biblical text with energy and vigor. This event illustrates Arthur's willingness to be controversial—in the name of Truth—especially where scriptural teaching and spiritual conviction are concerned.

   6. *Through Flaming Sword*, Newberg: Barclay Press, 1959, digested findings from Arthur's graduate work on Fox in ways accessible to the common reader.

   7. Published by Eerdmans, Grand Rapids. This valuable collection put in the hands of students and teachers alike essays, pamphlets and letters of early Friends helping one attain a far more representative picture of the early Quaker movement than would have otherwise been possible.

   8. *Tomorrow Is Growing Old, Stories of Quakers in Alaska*, Newberg: Barclay Press, 1978, is one of the most significant treatments of the religious history of Alaska. It is also written in narrative style, which suits the theological character of Eskimo spirituality.

forge him into a cadre of young scholars who since the 1950's have challenged the leading interpretation of Fox during the first half of the twentieth century. Rufus Jones had constructed an extensive platform arguing Fox and early Friends should be regarded in the category of European mysticism, implying the priority of an inward orientation of Quaker spiritual experience. Such a view, however, diminished the clear scriptural and at times the clear Christocentric experience of Fox and early Quakers. In his essay on evangelical Quakers in Francis Hall's *Friends in the Americas*[9] Arthur writes, "Of major importance has been the scholarly recovery of the evangelical perspectives of our early Quaker heritage. The labors of Canby Jones, Wilmer Cooper, Hugh Barbour, Maurice Creasey, Lewis Benson, the present writer, and others attest to the current recognition of the essentially Christ-centered character of normative Quakerism." In his many articles in the *Evangelical Friend*, addresses given at yearly meeting sessions, and contributions elsewhere Arthur has been a front-running interpreter of Quaker faith and practice.[10] He not only employs the power of the spoken and written word, but he also is a mender of damaged words and concepts, wresting them from parasitic usages and distorting abuse. While Truth transcends finite words, it also is conveyed by them—at times even effectively.

4. *Truth Experienced Through the Senses:* Creative leadership discerns needs quickly and makes adjustments accordingly. As a rationalist himself, Arthur also realizes not all people perceive or experience God's Truth intellectually. Revelation also comes through the senses, and God's Truth deserves to be expressed though such media as art, music, poetry and sculpture. After all, all Truth is the Lord's, and even the created order bespeaks his glories in ways transcending human words. Why shouldn't the keeper of the Garden also speak beyond words? Arthur's earlier explorations with painting and carving have given way to producing great numbers of black walnut clocks and sculptures, largely during the 70's and 80's.[11] To this day, the Religious Studies Department, the new Prayer Chapel and the Herbert Hoover Academic Building display evidence of Arthur's artistry with

---

9. Philadelphia, 1976, p.50. See also my treatment of this scholarly shift of opinion, including the commissioning of new introductions to the Braithwaite volumes of the *Rowntree Series* by Henry Cadbury, in my epilogue to Walter Williams' *The Rich Heritage of Quakerism*, Newberg: Barclay Press, 1987, pp.254-257.

10. Notice the Quaker course he designed bears both emphases: "History *and* Doctrine of Friends." Arthur's consistent emphasis upon sound Quaker historiography, faith and practice has been one of the foundational reasons for the ideological success of the Evangelical Friends movement. Without such considerations movements too easily lose historical perspective and become vulnerable to trend and short-lived convention.

11. Arthur writes in his autobiography (*Ibid.*, p.170), "As I worked in wood ... God seemed to move nearby, to look over my shoulder, and when I could not pray with words in formal settings, kneeling at bedside or at some church altar, I could discern the Spirit in the chips that flew from my chisel ... Eyes strained by introspection regained their ease by tracing grain and growth rings in the wood. Sculpting became an aide to spiritual insight."

wood.[12] Arthur also has written lucid poetry over the last two decades and has published many of these in book form.[13] He has written the text for musicals: the first being a musical dramatization of the life of George Fox and the second portraying the life of Jonah the prophet.[14] Even his spiritual autobiography contains a combination of suggestive poetry and lucid prose in each chapter. Through his versatile contributions, as well as his latest book,[15] Arthur reminds us that not only are many aspects of God's Truth best expressed artistically, but they are also experienced through the senses.

5. *Truth and Its Implications in the World:* The Word of God makes a difference for us personally but also in the world. During the Vietnam era Arthur, along with many other thoughtful Christians, came to be more and more concerned with the social implications of the evangelical faith. Peace instead of belligerence, simplicity rather than consumerism, justice above complicity, cultivating and not abusing natural resources, and service before selfishness all became themes clearly articulated and lived by Arthur Roberts from the 1960's forward. A critic of the man-made city and its struggle against the created order, Arthur became actively engaged in the work of seeking to make the world a better place for the glory of God and the betterment of humanity. Participating in the political arena has been a longstanding venture for Arthur Roberts, who served many years on Newberg Planning Commission and has been given added opportunity during retirement. He was elected to the Yachats City Council for a four-year term in 1988, and Governor Roberts appointed him to the Ocean Policy Advisory Council in 1992.[16] Arthur was a contemporary of Martin Luther King, Jr. at Boston University, and he has sought to transform systems redemptively, not just oppose them when flawed. In all, we learn from Arthur to consider civility a Christian responsibility while seeking to transform the kingdoms of this world into the Kingdom of God. The abandonment of that mission by many "Christians" falls short of the teachings of Jesus and the ministries of early Friends, according to Arthur Roberts. The Truth of Jesus Christ is both personal and social in its implications, and followers of

---

12. The 1661 Quaker Declaration to Charles II, "We deny ... all outward wars and strife and fightings..." is carved in walnut and displayed in the Hoover Academic Building, a rustic kneeling bench graces the new Prayer Chapel, and various artistic pieces by Arthur adorn the Religion suite in Ross Center.

13. Three of these collections are *Listen to the Lord*, Newberg: Barclay Press, 1974; *Move Over, Elijah*, Newberg: Barclay Press, 1967; and *Sunrise and Shadow*, Newberg: Barclay Press, 1984.

14. "Children of the Light" was written and first performed in 1983, and "Jonah ben Amittai" was first performed in 1987. Both were joint projects by Arthur Roberts and Dave Miller, who composed the musical scores.

15. *Messengers of God: The Sensuous Side of Spirituality*, Newberg: Barclay Press, 1996.

16. *Drawn by the Light*, Newberg: Barclay Press, 1993, pp.212-213.

Jesus must be willing to further his work in the world for which he died. As Arthur says at the close of his spiritual autobiography:[17]

> The four dimensions of time-space afford boundaries that lie within a larger world. Each of us lives within a world delineated overtly by articulated clusters of human relationships we call culture, or civilization—a fifth dimension. We live, too, in a realm hardly contained in the boundaries of reason but rather hinted at covertly in dreams and longings too intangible for words although strong enough to quicken our yen for the yet-to-be-revealed. Ultimately, however, I find my strongest sense of being in a seventh dimension—the Kingdom of God—which encircles all others and defines their meanings and their limits.
>
> This Kingdom Christ reveals so fully in the heart as well as in history, gives coherence to all circles of relationship. All belonging comes within the judgment of this perimeter, whether ethnic, or political, or social, or family, whether the tight circles of the inward self or the rippling circles of the social self ... Most of all, Jesus Christ, the Risen Lord, is here among us. We are Jesus' disciples. This place, this Kingdom, is not just a spot to visit occasionally, it is not a fantasy within a 'real world' of stuff and real-politik. The Kingdom of God is more real to me than the Pacific Ocean, or the animals I have known. The Kingdom is more real than America or Yachats or George Fox College. To put it another way, the Kingdom frames these geographical places to reveal the artistry of God.

Paul N. Anderson

---

17. *Ibid*, pp.229-230.

Biblical Studies

Ordinary Prophets, Extraordinary Lives

HOWARD R. MACY

I will propose in this essay that the lives of the prophets, or more precisely, the practical results of the spirituality of the prophets, can guide our own living as followers of Christ. They can supply insights which can help interpret our experience, and they can hold out vistas of possibilities for growth which we may not yet have realized.

As I sometimes warn my students, I should caution that understanding the prophets may corrupt your life. Just about the time you've caught on to what the prophets are doing, you discover that they've caught you. Once you know what the prophets knew by heart, a revolution begins which cannot fully be resisted or undone.

The Bible suggests that with the gift of the Spirit at Pentecost, God intended to initiate a revolutionary community of prophets. Moses once exclaimed wistfully, "Would that all the people of God were prophets" (Numbers 11:29). The prophet Joel later promised a day when the Spirit would enable all the people to dream dreams, to have visions, and to prophesy (Joel 3:1-2). And Peter explained to the puzzled crowd at Pentecost that the promise of Joel was even then being fulfilled. As Katherine Dyckman and Patrick Carroll write:

> "All of us Christians, not just some 'specially chosen,' are called to be deeply united to God in prayer and to speak out of that prayer with some strand of prophetic voice. Everyone is called to be both mystic and prophet" (*Inviting the Mystic, Supporting the Prophet*, 86).

The whole Christian community is called, in some measure, to prophetic life and witness. Understanding the practical spirituality of the prophets can help us understand how to follow this call.

Even to attempt to see the prophets as guides for discipleship may seem odd, however, because the reality of the prophetic life is so frequently obscured by caricatures which make the prophets seem wholly unlike ourselves. Unlike ourselves, for example, we may regard them as people who are particularly susceptible to paranormal experiences or particularly adept at taking dictation from God. Or we might see them as people like the "saints," whose level of devotion and obedience would melt down any device designed to measure normal human holiness.

Perhaps the most common caricature of the prophets is to present them as religious soothsayers, as purveyors of predictions, timetables, and secret codes revealing when the world will end. The average mom-and-pop Christian bookstore reveals how widespread this caricature is when it fills its so-called "prophecy" shelves with books which speculate coyly that the end of time is just around the corner.

Another common caricature which obscures the prophets is to see them as primarily social activists and town cranks. It is true that Jeremiah called himself a "man of strife and dissension" (Jeremiah 15:10), and that others stood in conflict with the powers that be. But it is not accurate to present the prophets primarily as social critics. Nor should we say that the personality characteristic that qualifies them to be prophets is being strident or perpetually grumpy.

Soothsayer and activist are caricatures on the opposite ends of a continuum, and neither one accurately portrays the prophets. Unfortunately, even more scholarly descriptions often obscure the prophets as well, by failing to take into account the passion, empowerment, and obedience that were essential to the prophetic experience. Through the various approaches of modern biblical criticism, we have learned a lot that is genuinely helpful about prophetic methods, speech forms, cultural assumptions, and even social role. On balance, however, the empirical, arm's-length analysis of the prophets offered by the history-of-religions approach has often proved antiseptic and sterile. It too easily betrays and trivializes the prophetic sensibilities and motivations. As an extreme example, one exceptionally skeptical scholar at a recent professional meeting wondered aloud whether the prophets even existed. There are happy exceptions to such weaknesses in biblical scholarship, of course. Abraham Heschel and Walter Brueggemann, for example, offer penetrating interpretations of prophetic experience.

Setting caricatures aside, who were the biblical prophets? What was their place in Israel? Consider this as a working definition: the prophets were people who signaled and embodied God's active presence and purposes in the world. They pointed to and were themselves flesh-and-blood messages of what God was up to.

We might also ask who the biblical prophets were in a more personal way. This essay's title, "Ordinary Prophets, Extraordinary Lives," suggests both my interest and my answer. We must be modest about an answer, since our direct evidence is limited. However, what we do know suggests that the prophets were just ordinary folk. Amos identifies himself as a shepherd and a person who tends sycamore fig trees. Micah, too, was from rural and small-town Judah. Elisha was plowing behind oxen when he was called to prophesy. Jeremiah grew up in a small village near Jerusalem. He was from a priestly family whose ancestor Abiathar had been kicked out of both Jerusalem and the high priesthood by Solomon. Scholars often suggest that Isaiah may have been from an important family, but that seems noteworthy largely because it's unusual.

These are ordinary people who learned to live with extraordinary faithfulness. As God became the Center of their ordinary experience, they were able to live with boldness and courage, with integrity and loyal love which modeled the call to faithfulness they urged on Israel. On balance, we should also say that, being ordinary, they lived this way often in the face of mystery and puzzlement, of fear and disappointment.

We should expect the prophets to be ordinary, of course. The Bible often shows how God delights in using unlikely people to do unexpected things. Think of Moses, Deborah, Gideon, David, Elijah, and many others. This is so common that it might be regarded as a literary motif, though, even as a motif, it is firmly grounded in the reality of the Israelites' experience.

In the Old Testament we have stories and written records of the messages of many of the prophets. Of others we have only names and the sketchiest vignettes. Many others we know nothing at all about, though the Old Testament is clear that there were many more than are mentioned specifically in the Bible. The evidence also suggests that prophecy was a diverse phenomenon in Israel. Apparently some had all or part of their livelihood from helping people seek God's guidance, from teaching, perhaps from interceding with God on behalf of others. Some were even on the government payroll in the service of the king. For others, like Amos, prophecy was their vocation but not their business. Some may well have trained for prophecy; others clearly did not.

Whatever else we may say, however, the prophets from whom we have stories and messages in the Old Testament were not merely filling a professional role or performing a socially constructed religious duty. They were people who operated out of an encounter with God which grounded and oriented their whole experience. We may describe four movements or stages which characterized the prophetic experience. They are encounter, vision, conversion, and witness. Perhaps they are not rigidly sequential, but I believe they helpfully suggest the transformation at work in prophetic spirituality.

Encounter

If we are to understand and learn from prophetic spirituality, we must begin by exploring the experience of *encounter*. In his classic work *The Prophets*, Abraham Heschel writes:

> "The prophets had no theory or 'idea' of God. What they had was an *understanding*. Their God-understanding was not the result of a theoretical inquiry, of a groping in the midst of alternatives about the being and attributes of God. To the prophets, God was overwhelmingly real and shatteringly present. They never spoke of Him as from a distance. They lived as witnesses, struck by the words of God, rather than as explorers engaged in an effort to ascertain the nature of God; their utterances were the unloading of a burden rather than glimpses obtained in the fog of groping" (I, 1).

Again from Heschel: "To the prophet, knowledge of God was fellowship with Him, not attained by syllogism, analysis or induction, but by living together" (I, 3).

Sometimes interpreters have described prophetic ideals or the achievements of ethical monotheism in the prophets without seeing them in the context of this encounter. Unfortunately, this misses entirely the root of the prophets' experience. The prophets did not discover or create a set of principles. And, though they cherished the traditions of Israel, they did not simply recall the guidance of Torah. They confronted, or better, were confronted by the Creator of the universe. They met face to face the One who, as Amos writes, "makes the Pleiades and Orion," (5:8, *New Jerusalem Bible*, here and in all quotations) who "forges the mountains, creates the wind, who reveals his mind to humankind, changes the dawn into darkness and strides on the heights of the world" (4:13).

We have relatively few reports of these confrontations – some direct reports of prophetic call, some reflections on the meaning of the prophetic vocation, and evidence in the prophets' speeches of understandings that can only be had at first hand. Though the reports are not abundant, they are remarkably consistent in what they portray. These encounters overwhelmed the prophets. The encounters were blind-siding, breath-sucking, gut-jarring; they were full of energy, creativity, and crazy surprise; they intermingled fear and attraction, tenderness and amazement. They had the same effect as Job's encounter when God completely overwhelmed him in the whirlwind speeches, and Job responded, "Before, I knew you only by hearsay, but now, having seen you with my own eyes, I retract what I have said, and repent in dust and ashes" (Job 42:5). Out of such experiences the prophets became "God-blinded souls," to use Thomas Kelly's phrase.

I believe it would be a mistake to see these encounters as conversion experiences in the sense of initiating a relationship of faithfulness to God. To extend the example of Job (who is not among the prophets), right after he says he has seen God with his own eyes, he repents; but we must remember that, in God's opinion, Job was already the most righteous person in the whole world. In that same light we may understand Isaiah's response to his vision of God enthroned, when he says, "Woe is me! I am lost, for I am a man of unclean lips and I live among a people of unclean lips, and my eyes have seen the King, Yahweh Sabaoth" (Isaiah 6:5). He is overawed by the holy immediacy of God. It is in the context of this experience that Isaiah accepts a prophetic mission. Reflecting on his own call, Amos also suggests the power of knowing God shatteringly present: "The lion roars, who is not afraid? Lord Yahweh has spoken: who can but prophesy?" (Amos 3:8)

Just as they are overmatched by God's presence, so they are overmatched by what God is asking of them. Often we hear the tone of astonishment and surprise. "Who me? Do what? Who am I to do this? Surely you have the wrong person! I'm too young. I'm a nobody. I can't talk. Why in the world would they believe me?" The language of resistance, born of a sense of inadequacy and fear, usually is answered by God's reassurance, tenderness, and unwavering command. "Go ahead and do what I say. Don't be afraid. I am with you." In the encounter, apparently the prophets are both drawn and compelled. It smacks of both attraction and coercion. Jeremiah, for example, says of his call, "You have seduced me, Yahweh, and I have let myself be seduced ..." (Jeremiah 20:7) and "When your words came, I devoured them: your word was my delight and the joy of my heart; for I was called by your Name, Yahweh, God Sabaoth" (Jeremiah 15:16). But he also says "You forced me..." "You have overpowered me: you were the stronger" (20:7). At some points the prophets seem to step forward to accept their role. At other points they seem to be dragged backward, kicking and screaming, into their vocation.

The encounter with God not only resulted in specific instructions or guidance, but the very fact of the encounter was the unshakable cornerstone in the prophets' conviction that God is fully present in the world in power and love. This was not hearsay, but immediate experience which undergirded their entire prophetic lives.

We should not view such encounters simply as one-time experiences, even though some of them represent a major turning point. Indeed, the prophet clearly carries on a continuing relationship of intimacy with God in which the prophet's life and ministry has its sustenance. Neither should we give the impression that all such encounters are dramatic. Part of the significance of Elijah's encounter with God at Mt. Horeb (or Sinai) is precisely that it did not share the lightning-and-thunder drama of Moses' meeting with God there some centuries before. Elijah experienced a terrifying storm and earthquake and fire, but God did not meet him in those. The encounter came, instead, in the "still, small voice," "the sound of gentle stillness" (1 Kings 19). It reminds us that God is not limited to pyrotechnics, audible voices, and wide-screen, technicolor visions. The inner voice, the whispered words, the profound sense of God's presence – all can be equally weighty. Whether dramatic or more hidden, these experiences of encounter give those who receive them a sense of rootedness. They help to reveal what is ultimately significant. They point the way to true north. And they are fundamental to prophets ancient and modern.

To anticipate a bit, we can identify such encounters in later persons whom we might regard as prophets. We might also reflect on the encounters with God that we ourselves have experienced and the role they play in setting our direction and loyalties.

Vision

After the encounter comes *vision*. This is the next major movement in a prophet's experience. Vision emerges from encounter with God in at least three ways: first, as a reordering of reality, of the nature of the world itself; second, as a new capacity for discernment; and finally, as a capacity to imagine what is yet possible, what Brueggemann refers to as the "prophetic imagination" (*The Prophetic Imagination*).

(1) The first of these types of vision, *a reordering of reality*, is fundamentally the same phenomenon that Paul refers to in Romans 12 as the "renewing of the mind." It is coming to a profoundly altered way of seeing the world. Goethe is quoted as saying, "Few people have the imagination for reality," and I believe it is true. Even when the abstraction of the prophets' ideas may not seem remarkably different, we need to recognize that a great chasm cuts between cognitive and experiential knowledge. To refer to Heschel again, these were not "ideas," which can be quite superficial, but "understandings." What the prophets learned from their experience of God deeply affected their world view and their behavior. In my study, I have concluded that most of the prophetic message and understanding of reality can be gathered under three great insights.

(a) The first is that the prophets understood *the nearness of God*. They knew that God was actively and notoriously present in the world with sovereign power. Nothing escapes God's notice. God notices the routine slights of justice that nobody else gives a second thought to any more. God sees the plight of hidden, vulnerable people as well as the hidden crimes of prominent people. Nothing is out of God's reach. The unrivaled superpower can be brought down in an instant, and its king can go directly from a lavish state dinner to Sheol where he'll be lunch for worms and maggots. So the prophets opposed those who scoff at God's power, thinking they can do whatever they want with impunity. They tried to lift the faltering trust of those who think that God's active presence in the world is not sufficient to meet their need. Because they had encountered God shatteringly present, the prophets were convinced of the nearness of God.

(b) The prophets were also convinced that *God's purposes in the world are loving*. As they encountered and walked in intimacy with God, their hearts were molded to God's heart, and they learned about loyal love, mercy, and compassion. They learned to delight in the things that God delights in – steadfast love, justice, and righteousness (Jeremiah 9:23-24). They learned that God is lovingly working to restore all of creation, and that even judgment and justice are part of mercy. Their visions of restoration and reconciliation are glimpses into the heart of Eternity. They are echoes of the home from which humankind wandered when we wanted to be out on our own. The prophets witnessed first-hand the God who pursues all of creation with love and who stands ready, arms open wide, to embrace us all back home.

(c) The third great insight of the prophets grows out of the first two. It encompasses the issue of *loyalty*. We could put it as a reasoned conclusion: if God is really among us acting in sovereign power and if God's purposes are loving, then to whom else or to what else would we even think of giving our loyalty? I suspect, however, that the prophets' insight here was born more of the direct experience of God's ultimacy and love than of logic. But it shaped both their own loyalty and their messages, which often called the people away from disloyalty and misplaced trust.

(2) A second kind of vision which grew out of encounter with God is *discernment*. It is the capacity to see things for what they are rather than for what they purport to be. It is the ability to see through deception and self-delusion and to call things by name. For example, Isaiah warns, "Woe, you who call evil good and good evil, who put darkness for light and light for darkness, who put bitter for sweet and sweet for bitter!" (Isaiah 5:20) Amos shocked the leaders of Samaria by telling them that the "treasures" in their secure mansions would better be called "violence" and "oppression" (Amos 3:10). What they thought was God's blessing for their good behavior Amos saw as wealth gained by ripping off the poor. With discernment, the prophets were able to see through ideology and dogma, through rationalizations and justifications, through religious and political pandering, and the many other ways humans can fool themselves and each other. They spoke out of that discernment to open new ways for people to understand their circumstances and their lives. They offered people the possibility of living in the freedom of truth rather than in the certain destruction of delusion.

(3) The third kind of vision we can call *"prophetic imagination."* This is the capacity to see what is yet possible under the power of God rather than

yielding to cynicism and despair or to a status quo which is death warmed over. It is the capacity to know deeply that seeing the possibility of reconciliation and of restoration is not merely lofty idealism or wishful thinking. Brueggemann writes: "It is the task of prophetic imagination and ministry to bring people to engage the promise of newness that is at work in our history with God" (*The Prophetic Imagination*, 62-3). It is Jeremiah buying a field while he is in prison and the Babylonians are conquering his homeland, including the field. Someday people will once again buy fields and plant and harvest in this land, he says (Jeremiah 32). It is Isaiah declaring that there would be a wide highway through the desert on which God would once again lead the Israelites safely to freedom (Isaiah 40). It is to hold out the real possibility that the future of our lives in the real world need not be bound by the patterns and failures of the past, but that it can be creatively ordered and empowered by the sovereign God who is with us in love.

Conversion

Encounter and vision lead to a third movement in prophetic experience, which is *conversion*. This is conversion in the sense of on-going and deepening personal transformation. This movement is as extensive and thorough-going as encounter and vision, but I'll treat only two aspects of conversion briefly here.

The first is that the prophet struggles toward a re-rooting of personal identity. The innate demands of loyalty to God above all else creates a new allegiance, a new orientation. And this is often awkward. The prophets knew the clumsy tension between living in a particular time and place but, at the same time, transcending that time and place. As they placed themselves as citizens under the reality of God's rule, they became bi-cultural or cross-cultural persons with the sort of vague in-betweenness that can bring. Their sense of the source of their lives and the object of their loyalty had radically changed, and this altered the personal, familial, and national identities they had previously held.

A second aspect of the prophets' conversion was a personal transformation which moved them toward congruence with reality as they had seen it, toward conformity to God's purposes in the world as they knew them to be. Our Old Testament examples of this in the prophets are limited, but the reasons for this movement are clear. One is that integrity and love require it. It is impossible to sustain intimacy with God and, at the same time, avoid being molded to God's character. Conversion is a natural movement driven by the encounter with God which deepens and clarifies the prophets' vision.

Further, one test of true prophets is whether their lives correspond to the messages they give. Jesus, for example, made that point when he said you can tell the nature of a tree by its fruit (Matthew 12:33-37). This is a practical matter, not just a matter of duty. Anyone who has experience with prophecy knows that one of the first assaults on a prophet, particularly on one who says uncomfortable things, is the charge of hypocrisy. "So what about you, old Goody Two Shoes?! You're not so wonderful yourself." And so on, in the hopes of dismissing the message by discrediting the messenger.

This is a charge that has bite, by the way, because a real prophet knows that, in some measure, such charges are true. Prophets, too, are drawn down by sin, or, at the very least, live in some measure as accomplices and beneficiaries of their culture's corruption. They feel keenly Isaiah's confession of complicity, "I am a man of unclean lips and live among a people of unclean lips." (Isaiah 6:5) For some, no doubt, this is an embarrassment which hinders them in telling the truth that they know. For many others it is reason to continue humbly in the process of conversion, relying on God to help bring their lives in conformity to their best vision.

Witness

The last movement of prophetic experience is also the best known, because the bulk of the prophetic material in the Bible flows from it. This movement is *witness*. Here the prophets communicate to others what they know of God's presence and purpose. Sometimes the process of conversion itself foreshadows witness, for a notable change in lifestyle or an act done simply out of personal integrity may, even unwittingly, deliver a powerful message. I think, for example, of John Woolman when as a young man he first declined to write a bill of sale for a slave. It was an action taken only out of conscience, but it could not go unnoticed.

But the witness of the prophets is not usually unwitting. They had to tell what they knew for the love of God and the love of their peers. Their witness was powerful. It was creative and filled with variety. They used all sorts of speech forms, many of them poetic. (The theologian Hans Urs von Balthasar writes that "what a prophet has to say can never be said in prose" [quoted in Brueggemann, *Finally Comes the Poet*, 4].) They used courtroom language, dirges, satires, thanksgiving songs, doxologies, proverbs, woe oracles, parables, and many other speech forms. They also used acted or life symbols to convey their messages. They performed mime and street theater, dressed (or undressed) in unusual ways, gave their kids weird symbolic names, sang protest songs, challenged false prophets to public contests, adopted habits or lifestyles that would grab people's attention, buried underwear, smashed clay pots, bought worthless real estate, and much more.

At least two things impress me about the prophets' witness. The first is the energy and creativity that the witness displays. These are not forms of witness that they borrowed from the latest edition of the *Prophet's Handbook*. They grow dynamically out of encounter and out of an ongoing life with the

Creator and Source of energy. Deeply grounded prophetic witness is not merely imitative.

In their witness, the prophets also impress me by the risks they took and the courage their witness required. Of course, they could get killed, which has its down side. Or they could be hunted by the military or thrown in jail. Or slandered, laughed at, and ostracized. Or they might have to live with the embarrassment of certainty, when they had to persist in speaking the word of God they knew for sure to those who thought they just made it up and hadn't even a wild chance of being right. Or there was the awkwardness of publicly taking on the reigning ideologies and deeply cherished idolatries. Such faithfulness required risk and courage.

Yet it is a witness that must be made, for it is the natural culmination that flows from the reality of God encountered. It is a way of signaling and embodying the reality that God is among us in power and love to restore life, individually and corporately, to its highest possibilities.

Questions to Explore

Let me offer only three brief suggestions about how this exploration of prophetic spirituality might meet our own communities of faith. First, as I have suggested that, in some measure, every Christian is called to prophetic life and witness, let me also suggest that the pattern I have outlined may serve as a way of thinking about our spiritual formation. Encounter, vision, conversion, and witness. I see a lot of examples of this movement in persons whose names you would recognize and in many whom you wouldn't know. What puzzles me, however, is how often this progression gets short-circuited. Do people brush up against encounter and pull back? Is authentic vision co-opted by ideology, rationalization, or the cherished idolatries of our culture? Is real conversion too threatening? Is witness too much of a risk? I have ideas, but I'm not sure about what stunts this process of spiritual growth.

Secondly, let me wonder whether we might be willing to be communities of vision. Can we be discerning enough to see through delusion or nonsense and call it by name, whether it be in the church, the college, the professional academy, the marketplace, or the other cultures and subcultures in which we live? Can we have the prophetic imagination to envision the new things that God might do in the world if we would live with courage and obedience?

Finally, I wonder whether we might even more intentionally be alternative communities of vision. In particular, can we be the kind of communities that enable and support the transformation, the conversion, the personal re-rooting, and the witness that authentic encounter with God will bring? I wonder whether we might even more intentionally become communities of prophets, signaling and embodying God's active presence and loving purpose in the world.

WORKS CITED

Brueggemann, Walter. *Finally Comes the Poet*. Minneapolis: Fortress Press, 1989.

———. *The Prophetic Imagination*. Philadelphia: Fortress Press, 1978.

Dyckman, Katherine Marie and L. Patrick Carroll. *Inviting the Mystic, Supporting the Prophet*. New York: Paulist Press, 1981.

Heschel, Abraham. *The Prophets*. New York: Harper and Row, 1962.

Resistance in a 'Culture of Permission'

Sociological Readings of the Correspondence with Persian Authorities in Ezra 1-7

DANIEL L. SMITH-CHRISTOPHER

"a dominator is sometimes also a donator...some colonizers
have acted like protectors of those they've colonized"
Albert Memmi, *Dependence*, 1984

The first six chapters of the book of Ezra center around an alleged correspondence between the Persian Emporer's court and the local authorities of Palestine under Persian rule. In her recent literary analysis of Ezra-Nehemiah, Eskenazi (1988) suggested that the letters that compose this correspondence, among the other documents reproduced in Ezra-Nehemiah, "demonstrate the power or propriety of documents as causative principles and significant forces in human events."[1] Without question, these letters were crucial to the editors of Ezra-Nehemiah. But why? What does the reproduction of this alleged official correspondence mean to the final editors of Ezra-Nehemiah?

While most studies of these letters have tended to focus on the historical sources of the letters and their authenticity (see esp. Clines, Williamson, Bickerman, and deVaux among others);[2] and what they can tell us about Persian policies (Galling, Margalith, Weinberg, Blenkinsopp),[3] the typical

---

1. Eskenazi, Tamara, *In An Age of Prose: A Literary Approach to Ezra-Nehemiah* (Atlanta: Scholars Press, 1988) 41.

view about the *reason for their inclusion by the editors* was that they were included in order to show God's power and authority over foreign rulers, and/or the positive relationship between the representatives of the Exile community (Sheshbazzar, Zerubbabel, Ezra, and Nehemiah) and the Persian court. As Ackroyd states in his classic study of the exile, the letters are: "...indicative of a point...namely that under God the Persian authorities were favourably disposed toward the re-establishment of the Jewish community."[4] While granting the importance of these lines of inquiry, it is the purpose of this study to take up this latter issue, that is, the redactional intention of including this correspondence in the final preparation of the books of Ezra-Nehemiah, and specifically the attitude toward Persian rule. This attitude begins with the correspondence with Persian authorities in Ezra 1-6, but continues to develop in the rest of Ezra and Nehemiah as well.

Attempts to draw conclusions about "attitudes" reflected in the Biblical text, however, may seem a hopelessly imprecise task for Biblical analysis, but it is hard to avoid the conclusion that such assumptions about an attitude reflected in texts, attitudes toward foreigners, women, foreign rulers, etc., are critical components of our understanding of the developing role and function of the Biblical material in general, and the Persian period in particular.

I. The Jewish Attitude to Persian Rule: Text and History

Contemporary scholars working on the Persian Period of Hebrew history are familiar with the assumption of most scholars of the twentieth century that Jewish attitudes toward Persian rule were generally compliant, indeed grateful. In his recent popular commentary, Holmgren reflects this general perspective in a most interesting manner. In his comment on Neh. 9:36-37, one of the most significant complaints against the Persians, Holmgren recognizes that this passage indicates a measure of resentment and unrest, but then continues at some length to maintain the general assumption about Jewish attitudes to Persian rule:

---

2. The classic argument now is Elias Bickerman's article, "The Edict of Cyrus in Ezra 1," *SBL*, 1946 (65) 249-275; Roland de Vaux, Ch. 4, "The Decrees of Cyrus and Darius on the Rebuilding of the Temple," in *The Bible and the Ancient Near East* (Doubleday: New York 1971) 63-96; H.G.M. Williamson, *Ezra,Nehemiah*, Word Biblical Commentary, (Word: Waco, 1985); Clines, D.J., *Ezra, Nehemiah, Esther*, The New Century Bible Commentary (Eerdmans and Marshall, Morgan & Scott: Grand Rapids and London, 1984) 7-12; 36-37, etc.

3. Kurt Galling, *Studien zur Geschichte Israels im Persischen Zeitalter* (Tübingen, 1964); Blenkensopp, *Ezra-Nehemiah* (SCM: London, 1988); Margalith, K., "The Political Role of Ezra as Persian Governor," *ZAW* 98 (1986), 110-112; Weinberg, Joel, *The Citizen-Temple Community* (Sheffield University Press: Sheffield, 1993).

4. Ackroyd, Peter, *Exile and Restoration* (SCM: London, 1968) 149.

To be 'almost free' is never enough; if you are a slave, 'almost free' means that you are still a slave. Under Persian rule the Jews were 'almost free.' Jews did not despise this 'almost free' existence, however, because under benevolent monarchs the Jews were free to return to the land and there to rebuild the temple and the city of Jerusalem. The writings of both Ezra and Nehemiah portray the Persian rulers as cooperative and fair...toward the Jewish community...[5]

This perspective is by no means limited to scholars of the Hebrew Bible. Eduard Lohse's classic New Testament introduction, *The New Testament Environment* (1976) also mentions the Persian policy that: "...afforded Judaism the opportunity to develop its own life with the express support of the government..."[6]

The key, then, is the supposed benevolence of the Persian emperors. It is true that there are passages from the Bible that would seem to support such assumptions. The most commonly cited passage is Deutero-Isaiah's (or some later editor's) enthusiastic bestowal of the term "Messiah" to Cyrus in Isa. 45:1. It is furthermore true that Jewish names turn up amongst the Murashu Documents, leading many scholars to conclude that under the Persians, business must have been good for at least some of the community members.[7] Finally, there is nothing in the Elephantine correspondence which suggests resentment, although it must not be overlooked that it was a military colony in the service of the Persians, and finding itself standing opposed to a hostile, local native Egyptian populace. In a sense, the Persians were the only "friends" they had!

In his provocative work, *In Search of Ancient Israel*, Philip Davies promotes his view that the post-exilic, returning community is not only under Persian encouragement and support, but may well have been an actual *creation* of Persian interests in having a loyal outpost on their Western front, facing the Mediterranean sea. While Davies suggests that this community's own belief that it had once lived in this land previous to being exiled by the Neo-Babylonian Empire may itself be Persian inspired fabrication to justify the establishment of this community over local indigenous objections, one need not go the whole way with Davies' historical skepticism about a pre-exilic 'ancient Israel' in order to appreciate the importance he lays on direct Persian involvement in the post-exilic community, and that community's loyal and diligent carrying out of their Persian overlord's designs in Pales-

---

5. See F. C. Holmgren, *Israel Alive Again: A Commentary on Ezra & Nehemiah* (Eerdmans: Grand Rapids, 1987), 134-135. See also F. C. Fensham, *The Books of Ezra and Nehemiah* (Eerdmans: Grand Rapids, 1982).

6. E. Lohse, *The New Testament Environment* (Abingdon: Nashville, 1976) 16.

7. Ran Zadok, *The Jews in Babylonia During the Chaldean and Achaemenid Periods* (Haifa, 1979) 80-86. Zadok, however, notes that very few Jewish names turn up as officials, or members of the upper eschelons of society. Nehemiah, he argued, was a clear exception to the rule.

tine. Davies analysis clearly depends on a compliant, dutifully pro-Persian Ezra and Nehemiah.[8]

Similarly, in his recent work, *Judaism in Persia's Shadow: A Social and Historical Approach*, Jon Berquist has also taken this assumption of positive relations between Ezra and Nehemiah with the Persian Empire to claim that the Persian period Biblical documents reflect Persian interests in maintaining an ordered society. Noting that it has long been assumed that the entire legal corpus of Ancient Israel was finally redacted in the Persian Period, Berquist makes the startlingly bold claim that:

> *Darius* [my emphasis, ed.] assembled these materials and promulgated them in order to support his own imperial project of legal standardization. Although there has been a variety of Israelite and later Yehudite religious texts and even though the editing sponsored by Darius might have changed only little within the texts, the Persian Empire published these documents in an attempt to maintain social order and to define the Yehudites by their own distinctive legal code, now enforced within the confines of the Persian imperial structure.[9]

Such a theory involves Berquist in a detailed argument to show how there was little if any resistance to Persian rulership over the Jewish community, and that the Persians themselves may have had a hand in the actual formulation of the Biblical documents at least in officially sponsoring the Jewish court officials (Ezra?) who were involved. While his arguments are too detailed and extensive to review here, suffice it to say that the current paradigm of studies in the Persian period involves significant assumptions about the *absence of notable resistance to Persian authority in Jewish lives in the period following the Persian conquest of Babylon in 539*, until the conquests of Alexander the Great in 333 BCE. Quite to the contrary, the emerging paradigm appears to be moving from an earlier consensus that the Persian authorities were at the least benevolent, to a new image of total cooperation and complicity in Persian Imperial designs on the west coast of Palestine, and Per-

---

8. I am still thinking over the implications of Davies' general arguments about pre-exilic Israel, as well as those of Thompson, Lemche, and others. Their impressive arguments deserve serious (and lengthy) consideration because it is clear that if they are correct, we are in for a major change in Hebrew Biblical studies, and the resulting theological reflection by those of us who remain concerned about biblical theology. See the recent debates, although at times perhaps a bit shrill, that suggest that these views are causing an appropriate stir: Iain Provan, "Ideologies, Literary and Critical: Reflections on Recent Writing on the History of Israel," *Journal of Biblical Literature*, 114 (4), 1995, 585-606; and in the same issue, Philip Davies, "Method and Madness: Some Remarks on Doing History with the Bible," 699-705, and Thomas L. Thompson, "A Neo-Albrightean School of History and Bibllical Scholarship?" 683-698.

9. See Jon L. Berquist, *Judaism in Persia's Shadow: A Social and Historical Approach* (Augsburg/Fortress: Philadelphia, 1995), 138.

sian sponsership of accompanying Jewish religious propaganda that later becomes the basis for "scripture."[10]

It is furthermore interesting to note that research on the court tales of the book of Daniel also frequently presume a positive view of Persian rulers, and even if they are written after the Persian Period, this is typically considered a reliable collective memory of the Jews in Diaspora.[11] Indeed, such a "positive view" is often used as an argument for dating the Daniel materials e.g., the stories must come from an era other than that of the hated Antiochus Epiphanes IV, because it is hard to accept stories of a benign foreign ruler in that time. But we can easily stray on this line. Clearly, the assumption about ancient Jewish positive attitudes about Persian rulers is not limited to work on Ezra-Nehemiah.[12]

It must be argued, however, that allowing such a perspective drawn from these few sources to dominate the interpretation of all Persian Period Biblical literature, and the Jewish experience of Achaemenid rule, would lead us to overlook important sociological and socio-psychological factors that are crucial for a modern assessment of the historical and ideological understanding of the Persian Period. To begin, let us consider the recent revisions to the historical picture of the Achaemenid rulers themselves.

In a recent analysis, Root contrasts the Persians' own self-image and propaganda as portrayed on official carvings, against actual practice:

---

10. It is still somewhat problematic for me, however, to accept that such efforts were marshalled by the Persian authorities to assemble religious materials for the Jews. Wasn't Persian military and financial support all the "justification" that a Persian outpost would really need?

All these questions may need to be seriously revised, however, in the light of Ruben Richard's new dissertation, "The Role of Imperial Decrees in Ezra-Nehemiah: An Ideological and Exegetical Analysis" (University of Cape Town: 1995). Although I just received this work, thanks to the kindness of Dr. Richards, I cannot comment at length, except to cite a representative statement that would place Richards' work along the lines of both Davies and Berquist:

> The religio-cultural text, Ezra-Nehemiah, lends religio-cultural legitimacy to the political decrees of the colonial empire, Persia, while the imperial decrees in turn provide political, military, and economic authority and legitimacy to the Golah-led reconstruction of post-Babylonian Palestine. Such a symbiotic relationship illustrates the ideological collusion of the Ezra-Nehemiah text with Persian colonial ideology. (iv).

We look forward to the publication of this important work, which clearly takes a different line of argument from the present essay.

11. So Collins, who writes that "the benevolence of the king is assumed," *Daniel* (Grand Rapids: Eerdmans, 1984); Wills, L., *The Jew in the Court of the Foreign King* in an otherwise very interesting study further presumes the positive view of the foreign rulers. This view is maintained in recent commentaries such as Andre LaCocque, *The Book of Daniel* (Atlanta: John Knox Press, 1979) 113; N. Porteus, *Daniel, A Commentary* (London: SCM Press, 1965), see p. 90; and O. Plöger, *Daniel*, Kommentar zum Alten Testament, (Leipzig: Gütersloh, 1965) 98.

The world was at peace on the walls of Persepolis as it never was in actuality. While news of the Persian sack of Miletus was striking terror in the Athenian soul, artisans from near and far were carving dreams in stone for Darius. It is easy to be cynical about this paradox between the actuality and the art of "Pax Persiana.' And yet, even to have conceived this vision of an imperial cosmos where the Four Quarters sing harmonious praises to the power of the king was something unprecedented in the ancient world: a haunting finale for the Pre-Hellenic East.[13]

In her important re-assessment of the implications of the famous "Cyrus Cylinder," Amelie Kuhrt concludes that:

> The assumption that Persian imperial control was somehow more tolerable than the Assyrian yoke is based, on the one hand, on the limited experience of one influential group of a very small community which happened to benefit by Persian policy and, on the other, on a piece of blatant propaganda successfully modelled on similar texts devised to extol a representative and practitioner of the earlier and much condemned Assyrian imperialism.[14]

Finally, in a recent form where the historical "image" of Cyrus was examined again, van der Spek repeats the older view, and then takes issue with it on the basis of the historical sources:

> In modern literature he is praised as an innovator who ruled an empire in a new way, and exercised religious tolerance and liberality towards the subjugated. This policy would have contrasted very favourably with the attitude of the Assyrian kings, who were notorious for their cruelty, their mass deportation and their imposition of Assyrian cults...
> This contrasting view, however, is quite incorrect. Cyrus and the other Persian kings ruled their empire in a way which was quite common in antiquity...
> Cyrus introduces no new policy towards subdued nations, but acted in conformity with firmly established traditions, sometimes favourable, sometimes cruel. Under his responsibility temples were destroyed, Ecbatana was plundered, after the battle of Opis Cyrus 'carried off the plunder (and) slaughtered the people.'[15]

---

12. In another work, I have begun to challenge the assumption of positive Jewish attitudes to Persian rule in the book of Daniel, but in general, I think it is fair to say that this assumption of Jewish attitudes needs to be re-examined in the light of the increasing historical skepticism with regard to supposed Persian benevolence, but also the role of "converting" the enemy in post-exilic literature. See my "Gandhi on Daniel 6: A Case of Cultural Exegesis", *Biblical Interpretation*, 1(3), 1994, pp. 321-338.

13. Margaret Cool Root, *The King and Kingship in Achaemenid Art: Essays on the Creation of an Iconography of Empire* [Acta Iranica IX], (E.J.Brill:Leiden,1979) 311.

14. Amelie Kuhrt, "The Cyrus Cylinder and Achaemenid Imperial Policy," *JSOT* 25 (1983) 94-95.

This historical reconsideration is beginning to have an impact on Biblical analysis. For example, Jenner considers the Cyrus decree of Ezra 1 itself to be a falsification by Darius who needed to legitimate a strong western flank where the Jewish temple would certainly serve his purposes. Furthermore, that Cyrus is called a Messiah should not be over-read, since, Jenner suggests, the attitude could have been much cooler than many modern interpreter's assume, since "...Cyrus, being in a position of dependency and obedience to JHWH, was no more than a useful tool in the service of Jerusalem."[16]

I would argue that the most important recent voice that questions the positive image of the Persians in the biblical material is the work of Kenneth Hoglund.[17] Hoglund argues convincingly for a re-assessment of the role of Nehemiah as a Persian official, whose task was more military than spiritual, and as concerned with the further imposition of Persian control over Palestine as it was with any free expression of local religion by the Jewish residents there:

> If correlations can be made between the larger imperial concerns over the security of the western territories, and the specific activities of Ezra and Nehemiah, then one may conclude that their missions did not represent a special disposition toward the postexilic community on the part of the Achaemenid court. Rather, their missions would represent a localized manifestation of a policy being conducted within the larger region of the western territories.[18]

In short, as Hoglund summarizes, "The appearance of these garrisons in the mid-fifth century is the indelible fingerprint of the hand of the Achaemenid empire tightening its grip on local affairs in the Levant."[19] But given these socio-political realities, what was the Jewish *attitude* about them?

It was Hoglund's attentiveness to the strong words of Ezra's prayer (which assert that the Jews were "slaves" under the Persians) that inspired my own investigation.[20] It is the task of this work, then, to take up material in Ezra-Nehemiah and argue that the redactional attitude toward the Persians can be read as decidedly negative, and thus requires that we re-think the editorial motivation in reproducing the alleged correspondence of Ezra

---

15. R.J. van der Spek, "Did Cyrus the Great introduce a new policy towards subdued nations? Cyrus in Assyrian perspective," *Persica* X (1982) 278-79 and 281-282.

16. K.D. Jenner, "The Old Testament and its Appreciation of Cyrus," *Persica* X (1982) 284.

17. Although now published, I used Hoglund's dissertation for this study, for which I am grateful to Kenneth Hoglund. Now published as *Achaemenid Imperial Administration in Syria-Palestine and the Missions of Ezra and Nehemiah* (Atlanta: Scholars Press, 1992). Beyond Hoglund, also see A. Kuhrt, *op.cit.* 83-97; R.J. van der Spek, *op.cit.* 278-83.

18. Hoglund, 351, 370.

19. Hoglund, 433.

1-7 as a prologue to the missions of Ezra and Nehemiah. An emerging issue in Ezra-Nehemiah studies, it seems to me, would be a thorough investigation into the entire field of complicity with Empire among minorities. This study is intended to open some of these questions.[21]

II. The Culture of Permission and the Royal Correspondence of Ezra 1-7

The royal correspondence in the book of Ezra is clearly an important aspect of the purpose of the work, Ezra-Nehemiah, as a whole. This is emphasized by Eskenazi, in her important work, In An Age of Prose:

> Instead of dismissing this characteristic as a clumsy splicing job, we must recognize it as one of the book's central themes: Ezra-Nehemiah is a book of documents...they demonstrate the power or propriety of documents as causative principles and significant forces in human events. The ultimate power behind the documents...is God. But God's messages, in Ezra-Nehemiah, are transcribed by divinely appointed human subjects...into writings which become the definitive forces in the unfolding reality.[22]

A careful examination of this correspondence, however, reveals a certain ambiguity precisely on the issue of the attitude of the Jewish community toward the Achaemenid emporers. What is striking about these documents is the power relations that are evident between the emperor, the local authorities, and the Jewish community. When one considers these documents as expressions of foreign prerogative over Jewish destiny, in short, as symbols of dominance, then an entirely different light is shed on the assessment of these documents, their role in the unfolding sequence of events in Ezra-Nehemiah, and indeed our appreciation of the attitude of the Jewish community from which we have the books of Ezra-Nehemiah, Daniel, Esther, and other materials that go back at least in part, I would argue, to the Persian experience.[23]

---

20. Colleagues have questioned me on this matter—weren't all citizens of Persian Imperial control called "slaves of the emporer" in a manner reminiscient of saying, "Servants of the King." However, the context of these comments in Ezra-Nehemiah leaves little doubt that a negative connotation to "slave" is intended here. See, now, T. Eskenazi, "...It is clear...that in this prayer, the speakers indentify with the slavery of Egypt most directly... ," Ezra-Nehemiah, Anchor Bible Commentary, Forthcoming (comments by personal correspondence, 1996).

21. During my recent sabbatical at the Chinese University of Hong Kong, I began to do some research in the period of Mongolian control over the Han Chinese in the so-called "Yüan Dynasty" of 1279-1368. The intellectual debates among the Han Confucian literati about what would, or would not, constitute complicity with the conquerors are directly relevant to a consideration of Biblical material during the Neo-Babylonian and Persian periods. I am hoping to write up some reflections on this research, and its possible bearing on issues related to the Persian Period. Contemporary social scientists have also occasionally written about these issues, most importantly Albert Memmi, Dependence (Beacon Press: Boston, 1984) and The Colonizer and the Colonized (Beacon Press: Boston, 1991).

22. Eskenazi, Prose 41-42.

But how can letters of permission, for which one would presumably be very grateful, be seen by an editor as negative symbols of dominance? One need only remind oneself of the ever-present requirement to carry "papers" in authoritarian regimes—and the resentment of the ubiquitous demand to produce them. Such registration papers, for example, became symbols of dominance and resistance in campaigns such as Gandhi's early symbolic act of burning the registration cards that were required of Asians in South Africa in 1906.[24] In his classic analysis of confinement, Erving Goffman mentions aspects of what I am calling a "culture of permission":

>...one of the most telling ways in which one's economy of action can be disrupted is the obligation to request permission or supplies for minor activities that one can execute on one's own on the outside...this obligation not only puts the individual in a submissive or suppliant role 'unnatural' for an adult but also opens up his line of action to interceptions by staff. Instead of having his request immediately and automatically granted, the inmate may be teased, denied, questioned at length, not noticed, or, as an ex-mental patient suggests, merely put off...[25]

Furthermore:

>...total institutions disrupt or defile precisely those actions that in civil society have the role of attesting to the actor and those in his presence that he has some command over his world that he is a person with "adult" self-determination, autonomy, and freedom of action.[26]

In his study of domination and dependence, Albert Memmi has pointed to an important social reality in the context of social or political domination and that is the concomitant dependence of the subordinate:

---

23. The question of dating this material would take us deep into another argument. Suffice it to say, at this point, that an "oral stage" of the Daniel and Esther stories has been argued in some detail by Ernst Haag *Die Errettung Daniels aus der Löwengrube: Untersuchengen zum Ursprung der biblischen Daniel-tradition* (Stuttgart:Katholisches Bibelwerk,1983), and Lawrence Wills, *The Jew in the Court (op.cit.)*, and the earlier forms of Ezra and Nehemiah, but especially Nehemiah, is a central task of Ulrich Kellermann's important monograph, *Nehemia: Quellen, Überlieferung und Geschichte* (Berlin:Verlag Alfred Röpelman:Berlin, 1967).

24. For the purposes of this study, I referred to Louis Fischer's more popular work, *The Life of Mahatma Gandhi* (Harper and Row: New York, 1950).

25. *Asylums: Essays on the Social Situation of Mental Patients and Other Inmates*, Erving Goffman (Aldine Publishing: Chicago, 1961). Goffman also cites Gresham Sykes, *The Society of Captives* (Princeton University Press: Princeton, 1958), Elie Aron Cohen, *Human Behaviour in the Concentration Camp* (New York: W. W. Norton, 1953), and Eugen Kogon, *The Theory and Practice of Hell*, (New York: Farrar Strauss, 1950?).

26. Goffman, 43.

Domination does not explain everything, even if it does almost always play a role in most human relationships and even if we are constantly obliged to resist the influence of those who are powerful. The behaviour of individuals and groups today is an indissoluble mixture of dependence and subjection, dominance and providing. Moralists and politicians may bemoan the fact and warn us about the voracity of those who are dominant, about the price they exact for their poisoned gifts. But they will never prevent individuals and nations who are in need from becoming more or less dependent on those who can provide for them. This in turn makes the strong even stronger.[27]

One could well argue that a narrow attention to rewards given to those dependent on the graces of the dominator must not blind us to the negative realities of the oppression that such relationships are built upon.

My thinking about the Royal correspondence in Ezra 1-7 was furthermore shaped by interviews conducted in Los Angeles with Japanese-Americans who are former internees during World War 2.[28] In these conversations, I was struck by the frequent mention of letters of permission allowing some of these internees to leave the camps and travel within the United States on personal or educational business. When I asked them what *their own* attitudes toward these letters were, they uniformly expressed gratitude and appreciation but then made an intriguing reference to the contempt which their children later held for these same documents of permission. For the children, these letters were insulting documents that "permitted Americans to be citizens of their own country." One thinks immediately of the phrase in Nehemiah 9:36, which has Ezra saying: "Here we are slaves to this day, *slaves in the land that you gave to our ancestors.*" In short, attitudes toward these documents differ radically between those who originally carried them, and those who stand and read such letters when they are framed in the Japanese-American Museum of Los Angeles. Thus, to return to the Biblical task, what we may well need to focus on is the attitude of the editors of Ezra-Nehemiah, and not those who originally 'carried' the letters. Stated in another way, the motivation to include this in a document intended to be kept and re-read may not have not have been as grateful as those who originally benefited from such letters.

With this in mind, reading the entire set of letters gives an interesting impression. To simply note the appearance of the term "decree" in these letters, and elsewhere in the Bible, is immediately revealing. The term occurs again and again in Ezra-Nehemiah, Daniel, and Esther. The vast majority

---

27. Memmi, *Dependence*, 10.
28. I have been developing a study methodology that involves interviews such as these—interviews focussed on a particular socio-cultural context—as a source of new directions for Biblical analysis. See also *Text and Experience: Toward a Cultural Exegesis of the Bible*, Ed. Daniel L. Smith-Christopher (Sheffield University Press: Sheffield, UK, 1995).

of instances of this term are commands of foreign emperors dealing with the Jewish minority. The terms translated into English as "decree" in Ezra-Nehemiah, Daniel, and Esther, are of course loan words from "Imperial Aramaic." They are terms from political and administrative vocabulary. This is hardly surprising since minorities quickly learn words like: "police," "immigration authorities," "papers," "command," "order," "authorized," etc.

The Jewish community, as such a minority, is trapped by the competing claims to authority made by the local non-Jewish officials and by the Persian court ("Who gave you a decree to build this house?" Ezra 5:3). The correspondence itself does not involve the Jewish community, but takes place, as it were, "over their heads," between the local authorities and the central Persian administration. These local non-Jewish leaders tell the Persian court, "We also asked them their names, for your information..." (Ezra 5:10). The implied threat is obvious. The books exhibit a heightened consciousness of a people not in control of their own lives: "I, Darius, make a decree," "You are permitted to go to Jerusalem," "I decree that any of the people... ," etc. etc. The Jewish community must appeal to the Persian court for permission at every turn, although they attempt to ease the sting by constantly referring to their own prophetic authority as decisive before mentioning Persian authority (Ezra 5:1-2; esp Ezra 6:14, where the prophets are mentioned prior to the authorization of Persian kings).

Given this sociological context, a consideration of some of the editorial insertions surrounding the correspondence should serve to illustrate the ambiguity of the Jewish attitude toward the Persian ruler, and warn us against hasty assumptions about positive and/or compliant attitudes. I will focus my comments on five major themes or texts: (a) The Introduction in Ezra 1, (b) the celebration of Passover in Ezra 6:16-22 and the concomitant Exodus typology, (c) the references to the prophets Haggai and Zechariah, (d) the appearance before the Emporer in 7 ("standing before the King"), and (e) the phrase, "we are slaves," found in prayers attributed to Ezra in both the books of Ezra and Nehemiah.

(a) Ezra Ch. 1

Already in Ezra 1:1, it is stated the the Lord "stirred" the heart of King Cyrus. Too much can be made of this. The term certainly does not suggest a special relationship with Cyrus, rather it merely is a conventionalized manner of speaking of God's ultimate control even of enemies. The same Hiphil form of the verb "to stir" ($h\bar{e}^c\hat{i}r$) is found in 1 Chron. 5:26, where Tiglath-Pileser III's heart is "stirred" by God, and in Isaiah 19:2 where Egyptians are "stirred" against Egyptians. David wonders why Saul's heart is "stirred" against him in 1 Sam. 26:19, and Ezra 4:15 speaks of sedition being "stirred up" in the city of Jerusalem.

The issue of God's use of foreign rulers is an important theme in the Bible, and does not, of course, always mean that for the Biblical writers their God uses an instrument toward which their God, or the Israelites themselves, necessarily hold in a positive light. Williamson, commenting on this opening section, suggests that Ezra 1:6 recalls the "despoiling of the Egyptians," the first of many such references to an Exodus typology (note Ex. 3:21-22; 11:2; 12:35-36; Ps. 105:37).

To be "stirred" by God is to be controlled by God to say that foreign rulers ultimately act under God's instruction is not to endorse the actions of the foreign ruler. It is to declare them tentative, *not based in their own power and authority*. If I can be permitted a longer-range illustration, the Johannine picture of Jesus, replying that Pilate would "have no power...unless it had been given you from above" (John 19:11) can hardly be taken to be a positive endorsement of the Roman occupation of Palestine.

(b) Exodus typology in Ezra-Nehemiah

In his recent commentary, H.G.M. Williamson argues repeatedly, and I think convincingly, for an underlying theme of "second exodus" present in many of the discussions about the return of the Jews to Palestine in the Ezra-Nehemiah texts.[29] This theme that is referred to in subtle ways such as the use of specific phrases or vocabulary that are uniquely associated with older Exodus-related narrative and poetry. But if this is the case, one may forgive the Persian monarch (and his local representatives in Palestine) for a certain irritation (if not open resentment) since such a notion casts his Persian Highness in the unflattering role of being the second Pharaoh over this second exodus. Indeed, the Exile community's attention given to the celebration of the Passover and Sukkot in the time of Zerubbabel may well be seen as supporting the local non-Jewish authorities in their concern, in the time of Artaxerxes, that Jerusalem is a "rebellious city, hurtful to kings and provinces" (Ezra 4:15).

Such a connection of the Passover and/or Sukkot festivities and Jewish political resentment at their subordination to foreign rulers is an issue that has had little consideration by scholars of Jewish history in the Achaemenid period.[30] In his discussion of the history of the passover and unleavened bread rituals, for example, De Vaux notes that these early rites (which he

---

29. Williamson, 16,93, and 296 especially.

30. The most recent work on Sukkot, for example, by Jeffrey L. Rubenstein, does not deal with this at all. See "The History of Sukkot during the Second Temple and Rabbinic Periods: Studies in the Continuity and Change of a Festival," Ph.D. dissertation for Columbia University, 1992. Rubenstein's discussion of the association between Sukkot and God's punishment of other nations who do not recognize the primacy of Jerusalem in Zechariah14 did not pursue the possible sociological implications of such a notion during the Persian and/or Hellenistic periods. The key here, however, may well be the association of Temple re-dedication, and international prominence over former enemies.

thought traced to nomadic rites and Canaanite precedents) became historicized as celebrations of the Exodus events, which dominate their use and interpretation in the Biblical text.[31] If this is the case, how is it that the Persian authorities actually seem to *support* the observance of a politically loaded festival? The question is all the more intriguing because the Persian authorities also intervene to allow the observance of Passover at the Elephantine fortress as well.[32] Cowley, one of the earliest scholars of the Elephantine material, himself seemed surprised at Persian interest in allowing the Passover.[33] That the celebration's implications were certainly known by non-Jews is clear from the opposition by the local Egyptians. As Porten suggests:

> ...a strict separation of religious and political motivations is artificial. The religious festival of Passover celebrated the political victory over the Egyptians. Any political resentment which the Egyptians, especially the Khnum priests, might have felt toward the Jewish representatives of Persian authority in Egypt would have been heightened by religious differences and the presence of a Temple to YHWH, the God of the Jews.[34]

While it is interesting to note the number of times that Josephus records mass incidents occuring during the Passover celebrations in Jerusalem, it would seem that this is likely due to the fact that crowds were available to be stirred up, rather than the precise nature of their gathering. However, there are also suggestions of a politicized celebration in Josephus. In Ant. IX 274-276, Hezekiah's Passover is read as part of his liberation from foreign power and his ignoring of the subsequent Assyrian threats. In Ant. XVII 214ff, there is trouble at Passover from those Jewish opponents of Roman interference in Judean affairs of faith.[35] Did Passover have a nationalist/political overtone?

---

31. Roland de Vaux, *Ancient Israel: Religious Institutions* (McGraw-Hill: New York, 1965) 488-493, V.2.

32. Cf. the famous "Passover Papyri" (Cowley #21) in A. Cowley (ed.) *Aramaic Papyri of the Fifth Century B.C.* (Oxford: Claredon, 1923).

33. Cowley, xxiii-xxv. The exact nature of the Passover rite at this time is, as Cowley already stated in 1923, difficult to know for certain. The letter, which dates from 419 (Darius II) shows the Persian authorities allowing the celebration of Passover which was apparently opposed by local Egyptians.

34. p. 282, Porten, Bezalel, *Archives from Elephantine: The Life of an Ancient Jewish Military Colony*, (Berkeley: University of California, 1968). Porten notes other negative Egyptian reactions to the Exodus account that are mentioned by Josephus (Ag. Ap. 1:14,73ff,26-31,227ff).

35. Furthermore, there is worry about trouble during Passover, also related to Roman lewdness with the Jewish crowds, in *Ant.* XX, 105ff. But this scene must be read within the politically loaded context of Roman occupation—where Roman insolence could clearly be interpreted as flaunting the Jewish subordination.

In his recent work, *Josiah's Passover: Sociology and the Liberating Bible*, Nakasone argues that the Josianic Passover was a calculated move to change Passover from a local family celebration designed to ritually distribute the local surpluses of agricultural and pastoral produce. Josiah centralized Passover in Jerusalem, argues Nakasone, where the economic and social benefits would accrue to the ruling elite. But this exploitation had to be religiously/ideologically justified. As Nakasone writes:

> It should not be forgotten that the religious reform was deeply involved in the national liberation struggle of the Israelite state against the Assyrian hegemony. This was the reason the main ideological support of the Deuteronomic religious reform was the Exodus tradition (Dt. 16:1-3), which was now used against Assyrians...given the national oppression by the Assyrians, the return to Yahwism, symbolized by the Exodus tradition could be intended to herald a national liberation that could assist the Jerusalemite ruling elite in the smooth operation of their economic policies.[36]

Nakasone's arguments about Josiah's "use" of the Exodus motif against the Assyrians is interesting, even apart from the acceptance of the socioeconomic theory which he proposes for Josiah's motivation. If the Josianic Passover had such political overtones, then certainly one could argue that the attempt to revive such a national celebration at the end of the Exile would draw the suspicion of the present ruling authorities. The absence of such suspicion is all the more interesting, and particularly with regard to the "Passover Papyri." It would serve to explain matters, however, if Cowley and others are correct in assuming that the very observance of a Passover at Elephantine, rather than in Jerusalem, reveals a rite that is not under the centralizing legislation of Josiah and is perhaps also therefore stripped of the nationalist overtones which it was to receive at that occasion.

Clearly, more work needs to be done on the nature of the Passover (as well as Sukkot) and its possible political overtones. To suggest that the Passover had *no* such nationalist overtones, and that it could not have been responsible for some of the accusations against the Jewish community in Ezra 6-7, is an argument based largely, I would suggest, on the continued assumption of an alleged positive Jewish attitude toward the Persian rulers which is precisely what we are challenging. Finally, one could well wonder whether the use of "the King of Assyria" in Ezra 6:22 should not be so easily dismissed as merely a neutral circumlocution for the Persian authorities.

---

36. Shigeyuki Nakasone, *Josiah's Passover: Sociology and the Liberating Bible* (Orbis Books: Maryknoll, N.Y., 1993) 106.

(c) The Authority of Haggai and Zechariah

In Ezra 5:1-2, and in reference to the Temple work in 6:14, the prophetic authority of Haggai and Zechariah are specifically mentioned before recognizing any authority of the Persian rulers. The indication seems to be that for the exile community, the true authorities are the prophets, and the Persian monarch is secondary. Indeed, after a lengthy demonstration of the power of the emperor to allow the Temple construction to get underway, it seems a bit ungrateful to suggest that the elders of the Jews "prospered through the prophesying of the prophet Haggai and Zechariah" (Ezra 6:14, cf. 5:1-2). Their success was by the command of the God of Israel, and then finally recognition is given to three kings of the Persians.

Haggai and Zechariah are, of course, the two prophets that we have from the period immediately following the return of exiles to Palestine (other prophets are mentioned negatively, Neh. 6:14). Attention to the rebuilding of the Temple as a theme in both Haggai and Zechariah should not distract us from the strong nationalistic language used in both prophets. Haggai refers to God's plan to "overthrow the throne of kingdoms; I am about to destroy the strength of the kingdoms of the nations." This is followed by the historically significant allusion to God's overthrowing "the chariots and their riders; and the horses and their riders" (Haggai 2:22). Zechariah, too, may refer to punishment of the nations that caused the exile rather than the Persians (2:8) "the nations that plundered you," but the implications of the rise of Jerusalem's notoriety and majesty, though peaceful, is surely the reduction in importance of other nations and peoples (as in Zech. 14).

What is clear is that the respect shown toward the authority of Haggai and Zechariah cannot overlook *their* political claims about the world authority of Jerusalem and of God's intentions toward Jerusalem. That such an implied revolution would be largely nonviolent makes the negative attitude toward current Persian rule no less militant in its hope for liberation from foreign control.

It is clear that these arguments can be supported from evidence drawn elsewhere in Ezra and Nehemiah.

(d) Appearances before the King

It is interesting to note the frequency with which the narrators of Persian Period stories emphasize the significance of 'standing before' the foreign king. In Daniel 1:5,19 the appearances before the King are the "frame" scenes for the story as a whole. Daniel and his friends "stood before the King" for the first time when introduced to their challenge, and then when they are successful and rewarded.[37] Furthermore, Esther and Mordecai (who "stands" rather than bows before Haman), as well as Ezra and Nehemiah, had their turn to "stand before the king." The scene, in cinematographer's terms, is dramatic and crucial. Rarely do these figures "stand before" some lower official, which would more likely have been the case, historically.[38]

That these "scenes" are unique is clearer when compared to the mention of "bowing" or "doing obeisance," which is more common in the Deuteronomic Historian, 1 Sam. 24:8; 28:4; 2 Sam. 1:2, 9:6,8, 14:4,22,33, etc.

> In his work on the Court Tale genre of the Bible, Wills states that: In Asia Minor, Mesopotamia, and Israel, the power of the centralized court evidently captured the imagination of the masses...The gracious gifts to be received or the terrible punishments to be inflicted here were greater than anywhere else... .[39]

Yet, the wise, according to Proverbs, would avoid such appearances before powerful rulers:

> Do not put yourself forward in the king's presence
>   or stand in the place of the great;
> For it is better to be told, 'Come up here'
>   than to be put lower in the presence of a noble (Proverbs 25:5-7).

Both the Ezra and Nehemiah stories include significant appearances before the King. In the Nehemiah text, the relationship of Nehemiah to the King should not distract us from the language of fear. In Neh. 2:2, Nehemiah is "very much afraid" (wā'îrā' harbēh mə'ōd). Fear of the authorities and their opposition appears in 4:14, and Nehemiah's own fear of local opposition is mentioned in 6:14,16. The fear of the king is mentioned in Daniel 1:10. Nehemiah says grant "mercy" before "this man."[40] The term mercy (ḥesed) is found also in 1 Kg. 8:50, Daniel 1:9, and Psalm 106:46, as well as 2 Chron. 30:9 in cases of God's assurance before intimidating power.

---

37. Also note that in Daniel 2:2, Nebuchadnezzar's advisors come to his presence, and stood before the King before the Jewish resistors are introduced. These resistors will "stand" rather than bow before the image of the King. Similarly, in Daniel 10:11-12 Daniel is to stand before God's messenger.

38. There are some "standing before the King" scenes in the Deuteronomic Historian (note 1 Kings 1:28—Bathsheba called to stand before the King;1 Kings 3:16—two prostitutes stand before the king; and note1 Kings 18:15—Elijah points out that he stands before God (rather than merely the King?), and also 17:1. Elisha says the same in 2 Kings 3:14.)

In the narratives, it is more typical to mention that someone was "before" the King (no mention of standing), or simply going to the King, with no court scene mentioned at all.

39. Lawrence Wills, The Jew in the Court, 19-20.

40. Blenkinsopp wonders if the use of (hā'îš hazzeh) "this man" is a slightly pejorative term. Kellerman, however, compares it to other uses of court-room language where one imagines a gesture toward the person being accused. See Kellerman, Nehemia, 55.

It is similar, therefore, to the granting of *ḥesed* before Ezra. What is clear, however, is that Nehemiah is seriously intimidated by the emperor's power.

When, in Ezra 7, the letter from Artaxerxes is completed, there is a significant response on the part of the writer (vv. 27-28) which is frequently taken to indicate the favorable attitude of the Jews toward the Persian monarch. Blenkinsopp, for example, notes that "we note once again the theme of the benevolence of the Persian kings."[41] Williamson states that this reaction is one of "praise and thanksgiving."[42] On the other hand, Rudolph commented on a certain "characteristic" attitude of Ezra, who spontaneously broke into thanks at hearing the orders of Artaxerxes, but thanks directed to God rather than the King, who was simply influenced by God's power.[43] Rudolph's comment points in an alternative direction. I would argue further that, especially in the Ezra material, a more forceful picture emerges from a consideration of this passage. In Ezra, as in other exilic works, we are invited to picture the lowly exile (always introduced as a member of the minority Jewish race) standing before the majestic presence of the Persian monarch:

> Blessed by the Lord, the God of our ancestors, who put such a thing as this into the heart of the king to glorify the house of the Lord in Jerusalem, and who extended to me steadfast love before the king and his counselors, and before all the king's mighty officers. I took courage, for the hand of the Lord my God was upon me... (Ezra 7:27-28a)

Three elements of this passage are worthy of note. First, briefly, the fact that Ezra was protected by "the hand of God" is an aspect of the Ezra narrative material that we encounter in other places—and especially in 8:22-24 where God's hand protects Ezra from enemies, and seems an interesting version of the Deuteronomic phrase of God's "mighty hand and outstretched arm" (cf. Neh. 2:8).

Second, Ezra took "courage." This may simply be a manner of speaking about "being encouraged" as having one's spirits lifted. But it can easily be a more serious matter, suggesting that God "strengthened" Ezra during a life-threatening encounter. After all, *hithazzaqtî*, the Hithpa'el (reflexive) form of *ḥāzaq*, "to be empowered," is often used in preparation for warfare, particularly in late Hebrew sources. 2 Chronicles 15:7, Asa is to "take courage" in a time of danger (note similarity of 15:2 and Ezra 8:22-24). In 2 Chron. 23:1 Jehoida "takes courage" as preparation for battle, and similarly with Amaziah in 25:11 (so also 2 Chron. 19:13). Israel is to "take courage" because of their near relief in Isa. 41:6-7. In short, such a phrase is indeed

---

41. Blenkinsopp, 160.
42. Williamson, 105.
43. Rudolph, 77.

curious if Ezra was to appear before a sympathetic, enlightened Persian ruler. More likely, he feared for his life (note the specific mention of the "mighty officers" in the King's presence). The military imagery that is being used by the narrator suggests a form of "spiritual" warfare against an enemy that is feared.

Third, and finally, Ezra was the object of ḥesed, which is typically translated as "steadfast love." The full extent of the term, however, is summarized by Sakenfeld in her suggestive, though cumbersome, definition of the term as: "deliverance or protection as a responsible keeping of faith with another with whom one is in a relationship."[44]

In most of the late sources, ḥesed appears to be in the context of praise for the building or re-building of the Temple (1 Chronicles 34, 41; 2 Chron. 5:13; 7:3,6, and Ezra 3:11, and it appears also in Psalm 100). But in Psalms 118, 106,107 and most especially in 136, note that ḥesed is the particular power of God to deliver Israel from her enemies (see also 143). In Jeremiah 33:11, the restoration after exile is clearly the intended result of God's ḥesed "for I will restore the fortunes of the land... ." Finally, the shout of praise for God's ḥesed is associated with the miraculous defeat of enemies in 2 Chron. 20:21, which is also associated (by the act of fasting) to Ezra 8:21-23, with God's deliverance from enemies of Ezra.[45] Similarly, in Daniel 1:9, God made Daniel the object of ḥesed and raḥămîm (mercy) before the head of the eunuchs. The term is closely associated with mercy, according to Sakenfeld (cf. 1 Kings 8:50, "and forgive your people who have sinned against you, and all their transgressions that they have committed against you, and grant them compassion in the sight of their captors, so that they may have compassion on them..."; Neh. 1:11—Nehemiah is thankful for mercy when he was before "this man," the ruler and Ps. 106, against people before their captors.)

One of the most powerful examples of this motif of ḥesed as God's deliverance from the power of enemies is the liturgical use of the phrase, "His ḥesed endures forever." As Sakenfeld states:

> This liturgical expression is used in association with a great variety of circumstances, ranging from deliverance of individuals from sickness (Ps. 107:17ff) or from perils of the high seas (Ps. 107:23ff) all the way to a generalization to the magnalia dei for the community, including not only deliverance from Egypt and the Amorites but even the creation of the world itself (Ps. 136).[46]

---

44. Katherine Doob Sakenfeld, *The Meaning of Ḥesed in the Hebrew Bible: A New Inquiry*, (Missoula: Scholars Press, 1978) 233.

45. See my study on fasting in this material, and its military associations: "Hebrew Satyagraha: The Politics of Biblical Fasting in the Post-Exilic Period (Sixth to Second Century B.C.E.)" *Food and Foodways: An Interdisciplinary Journal* (Paris/N.Y.) 1993, Vol. 5(3), 269-292.

46. Sakenfeld, 167.

But Psalm 107 speaks primarily of liberation from the results of exile and the treatment by Israel's enemies. In this context, imprisonment, sickness, bring adrift on the seas (e.g., Jonah) are all metaphors for separation from God as preeminently expressed in the foreign existence of Exile (In fact, some of these metaphors are often used in the context of speaking about exile: Isaiah 61). Nevertheless, I would agree with Sakenfeld's concluding statement on *hesed* in the Psalms, which is "predominantly associated with deliverance rather than any special blessing."[47] Finally, Sakenfeld suggests that

> This nuancing of *hesed* as 'delivering power' reaches its height in a series of texts in which it paralleled with "strength." Prominent among these is Exodus 15:13:
>> You led in your *hesed*
>> The people whom you redeemed
>> You guided in your strength
>> to your holy encampment.[48]

The result of this analysis of *hesed* in the context of Ezra's (and, in a similar phrase, "mercy" in Neh. 1:11) appearance before the Persian monarch forces us to conclude that the passage assumes the necessity for God's delivering action against an enemy. That the result was the King's permission should not minimize the implied "spiritual warfare" that is assumed in the Ezra passage. Praise was directed to God's delivering power, not to the Persian Monarch's good intentions.

(e) "we are slaves"

In both Ezra 9:7-8 and Neh. 9, the editors have Ezra referring to the condition of the Jews as "slavery." So startlingly abrupt is Neh. 9:36-37, with its complaint of the burden of Persian taxation and its mention of enslavement that many modern scholars place this entire prayer into a later era than the rest of Ezra-Nehemiah. Hoglund, for example, suggests that:

> It is this enhanced control and domination of the community that resulted in the anti-Persian sentiments scattered throughout the narratives of Ezra-Nehemiah. The author of the biblical narratives, writing perhaps a generation after the reforms, senses that the community has been radically transformed as the result of the actions of these two imperial officials, yet holds the empire responsible for the sense of powerlessness that pervades the community.[49]

---

47. Sakenfeld, 218. See also Katherine D. Sakenfeld's more recent summary statement of her work on *Hesed in the Bible: Faithfulness in Action: Loyalty in Biblical Perspective*, (Fortress Press: Philadelphia,1985).

48. Sakenfeld, *Hesed*, 221.

That Neh. 9 could have been added later than the earlier Ezra and Nehemiah memoirs is argued on wider grounds than this attitude of Neh. 9:36-37. However, I would argue that this "attitude" must no longer serve as evidence for a clear demarcation of Neh. 9 from the rest of the Ezra-Nehemiah material. This passage is only more forthrightly stating an attitude that, as we have seen, is implicit in more subtle passages elsewhere. An excellent example is Ezra 9:7. Blenkinsopp notes that:

> the final phrase 'as is the case today'...may seem out of place and contrary to the otherwise benign view of Persian rule in the book; it would certainly be inappropriate in a document destined for Persian consumption. But it would be a mistake to make too much of this prudential attitude...[50]

When taking on the idea that the missions of Ezra and Nehemiah were intended to induce loyalty in the Jewish community, Hoglund dryly comments, in reference to Ezra 9:8-9 and Nehemiah 9:36-37 that:

> if the missions of Ezra and Nehemiah were commissioned by the Achaemenid court to induce loyalty in Yehud, the narratives of Ezra-Nehemiah suggest that the reformers themselves were unaware of this goal...[Ezra 9:8-9 and Neh. 9:36-37]...hardly seem conducive to engendering greater loyalty toward the empire.[51]

Blenkinsopp, also, as we have noted, leans toward a reasessment of the Persian policies:

> In spite of the pro-Persian sentiments in Isa. 40-48 and favorable allusions to the Persians' providential role in Ezra-Nehemiah, there is no reason to believe that their rule was significantly more benign than that of their Semitic predecessors. The allusion to military conscription, forced labor, and the requistioning of livestock recall references elsewhere to the heavy burden of taxation during the early Persian period (Ezra 4:13; 7:24; Neh. 5:4). One of the worst aspects of imperial policy under the Achaemenids was the draining away of local resources from the provinces to finance the imperial court, the building of magnificent palaces, and the interminable sucession of campaigns of pacification or conquest...the prayer is therefore, by implication, an aspiration toward political emancipation as a necessary precondition for the fulfillment of the promises.[52]

These passages, finally, are only the most forthright indication of that which we have already noted: the attitude of Ezra-Nehemiah to Persian rule was

---

49. Hoglund, 43.
50. Blenkensopp, 183.
51. Hoglund, 144.
52. Blenkinsop, 307-308.

not a grateful subservience to enlightened foreign emperors and certainly not a community which gratefully and dutifully owes its very existence to Persian benevolence. There are simply too many 'tooth-marks' on the Persian hands that fed them!

Summary: Ezra-Nehemiah and Religious Resistance

The arguments presented here may not be convincing when considered in isolation—no one nuance or phrase serves to clearly establish a hostile attitude toward Persian rulers. Taken as a whole, however, I believe that we can conclude that the attitude of Ezra-Nehemiah toward their Persian overlords is one of neither gratitude nor warmth. Their attitude is both the realistic assessment of forced subservience, and in response, a faithful non-violent resistance to any idea that Persian power or authority is greater than God's spiritual armament of the faithful. Thus, the editors of Ezra and Nehemiah propound a subversive theology that reserves recognition of authority to God first and foremost. Such a theological politic can breed independence as effectively as violent revolution, and an understanding of the meaning of spiritual and ideological resistance to subordination may lead to a reassessment of our readings of Ezra-Nehemiah. These arguments may be taken as a suggestion that perhaps we need to be more attuned to the subtle varieties that social resistance can take among occupied peoples. It would be a matter of presumptive bias, I would argue, to presume that no significant resistance is taking place if we do not clearly see a Mattathias, burning with zeal, killing a king's officer.

Quaker History

The Relation between Content and Experience

In George Fox's Theology of Encounter[1]

PAUL N. ANDERSON

The kerygmatic[2] message of George Fox may be described as a "theology of encounter." Not only did it call for a transforming encounter with God through the pneumatic power and presence of the resurrected Lord, but Fox's spiritual insights were gained largely by means of such encounters which he called "openings." The focus of this paper is to explore the connection between salient aspects of Fox's kerygmatic message and their epistemological origins within his spiritual experience; in other words, to assess the relation between content and experience in George Fox's theology of encounter.

In order to investigate this topic we shall confine our study primarily to the events leading up to Fox's 1652 sermon on Firbank Fell, considering first the contents of the sermon as recorded in his *Journal*, and second, Fox's

---

1. An earlier form of this paper was delivered at the George Fox Tercentenary Conference in Lancaster, England, March 1991.

2. The reason I use the word "kerygma" here (from the Greek word, *keryssein*, "to proclaim"—see C.H. Dodd, *The Apostolic Preaching and Its Developments*, Grand Rapids: Baker, 1936, reprinted in 1980, esp. pp.7-35). Fox considered himself in continuity with the original proclaimers of the Gospel message, and yet, his message focused not just on the eschatological events of the past (what God *has done* through Christ at the dawning of the New Age) but upon the eschatology of the present and impending future: what God *is doing*—and yet *would be doing*—through Christ in this new day of Visitation. To continue with Dodd's language, Fox not only proclaims a "realized eschatology," but he has experienced it, and these encounters form the content of his further proclamations.

anteceding openings which formed the experiential basis for his insights and convictions. Finally we shall make several observations regarding connections between the two and their implications.

I. Content

George Fox's sermon at Firbank Fell marked a turning point in the Quaker movement.[3] Indeed, it was largely that event, holding an audience of over one thousand captive for three hours, that marked the transition from a cluster of isolated searchings to a groundswell movement endeavoring to influence the known world. It is also here in Fox's *Journal*[4] where we find his clearest and fullest articulation of his message up to that point, and one of the clearest anywhere in his *Journal*. This being the case, Fox's sermon at Firbank Fell provides at least an adequate starting place for identifying some of the basic tenets of his kerygmatic message. These are as follows:[5]

1. Steeplehouses are "no more holy than that mountain;" temples (and "dreadful houses of God") "were not set up by the command of God nor Christ;" nor were their priesthood and tithe systems divinely ordained. Rather, "Christ was come, who ended the temple, and the priests, and the tithes, and Christ said, 'Learn of me', and God said, 'This is my beloved Son, hear ye him.'"

2. The Lord had sent Fox with "his everlasting gospel to preach, and his word of life to bring them off all those temples, tithes, priests and rudiments

---

3. Ernest Taylor (*The Valiant Sixty*, York: Sessions, 1947, third ed. 1988, p. 18) puts it this way: "These meetings at Firbank and Preston Patrick changed the whole prospect. Fox went up Wensleydale as a solitary enthusiast. The following few days gave him a band of zealous workers, who went forth on Gospel service in two's and three's."

4. Not only in Fox's *Journal* are the Sedbergh/Firbank Fell events reported as pivotal, but they are also described as highly significant to such formative leaders as Thomas, Ann and John Blaykling, Frances Howgill, Richard Robinson, Joseph Bains, John Auldland—and apparently *even* judge (Colonel) Gervaise Benson and Major Bousfield were somewhat convinced. Also, many others appear to have been reached as suggested by a letter from Sedbergh Meeting concerning Fox's arrival in the Northwest (reprinted in Hugh Barbour and Arthur Roberts, eds., *Early Quaker Writings: 1650-1700*, Grand Rapids: Eerdmans, 1973. pp.59-61). This letter describes the proclamation/event as follows:

And upon the first day following, G. F., being accompanied with the said John Blaykling, went to Firbank Chapel, where F. Howgill and John Auldland preached in the forenoon to a seeking and religious people there separated from the common way of national worship. The said G. F. bore till they had done, and when the meeting broke up, gave notice of a meeting afternoon the same day intended, hard by the said chapel; whither many did resort, and then and there the said G. F. was opened in a living testimony by the word of life to the reaching God's witness in many hearts and the said J. A. was then fully convinced of the Truth, with many more. (p.60)

5. Citations taken from *The Journal of George Fox*, John L. Nickalls, ed., London: Religious Society of Friends (minor revisions, 1975), p. 109.

of the world, which had gotten up since the apostles' days and had been set up by such who had erred from the spirit and power the apostles were in..." Rather, the goal is that they "might all come to know Christ their teacher, their counsellor, their shepherd to feed them, and their bishop to oversee them and their prophet to open to them, and to know their bodies to be the temples of God and Christ for them to dwell in."

3. The work of those "who make a trade of their words and have put them into chapter and verse" is apostasy and is of the same fallen character as the false prophets, chief priests, scribes and Pharisees such as "the prophets, Christ, and his apostles cried against." Rather, Fox says, "I turned them to Christ the substance," expositing both the parables and Epistles to them.

4. People were turned from darkness and the power of Satan to the Light and the spirit of God, "that they might believe in it and become children of the light." Thus, Fox declares his hope that "with the spirit of Truth they might be led into all the Truth of the prophets', Christ's and the apostles' words."

Indeed, the program of Fox's ministry is largely represented in digest form within the outline of this important sermon, and from these motifs several observations may be made:

1. Within each set of points there are both *deconstructive* and *reconstructive* elements. Fox is called to bring people "off" their dependence on outward forms, institutions and leaders, turning them "to" Christ the substance and fulfillment of all religious convention.

2. The deconstructive emphases of Fox are set in clear contradistinction to conventional religious understandings and practices. Christocentric emphasis applies a radical interpretation of the past (the original, authentic church) in a way which corrects the present and prepares the way for the future. In this sense Fox advocates a *radical restoration* of basic and authentic Christianity.

3. Generally, the sermon falls into two halves (paragraphs) which address two kinds of authorities challenged by Fox: the *institutional priests* (advocating the authority of the church) and the *dissenting preachers* (advocating the authority of the scriptures). While the latter is more subtle, the two authorities of the church and the scriptures are seen here to be challenged by Fox in deference to the pneumatic power of the resurrected Lord. We see this agenda being hammered out before and after this sermon as well.

4. The issue at stake here, however, is not Christ *versus* the scriptures, nor the Spirit of Christ *versus* ecclesiastical authority. Rather, the issue is one of *Christocracy*: how the risen Christ leads *within* the church redemptively (not coercively) and how the leadings of the Spirit of Christ may be embraced and obeyed as discerned adequately *through* the scriptures—let alone through the personal leading and the sense of the gathered meeting.

Making these sources of authority truly dynamic—and thus truly authoritative—is the Spirit of Christ who works through them, but also beyond them. This eternal Christ is proclaimed to be present and available, waiting to be encountered and thus enlivening the church, teaching the reader of the scriptures and becoming the true Shepherd of the flock.

In these and other ways Fox's sermon on Firbank Fell represents in digest form an outline of his Gospel message, and in many ways the rest of his ministry reflects the unfolding story of how the message is delivered and variously received. One finds this story narrated in the *Journal*, but it also comes through clearly in his epistles. For the purposes of this essay, however, the discussion will be confined to treatments in Fox's *Journal*.[6]

II. Experience

As well as these motifs, summarized as the digest of a three-hour sermon, one may also trace their development within the experience of George Fox if his journal may even come close to a reliable guide.[7] Obviously, there are problems with evaluating the veracity of any historical or literary document, especially an autobiographical journal which has been extensively edited. But even if there is only a literary relationship (and it is highly doubtful this is *all* there is) there still exists a suggestive connection between the content of Fox's message and the insights gained from his spiritual encounters. So, let's proceed with the exploration. In doing so, consider a terse digest of Fox's openings and reports of his ministry between 1643 and 1652, which begin with Fox's early searchings and debates with religious leaders. What we find in this, the beginning of his ministry, is that his experiential sojourn traverses at least five phases as Fox moves from seeker to an apostle with a message. What one also finds, however, is that *each* of the points articulated in the Firbank proclamation is anticipated in the prophetic openings of George Fox between 1635 and 1652. A selection of these are as follows:

Phase one: Fox becomes a seeker of truth; the Lord opens to him the way of truth. Here we see the young seeker exploring answers to his questions,

---

6. In that sense, the discussion limited to treatments in Fox's *Jounal* offers clear parameters within which the discussion can be meaningfully confined and carried out.

7. In many ways, the issue of the "historical George" is parallel to issues associated with quests for the "historical Jesus." While Fox was the primary writer of the *Jounal* (as a contrast to Jesus' being represented later in the gospels by later writers), the three levels of original events, developing memory (tradition) and final writing/editing remain for both figures. Whether or not events happened entirely the way they are represented in Fox's *Journal* (and obviously *some* embellishment and stylizing must have occurred), certainly the ways they are portrayed are significant in and of themselves. They reflect at least the selective memory of highlights and their relation to events preceding and following. That relation in and of itself is significant, although such by no means affects the historical reliability between the events and their later reporting.

assessing the validity of posed solutions, and finally responding to the divine initiative experientially.

1635— Eleven years of age—"The Lord taught me to be faithful in all things...inwardly to God and outwardly to men, and to keep to 'yea' and 'nay' in all things."[8]

1643— In response to coercive appeals to drink in excess and the disappointing example of "professors" of faith— "...the Lord...said unto me, 'Thou seest how young people go together into vanity and old people into the earth; and thou must forsake all, both young and old, and keep out of all, and be as a stranger unto all.'"[9]

1646— "...A consideration arose in me, how it was said that all Christians were believers, both Protestants and Papists; and the Lord opened to me that, if all were believers, then they were all born of God and passed from death to life, and that none were true believers but such..."[10]

—Following earlier debates with four priests—"At another time...the Lord opened unto me that being bred at Oxford or Cambridge does not fit and qualify men to be ministers of Christ; and I stranged at it because it was the common belief of people."[11]

1647— "At another time it was opened in me that God, who made the world, did not dwell in temples made with hands...or dreadful places, and holy ground...but that his people were his temple, and he dwelt in them."[12]

— Versus Nathanael Stephens regarding dependence on priests— "But I brought them Scriptures, and told them there was an anointing within man to teach him, and that the Lord would teach his people himself."[13]

— "But as I had forsaken all the priests, so I left the separate preachers also, and those called the most experienced people; for I saw there was none among them that could speak to my condition. And when all my hopes in them and in all men were gone, so that I had nothing outwardly to help me, nor could I tell what to do, then, Oh then, I heard a voice which said, 'There is one, even Christ Jesus, that can speak to thy condition', and when I heard it my heart did leap for joy."[14]

---

8. *Journal*, Nickalls ed., pp.1-2.

9. *Ibid*, p. 3.

10. *Ibid*, p. 7, certainly a radical notion for its time!

11. *Ibid*, Fox describe how this opening "struck at" Priest Stephens' ministry (twice) and the ministries of the priests, but that it also went against the grain of the dissenting preachers.

12. *Ibid*, p.8; clearly a reflection of Fox's taking to heart the New Testament teaching on the theme, as Fox himself states within the above paragraph, "...for both Stephen and the Apostle Paul bore testimony that he [God] did not dwell in temples made with hands...".

13. *Ibid*. Notice that authorities of both church and scripture are challenged in the name of scriptural teaching on the authentic character of the church. In that sense, Fox is challenging these authorities in the name of biblical ecclesiology. Notice, however, that the "hollow trees and lonesome places" event serves in the ministry of Fox a function similar to the Temptations of Jesus in the wilderness (pp. 9-10), although the testing motif also continues later in his *Journal*.

Phase two: The seeker becomes a finder; encounter is transforming. At this point, Fox comes to see purpose in his search, which gravitates around the calling for all persons everywhere to come into full dependence on Christ and the saving/revealing initiative of God alone.[15] During this phase Fox also reflects upon his own temptations and inclinations away from the truth. This phase furthers the "hollow logs and lonely places" motif as Fox's wilderness experience in preparation for his public ministry continues.

1647— Fox testifies: "My desires after the Lord grew stronger, and zeal in the pure knowledge of God and of Christ alone, without the help of any man, book, or writing. For though I read the Scriptures that spoke of Christ and of God, yet I knew him not but by revelation, as he who hath the key did open, and as the Father of life drew me to his Son by his spirit."[16]

— Likewise—"And I found that there were two thirsts in me, the one after the creatures, to have gotten help and strength there, and the other after the Lord the creator and his Son Jesus Christ. And I saw all the world could do me no good."[17]

— At another opening—"...I therein saw clearly that all was done and to be done in and by Christ, and how he conquers and destroys this tempter, the Devil and all his works, and is atop of him, and that all these troubles were good for me...My living faith was raised, that all was done through Christ, the life, and my belief was in him."[18]

— "Then after this there did a pure fire appear in me; then I saw how he sat as a refiner's fire and as the fuller's soap; and then the spiritual discerning came into me, by which I did discern my own thoughts, groans and sighs, and what it was that did veil me, and what it was that did open me... The divine light of Christ manifesteth all things and the spiritual fire trieth all things, and severeth all things...Therefore, keep daily to the cross, the power of God, by which ye may witness all that to be crucified which is contrary to the will of God, and which shall not come into his kingdom."[19]

---

14. *Ibid*, p. 11. This is the classic account of Fox's encounter with the divine voice, and his ministry becomes irreversibly focused on the Christocentric heart of the Gospel. It begins a new phase of his experience and calling.

15. Fox puts it: "Then therefore the Lord did let me see why there was none upon the earth that could speak to my condition, namely, that I might give him all the glory; for all are concluded under sin, and shut up in unbelief as I had been, that Jesus Christ might have the pre-eminence, who enlightens, and gives grace and faith, and power...And this I knew experimentally." *Ibid*.

16. *Ibid*. Notice the degree to which the medium and message are one.

17. *Ibid*, p. 12. Fox's "temptations" here have to do with trusting in any means of human instrumentality instead of the saving initiative of God. It is the desire for certainty versus the calling to faith. The way forward for Fox is to "wait patiently upon the Lord, whatsoever condition you be in..."

18. *Ibid*, p.14.

19. *Ibid*, pp.14-18.

— "...In this I saw the infinite love of God. I saw also that there was an ocean of darkness and death, but an infinite ocean of light and love, which flowed over the ocean of darkness. And in that also I saw the infinite love of God; and I had great openings.

And as I was walking by the steeplehouse side, in the town of Mansfield, the Lord said to me, 'That which people do trample must be thy food.'"[20]

— "And the same eternal power of God, which brought me through these things, was that which afterwards shook the nations, priests, professors and people. Then could I say I had been in spiritual Babylon, Sodom, Egypt, and the grave; but by the eternal power of God I was come out of it, and was brought over it and the power of it, into the power of Christ. And I saw the harvest white, and the Seed of God lying thick in the ground, as ever did wheat that was sown outwardly, and none to gather it; and for this I mourned with tears."[21]

This concludes the second phase of George Fox's sojourn: his time of temptation and testing—even worrying that he may have sinned against the Holy Ghost. He reports triumphantly regarding such "buffeting," "Thus, by the power of Christ, I got over that temptation also."[22] The third phase of Fox's sojourn relates to the testing of the world, his ongoing transformation and his calling to turn people from darkness to light.

Phase three: Fox receives his calling to proclaim the Day of the Lord and to preach repentance. The year is now 1648, and the shift is clear between the Lord's dealing with Fox personally and his awareness of divine visitation upon multitudes of others. In the following citation one can almost sense a new age dawning, as far as the eschatological awareness of Fox is concerned.

1648— "...I saw there was a great crack to go throughout the earth, and a great smoke to go as the crack went and that after the crack there should be a great shaking. This was the earth in people's hearts, which was to be shaken before the Seed of God was raised out of the earth. And it was so; for the Lord's power began to shake them, and great meetings we began to have, and a mighty power and work of God there was amongst people, to the astonishment of both people and priests..."[23]

— to the assorted preachers in the steeple house of Leicester who were trying to silence a woman Fox declared, "'Dost thou call this place... or mixed multitude a church?' For the woman asking a question, he ought to have answered it, having given liberty for any to speak.' ...I told him the church was the pillar and ground of Truth, made up of living stones, living members, a spiritual household which Christ was the head of, but he was

---

20. *Ibid*, p.19.
21. *Ibid*, p.21.
22. *Ibid*.
23. *Ibid*, p.22.

not the head of a mixed multitude, or of an old house made of lime, stones, and wood."[24]

— "Now was I come up in spirit through the flaming sword into the paradise of God. All things were new, and all the creation gave another smell unto me than before, beyond what words can utter. I knew nothing but pureness, and innocency, and righteousness, being renewed up into the image of God by Christ Jesus, so that I say I was come up to the state of Adam which he was in before he fell."[25]

— "...The Lord opened to me three things relating to those three great professions in the world, physic, divinity (so called), and law. And he showed me that the physicians were out of the wisdom of God[,]...that the priests were out of the true faith which Christ is the author of, ...[and] that the lawyers were out of the equity and out of the true justice and out of the... perfect law of God."[26]

— "I saw also how people read the Scriptures without a right sense of them, and without duly applying them to their own states...They could not know the spiritual meaning of Moses', the prophets', and John's words, nor see their path and travels, much less see through them and to the end of them into the kingdom, unless they had the Spirit and the light of Jesus; nor could they know the words of Christ and of his apostles without his Spirit."[27]

About this time in the *Journal* one identifies a shift from clusters of insight-producing encounters to more of a programmatic phase of Fox's apostolic mission. This phase is characterized by Fox's awareness of his mission marked by the introductory phrase, "Now I was sent to..." followed by a statement of purpose. This marks a fourth stage in the religious experience and ministry of George Fox.

Phase four: Fox is sent as an apostle, commissioned to bring specific messages to particular audiences. Especially significant during this phase as it relates to the thesis of this essay is the fact that insights from earlier openings become the substance of later missions and commissionings. One is not surprised to observe George Fox seeking to be a steward of his understandings of truth, but one gets the sense that the openings themselves become factors in subsequent callings. More generally, every spiritual encounter becomes a spiritual calling as the individual lives out of the newness of transformation. Notice especially the interplay between the "I was sent..."

---

24. *Ibid*, p.24.

25. *Ibid*, p.27. Clearly one of Fox's most transformative openings until now, this passage represents the Quaker conviction that Christ not only saves but also renews the individual radically. See Arthur Roberts' important treatment of George Fox's message and ministry as understood through the lens of this passage: *Through Flaming Sword*, Newberg: Barclay Press, 1959. It was Roberts' first book.

26. *Ibid*, p.28.

27. *Ibid*, pp.31-32.

passages, implying apostolicity (meaning "sentness"), and the "I was to..." passages, implying the mission to be accomplished. Thus, Fox declares:

— "Now I was sent...to turn people from darkness to the light that they might receive Christ...And I was to bring people off from all the world's religions, which are vain, that they might know the pure religion, and might visit the fatherless, the widows and the strangers, and keep themselves from the spots of the world."[28]

— "And I was to bring people off from Jewish ceremonies, and from heathenish fables, and from men's inventions and windy doctrines, by which they blowed the people about this way and the other way, from sect to sect; and all...their vain traditions, which they had gotten up since the apostles' days, which the Lord's power was against..."[29]

— "Moreover when the Lord sent me forth into the world, he forbade me to put off my hat to any, high or low; and I was required to 'thee' and 'thou' all men and women, without any respect to rich or poor, great or small."[30]

After these series of openings one detects a shift from Fox's perception of his calling and openings to the emergence of debates with others along the way. Clearly he responds to the situations and postures of those he meets, but he addresses them directly, and his formulation of his own message—derived from his experiences—becomes apparent. This leads to the final phase of his beginning ministry, from which his later service takes root.

Phase five: Fox engages those he meets along the way and begins the more public kerygmatic work of his ministry. All of this appears to be spurred on by the words of the Lord to Fox in 1649 regarding the "great steeplehouse" of Nottingham: "Thou must go cry against yonder great idol and against the worshippers therein."[31] This command from the Lord seems to begin a new stage in Fox's ministry as his message comes into dialogue with alternative views, and he declares his kerygma openly. He also spends time in prison for the first time, which sensitizes him to issues he later addresses during the Derby imprisonment. Notice the following episodes:

1649— Interrupting the preacher of Nottingham and correcting his exegesis of II Peter 1, "He took for his text the words of Peter...[and] the Lord's Power was so mighty upon me, and so strong in me, that I could not hold, but was made to cry out and say, 'Oh, no, it is not the Scriptures,' [that Peter alluded to as the 'sure word of prophecy' in the text] and was commanded to tell them God did not dwell in temples made with hands. But I told them what it was, namely, the Holy Spirit, by which the holy men of God gave forth the Scriptures, whereby opinions, religions, and judgements

28. *Ibid*, pp.34-35.
29. *Ibid*, p.36.
30. *Ibid*.
31. *Ibid*, p.39.

were to be tried [explicit in the Petrine text]; for it led into all Truth, and so gave the knowledge of all Truth."[32]

During this next section of his *Journal*[33] Fox continues to engage religious and civil authorities, and especially prevalent is the phrase, "I was moved..." as related to specific confrontations and messages. While in jail at Nottingham, Coventry and Derby, Fox becomes moved with compassion for those forced to endure such conditions and becomes an advocate for more humane conditions. He writes to judges, priests and magistrates regarding the need for true justice to prevail and arguing the authentic (spiritual) character of authority. In these letters Fox also sought to convince authorities of the Gospel truth he had received, and in a very real sense, his Derby imprisonment gives rise to his expanding kerygmatic ministry by means of the written word.[34] This year of imprisonment must have also have given Fox much opportunity to reflect upon his openings and message, and the connections between his message delivered at Derby before his imprisonment and later proclamations are evident:

1650— At Derby, before the magistrates: "I said God moved us to do so [to come 'thither'], and I told them, 'God dwells not in temples made with hands.' I told them also all their preaching, baptism, and sacrifices would never sanctify them, and I had many words with them. And I told them they were not to dispute of God and Christ, but to obey him."[35]

Between 1649 and 1652 Fox has several bouts with Ranters, "professors" (of faith), and the likes of Priest Nathanael Stephens and Judge Gervaise Benson and is given ample opportunity to sharpen his message— often out of the duelling of scriptural and theological debates characteristic of his adventures. Central to these debates, however, is the emphasis: "Nay, we are nothing, Christ is all."[36] Some of the more notable citations are as follows:

1651— In jail, Fox's response to Cromwell's offer to release him in exchange for his military service: "But I told them I lived in the virtue of that life and power that took away the occasion of all wars, and I knew from whence all wars did rise, from the lust according to James's doctrine."[37]

1652— "As we went I spied a great high hill called Pendle Hill, and I went on the top of it with much ado, it was so steep; but I was moved of the Lord to go atop it...and there atop it I was moved to sound the Day of the

---

32. *Ibid*, p.40.

33. Chps. III-V; see pp. 44, 48, 49, 51, 62, 66, 73, 74, 79, 84, 95, 98, and especially 104.

34. *Ibid*, pp.52-70.

35. *Ibid*, p.51.

36. *Ibid*, p.56. Emphases on the Spirit who inspired the Scriptures and appeals to justice and righteousness are also directly Christocentric themes. The Spirit of Christ is the source of inspiration for believers, according to Fox, and his indwelling Spirit produces righteousness in the life of the believer.

37. *Ibid*, p.65.

Lord; and the Lord let me see a-top of the hill in what places he had a great people to be gathered...And the Lord opened to me at that place, and let me see a great people in white raiment by a river's side coming to the Lord..."[38]

By now things are really coming to a crescendo. The authenticating role of the attestations by Robinson and Howgill are striking. Robinson declares that Fox "came from the Lord," and Howgill testifies with biblical overtones, "This man speaks with authority and not as the scribes." In between these testimonials Fox summarizes his message, which is indeed parallel to the Firbank Fell sermon, and a digest of his openings thus far. This is the "kerygmatic nugget" preached at the Sedbergh fair:[39]

— "There I declared the everlasting Truth of the Lord and the word of Life for several hours, and that the Lord Christ Jesus was come to teach his people himself and bring them off all the world's ways and teachers to Christ, their way to God; and I laid open all their teachers and set up the true teacher Christ Jesus; and how they were judged by the prophets, Christ, and the apostles; and to bring them off the temples made with hands, that they themselves might know they were the temples of God."

A few pages later, then, his sermon at Firbank Fell is quoted in digest form.

To summarize this section, Fox's openings from 1643-1652 suggest a five-phase progression by which content and experience are interwoven and intricately related to each other: In phase one, the seeker phase, young Fox can be seen as exploring his understanding of truth in dialogue with religious authorities who ought to know better but don't. He becomes distrustful of conventional answers to spiritual questions and finds himself directed again and again to Christ Jesus. Phase two begins when the seeker becomes a finder. His full dependence is on Christ, but he undergoes difficult testing and temptations. He weathers these successfully by the power of the Seed who bruised the serpent's head, and phase three shows Fox experiencing the sanctifying, or transforming work of Christ, simultaneous to the testing of the world. Phase four begins Fox's apostolic mission whereby he is called to turn people from their false securities to the spiritual presence of Christ, and we can identify the planks of a platform being laid and refined for further use. Phase five begins, then, with the kerygmatic aspect of his message and the fulfillment of his envisioning a great people to be gathered. The digest of the three hour sermon at Firbank Fell serves literarily as the ideological manifesto which launches the neo-apostolic movement.[40]

---

38. *Ibid*, p.104.
39. *Ibid*, pp.106-107. In this passage especially the heart of Fox's emerging kerygma becomes apparent. Themes sounded beforehand and in the forthcoming sermon here come together with terse clarity.

III. Interpretation

Now for interpretation. The above openings and reports document in clear ways some of the specific occasions and contexts within which Fox's kerygmatic content has come together prior to his Firbank Fell proclamation as described in his *Journal*. Nearly every phrase in the reported Firbank Fell sermon appears within the previous hundred-plus pages of his *Journal* as having reflected either openings received from the Lord or discoveries made out of debates with others and from personal experience. This fact suggests implications not only about the content of Fox's messages, but also about the epistemological origin of that content, which also relates to the message itself. Not only is his message *about* human/divine encounter, but it also *arises out of* human/divine encounter, and it is designed to *lead the hearer/reader into* such a reality as well.

Finally, a bit of brief analysis deserves to be rendered regarding the ways in which these knowings are formed. Fox's openings appear to emerge from basically three kinds of dialogues, the first two involving a thesis-antithesis-synthesis dialectic (the root of "dialectic" *means* "dialogue") and the third involving another kind. Especially during phase one, the *external and conversational dialectic* is clear between one of Fox's emerging beliefs (thesis), opposing views often represented by priests, preachers or conventional assumptions (antithesis), and the Truth made manifest by Fox's convincing argumentation or a divine opening (synthesis). Or at times, the dialectical roles are reversed. Here the conventional view of another is the thesis, to which Fox's "opening" or insight becomes the antithesis, leading to further deliberation as part of a synthesizing conversation that ensues.

A clear example is the section where young George, who already knew pureness and righteousness, was challenged sequentially by four priests. At the end of it Fox saw that his answers were often better than theirs, and one First-day morning the Lord "opened to him that being bred at Oxford or Cambridge was not enough to fit and qualify men to be ministers of Christ." This is an experiential dialogue, whereby Fox's belief that trained priests ought to know something about the ways of God was severely challenged by his experience. Out of this crisis came the opening that Christ was sufficient. Fox had similar socio-religious dialectical encounters with dis-

---

40. More could be done here by applying James Fowler's six stages of faith development (*Stages of faith Development; the Psychology of Human Development and the Quest for Meaning*, San Francisco: Harper & Row, 1981; and *Becoming Adult, Becoming Christian*, San Francisco: Harper & Row, 1984. See also Craig Dykstra and Sharon Parks (eds.), *Faith Development and Fowler*, Birmingham, Alabama: Religious Education Press, 1986; and Jeff Astley and Leslie Francis (eds.), *Christian Perspectives on Faith Development; A Reader*, Grand Rapids: Eerdmans, 1992), especially regarding the moves from synthetic-conventional to individuative-reflective faith and on to conjunctive and universalizing stages of faith development, but we'll leave that for another exploration.

senting preachers and the conventional notions of his contemporaries, and at times he found himself being opened to new understandings precisely because conventional answers seemed lacking.

The second kind of dialectic may be seen especially clearly during the second phase of Fox's sojourn. It involves an *inward and reflective dialectic,* involving dialogue of mind and soul, juxtaposing personal expectations and their failure to actualize. Such is the essence of theological reflection, and followed by this sort of dialogue is often a transforming spiritual encounter in the experience of George Fox. This sort of dialogue is an existential one because it deals with the essence of the human struggle to maximize the good, tempered by its frustrations and its learnings. After encountering the risen Christ, and feeling his heart leap for joy, Fox sinks into an abyss of depression and frustration. Parallel to the Apostle Paul in Romans 7, Fox believes he is called to a life of purity and righteousness but finds himself sorely tested and tempted to despair—especially in the face of his religions opposition. However, in the midst of his struggles it is opened to him that the head of the serpent was bruised by Christ the Seed and Word of God. Thus, "And this inward life did spring up in me, to answer all the opposing professors and priests, and did bring in Scriptures to my memory to refute them with."[41] Within this sort of cognitive dialogue Fox comes to a spiritual conviction as a result of experiencing spiritual triumph over temptation in his own life, and this knowing enables him to proclaim its veracity to others.

The third dialogue may be seen especially clearly in Fox's third and fourth phases, but it is also common throughout his Journal. This is a *revelational and unmediated dialectic,* and it involves a human/divine dialogue whereby God, or Christ, or the Holy Spirit initiates, humans respond, and that response produces an effect commensurate with the faithfulness of the response.

Like the other dialogues, the revelational dialectic is precipitated by crises which call for resolutions, but as Fox matures in his spiritual sojourn the means by which this encounter happens become more finely tuned. Whether attending the living voice of Christ personally, or reading the scriptures prayerfully, Fox comes to know "experimentally" what he has encountered and proclaimed: *Christ is come to teach his people himself.* There is no need for human or conventional mediation, and this is where experience leads to content—and back to experience again. Fox also facilitates this movement for others by creating an experiential dialectic in the lives of his hearers/readers by means of his written and spoken ministries.

Challenging the conventional notions (theses) that God's Truth is disseminated solely through the priests and the preachers (the church and the scriptures), Fox declares antithetically that these are insufficient. Rather, the

---

41. *Ibid,* p.13. Notice the clearly antithetical corrective, characteristic of this sort of dialogue.

true source of Christ's leadership is through the Holy Spirit. Christocracy (the leadership of Christ) *may* be effected through the church and the Scriptures, but only if Christ's Spirit is at work within and through the leaders and the led, as well as the writings and the readers. And Fox pushes forward, lest such a synthesis become just another conventional notion needing to be overturned by new revelation. He calls seekers to encounter the risen Christ in their own lives as the experiential test of his kerygma's veracity.[42]

Therefore, as all three of these dialectical processes suggest, George Fox's theology of encounter arises out of the experiential character of his own religious sojourn, and this essay seeks to demonstrate something of the way his testimony to that effect may have occurred. Virtually all tenets of his message have been discovered by means of Fox's own spiritual openings, which emerged as the insights gained from socio-religious, existential and revelational dialogues. Challenges produce crises which lead to synthesizing discoveries, and yet discoveries also lead to new crises and further conversations and openings. Not only does Fox's message call for a transforming encounter with the risen Christ, but such encounters serve as the epistemological origin of the message, and expectant waiting before the Lord provides the experimental laboratory wherein the potentiality of the message becomes actual. Thus, the human-divine dialogue continues as believers become open to the transforming Word of God.

Experience and content go hand in hand in George Fox's theology of encounter. Content emerges from experience and literally becomes a spiritual calling to reproduce that which it represents: a transforming encounter with the resurrected Lord. This is both the content and the experience underlying George Fox's theology of encounter. Not only does this relationship demonstrate Fox's claim, "this I knew experimentally," but it also evokes such experimentation in the hearts and lives of others. It thus becomes that which it proclaims.

---

42. More could be done here, applying James Loder's five steps of any knowing event (see *The Transforming Moment; Understanding Convictional Experiences*, San Francisco: Harper & Row, 1981) to the epistemological character of Fox's openings. Any knowing event, says Loder, begins with a crisis, a jolt which is followed by a time of scanning. When the mind locks onto a suitable image this produces a constructive act of the imagination, which is then tested and confirmed. Confirmation brings the "aha" experience of verification, and this leads to reflection.

William Penn and the Scriptures

William Penn was a prolific writer, and, following the practice of the period, he drew upon countless authorities to support his arguments and strengthen the points he wished to make. While he is often remembered for his familiarity with the classics, with church fathers and political philosophers, we should remember that he referred to the Scriptures, and quoted from them more frequently than all other sources combined.

Penn was born during the Civil War in 1644 near the Tower of London and christened in October in All Hallows Barking, the Anglican parish church overlooking the Tower. His father, Captain William Penn, a naval officer, happened to be up the Thames that month having his ship outfitted for a new campaign. He was able to see mother and child, and take his son to the church for christening. His mother, Margaret Jasper Vanderschuren, was a well-to-do young widow who had fled to London when war broke out in Ireland between the Catholics and Protestants and had married the handsome captain in 1643.

The young officer in Parliament's navy, who was soon promoted to the rank of rear admiral, decided to move his small family out of London and obtained a house at Wanstead, in Essex, some ten miles northeast of the city. When he was old enough, young William was enrolled in the Latin school at Chigwell nearby, and studied there until the family moved temporarily to Ireland in 1656. He studied with a tutor during the next four years, and also heard his first Quaker, Thomas Loe, during this period.[1]

In 1660 Admiral Penn took an active part in restoring Charles II to the English throne. He was knighted for his efforts and enrolled his son in Christ Church at Oxford, a stronghold of royalist sympathies. Young William became involved with the nonconformist preacher and scholar Dr. John Owen who opposed the Anglican return to power with the Crown, and was sent down or expelled in 1662. When his father shipped him off to the continent, hoping he would forget his radical religious ideas Penn enrolled for a year in the Huguenot Academy at Saumur, on the Loire, where he studied religious and political philosophy and theology with Moses Amyraut. Thus, when William Penn joined Quakers in 1667 he had accumulated a wide classical and religious education which made him extremely valuable to the hated sect, for he was prepared to serve as a worthy defender of Friends against their religious opponents and persecutors.

His first publication as a Friend, *Truth Exalted* (1668), a fifteen page tract in which he rejected all other religious movements, and proclaimed the virtues of the despised Quakers, contained more than fifty references to the Scriptures.[2] His next publication, *The Guide Mistaken* (1668), a rejoinder to the Anglican priest Jonathan Clapham, who had said that Quakers and a list of other religious groups and churches, could never attain salvation, was strengthened by more than sixty references to the Bible.[3] In his third publication, *The Sandy Foundation Shaken* (1668), written after he and George Whitehead (1635-1723) had debated the Presbyterian Thomas Vincent and several other clergymen, about the nature of the Trinity and the Atonement, got Penn in trouble with the authorities and he was imprisoned in the Tower of London for blasphemy. In the pamphlet he used the Scriptures to refute the doctrine of the Trinity espoused by Vincent, as well as the doctrine of the Atonement advanced by the Presbyterian preacher.[4] After eight months in the Tower, Penn issued *Innocency with Her Open Face* (1669) by way of explanation that he had not meant to deny the Divinity of Christ in his earlier tract, and that he did believe in the Trinity, but not in the way his opponents had defined it. He referred to the Scriptures forty times in this pamphlet.[5] Even in his early years as a Friend Penn was writing essays on

---

1. *William Penn* (1957), by Catherine Owens Peare, is the best biography for Penn, but it should be supplemented by the extensive annotations in *The Papers of William Penn* (1981-1987). The first four volumes of this set were edited by Mary Maples Dunn and Richard S. Dunn, and Volume 5, a bibliography of his published writings was prepared by Edwin B. Bronner and David Fraser. (Hereafter, *PWP*)

2. In 1726, eight years after Penn's death, Joseph Besse issued a two volume folio *Collection of the Works of William Penn*, which was reprinted in 1974. This contains 77 titles and includes all of Penn's important published writings. (Hereafter referred to as *Works*): *Truth Exalted*, 1:239-248. Volume 5 of *The Papers of William Penn*, an annotated, illustrated interpretive bibliography of Penn's published writings, including those volumes to which he contributed, 135 in all, will be used extensively in this paper. *Truth Exalted*, 90-93.

3. *Works*, 2:1-31; *PWP* 5:94,95.

4. *Works*, 1:248-266; *PWP*, 5:96-99. Hugh Barbour discussed the biblical arguments used by Penn in his article "The Young Controversialist," 20, in *The World of William Penn* (1986), edited by Richard S. Dunn and Mary Maples Dunn. Melvin B. Endy, *William Penn and Early Quakerism* (1973), 297.

ethics such as *No Cross, No Crown* (1669) and religious liberty such as *The Great Case of Liberty of Conscience* (1670), in addition to religious tracts to defend Quaker beliefs against their opponents. He used the Scriptures to uphold his arguments in both of these essays, along with appeals to reason and to the writings of classical authors, to church fathers and seventeenth century authorities. In *No Cross, No Crown*, while opposing hat honor and other practices of showing respect, he referred to the Bible numerous times.[6] His first comprehensive defense of religious liberty included numerous citations of the Scriptures in Chapter III: "[persecutors] oppose the plainest Testimonies of Divine Writ that can be, which condemn all Force upon Conscience."[7]

Penn's manuscript correspondence also contained many scriptural references, especially during the years when he spent much of his time defending Friends from their detractors. In Volume 1 of *The Papers of William Penn*, covering the years until the end of 1679, the index contains nine lineal inches of references to specific verses in the Bible. After listing two inches of references in Volume 2, covering the years 1680-84, the rounding of the "Holy Experiment," the editors decided to omit references in subsequent volumes.

Many of the scholars who have written about Penn in recent decades, including Edward C.O. Beatty, *William Penn as Social Philosopher* (1939), Vincent Buranelli, *The King and the Quaker, A Study of William Penn and James II* (1962), Mary Maples Dunn, in *William Penn, Politics and Conscience* (1967), Joseph Illick, *William Penn the Politician* (1965), and Catherine Owen Peare, *William Penn* (1957), virtually ignored Penn's use of the Scriptures. On the other hand, Melvin B. Endy, in *William Penn and Early Quakerism* (1973) devoted a good bit of space to studying the way in which Penn, and Quakers generally in his period, regarded the Bible and used it. Hugh Barbour has also written about Penn's understanding of the Scriptures and his use of the Written Word, especially in his introductory material in *William Penn and Religion and Ethics* (1991).

What did William Penn believe about the Scriptures, and why were his beliefs, and those of other Friends attacked so relentlessly by other church leaders? The Quaker emphasis on the Inward Light meant that other sources of authority were given a secondary place. Catholics looked to Church traditions and the pronouncements of Church fathers for guidance

---

5. *Works*, 1:266-271; *PWP*, 5:100, 101.

6. The 1669 edition is not in *Works*, but may be read in Barbour's *William Penn on Religion and Ethics* (1991), 39-113. *PWP*, 5:102-104.

7. *Works* 1:443-467; *PWP*, 5:112-117. This essay may also be read in the Everyman Paperback Classic, *William Penn's The Peace of Europe, The Fruits of Solitude and Other Writings* (1993), edited by Bronner, 153-186. This new collection of ten of Penn's most important and most readable essays, is available in an inexpensive edition in the United States as well as in Great Britain.

and authority. Protestants, rebelling against the teachings of the Roman Catholic faith, turned to the Scriptures as their source of authority. Friends declared that true authority was found by a personal encounter with Christ through the indwelling spirit, the Inward Light, not from the words of men or the words printed on a page of the Bible.

In *Primitive Christianity Revived in the Faith and Practice of the People Called Quakers* (1696) Penn draws upon the writings of John, what he calls "the blessed Scriptures of Truth," to prove the primacy of the Christ Within or Light Within. "In the Beginning was the Word, and the Word was with God, and the Word was God."[8] More than two decades earlier, in *The Spirit of Truth Vindicated* (1672), written to defend George Fox who was in America, Penn had used the Scriptures to defend the belief of Friends that while the Light Within was the ultimate authority, the Bible was also an expression of the True Spirit.[9]

Hugh Barbour, in *William Penn on Religion and Ethics* calls our attention to a defense of the value of the Scriptures in Penn's volume *An Address to Protestants* (1679): "All Scripture is given by Inspiration of God and is profitable for Doctrine, for Reproof, for Correction, for Instruction in Righteousness, that the Man of God may be perfect, throughly [sic] furnisht unto all good Works." (This quotation is from II Timothy 3:16,17).[10]

At the same time, as Endy pointed out, the Bible was often misused by clergymen and others seeking to prove a particular doctrine or practice. "Scripture, according to Penn, had yielded so many contradictory answers to important questions that exegetes had been able to find there whatever they wished to discover. They seemed to devote most of their time to writing tracts to prove that Scripture contained only the answers which they had found."[11] Penn wrote in *Reason Against Railing* (1673), "That the Scriptures are Unintelligible without it {i.e., the Inner Light} is easily prov'd from the variety of Judgments that are in the World about most of the Fundamental Doctrines contained therein."[12] Endy went on to refer to *The Invalidity of John Faldo's Vindication* (1673), in which Penn wrote, "Wherefore since the Scriptures themselves testify to the Spirit, as the great Judge, Rule and Leader, especially under the New Covenant, when the Law is not written on Tables of Stone (much less Paper) but of Flesh, to wit, the Hearts of the Sons and Daughters of Men, the Spirit, and not the Scriptures must be the rule of Faith and Judge of Controversy."[13]

---

8. *Works*, 2:856; *PWP*, 5:434-437; Everyman, *Penn*, 231.

9. *Works*, 2:135ff.; *PWP*, 5:137,138; Barbour, "The Young Controversalist," 22, *The World of William Penn*.

10. p. 463. It may be found in *Works*, 1:756, and *PWP*, 237-242, which points out it went through two editions, seven printings in all by 1692. Barbour had written about this earlier in *Quakers in Puritan England* (1964), 157-159.

11. *William Penn and Early Quakerism*, 154, 155.

12. *Works*, 2:508; *PWP*, 5:160-162.

On occasion Penn went further in his comments about the Scriptures, suggesting inconsistencies and weaknesses in the compilation of the accepted texts and books in the Bible. Melvin Endy pointed out that Penn, from the 1670's wrote of "its contradictions and barbarities, the likelihood of lost books, textual corruptions, poor copying and translating... ." He also pointed out that the writings in "the New Testament canon were scattered and uncollected for several centuries."[14] Despite such criticism Penn strongly supported the use of the Scriptures, as long as they were measured against the Spirit. He rejected the Protestant idea that the Spirit was found in the Bible, that "one could buy the Spirit from a bookseller." He added, "one needed the guidance of the Spirit to ascertain the true meaning of the Scriptures because of its lack of clarity, its contradictions, and other characteristics making it unsuitable as a rule of doctrine."

In summarizing this section of his book Endy wrote, "Penn, then, emphasized at different times both the inadequacies of Scripture and its usefulness." He added, Penn believed "it was important to state clearly that the Spirit was the agent, Scripture the subordinate means, and that the Spirit could bring Christ to a man independently of Scriptures."[15]

In *A Key Opening the Way* (1692) Penn wrote that Friends regard the Scriptures as "given forth in former Ages by the Inspiration of the Holy Spirit...ey are profitable for Doctrine, for Reproof, for Correction, for Instruction in Righteousness, that the Men of God may be perfect." He went on to deny that the Scriptures were The Word of God, that is, the sole Word of God; that was to claim more than Quakers could accept.[16] Penn's use of the Scriptures to prove the primacy of the Inward Light in 1696 in *Primitive Christianity Revived* has already been mentioned.

Three of Penn's best loved writings are *Some Fruits of Solitude* (1693), *More Fruits of Solitude* (1702), and *Fruits of a Father's Love* (1726, but probably written in 1699).[17] These collections of aphorisms or maxims, some 900 in all offer good advice, pertinent observations on life, and in the third volume, extended advice to his children about how they should conduct themselves.

While he clearly relied on the Scriptures as an important source of his writing, he seldom referred directly to the Bible in his Maxims. In *Some Fruits* he called upon his readers to be like Christ, and suggested using the Scriptures as well as the Inward Light to gain a better understanding of God's Will in this regard.[18] In *More Fruits* he used the familiar thirteenth

---

13. *Works*, 2:337; *PWP*, 5:167-169.

14. *Penn and Early Quakerism*, 207-215.

15. Ibid., 215.

16. *Works*, 2:778-791, particularly 781, 782; *PWP*, 5:387-395. This popular tract went through thirteen printings during Penn's lifetime.

17. These three titles are included in Everyman's *Penn*, 23-118.

chapter of I Corinthians, about the importance of charity or love to emphasize his points. He paraphrased this passage rather than quoting it exactly, a
practice he often followed.[19] In *Fruits of a Father's Love* Penn gave many
scriptural references in addition to strongly recommending the daily reading of the Bible.[20]

While seeking to emphasize the importance of the Bible to his children
Penn told them that "from my youth I loved to read [the Scriptures, and
they] were ever blessed to me." He added that they should read "the Old
Testament for history chiefly, the Psalms for meditation and devotion, the
prophets for comfort and hope, but especially the New Testament for doctrine, faith and worship... ."[21] He continued by referring to the source of
the Scriptures and their importance in revealing the Will of God.

When Penn was asked by his young friend John Rodes (1670-1743) to
suggest readings in various areas, Penn mentioned the Bible before any
other titles in several categories, particularly in the area of ethics and international policy.[22] His other suggestions included classical authors such as
Seneca, Plutarch, Epictetus and Tacitus, scientific writers such as Francis
Bacon and Robert Boyle, and renaissance authors such as Thomas More
and Machiavelli.

The second, and completely revised edition of *No Cross, No Crown*
(1682) has been read by Friends and others more frequently than any other
of Penn's titles, though it has not been as popular in the present century as
earlier. We are told that it sat on shelves in meetinghouses and in Quaker
homes along with Fox's *Journal* and Robert Barclay's *Apology*.[23] It is often
remembered because Penn quoted from nearly 150 men and women in the
second part of the book, more than half of whom were from the classical
period, including twelve women. The balance of the authorities Penn
quoted were early church leaders before the Reformation, and political,
philosophical and religious figures from the period after that earthshaking
event. However, it is worth noting that Penn cited more than 600 scriptural
passages in the first half of the book. More of these references were from
the New Testament than the Old, but he referred to many of the books in
the Old Testament from Genesis to Malachi.

While William Penn had a broader educational experience than any
other seventeenth century Friend, and also moved more freely in all circles
of society than any other member of the new sect, he kept in the main-

18. Ibid., 56; *PWP*, 5:401-409; *Works*, No. 469, 1:840.

19. Everyman, *Penn*, 86; *PWP*, 5:493, 494; *Works*, No. 295, ff., 1:858.

20. Everyman, *Penn*, 89-118, especially 94; *PWP*, 5:514-516; *Works*, 1:893-911, especially 896.

21. Everyman, *Penn*, 94.

22. *PWP*, 5:42, and Sophie F. Locker-Lampson, editor, *A Quaker Post-Bag* (1910), 4-6.

23. *PWP*, 5:287-294; *Works*, 1:272-439; *No Cross, No Crown* (1981), introduction by Norman Penney, and foreward by Barbour.

stream of Quaker belief and practice. His familiarity with classical authors, with church history, and with contemporary thought did not keep him from remaining thoroughly familiar with the Scriptures, and from using the Bible in most of his writings. Even though he had become familiar with some of the inconsistencies in the Scriptures which makes him a forerunner of what was to be called "Higher Criticism" in the last century, this did not deter him from extensive use of the Bible, nor did it diminish his deep appreciation for it.

His last recorded words, found in the biographical notes prepared by his editor, Joseph Besse (c.1683-1757), were delivered to two friends who went to visit Penn in Ruscombe in 1716, four years after his serious strokes. As they were leaving he bade them good-bye with these words paraphrased from the Scriptures: "My Love is with you; The Lord preserve you, and remember me in the Everlasting Covenant."[24]

---

24. *Works*, 1:150. The phrase "the Lord preserve thee" is in Psalms 121:7,8 and the words "Everlasting Covenant" are found in several places in the Old Testament as well as in Hebrews 13:20.

Religion and Ethics in the Thought
of John Bellers

T. VAIL PALMER, JR.

T he lives and writings of seventeenth- and early eighteenth-century
Friends have had an enormous impact on later generations of
Quakers. They have also received due attention from church historians. George Fox's *Journal* has achieved a measure of fame as a Christian
devotional classic. Beyond this, only two of these early Friends have
received significant attention, after their time, in circles beyond the Quaker
family. One of these Friends, William Penn, is well enough known to need
no further comment. The other one is John Bellers. His writings have had
their chief impact on Socialist and Communist thinkers. Robert Owen,
early nineteenth-century utopian socialist, acknowledges Bellers as an
important source for his thought. Karl Marx cites Bellers in several footnotes in *Das Kapital*; in the most famous of these he calls Bellers a "veritable
phenomenon" or a "phenomenal figure in the history of political economy."[1] The revisionist Marxist historian, Eduard Bernstein, develops Marx's
footnoted hints into a full chapter on Bellers in his study of radical reli-
gious-social movements of the seventeenth century: *Cromwell and Communism*.

What was the source of Bellers's social-political insights, which received
such significant attention in later centuries? Quakers today often suggest
that the religious experiences of Quakers are the source from which they
derive their significant social and ethical insights, including the remarkable,
sometimes unique, corporate Quaker social "testimonies." Would this sug-

---

1. Karl Marx, *Capital*, tr. Eden and Cedar Paul, Everyman's Library No. 848 & 849
(London: J. M. Dent & Sons, 1930), Vol. 1, p. 527, n. 1.

gestion account for Bellers's social-economic insights? Or would an analysis of his thought point to some other source?

John Bellers (1654-1725), a second-generation Quaker, was the author of a number of writings, most of them proposing specific social reforms: employment for the poor, a council of European states, maintenance of permanent lists of qualified voters, publicly supported hospitals for treatment of the poor and for medical research, education for the children of the poor. Although he directed in his will that his books were to be collected and reprinted in a single volume, this was not done. Robert Owen reprinted his "Proposals for Raising a Colledge of Industry" in 1818.[2] A. Ruth Fry reprinted substantial excerpts from most of his writings in a single volume in 1935.

Bellers's writings present remarkable contrasts to those of Edward Burrough and other first-generation Friends. The style of George Fox, Burrough, and other Friends of their generation, tends to be turbid, repetitive, and long-winded. Bellers's style, in comparison, is brisk and crisp, with some of his arguments reduced nearly to outline form. Probably few modern readers would require his apology lest "some may think me too short in Expression."[3]

There is a distinct drop in religious temperature from the thunder and the consolation of Burrough's enthusiasm[4] to Bellers's calm, even bland rationality and his tendency to reduce all religions to their lowest common denominator. On the other hand, where Burrough's proposals for social action are usually brief and undeveloped, and often seem to be rather incidental outworkings of the basic thrust of his radical Christian theology, Bellers's entire attention is devoted to spelling out in specific detail his proposed social reforms; and these proposals are dotted with remarkable, if occasionally idiosyncratic, insights into the nature of the forces at work in human society.

Moreover, Burrough makes quite different ethical proposals to Friends and to others;[5] he clearly expects a stricter standard of righteousness within the church of the faithful than among those whom he thinks to be only nominally Christian. In contrast, Bellers often addresses identical proposals

---

2. For a discussion of the interest of Robert Owen and of Marxist writers in John Bellers, see T. Vail Palmer [Jr.], "A Revisionist Revised: A New Look at Bernstein's *Cromwell and Communism*," in D. Neil Snarr and Daniel L. Smith-Christopher, eds., *Practiced in the Presence: Essays In Honor of T. Canby Jones* (Richmond, IN: Friends United Press, 1994), pp. 52-57.

3. *John Bellers, 1654-1725: Quaker Economist and Social Reformer. His Writings Reprinted, with a Memoir by A. Ruth Fry* (London: Cassell and Co., 1935), p. 56 (hereafter referred to as Bellers, *Writings Reprinted*).

4. T. Vail Palmer, Jr., "Quaker Peace Witness: the biblical and historical roots," *Quaker Religious Thought*, Vol. 23, Nos. 2 and 3 (cumulative numbers 68 and 69, June 1988), pp. 40-41 (hereafter referred to as Palmer, "Peace Witness").

5. *Ibid.*, p. 44.

to Friends and to others, and even when appending different covering notes to Friends and to, say, members of Parliament, he uses similar arguments in both instances.

Bellers's religious views can be characterized as rationalist and eclectic in their emphasis. He is concerned to point out what it is that the various Christian groups hold in common. Thus, in making "A Proposal for a General Council of all the Several Christian Persuasions in Europe," he recommends that "first, they should take an Account what Things all the several Religious Perswasions in *Europe* agree in. And then it will appear, That those two Essential Articles of Loving God and their Neighbours, will be two of them."[6] His tendency to stress the points which Christians can agree on and to avoid religious controversy can be seen in the reasons he gives for distributing Robert Barclay's *Apology* "to all the Parliament-Men, Ministers of State, and Magistrates, &c. in the Nation." In contrast to many early Quaker writings, Barclay's book, "being rather a Peaceable than a Controversial Declaration of our Principles, it finds the easier Acceptance with some that love not Controversy, without publishing our Adversaries Books,[7] which Books of Controversy do."[8]

Bellers draws with approval on religious ideas proposed by a number of authorities in various ages and places. After quoting a page-long argument from Isaac Newton, he sums it up by commending "this Excellent Philosopher" for his "bright and pure Demonstrations of a *First Cause*."[9] He quotes for inspiration from the works of the since-forgotten poets, Edmund Waller and Edward Young.[10] He can quote from Solomon and Confucius as joint authorities on the advantages to a kingdom of promoting the work of "Men of useful Genius's."[11] Yet another quotation suggests Bellers's appropriation of the thought of two great mystics; he quotes in its entirety "A Short Dia-

---

6. Bellers, *Writings Reprinted*, p. 99.

7. Typical early Quaker practice, in controversial writing, was to quote in full the objectionable sentence or paragraph from the opponent's document, and then to refute it. In this way, these controversial tracts literally involved "publishing our Adversaries Books," bit by bit, within the Quaker books refuting them!

8. John Bellers, *An Abstract of George Fox's Advice and Warning, to the Magistrates of London, in the Year 1657. Concerning the Poor. With Some Observations thereupon, and Recommendations of them to the Sincerely Religious, but more particularly to the Friends of London, and Morning-Meeting of these Times* (London: Assigns of J. Sowle, 1724), p. 17 (hereafter referred to as Bellers, *Abstract*).

9. Bellers, *Writings Reprinted*, pp. 140-141.

10. *Ibid.*, pp. 123, 135-136, 140.

11. John Bellers, *An Essay Towards the Improvement of Physick: In Twelve Proposals. By Which the Lives of many Thousands of the Rich, as well as of the Poor, may be Saved Yearly. With an Essay for Imploying the Able Poor; By which the Riches of the Kingdom may be Greatly Increased; Humbly dedicated to the Parliament of Great Britain* (London: Assigns of J. Sowle, 1714), pp. 18-19.

logue between a Learned Divine and a Beggar,"[12] which was originally, as he puts it,

> above 300 Years ago, then writ by John Taulerus, and since printed in Doctor Everrard's Works (Part 2d p. 451) who was a Religious Dissenter, in King James the First's Time.[13]

Bellers's own theology or philosophy of religion is summarized on several occasions in his detailing, in philosophical terms, of a number of the attributes of God:

> God is from Eternity to Eternity, without Beginning of Time, or End of Life.... He is infinite and omnipresent, ...omnipotent in Power, being able to do all things, ...omniscient.... His Being is invisible, immaterial Life and Spirit, Light and Glory.[14]

> God only (who is Light) can penetrate Men's Souls, and beholds the most inward Thoughts and Desires thereof...God is in all Places, and fills all things, ...so pure invisible and intellectual a Spirit.[15]

> The only Wise God, Omnipotent and Eternal.[16]

He even concludes an epistle to a Quaker quarterly meeting with a prayer in which God is addressed in similar terms:

> Thou Holy, Almighty and Eternal God! Who fills Heaven and Earth with thy Presence. ...Thou know'st our Wants and our Necessities;...Thou inexhaustible Fountain and Fulness of all our Mercies and Blessings! ...

> Thy Will, O Lord! is united to infinite Wisdom and omnipotent Power. ... Words are to few, and all the Languages in the Universe are not sufficient, ...fully to set forth the Glory of thy Majesty! the Might of thy Power, Or the Excellency of thy Wisdom! Thou unexpressible Being! Who art GOD over All; Blessed in thy Self for ever and ever.[17]

God, to Bellers, is the Creator; but man can play a role in helping to complete his creation. The work of making the lot of mankind more comfortable, for instance, "will be instrumental in God's hand in finishing his Creation (Man being the Head of it)."[18]

---

12. Bellers, *Writings Reprinted*, pp. 155-158.
13. *Ibid.*, p. 154.
14. *Ibid.* p. 78.
15. *Ibid.*, p. 79.
16. *Ibid.*, p. 92.
17. John Bellers, *An Epistle to the Quarterly-Meeting of London and Middlesex* (no place, no publisher, 1718), p. 15 (hereafter referred to as Bellers, 1718 *Epistle*).

Bellers's appreciation of philosophy does not extend to the point that, for him, philosophy or knowledge is an end in itself; rather, "the great end of all true Philosophy, whether *Experimental* or *Moral*, is to improve the Happiness of Men, either of Body or Mind, in the Things of *this* World or of the *next*."[19] In light of this ultimately pragmatic statement, it is perhaps not surprising that Bellers should so frequently include pragmatic or prudential appeals at the heart of his arguments for social reform: "Next to the Love of God, and of Vertue, Interest and Rewards are the best Preventions of Vice."[20]

He can even appeal to London Friends, some of whom, like Bellers himself, could remember their own imprisonments and other sufferings for their faith: "Except we make those Poor our Friends, which we may and ought to take Care of: Such Poor may come to be a vicious and distrest Mobb, and ready Instruments in the Hands of our Enemies to bring much Sufferings upon us."[21]

It will not be necessary here to summarize in detail the nature of Bellers's social-reform proposals. Many writers have done so; in particular, William C. Braithwaite, A. Ruth Fry, Eduard Bernstein, Karl Seipp, and Philip S. Belasco have done so at some length.[22] But it will be worth repeating a few of his more remarkable insights, which have contributed to the development of social thought.

One principle emphasized by Bellers in his social thought is the value of human life: "The Life of a Man is of greater Value with God than many Pounds, and ought to be so with Men."[23] More specifically, Bellers suggests that the value of human life, which he thus states in economic or monetary terms, should be expressed in the labor which people perform; in his "Proposals for Raising a College of Industry,"[24] he suggests, "This Colledge-

---

18. Bellers, *Writings Reprinted*, p. 38.

19. *Ibid.*, p. 139.

20. *Ibid.*, p. 74.

21. Bellers, *Abstract*, p. 9.

22. William C. Braithwaite, *The Second Period of Quakerism*, 2d ed. prepared by Henry J. Cadbury (Cambridge: At the University Press, 1961), pp. 571-594; A. Ruth Fry, "John Bellers, Quaker, Economist and Social Reformer," in Bellers, *Writings Reprinted*, pp. 5-28; Eduard Bernstein, *Cromwell and Communism: Socialism and Democracy in the Great English Revolution*, trans. H. J. Stenning (New York: Augustus M. Kelley, 1966 [reprint of 1930 1st ed.]), pp. 253-280; Karl Seipp, *John Bellers: Ein Vertreter des frühen Quäkertums* (Nürnberg: Quäker-verlag, 1933); Philip S. Belasco, *Authority in Church and State* (London: George Allen & Unwin, 1928), pp. 96-107; Philip S. Belasco, "John Bellers," *Economica*, Vol. 5 (no. 14, June 1925), pp. 165-174.

23. Bellers, *Writings Reprinted*, pp. 76-77.

24. It is difficult to characterize Bellers's famous "Colleges of Industry" according to any simple model. They include some ideas of a modern co-operative community or community of labor, some aspects of a modern paternalistic industry-related community (like Bournville, England, or Hershey, Pa.), and some aspects of a vocationally-oriented boarding school.

Fellowship will make Labour, and not Money, the Standard to value all Necessaries by."[25]

Bellers was not the first thinker to propose a labor theory of value. John Locke, for example, had already formulated such a theory. Bellers's version of the labor theory of value, however, is formulated in his own peculiar way, which comes closer than does Locke's version to anticipating the later development of this theory as a basic component of Karl Marx's economic analysis. In particular, Bellers is concerned to show how the wealth of the rich has no other source than the labor of the poor: "The Labour of the Poor being the Mines of the Rich."[26] "The rich have no other way of living, but by the labour of others; as the landlord by the labour of his tenants, and the merchants and tradesmen by the labour of the mechanicks, except they turn levellers, and set the rich to work with the poor."[27]

A central point which Bellers keeps emphasizing is to dispute any idea that money can be considered the source of value or of wealth; money is at most a medium of exchange or a measure of wealth:

> Land, Stock upon it, Buildings, Manufactures and Mony, are the Body of our Riches; and of all these, Mony is of least use, until it's parted with; ...Mony is unprofitable to a private Person but as he disposeth of it, for something more valuable; ...as Mony increaseth in quantity, it decreaseth in Value in a Country, except the People and Stock increase in proportion to the Mony.
> Mony hath two Qualities, it is a Pledge for what it is given for and it's the Measure and Scales by which we Measure and Value all other things.[28]

At one point Bellers may seem to be suggesting a "population theory of value," at least as far as the source of the value of land is concerned: "It being the multitude of people that makes land in Europe more valuable than land in America, or in Holland than Ireland."[29] However, even here Bellers means that a larger population increases the value of land, because it provides a greater quantity of labor to make the land productive; his statement is given as a reason for his argument that putting the unemployed poor to work in England would increase the wealth of the nation.

---

25. *Ibid.*, p. 37.
26. *Ibid.*, p. 38.
27. John Bellers, "Proposals for Raising a Colledge of Industry in all Useful Trades and Husbandry, with Profit for the Rich, A Plentiful living for the Poor, and A Good Education for Youth. Which will be Advantage to the Government, by the Increase of the People, and their Riches," in Robert Owen, *New View of Society*, reprint from edition of 1818, London (New York: AMS Press, 1972), p. 35 (hereafter referred to as Bellers, "Proposals").
28. Bellers, *Writings Reprinted*, pp. 69-70.
29. Bellers, "Proposals," p. 32.

With all of his emphasis on the wealth of the rich as being essentially parasitic on the labor of others, John Bellers does not propose that such wealth should be eliminated. On the contrary, he specifies that the "Colleges of Industry," which he proposes as means of putting the unemployed to work, should be established by the wealthy, who should expect to make a profit from their investment in such Colleges. His reasoning, on this point, is pragmatic: "A thousand pound is easier raised where there is profit, than one hundred pound only upon charity; people readily employing all their estates where there is profit, when they will not give a tenth of it to the poor."[30] Profit is stronger as a motive than are love and charity; therefore we have to appeal to that motive, even when we want to accomplish goals that are essentially altruistic: "However prevailent Arguments of Charity may be to some, when profit is joyned with it, it will raise most Money, and consequently provide for most People; hold longest and do most Good: For what Sap is to a Tree, that, Profit is to all Business, by encreasing and keeping of it A-live."[31]

Bellers uses a similar pragmatic argument in arguing for freedom of religion: "There being no Necessity, to force Creeds: but to perswade to Charity; in order to make a Kingdom prosperous, Men good Subjects to their Princes, and Friends to their Neighbours: those Countries and States thriving best where they are most easy about Ceremonies, while the most rigid are much less populous; *Holland* is an Instance of the First, and *Spain* of the latter."[32]

To his pragmatic arguments for the establishment of colleges of industry for the poor, Bellers adds an emphasis on the responsibility of the rich: to whom much is given, from them much will be required. Thus he writes to his fellow-Quakers: "We having more Friends of Industry, in Trade and of good Estates among us now, than in any Time since we were a People, and consequently the Account that must be given for those Estates will be so much the greater."[33]

At this point, however, we find that Bellers has implicitly appealed to a biblical standard of judgment (Lk. 12:48). Elsewhere his dependence on biblical sources is more open and explicit. Even his appeal to labor, rather than to money, as the source of value is dictated, at least in part, by his attention to the Christian Scriptures: "This Colledge-Fellowship will make Labour, and not Money, the Standard to value all Necessaries by; and tho' Money hath its Conveniences, in the common way of living, it being a Pledge among Men for want of Credit; yet not without its Mischiefs; and call'd by our Saviour, The *Mammon of Unrighteousness*."[34]

---

30. *Ibid.*, p. 35.
31. Bellers, *Abstract*, p. 15.
32. Bellers, *Writings Reprinted.*, p. 99.
33. Bellers, *Abstract*, p. 8.

His appeal to Christian revelation even sets limits to his eclecticism; there comes a point where Jesus must supersede any non-Christian authorities, as the moral pattern: "Never mention those Heathen Heroes, such as *Alexander, Caesar* or *Hannibal,* for Patterns to be Imitated by Christian Princes, who Sacrificed the Lives of Thousands, to their restless Ambition and Honour; But let the Holy Jesus, who went about doing good, be the Example for all Christian Princes to Imitate, which will Increase their Subjects, and add lasting Glory to themselves, and a happy Peace to both."[35]

The extent of Bellers's dependence on the Bible is greatly obscured if one reads only the extensive excerpts from his writings in the volume by A. Ruth Fry. The original printings of his writings frequently include long lists of Bible passages, often quite brief, which Bellers apparently considers relevant to his arguments. The number of clear biblical references, both in the text of his writings and in the appended lists of supporting passages, strongly suggested to me that an analysis of Bellers's use of the Bible might afford some clues to the relationship between religion and ethics in his thought.

In the works of Bellers which I could find, I counted 317 biblical references; 242 of these were from the New Testament, 75 from the Old Testament. Certain books are clear favorites. Bellers quotes 38 times from the Gospel of Luke; other books from which he quotes 20 or more times, in order of decreasing frequency, are the Gospel of Matthew, the Gospel of John and the book of Proverbs, and the First Epistle of John.

There are four passages which Bellers quotes four or more times each: Luke 16:19-31, six times (the parable of the rich man and Lazarus); Luke 16:9 ("And I say unto you, Make to yourselves friends of the mammon of unrighteousness; that, when ye fail, they may receive you into everlasting habitations." KJV); Matthew 25:31-46 (the parable of the sheep and the goats at the great judgment); and Acts 17:23-28 (from Paul's speech on Mars Hill in Athens: "God...dwelleth not in temples made with hands; ...and hath made of one blood all nations of men; ...they should seek the Lord... and find him; though he be not far from every one of us." KJV).

The most remarkable aspect of Bellers's biblical references is the fact that a few themes recur frequently in his quotations. His greatest emphasis is on the general theme of the last judgment or of judgment after death; 58 of his quotations reflect this eschatological theme. Bellers does not dwell much, in the references he chooses, on when the judgment will occur: at the moment of death or at the end of history, in the imminent or indefinite future. The theme running through these passages is the simple idea that a future judgment will come.

---

34. Bellers, *Writings Reprinted.*, p. 39.
35. *Ibid.*, p. 97.

Another significant theme in Bellers's biblical quotations is an interest in the poor and the afflicted. Forty-three of his references comfort the poor, condemn the rich, or call for aid to the poor and afflicted. Nearly half of these passages (21) also reflect the theme of judgment, the ideas that the rich will suffer after the final judgment, that final rewards will go the poor or to those who help the poor and suffering in their distress.

Another theme, much emphasized by Bellers, is that of spirit; 49 of his quotations refer to the Spirit of God or to man's spirit. The biblical theme of light is emphasized in 27 quotations. The importance of wisdom, reason, understanding, knowledge is the theme of 27 quotations. The proposition "in" is central to 25 quotations—in the sense that in these passages God or Christ, revelation or the knowledge of God, light or God's Spirit is said to be **in** man.

A significant number of Bellers's biblical references have to do with certain ethical attitudes. Thirty of these passages advocate love—love of the brother, of the neighbor, of one another. Anger is condemned or warned against in 19 quotations.

Other themes appear in the Bible passages quoted by Bellers, but far less frequently than do those I have listed. It is clear, then, that his use of the Bible is highly selective and represents strong, central religious concerns in his thinking. It is not surprising that many of these themes are also emphasized in the text of his writings.

Thus Bellers emphasizes the eschatological sanction for morality, the idea that our behavior will be rewarded or punished at the final judgment:

> Happy will those Princes and States be, who shall be Instruments, in settling such a Peace in Christendom, for as it will give them the greater Assurance of Crowns Eternal hereafter.[36]

> Whether at the Great Day of Judgment, where the most secret things shall appear, much more the most publick: There will be any Crime so aggravataed, as that of having been an Enemy to Settling and Establishing the Peace of Europe, that might have prevented the destruction of such a vast body of Christians, as then will appear.[37]

> God...made Men in Order to Raise or Create Angels (from such of them as should attaine the Resurrection) or Beings, equal to Angels. ...

> Therefore the Raising and Reformation of Mankind to prepare them for that happy State, is the Duty and Business of all Degrees of Mankind; As... the Rich as General Stewards to Imploy, and Relieve, and the Ministers to Instruct the Poor and their Children; ...by which making Friends of the

---

36. *Ibid.*, p. 95.
37. *Ibid.*, p. 97.

Mammon of Unrighteousness, it will add to the Glory and Happiness of your Mansions, Eternally in the Heavens.[38]

In introducing his quotation of the "Dialogue between a Learned Divine and a Beggar," Bellers begins, "I shall add the Substance of an Excellent Discourse (as an Addition to mine, Of the Value of the Poor) of a poor Man in *Germany*, above 300 Years ago."[39] In light of this introduction and of his emphasis on the poor in his biblical references, Bellers doubtless quotes this dialogue not because of any interest in the mysticism of Tauler and Everard but because of the emphasis in the dialogue on the poor beggar as a fount of religious wisdom.

The themes of light, of wisdom, and of the knowledge of God in man are all reflected in a passage in which Bellers asks, regarding God,

> Cannot he cause a Light revealing himself, to spread thro' the inmost recesses of our Souls? ...

> He that really believes the Existence of an *All-comprehending, Omnipotent, Intelligent Being*, can he disbelieve even the very probability of his Working thus in our Minds? ...

> Is not therefore *Inward Light*, or *Divine Irradiation*, (how weakly or uncautiously soever, some may have explained it) a Doctrine that plainly results, from the Necessary *Omnipresence* of God, and the Intellectual Nature of Humane Souls?[40]

In his "Proposal for a General Council of all the Several Christian Persuasions in Europe,"[41] Bellers urges (in contrast to an earlier similar proposal by Henry IV of France) the inclusion of the Russians and the Turks in the council, on the grounds that "the *Muscovites* are Christians and the *Mohometans* Men, and have the same faculties, and reason as other Men."[42] Bellers's emphasis on the essential rationality of human nature is also found in the following description of the soul: "The Soul of Man is the most invisible, spiritual, and intellectual Part of this Creation."[43] He also insists on the divine source of human rationality and knowledge: "As the *First Being* which created all Natural ones was Divine, so in all Ages and Countries of the World, those *Original Illuminations* in Men, which explain'd the Method of Nature, must flow from that Fountain of Light which first put Nature into Order."[44]

---

38. Bellers, *Abstract*, p. 3.
39. Bellers, *Writings Reprinted*, p. 154.
40. *Ibid.*, p. 142.
41. *Ibid.*, p. 99.
42. *Ibid.*, p. 103.
43. *Ibid.*, p. 78.

For Bellers, the doctrine of Inward Light implies not only the rationality of human nature but also its nobility and capacity for reform. He writes in a broadside to criminals in prison: "Consider the Nobility of your Nature, being of the same Species with other Men, and therefore capable by a thoro' Reformation to become Saints on Earth, and as Angels in Heaven to Reign with our Saviour there."[45]

Bellers's accent, in his biblical references, on the importance of love in the religious life, comes out in frequent references in the text of his writings to love or charity as one of the prime essentials of true religion:

Every Man may esteem the Value of his Religion in proportion to the Love he finds toward God and his Neighbours, for on those depend all true Religion, and one of the greatest Marks that we sincerely love God is, when we use our Endeavours for the good and happiness one of another.[46]

Since we are become a considerable Body in the Nation, there is a Duty incumbent on this Body, to exert it self in all Christian Offices to propagate Vertue, Charity and Piety among Men; Good Examples being more convincing than Precepts.[47]

At times Bellers writes more broadly of virtue or morality as the essence (from an objective point of view) of true religion: "Immorality in the Professors of any Religion makes them the greatest Enemies and Ruin of that Religion which they profess."[48]

More specifically in such contexts, he sometimes equates charity and virtue with care for the needs of the poor:

The ill Morals and Miseries of the Poor, are scandalous to our Religion to the last Degree, Charity and Virtue being the greatest Ornaments and Excellencies of Christianity.[49]

[George Fox] charged the Citizens from the Lord to take care of the Poor, and as the Charge and Message to the Citizens was then General, so it remains a Duty and Obligation upon the Citizens to all Generations, and more especially upon such as shall profess themselves to be the Servants and People of God....

A good economy in managing of the Poor, will make us as the Loaves and Fishes which our Saviour blest to a very great Increase.[50]

---

44. *Ibid.*, p. 139.
45. *Ibid.*, p. 166.
46. *Ibid.*, pp. 164-165.
47. *Ibid.*, p. 148.
48. *Ibid.*, p. 56.
49. *Ibid.*, p. 57.

Charity, love, virtue, according to Bellers, have their foundation in resignation to the will of God, which is the essence of religion from a subjective viewpoint: "*Resignation* (in Love and Humility) to the Will of God, is one of the most Essential *Invisible* Parts of true Religion (as Acts of *Charity* is of the *Visible* Parts)."[51] The heart of the prayer in his quarterly meeting epistle is an aspiration to subject the will to God: "Do thou inable us, O Lord! to prostrate our selves in deep Humility before thee, with our Wills subjected and resign'd unto thy Holy Will in all things, that we may, with Sincerity, say, Thy Will be done on Earth as it is done in Heaven."[52] Bellers even advises that subjection of the will be made an important part of the education of children: "The will being the greatest enemy a man hath, when it is not subject to the will of God; How valuable is it then for a child's will to be kept under another's direction than its own? It will be the less difficult to submit it to the will of God, when grown a man, especially if season'd with religious lessons of scriptures, &c."[53]

Bellers's social insights spring from a combination of an understanding of man as essentially rational; a rationalistic interpretation of religious truth; a pragmatic orientation toward human happiness, particularly eternal happiness after the last judgment; and a deep compassion for the sufferings of the poor. What is the origin of these wellsprings of thought and feeling in his own religious life?

Most likely, Bellers drew his deepest insights from his life and experience within his own religious body: the Society of Friends. His basic philosophy of religion and views on human nature are spelled out in a 1699 pamphlet whose title aptly summarizes his approach to these matters: "Essays About the Poor, Manufacturers, Trade, Plantations, & Immorality, And of the Excellency and Divinity Of Inward Light Demonstrated from the Attributes of God, and the Nature of Man's Soul, as well as from the Testimony of the Holy Scriptures."[54] This pamphlet concludes with a long list of Scripture passages, which he organizes under three headings: "Of God's Manifestation in Men," "Of Christ's Manifestation in Men," and "Of the Holy Spirits Manifestation in Men."[55] This understanding of the Inward Light as implying a philosophical understanding of the attributes of God and a view of the essential rationality of the human soul can hardly be found in the writings of early Friends during the first decade of their history. On

---

50. Bellers, *Abstract*, p. 7.

51. Bellers, *Writings Reprinted*, p. 158.

52. Bellers, 1718 *Epistle*, p. 15.

53. Bellers, "Proposals," p. 29.

54. Bellers, *Writings Reprinted*, p. 53.

55. John Bellers, *Essays About the Poor, Manufactures, Trade, Plantations, & Immorality, And of the Excellency and Divinity of Inward Light Demonstrated from the Attributes of God, and the Nature of Mans Soul, as well as from the Testimony of the Holy Scriptures* (London: T. Sowle, 1699), pp. 23, 24, 25.

the other hand, such ideas had appeared among Friends by Bellers's day, notably as one strain of thought in the writings of William Penn, whose association with Bellers on more than one occasion is clearly documented.

Bellers's passionate interest in the plight of the poor may well have its source in a series of actions that do go back to the earliest period of Quakerism. I have elsewhere described Edward Burrough's role in the setting up of organizations to take care of poor Friends in London, particularly by providing employment for them.[56] In 1671 the Six Weeks Meeting was established in London; this Meeting took over responsibilities for the care of the poor. In 1677 the Six Weeks Meeting instituted a scheme to buy flax and employ poor Friends in spinning it. In 1680 that body appointed John Bellers as treasurer of the funds provided for this plan. This was apparently his first official responsibility within the Society of Friends. He served in this capacity until 1684, when the plan was apparently discontinued. Involvement in this program must have deeply impressed the young Bellers (25 or 26 years old when first appointed) with the sufferings of the unemployed, with their capacity for achievement when given an opportunity, and with the value of providing opportunities for them in the form of specific plans and programs. In 1696, twelve years after the end of his involvement in the flax-spinning enterprise, he published his famous "Proposals for Raising a College of Industry."

This analysis of the likely sources for Bellers's social ethics is borne out by studies I have made of the religion and ethics of three other Quaker writers: Edward Burrough, Jonathan Dymond, and Richard Ullmann. In all four cases, it is clear to me that individual religious experience is *not* the source for their social or ethical views. What does appear to run through all four of them is a grounding of their social ethics in the *life of the Christian community*. I use this phrase in its broadest sense to refer both to the contemporary life of the community, in the writer's own time, and to the previous life of the community, as recorded in Scripture and in the tradition of the church. In Dymond's thought, I found a "basic, unstated premise": "The Will of God is…the final standard of right and wrong, but the fundamental, authoritative source for our knowledge of God''s Will is…the *received tradition* of the Religious Society of Friends."[57] The thought of Burrough, as that of George Fox, is based on an empathetic reading of the New Testament: "Fox and Burrough…had entered sympathetically and imaginatively into the New Testament community and were reliving its sacred history."[58] Ullmann draws heavily on his interpretation of seventeenth-cen-

---

56. Palmer, "Peace Witness," pp. 46-47.

57. *Ibid.*, pp. 51-52.

58. T. Vail Palmer, Jr., "Early Friends and the Bible: Some Observations," *Quaker Religious Thought*, Vol. 26, No. 2 (cumulative number 80, March 1993), p. 44 (hereafter referred to as Palmer, "Observations").

tury Quakerism as a major source for his own theology and ethics.[59] And Dymond's ethics spring directly out of his involvement in Quaker committee work!

What is the enduring value of Bellers's own proposals? It has been aptly said that his "schemes were always too good to work, but not fantastic."[60] Surprising insights crop up here and there in his work; but they remain isolated insights, not tied together into any comprehensive system of thought. He thus has no way of sorting out the insights from the commonplace sentiments that also proliferate in his writings. He is, in the final analysis, a second-generation Quaker, with all that implies. He lacks the "fantastic" apocalyptic vision that empowered the first generation. Nor does he have their deep empathy with the biblical writers. For Bellers, even more than "for Penn the Bible seems to have become primarily a handbook, a collection of resources and guidelines."[61] Marx may well have caught the nature of Bellers's enduring contribution to political economy—by summarizing it in a few appreciative footnotes.

---

59. T. Vail Palmer, Jr., "Religion and Ethics in the Thought of Richard Ullmann," to be published.

60. Hugh Barbour and Arthur O. Roberts, ed., *Early Quaker Writings: 1650-1700* (Grand Rapids, Mich.: William B. Eerdmans Publishing Company, 1973), p. 451.

61. Palmer, "Observations," p. 48.

The Business of Our Lives

Reflections on A Plea for the Poor

TOM HEAD

I view John Woolman's *A Plea for the Poor* through the eyes of my own experience. In particular, two aspects of my experience shape my vision: that of being an economist and that of being a Quaker. The economist in me is sensitive to statements about prices, wages, rents, production, distribution, equality, inequality, contracts, poverty and wealth. The Quaker in me responds especially to the language of the spirit. When Woolman speaks of God, the Creator, our Redeemer, Jesus Christ, pure wisdom, Divine love, tender mercies, universal love, the Fountain of universal light and love, our Lord, our Saviour and so on, the life of the spirit is the context for my understanding and interpretation. Both streams of experience—economy *and* spirituality—are found in Woolman and are integrated in authentic and powerful ways. Thus, Woolman speaks to me as few others do.

I also want to acknowledge at this moment that I reflect upon *A Plea for the Poor* with elements of both nostalgia and gratitude. It was twenty-five years ago that I first encountered the writings of John Woolman. The occasion was my first visit to George Fox College. I was being interviewed by Arthur Roberts, then Dean of the College, for a teaching position. I suppose we talked about whether or not I had read John Woolman. Although I had a faint awareness of Woolman as a Quaker who worked to end slavery among Friends, I had not seen his writings and made no connection between his work and my professional life. Arthur pulled a paperback copy of *The Journal of John Woolman and A Plea for the Poor* off his office bookshelf, handed it to me, and said something like "If you're going to teach

Economics at a Quaker college, you ought to read this, especially *A Plea for the Poor*." On that day I had not yet completed interviewing, and it was to be some time before I had a teaching contract in hand, but, accurately or not, I look back on that moment as the start of my work at George Fox College. I remember carrying that borrowed book along with me on an outdoor excursion late in the spring or early summer and first reading *A Plea for the Poor* somewhere along a wooded trail in the Pacific Northwest. When I took up my teaching duties at George Fox College the following fall, I returned Arthur's book to him with a sense that this would not be the last time I would encounter John Woolman.

While these personal experiences heighten my interest in Woolman and inform my reading of him, I am also aware that I lack some experiences that would serve me well at this moment. I am neither an historian nor a literary scholar, and I feel these deficiencies acutely when I try to decipher some of the more inaccessible portions of John Woolman's works. Fortunately, so much of Woolman's writing is timeless, or nearly so, and my inability to comprehend dense or archaic passages does not totally keep me from catching his powerful sense of things.

Woolman's Economic Model

As I return to John Woolman's *Journal* and *A Plea for the Poor* from time to time and recommend them to students as significant documents in the history of economic thought among Friends, I am brought to the question of whether or not John Woolman offers anything close to what we could call an economic theory or model. The more I read him, the more I think he does, and *A Plea for the Poor* is a good place to find the kernel of that model.

Economists typically work with a model of human behavior which assumes that the business of our lives is the maximization of welfare or well-being. As a broad, general approach, the idea of utility maximization is not altogether wrong or inappropriate, for the model builders allow for the broadest assortment of economic goods and services to be fed into our utility functions, constrained only by society's sense of what is legal and ethical, often a rather fuzzy constraint. If fast cars and fancy clothes are our passion, then so be it. But if community development and acts of kindness give us pleasure, then the model will acknowledge those as well. Whatever economic agents deem to be the source of well-being, the economist will accept. These given preferences will then be used in the process of moving toward an optimal allocation of resources.

Prevailing economic thought understands itself as describing what is, as opposed to what ought to be. It does explain a great deal of economic behavior, both selfish and altruistic. Modern economic thought does a fairly decent job of explaining how we improve our well-being, how we build our wealth, etc. However, the acceptable discussions are usually confined to what is called positive economics (what is), in contrast to normative economics (what ought to be). Many will say that positive economics is the only form of economics, especially the only form of economics that qualifies as a science since only positive statements are testable ones, the only ones which can be rigorously investigated and thus proven to be right or wrong.

John Woolman offers some observations that are decidedly in the form of positive statements, and he subjects them to testing by the best evidence he can bring to the fore, but few of these discussions stand out as profound or memorable. Instead, it is the more normative statements which form the core of his observations about the business of life. His more important and more lasting contribution is not in the form of the value-free propositions found in modern economics but in the form of value-laden propositions about the design of creation.

In *A Plea for the Poor*, we discover not the economics of the moment but the economics of all time. Here, in one rich paragraph, is Woolman's sense of what our real business is:

> Our gracious Creator cares and provides for all his creatures. His tender mercies are over all his works, and so far as true love influences our minds, so far we become interested in his workmanship and feel a desire to make use of every opportunity to lessen the distresses of the afflicted and to increase the happiness of the creation. Here we have a prospect of one common interest from which our own is inseparable, so that to turn all we possess into the channel of universal love becomes the business of our lives (p. 227).[1]

For Woolman, our own individual interests—the stuff of utility maximization—derives from a common interest, a world designed with care and provision for all. Acting consistently with this design, all we possess becomes not the source of mere personal well-being but of the happiness of all creation.

To the modern ear, it all sounds rather soft, idealistic, or even deluded. It may have sounded so to many people in Woolman's time, too. Seeing beyond 'me' and 'mine' has long been a struggle. So often we fail to "consider the connection of things" (p. 233). But Woolman's writings suggest that if we fail to see how our own economic destiny is related with the whole, we will ultimately not be well off. Is he right? Is this true?

---

1. All page references are to *The Journal of John Woolman and A Plea for the Poor*, The John Greenleaf Whittier Edition Text of 1871, New York: Corinth Books, 1961. While Phillips P. Moulton's excellent edition of *The Journal and Major Essays of John Woolman*, New York: Oxford University Press, 1971 is now a scholarly standard, I have returned in this paper to the text of my first reading of Woolman.

While it takes many ways of knowing to evaluate the truthfulness of his viewpoint, I would suggest that psychology may yield far more evidence than does economics. Who are the people most fulfilled in life? happiest? most content? most filled with a sense of meaning and purposefulness? Is it the group of people with ever-increasing amounts of wealth and power? I think not. I think it is more likely to be those who "become interested in his workmanship," those who deeply sense how things work.

How Do Things Work?

Early in *A Plea for the Poor*, John Woolman chronicles many things that are not working. He identifies people who are needlessly unemployed. He finds others who are overworked, "who labor harder than was intended by our gracious Creator" (p. 224). He is also pained by the way animals are treated: "Oxen and horses are often seen at work when, through heat and too much labor, their eyes and the motions of their bodies manifest that they are oppressed" (p. 224). Something is not right here.

In what sense are things not right? Is it in a normative sense; that is, do we not like the way things are? Or, is it in a positive sense; that is, do we see a system that is not performing as designed, a system that is not working. Or is it both? While I can easily make the distinction between positive and normative in the classroom, I do not find it so easy to make when reading John Woolman. *A Plea for the Poor* simply does not conform. At the heart of John Woolman's understanding of economics is the idea that we live in a created order and that there is purposefulness and meaning in its design. While I do not sense a reluctance in his thought to permit individual variation, and thus the stuff of economic preferences and economic freedom, I also do not sense that he is willing to accept the notion that individual preference is the whole of the story.

There is a design, and John Woolman diagnoses our failure to attend to the logic and requirements of that design as the source of our economic difficulties. He does so in language that is inviting and powerful. Consider a sampling of the language that he uses in *A Plea for the Poor*:

...[tenants] often find occasion to labor harder than was intended by our gracious Creator (p. 224)

... business which is foreign to the true use of things (p. 225)

... regulate their demands agreeably to universal love ... (p. 225)

...discourage those branches of business which have not their foundation in true wisdom (p. 225)

To be employed in things connected with virtue... (p. 225)

... while they live answerably to the design of their creation... (p. 226)

... acts contrary to the gracious designs of Him who is the owner of the earth...(p. 226)

Goodness remains to be goodness, and the direction of pure wisdom is obligatory on all reasonable creatures. (p. 226)

...greater toil or application to business than is consistent with pure love...
(p. 226)
...the right use of things...(p. 227)
...that use of things prescribed by our Redeemer...(p. 227)
...the man whose mind is conformed to universal love...(p. 228)
...Am I influenced by true charity in fixing all my demands? (p. 228-9)
...increase labor beyond the bounds fixed by Divine wisdom...(p. 233)
...consider the connection of things...(p. 233)
...that state of being in which there is no possibility of our taking delight in
anything contrary to the pure principle of universal love (p. 235)
...the impossibility of our taking pleasure in anything distinguishable from
universal righteousness...(p. 235)
...to act agreeably to that Divine wisdom which he graciously gives to his
servants (p. 236)
To labor for an establishment in Divine love, in which the mind is disen-
tangled from the power of darkness, is the great business of man's life...
(p. 236)
...a closer application to business than our merciful Father designed for
us...(p. 246)

To labor for a perfect redemption from this spirit of oppression is the great business of the whole family of Christ Jesus in this world (p. 249). Throughout *A Plea for the Poor* John Woolman raises our sights, speaking in lofty words of the highest of concepts, the universal wisdom that informs, directs and inspires right living.

In short, to know how things work requires religious knowledge. It is here that the line between positive economics and normative economics is blurred. As Woolman seeks to understand the nature and causes of oppression, he returns again and again to spiritual wisdom. His explanation, to put it simply, is that oppression occurs when human action moves too far out of balance. "While our spirits are lively, we go cheerfully through business; either too much or too little action is tiresome, but a right portion is healthful to the body and agreeable to an honest mind" (p. 227). In Woolman's world-view, labor is a very good thing and clearly part of the created order, but too little or too much leads to failure and misery. The system has a logic: "Divine love imposeth no rigorous or unreasonable commands..." (p. 229).

Conclusion

Are the thoughts of John Woolman, writing over two hundred years ago, relevant to the global economy today? While some would write him off as a sentimental fool, others in this postmodern era would be open to the wisdom that comes through in a world-view that so fully integrates faith and economics. A John Woolman writing today would still find oppression in our betrayal of the Third World, in multiple environmental crises, in threats to human rights and civil society. A John Woolman today would plea for the poor, plea for the alienated, plea for the children, plea for the victims of war, and plea for the earth. A John Woolman today would, as the bumper sticker says, think globally and act locally, for that is what the John Woolman of the 18th Century did, and his thoughts and actions are of the caliber that transcend historical details and reach across the years to offer a model of the way to be.

I want to end by telling a story about my youngest son, Eliot Arthur Head, whose middle name honors the spiritual impact of Arthur Roberts on our lives. I was talking with Eliot one day a couple years ago about well-known Quaker figures. We were discussing what people such as George Fox and William Penn had done. When I asked, "What did John Woolman do?" I was expecting to hear answers such as: He fought against slavery, he wrote a journal, he wore funny clothes, he was a tailor, or perhaps he took care of an orchard. Instead, then eight-year old Eliot blurted out, proudly and without hesitation, that he knew the answer: "John Woolman wrote receipts." To Eliot, this is what John Woolman did; he wrote receipts!

Eliot was remembering the story we had read together in which John Woolman was asked by his employer to draw up a bill of sale for the purchase of a slave. In Eliot's mind, John Woolman wrote receipts, sometimes very memorable receipts. John Woolman had never been involved in such an economic transaction before, and he felt paralyzed as he started to write. At 23 years of age, doing his day's work, he recognized that he was doing something violating his Christian religion, something inconsistent with the business of our lives. He went on and did the work he was assigned, but the course of his life was profoundly changed by the events this incident set into motion.

The thing that struck me about Eliot Arthur's answer is that *we all write receipts*. That is, we all do some little thing in the economy. It is all connected. And it all must ultimately find harmony with "that use of things prescribed by our Redeemer" (p. 227). We can all stop in the face of oppression, examine our actions, and turn toward the true use of things. We all have the opportunity to attend to that deeper Source of economic wisdom and to redirect the business of our lives toward a healthful and sustainable economy. For John Woolman, the religion of our lives and the business of our lives were not two separate realms. His plea is one of wholeness, and I return to this text once again with deep gratitude for the wholeness of another man, our teacher, colleague and friend Arthur Roberts.

Anthony Benezet, the True Champion of the Slave

IRV A. BRENDLINGER

A nthony Benezet was the greatest eighteenth century influence on the ending of British slavery and the slave trade. While names such as Wilberforce, Sharp and Clarkson ring with familiarity as champions of the slave, it is Benezet who occupies the position of foundational influence on these men and the entire cause. To substantiate this claim I shall briefly introduce his life and examine his antislavery activities and influences. However, it is most fitting to begin with his death and the public response to it. In this scene we receive a clearer vision of his life.

Philadelphia. May 3, 1784.

Anthony Benezet was dead. The funeral would be May 4, 1784, the day after his death. He would be mourned by hundreds of people, people of all social standings and educational levels, of diverse religious persuasions, of a broad variety of vocations, but most indicative of his life's accomplishments, by people of different races. For an eighteenth century Philadelphia funeral to be so attended is a clear statement of the unique character and accomplishments of the man being honored. A contemporary observed

> the greatest concourse of people that had ever been witnessed on such an occasion in Philadelphia, was present, being a collection of all ranks and professions among the inhabitants, thus manifesting the universal esteem in which he was held. Among others who paid that last tribute of respect, were many hundred black people, testifying by their attendance, and by

their tears, the grateful sense they entertained of his pious efforts in their behalf.[1]

Even more revealing of Benezet's core values is his will, reviewed five days before and completed on the very day of his death. After providing for the ongoing support of his wife through trust of his possessions or sale of his property if the interest from the trust were not sufficient, he instructed that a permanent trust be established to

> employ a religious minded person or persons to teach a number of Negroe, Mulatto, or Indian Children to read and write, Arithmetic, plain Accounts, Needlework &c. And it is my particular desire founded on the experience I have had in that service that in the choice of such a tutor special care may be had to prefer an industrious careful person of true piety, who may be or become suitably qualified, who would undertake the service from a principal [sic]of Charity to one more highly learned not equally so disposed.[2]

With an eye to the individual as well as the group and the institution, the last sentence of the will reads, "And I leave unto Margaret Till an appresst & much afflicted black woman [...] the sum of five pounds."[3]

Not only was Benezet concerned for the individual and a system of education, but he provided also for legal assistance for those trying to break the bonds of the institution that produced and perpetuated the causes of degradation, the institution of slavery:

> I also give unto James Star & Thomas Harrison the sum of fifty pounds in trust for the use of a certain Society who are forming themselves for the relief of such Black People & other who apprehend themselves illegally detained in Slavery to enable them to employ lawyers &c. to appear on their behalf in law & in all other cases afford just relief to these oppressed people.[4]

We will now take a closer look at the individual so honored by both blacks and whites at his funeral, the one who focused purposefully and almost exclusively in his will on the needs of black people.

---

1. Roberts Vaux, *Memoirs of the Life of Anthony Benezet*, (Philadelphia: James P. Parke, 1817), p. 134.

2. "The Will of Anthony Benezet," Pemberton Papers, Historical Society of Pennsylvania, cited in Brookes, p. 166

3. Ibid., cited in Brookes, p. 167.

4. Ibid.

I. Benezet's Life[5]

Anthony Benezet was born in St. Quentin, France, 31 January, 1713. He was a descendant of the legendary Benezet reputed to have received God's instructive vision of building the bridge across the Rhone at Avignon in the 12th century. This Benezet was canonized and the bridge was named "St. Benezet's Bridge."[6] Later generations of Benezets became Protestants, some of whom were persecuted and even martyred for their faith. When Anthony was only two years old, his Huguenot father's property was confiscated in Catholic France. His parents, Stephen and Judith, fled to Rotterdam with their two year old son, Anthony and their four year old daughter, Marie Madelaine Judith. Brookes relays an interesting event in the escape:

> They secured as their guide in the hazardous enterpise a clever youth, who used coolheaded strategy at one of the military outposts which then skirted the frontier. The youthful companion, approaching the sentinel at the border, displayed a gun which he was holding in one hand and a bag full of gold in the other, and naively said: "Choose! either you will allow these good people, who are victims of persecution, to pass, and you will be rewarded--or resist, and you shall die!"[7]

Obviously, the ploy succeeded, although one wonders how Benezet would have considered it in his adult, Quaker life! The journey would have been not only dangerous but also difficult, covering 170 miles in 12 days, with the young mother pregnant. She delivered three and a half weeks after their departure, but the child died within three months.[8]

The following August, 1715, the family left Rotterdam for England, staying one month in Greenwich before finding more permanent lodging in London. They remained in London for 16 years. Stephen was naturalized in England and prospered sufficiently so that upon emigrating to America he was able to purchase 1,000 acres and a brick home in Philadelphia. By now the family had increased to seven children, with an additional five hav-

---

5. The biographical section on Benezet is extracted largely from the thorough and excellent source, *Friend Anthony Benezet* by George S. Brookes, 1937.

6. The story of this legend can be found in Brookes, pp 2-3.

7. Ibid., p. 14 (citing Jacques Pannier, *Antoine Benezet, un Quaker en Amerique*, Toulouse, 1925)

8. Ibid., pp. 14-15. The departure date from St. Quentin was 3 February, 1715. Years later Anthony would reflect on his Huguenot heritage: "It was by the intolerants that one of my uncles was hanged, that an aunt was sent to a convent, that two of my cousins died at the galleys and that my father, a fugitive, was ruined by the confiscation of his goods." This quotation is contained in a letter from Francois, Marquis de Barbe'-Marbois, quoted in full in Brookes, pp. 451ff.

ing died in England.[9] Anthony was 18 years of age and had received some education in business (mercantile).

Before we leave Anthony's family, it is interesting to note that his father, Stephen had both Quaker and Moravian acquaintances. In London he was familiar with the Quakers who supported the school that Anthony probably attended (in Wandsworth), and he actually joined the Quakers.[10] Stephen also knew Peter Bohler,[11] the Moravian so influential a few years later in John Wesley's life.[12] Once in America, Stephen joined the Quakers (Philadelphia Meeting). Eventually, however, his Moravian connections became stronger. Both Spangenberg and Zinzendorf stayed in the Benezet home, and in 1743 Stephen left the Quaker meeting and became a Moravian. When a Moravian congregation was formed in Bethlehem, Pennsylvania, he became the first treasurer and covered the cost of the first catechism printing. In 1743 he also moved from Philadelphia to Germantown (now, in the NW part of Philadelphia). At this time he became a trustee of the Charity School, whose purpose it was to educate poor children without payment. The Charity School later became the College of Pennsylvania, and eventually the University of Pennsylvania.[13] In 1751 Stephen Benezet died; his funeral was preached by the Presbyterian, Gilbert Tennent.[14]

Anthony, on the other hand, after arriving in America at age 18 (1731) soon joined the Quakers.[15] Five years later, age 23 (1736), he married Joyce Marriott (also age 23), who had been recognized by the Philadelphia Monthly Meeting as a Quaker minister since she was eighteen years old.[16]

---

9. Brookes, passim.

10. Brookes, p. 17, 19

11. Ibid., p. 19

12. Peter Bohler is the Moravian whom John Wesley asked in May of 1738, before his Aldersgate experience, if he should quit preaching because he was not fully assured of his own faith. Bohler resonded with the encouraging words: "Preach faith till you have it; and then, because you have it, you will preach faith" (*The Works of John Wesley*, Jackson Edition, 1872, Vol. l, p. 86).

13. Ibid., p. 21. Closer examination reveals that the Charity School was founded in 1740 but didn't function as a school, rather as a "house of Publick Worship." The building was called the "New Building," located on Fourth Street near Arch, and George Whitefield preached there in November,1740. One of the original trustees , from 1740, was Benjamin Franklin. In 1751 a "Publick Academy," which had been envisioned by Franklin in 1749, opened in the "New Building." Franklin served as the president of the board until 1756. It was this institution which offered free education to the poor and later became the University of Pennsylvania. It is fascinating to trace the University of Pennsylvania to the building housing the Charity School of which Anthony Benezet was a Trustee. (*Encyclopedia Britannica*, Eleventh Edition, 1910-1911, Vol . 21, p 115). It is also interesting to realize that Stephen Benezet had been a fellow trustee with Franklin in 1743.

14. Ibid., pp. 21-2

15. Ibid., p. 16. Henry Van Etten, *George Fox and the Early Quakers*, p 124, indicates that four years earlier in England he had joined the Quakers, but that is not verifiable. Brookes, p. 16, mentions that Roberts Vaux *(Memoirs)* gives the same view.

Anthony and his new bride spent the next three years in the Philadelphia area, but he had no clear vocational direction. During this time a daughter was born to them, but she died within her first year. In 1739 the couple moved to Wilmington, Delaware where Anthony pursued a manufacturing career. This enterprise was short lived; they returned to Philadelphia within six months.[17]

In 1739, the year after Wesley's Aldersgate awakening in London, Benezet embarked on the career that he would follow for the rest of his life. He began teaching school at Germantown. During this time he also served as proofreader in a printing office that produced a German newspaper, tracts, books, almanacs and a Bible. Thus, it appears that he was fluent in German, English and French. He remained at the Germantown school for three years, until 1742, when he began teaching at the Friends' English School of Philadelphia (also known as the Philadelphia Public School, English, and later as the William Penn Charter School). His annual salary was 50 pounds.[18] He remained at the post for twelve years (until 1754), and during his fourth year was encouraged by the completion of a new school house, located at the southeast corner of 4th and Chestnut.[19] During his second year of teaching in Philadelphia, his son, Anthony, was born, but the infant tragically died after only six days.[20] For the first three years of teaching in Philadelphia, the Benezets lived in Germantown, probably about eight miles from the school on Chestnut. In 1745 they moved nearer the school and in 1753 they purchased a house on the north side of Chesnut, very near the school.[21] It was during this period that Benezet began a special and unusual teaching ministry that continued for twenty years. From 1750 to 1770 he used his evenings to teach black persons in his home. The curriculum included the basics of education as well as principles of the Christian faith.[22] In 1770 Benezet persuaded the Quakers of Philadelphia to construct a school building solely for the purpose of giving black children a free education. Funds were contributed by Benezet's personal friends, Philadelphia Quakers and London Quakers and from his own private resources.[23]

In 1754, Benezet resigned his position at the Friends' School, apparently for reasons of needing a less strenuous schedule. Within one month, however, he was back teaching, but this time at a Quaker school for thirty girls, who each paid tuition of 40 shillings. Classes were mornings only and Benezet's salary was 80 pounds for the year. This position lasted only for a

16. Ibid., p. 24.
17. Ibid., p. 27.
18. Ibid., pp. 28-30.
19. Ibid., pp. 33-34.
20. Ibid., p. 27.
21. Ibid., p. 36.
22. Ibid., p. 45.
23. Ibid., p. 47.

year and 1755 found Benezet serving as an Overseer of the Public Schools and taking the position of manager of the Pennsylvania Hospital in Philadelphia. [24] Two years later, when the teacher of the girls' school resigned, Benezet returned, under the arrangements of the newly resigned teacher: tuition of 30 shillings per girl and a salary of 20 pounds for the year.[25] After nine years, in l766, he resigned for health reasons.[26] At that time he moved to Burlington, New Jersey where he had built a home some two years earlier. Both he and Joyce were active in the Burlington Monthly Meeting, she as a minister and he as an elder.[27] Although he used the respite to write, it appears that he was not happy away from teaching. Nine months later he returned to Philadelphia to resume teaching, leaving Joyce in Burlington. He taught twelve poor girls for an annual salary of 20 pounds.[28]

Benezet remained at this teaching post until 1782, when he was 69 years old. At this time the Negro school[29] which he had initiated in 1770 was without a teacher. Rather than allow it to stop functioning, Benezet resigned at the Girls' School in order to give his last two years to the Negro school. He would have made the change a year earlier had he not been dissuaded by friends who were concerned that the task would be too strenuous for him.[30] The curriculum included reading, writing and arithmetic.[31] So it was that Benezet spent his last years teaching, and more particularly, teaching those he had worked so hard to liberate, as we shall discuss in the next section. However, before leaving the biographical section which has focused on his teaching career, it would be well to look briefly at the spirit and wisdom of the man as reflected in some his teaching experiences.

Anthony was clearly a man ahead of his time. In an age that saw corporal punishment as not only necessary for classroom order but also as beneficial to the student, Benezet had a different approach. He frequently used creativity to help his students progress past their inappropriate behavior rather than simply reacting with punishment.[32] He scheduled times of recreation and exercise to break up the study day.[33] In an age that saw speech and hearing deficiencies as problems to be punished, Benezet was moved with compassion. On one occasion a girl who was deaf and dumb

---

24. Ibid., p. 38. He served as hospital manager for one year, elected in 1757 (Brookes, p 39, f.n.23)

25. William Penn Charter School Records, cited in Brookes, p. 40

26. William Penn Charter School MS Records, cited in Brookes, pp. 42-3

27. Brookes, p. 44

28. Ibid.

29. Although the term "Negro school" would not be appropriate in the twentieth century it is used here because it was the normal designation in the eighteenth century and also was the term Benezet used.

30. Ibid., p. 48.

31. Ibid., p. 47. The first teacher at the Negro school was Moses Patterson; John Houghton immediately preceded Benezet as master (pp. 47- 48).

was enrolled in his school. Brookes indicates that "he devised plans whereby he could instruct her, and [...] after two years of tuition, accompanied by faith and patience and perseverance, she was enabled to share in a degree the fellowship of society denied her by an age which despised such unfortunate children, and sometimes put them to death."[34] In an age that was only just beginning to see the value of high quality education for children, Benezet wrote a tract proposing numerous innovations which have since become normative: a fixed and livable income so a stable teacher, even one having a family, could establish a permanent career in contrast to the customary low wage that attracted only transient, single teachers; a home, garden, orchard and stable be erected on the school property for the teacher; the giving of money by the community so a fund could be established, rather like an endowment which would provide for a teacher's salary and for educational expenses of the poor. For children who lived too great a distance from school to attend, he offered the plan of their boarding with the school master, thus giving him a financial increase from the board and giving them an otherwise impossible opportunity.[35] Finally, in an age that saw black people at worst as less than human, at best, inferior to the white race, Benezet transcends the 18th century prejudices by openmindedly observing reality. He speaks on this topic best for himself:

> I can with truth and sincerity declare, that I have found amongst the negroes as great a variety of talents as amongst a like number of whites; and I am bold to assert, that the notion entertained by some, that the blacks are inferior in their capacities, is a vulgar prejudice, founded on the pride of ignorance of their lordly masters, who have kept their slaves at such a distance, as to be unable to form a right judgment of them.[36]

Motivated by a genuine concern for fellow human beings, Benezet tuned his heart to their needs and became resourceful and innovative in trying to respond to those needs. As a result, his reputation as an effective and

---

32. Brookes gives a delightful example, p. 34. It seems that two boys constructed a miniature pillory (a sort of stocks) and placed a tortured mouse in the pillory on Benezet's desk. The following poem was attached: "I stand here, my honest friends, For stealing cheese and candle-ends." Of course, the test was to see how the teacher would respond. Rather than react in anger and punish the boys, once they were identified, Benezet pointed them out as examples of compassion, comparing them to most who would have killed the mouse for its theft. Rather than punishment, it was a lesson in compassion.

33. Letter from Deborah Logan, former Benezet student, to Roberts Vaux, about 1825 (in Brookes appendix, pp. 466-470).

34. Ibid., p. 42

35. *Some Observations Relating to the Establishment of Schools* Submitted by the Committee, Anthony Benezet and Isaac Zane, to the Yearly Meeting of the Society of Friends, 1778 (contained in Brookes, pp. 492ff).

36. Brookes, pp. 46-47, citing Roberts Vaux, *Memoirs of Anthony Benezet*, p. 30

compassionate teacher extended far. And the same genuine concern for others caused Benezet's influence to go beyond the structure and the discipline of the classroom. It caused his eyes to be open to the injustices that society caused, perpetuated and rationalized.

II. Benezet and Slavery

It is difficult for us of the twentieth century to imagine the injustices of the eighteenth century when the church as an institution and the overwhelming majority of Christians unequivocally supported the enslaving of one race by another. The atrocities are incomprehensible to us, with the number of black persons victimized being perhaps three times greater than the number of Jews later killed in the holocaust. There were, however, voices in the wilderness, those solitary persons of sensitive conscience who could see beyond the social conventions and the Biblical hermeneutic of their day to a greater truth. And there were even fewer who not only could see, but were also willing to act, taking whatever steps possible to change the situation of the oppressed. Such individuals are rightly termed "prophets," those who speak forth the truth, who act upon that truth and who inspire others also to see and act upon God's truth. By this definition Anthony Benezet was a prophet. In this section, a brief introduction to Benezet's antislavery writings will be made, followed by an exploration of his influence on other antislavery activists and an assessment of his significance in the antislavery fight.

Before perusing the content of some of Benezet's antislavery writings, it is helpful to list them in chronological order, setting them in the overall context of his life:

1754 *The Epistle of 1754, Presented to the Yearly Meeting of the Society of Friends*, written during his final (12th) year at the Friends' English School of Philadelphia (William Penn Charter School) and a year after he had moved into his own home on Chestnut Street.

1759 *Observations on the Enslaving, Importing and Purchasing of Negroes with some Advice thereon extracted from the Yearly Meeting Epistle of London for the Present Year*, written while he was teaching at the Quaker Girls' School in Philadelphia.

1762 *A Short Account of that Part of Africa Inhabited by Negroes*, written while still at the Girls' School.

1766 *A Caution and Warning to Great-Britain, and Her Colonies, in A Short Representation of the Calamitous State of the Enslaved Negroes in the British Dominions*. 1766 was the year Benezet moved to Burlington, New Jersey, devoting himself to writing and not teaching for a brief tenure of only nine months. This forty-five page tract is almost exclusively extracted from *A*

Short Account, but some of its content is also included in *Some Historical Account*.

1771 *Some Historical Account of Guinea, Its Situation, Produce and the General Disposition of its Inhabitants with an Inquiry into the Rise and Progress of the Slave Trade*

1772 *A Mite Cast into the Treasure: or, Observations on Slave-Keeping*

1778 *Serious Reflections affectionately recommended to the well disposed of every religious Denomination, particularly those who mourn and lament on account of the Calamities which attend us.* Benezet wrote the three documents from 1771 - 1778 while teaching a small number of girls at the Girls' School in Philadelphia.

1783 Letter sent to Queen Charlotte of Great Britain.

1784 *The Case of our Fellow-Creatures, the Oppressed Africans, respectfully recommended to The Serious Consideration of the Legislature of Great-Britain, by the People called Quakers.* The final two pieces were written while Benezet was teaching at the Negro school he had initiated in Philadelphia, the last tract composed in the year of his death.

Benezet's first writing on slavery, *The Epistle of 1754*, is a brief (three page), but clear statement against slavery and the slave trade intended to motivate Quakers to take consistent action against slavery.[37] He begins by acknowledging the fact that the Yearly Meeting has opposed the importing and buying of slaves, but in spite of that the number of slaves among Quakers has increased. He then specifies the reasons slavery should not be allowed among Friends:

— "To live in ease and plenty by the toil of those whom violence and cruelty have put in our power, is neither consistent with Christianity nor common justice,"

— "where slave-keeping prevails, pure religion and sobriety declines,"

— to enslave another clearly contradicts Christ's command that we "love one another as I have loved you,"

— separation of slave husbands from their wives promotes adultery,

— slavery tends to "lessen our humanity,"

Finally he implores fellow Quakers to examine their motives in keeping slaves. If their motives are anything other than for the slave's own good, then the "love of God" and the "influence of the Holy Spirit" are clearly "not the prevailing principle in you... ."[38] It is obvious from the rest of the

---

37. *The Epistle of 1754 Presented to the Yearly Meeting of the Society of Friends*, reprinted completely in Brookes, pp. 475-477

Epistle that the slave's own good is never the primary motivation for slavery. Some of the themes he developed more fully in subsequent tracts are found in seminal form here.

While each of the tracts is valuable, the most significant are *A Short Account*, 1762, *Some Historical Account of Guinea*, 1771, and *A Mite Cast into the Treasure: or, Observations on Slave-Keeping*, 1772. In the eighty pages of *A Short Account*, Benezet states early his threefold purpose. He intends 1) to show how evil slavery is: it subverts our relationship both to God and to our fellow human beings, 2) to discount arguments in support of slavery so as to prevent those considering involvement, and finally 3) to demonstrate the danger to those already involved in the business.[39] To reinforce his arguments, Benezet quotes numerous persons who have travelled in Africa and witnessed African culture and the capturing of slaves. His arguments include the horrendous nature of both the processes which enslave Africans and the "seasoning" which makes them fit slaves. Little is left to the imagination.[40] By contrast, he points to the high level of culture, intelligence and industry of the native Africans. Quoting philosophers such as George Wallace and Francis Hutcheson, he butresses his argument with the principles of liberty and the foundation of human benevolence. Also using the Bible, Benezet recalls the New Testament story of the debtor who cast into prison a fellow who was indebted to him. Benezet challenges: "think then, and tremble to think, what will be your Fate, who take your fellowservants by the throat, that owe you not a penny, and make them prisoners for Life."[41] Closing the tract on the topic of the problem of riches compared to the needs of the poor, Benezet calls to mind the parable of the rich man and Lazarus.[42]

Some Historical Account of Guinea (1771) is a lengthier treatment (some 143 pages) of the problem of slavery that again quotes African travelers, philosophers and theological writers. Benezet introduces the work by stating his purpose to "republish most serious parts of said tracts" so those of influence may "put a stop to any further progress" of slavery and the slave trade.[43] He makes a very strong case for the natural state of Africans, noting their excellent qualities which are only ruined by contact with Europeans.

---

38. Ibid.

39. Benezet, *A Short Account*, p. 6

40. For example, Benezet cites a method utilized to persuade slaves to eat: they were forced to eat pieces of a fellow slave who had been chopped up, the fate they could all expect if they failed to eat. After an attempted slave revolt, slaves were forced to eat the hearts and livers of some of the rebels and then forced to watch the execution of a woman, hanged by her thumbs. This account is contained in *A Short Account*, p. 49, *Some Historical Account*, p. 124 and *A Caution and Warning*, p. 27

41. Ibid., pp., 62-3

42. Ibid., pp. 79-80

43. Benezet, *Some Historical Account of Guinea*, p. ii

He repeatedly appeals to the humanity and sympathy of the reader as he explicitly describes inhuman atrocities inherent in slavery. He adds the future judgment and retribution of God in case the appeal to humanity is not sufficient. For practical consideration and to give evidence to the reality of the overwork and insufficient care of slaves he gives the statistics of necessary slave replacements. Repeatedly he cites "gain" as the predominant motive for slavery and notes the ability of slaveholders to "justify" the practice by means of their hardened hearts. He quotes the French philosopher Montesquieu to show that slavery is harmful to both the slave and the master. Quaker John Woolman is cited giving five principles that oppose slavery (pp. 74-75) and Benezet takes an unequivocal position on negro equality. He then appeals to the British legal system to show that slavery is inconsistent with the foundational laws of the empire. Finally, he answers objections to negro equality and sets forth three proposals to deal constructively with the ending of slavery and the subsequent adjustment of the work force.

A short, but pithy tract, published in 1772, addresses the major issues of slavery: the equality of negroes and whites, the problem of overcoming prejudice, how the slave trade fuels the institution of slavery and how slavery and Christianity are completely incompatible. In *Observations on Slave Keeping*, Benezet[44] marshalls a number of forces to drive home his points, including Bible quotations, allusions to Biblical pericopes, threat of God's judgment, quotations of John Locke and explanations of how difficult it is to overcome prejudice. He begins his argument by asserting the strength of prejudice when associated with a vested interest. This appears to be an attempt to disarm the reader by rocking the foundation of his or her position: "The power of prejudice over the minds of mankind is very extraordinary; hardly any extreams [sic] too distant, or absurdities too glaring for it to unite or reconcile, if it tends to promote or justify a favourite pursuit."[45] With time and reinforcement, he explains, such prejudice becomes "so rivited" that even religious people cannot "hear the voice of impartial justice."[46]

Benezet then quotes scripture encouraging aid on behalf of the poor (Proverbs 31:8-9), adherence to the Golden Rule and recognition of the Biblical prohibition against stealing a man, which was a capital offense (Exodus 21:16).[47] Five pages from the end he offers a threat based on a biblical story: "But if, with Dives, thou art preferring this world's treasure [a

---

44. While the a title page does not list an author, there is sufficient evidence for Benezet's authorship, including style, consistency of argument bases and the fact that the tract is bound together with other Benezet writings. The full title of the tract is: *A Mite Cast into the Treasure: or, Observations on Slave-Keeping.*

45. Benezet, *Observatiions on Slave Keeping*, p. 3.

46. Ibid.

47. Ibid., p.5

reference to slavery as purely fueled by profit motive] to that which ought to be laid up in heaven,—I fear thou will share his lot in the conclusion."[48]

Throughout the tract statements appear that assert human equality. One wonders if his experience of teaching black persons in Philadelphia enlightened his understanding. He reflected, "they are equally the work of an Almighty hand, with a soul to save or loose [sic]." The implication was obvious: "every individual of the human species by the law of nature comes into the world equally intitled [sic] to freedom at a proper age."[49]

To defend slavery for the sake of Christianity (to evangelize Africans) was to Benezet tantamount to describing the Spanish Inquisition as an expression of love.[50] The tract concludes with quotations of John Locke that clearly promote personal liberty and responsibity: "Every man has a property in his own person, this nobody has a right to but himself, the labour of his body, and work of his hands are his own." "For one man to have an absolute arbitrary power over another, is a power which nature never gives"[51] Such perspectives clearly imply an understanding of human equality, liberty and the responsibility to effect justice that are beyond the norm of the eighteenth century. The tract remains good reading and retains its relevance two and a quarter centuries later! This fact may speak to either Benezet's unusual foresight or human slowness to grasp reality.

Much more could be said about Benezet's writings, but this brief survey reveals both the flavor and the thoroughness of his approach. While not normally prooftexting from the Bible, he reflected its principles and was particularly skillful in utilizing parables and other pericopes. He occasionally used scripture either to introduce or to tie together his argument. It seems as if the biblical ethic of love and mutuality were the underpinnings of his entire antislavery endeavor. However, he did not stop there. Benezet's wide reading is graphically revealed by his frequent and relevant citing of such philosophers as Locke, Wallace, Hutcheson and Montesquieu. In fact, one of his major contributions is that he took the philosophical arguments against slavery of such individuals and made them available to the populace, showing the relevance of academic thought to a practical problem. Sound philosophical insight was no longer isolated in the cloister but applied to life. Individuals not accustomed to reading philosophy could benefit by discovering it in Benezet's writings in a form that could be understood in the context of a societal dilemma. This blending of biblical and philosophical insight with a tenacious drive to effect change significantly influenced other antislavery activists. He not only wrote for the general population but was also eager to influence those with political power, as may be seen in his let-

---

48. Ibid., p. 18
49. Ibid., pp. 9,19-20
50. Ibid., p. 20
51. Ibid., pp. 22-23

ter to Queen Charlotte of England in 1783. The letter introduces the accompanying antislavery tracts and encourages the queen to consider the plight of the slaves and the "divine displeasure" that may occur to the nation that promotes such injustice.[52]

In a way that seems quite extraordinary, Anthony Benezet exerted an influence on individuals who became significant in the fight against slavery that is far out of proportion to his learning, his office or his location. As one examines key figures who brought about the end of British slavery and the slave trade, there is an unusual frequency with which Benezet's life intersects with theirs through his writing. Not all influence can be traced, but there is evidence that Benezet was a key factor in the antislavery work of Granville Sharp, Thomas Clarkson, and John Wesley on the English side, as well as a number of persons on the American side.

Granville Sharp was a dominant antislavery activist in England who represented slaves in lawcourts. His work resulted in triumphs which eventually led to the benchmark Somerset case in 1772 (Sharp represented James Somerset), after which slave owning in England proper was no longer legal. He entered the cause by advocating for Jonathan Strong, a runaway slave in 1767. At that time he became acquainted with the writing of Benezet. In Sharp's words, "When G.S. was involved in the first law-suit [...] in 1767, he accidentally met with a copy of this book [probably Benezet's 1762 *A Short Account*] on a stall, and, without any knowledge whatever of the author, caused this edition to be printed and published."[53] From this point the two men corresponded regarding slavery and the slave trade, and it is probable that this correspondence was a major factor in Sharp's increasing successes in the abolition of slavery in England.[54]

Thomas Clarkson became the dominant researcher in the cause, supplying the abolitionists, especially William Wilberforce, with primary material for the extensive anislavery battle in Parliament. Clarkson entered the cause, however, as the result of the senior essay contest at Cambridge, 1785. The assigned topic was, "Is it right to enslave men against their will?", an issue about which Clarkson knew little and was not deeply concerned. Benezet's 1771 tract, *Some Historical Account*, had been circulated in England that very year, and Clarkson discovered it in researching for his essay. Clarkson not only won the contest but he altered his vocational plans from ministry to give his life to antislavery work. His own comment establishes

---

52. The letter is quoted in Thomas Clarkson, *The History of the Rise, Progress and Accomplishment of the Abolition of the African Slave Trade by the British Parliament*, Vol. 2, pp. 172-175.

53. Prince Hoare, *Memoirs of Granville Sharp, Esq.*, London, Henry Colburn and Co., 1820, p. 97. Hoare notes that two years later, 1769, when Sharp published his first tract against slavery, *The Injustice and dangerous Tendency of tolerating Slavery*, Benezet republished it in Philadelphia with no knowledge that Sharp had republished his *Short Account*.

54. Ibid., p. 115

the significance of Benezet in his initial research and in discovering his new life direction: "In this precious book I found almost all I wanted."[55]

John Wesley's entering the battle against slavery can be connected directly to Benezet's influence. Wesley's journal entry for 12 February, 1772 states:

> I read a very different book, published by an honest Quaker, on that execrable sum of all villanies, commonly called the Slave Trade. I read of nothing like it in the heathen world, whether ancient or modern: And it infinitely exceeds, in every instance of barbarity, whatever Christian slaves suffer in Mahometan countries.[56]

Frank Baker indicates that,

> Immediately he became Benezet's ally in this great campaign, and a month or two later Benezet wrote to Granville Sharp: "My friend, John Wesley promises he will consult with thee about the expediency of some weekly publications in the newspaper, on the origin, nature, and dreadful effects of the slave trade."[57]

Two years later Wesley published his *Thoughts Upon Slavery*. In this work the influence of Benezet can be most clearly seen. More than half of the tract is so fully dependent on Benezet's *Some Historical Account* that Stanley Ayling accused Wesley of blatant plagiarism.[58] The purpose of this article is not to address the question of plagiarism,[59] but to explore the influence of Benezet. Wesley did indeed avail himself of Benezet's material. The path of Benezet's influence followed these lines: It appears that Wesley wrote Sharp of his desire to publish against slavery and Sharp supplied Wesley with "a large bundle of Books and Papers on the subject," including Benezet's tract.[60] Sharp then responded to Wesley with an evaluation of Wesley's unpublished manuscript. The letter indicates "great satisfaction" and that no "alteration is necessary." It also acknowledges that "you have very judiciously brought together and digested [...] some of the principal Facts cited by my Friend Mr. Benezet and others."[61] After Benezet saw Wesley's published tract, he

---

55. Thomas Clarkson, *The History of the...Abolition of the African Slave Trade*, Vol I, p. 207.

56. John Wesley, *The Journal of John Wesley*, Jackson Edition, vol III, p. 453.

57. Frank Baker, *The Relations Between the Society of Friends and Early Methodism*, London, 1949, p. 22.

58. Stanley Ayling, *John Wesley*, London, 1979, p. 283.

59. For a discussion of Wesley and plagiarism, see Brendlinger, *A Study of the Views of Major Eighteenth Century Evangelicals On Slavery and Race*, unpublished Ph.D. Thesis, University of Edinburgh, l982, pp. 389 - 392.

60. Letter from Sharp to Benezet, 7 January, 1774, quoted in Roger Anstey, *The Atlantic Slave Trade and British Abolition 1760-1810*, London, Macmillan, 1975, p. 240.

wrote Wesley a complimentary letter and had the tract republished in America.[62] The reality, however, is that not only did Benezet influence Wesley, but also through Wesley his own influence continued to spread. Wesley's tract reached three editions in 1774, a fourth in 1775 and a fifth in 1776. A copy was found among the 354 books of George Washington's library.[63] Even beyond the tract, Benezet's influence on Wesley and through Wesley continued. In a letter that Wesley wrote to the Monthly Review, November, 1774, he quoted American newspaper advertisements offering rewards for the severed heads of runaway slaves. Benezet had sent the ads to Wesley in a letter of May, 1774.[64] The expansive mix of influence can be seen in future interconnections as Wesley corresponded with Thomas Clarkson, Granville Sharp and eventually William Wilberforce.

Through his writings Benezet was able to attract significant and influential people to the antislavery cause. Sharp, Clarkson and Wesley are formidable examples. On the other side of the Atlantic his influence can be seen in his relationship with Benjamin Rush and Benjamin Franklin, among others, whom he enlisted to the cause. Further, within his own denomination he was a key thinker in shaping Quaker policy on slavery and the slave trade. He helped translate the ideals and values of George Fox and John Woolman into specific practice for Yearly and Monthly Meetings. His ability to blend philosophical concepts with Biblical principles and passages and apply them persuasively to elicit an empathic human response enabled him not only to effect change within the Society of Friends but also to transcend denominational and geographical boundaries in his concern for human justice and dignity. Roger Anstey aptly states that Benezet brought "the moral philosophy of the age, with all its appealing emphasis on liberty, benevolence, happiness, justice, and so forth, to the support of a position reached on religious grounds, and so makes a more comprehensive case to the world at large."[65] In light of all of these facts it is difficult to overstate the importance of Benezet.

Summation: the Contribution

What gives one life such a clear sense of direction and such a persistent pursuit of that direction, especially when it stands in direct opposition to the cultural norms and the overwhelming Christian opinion of the day? In reading both the tracts and correspondence of Anthony Benezet, it becomes

---

61. Letter from Granville Sharp to John Wesley, undated, but datable to early 1774, in private collection of Wesley College Library, fo. 314, used by permission of Dr. Dairmaid MacCulloch.

62. Letter from Benezet to Wesley, 23 May, 1774, quoted in Brookes, p. 85.

63. John S. Simon, "George Washington's Library" WHS *Proceedings*, Vol. XIII, p. 1.

64. Letter from Benezet to Wesley, 23 May, 1774, quoted in Brookes, p. 105.

65. Anstey, *The Atlantic Slave Trade*, p. 217.

clear that his foundational and consistent motivation was his Christian faith. While it would be exciting to discover one theological distinctive or unique hermeneutic on which his entire system pivoted, such is not the case with Benezet. His response was simply one of common sense and the practical application of the overarching principles of Christianity, particularly the love of God and the love of neighbor. Granted, his Quaker pacificism stood in direct conflict to all of slavery because slaves were both taken and retained by an "act of war." Yet even his pacifism was subsequent to the more central truth of love of neighbor. Genuine love *demands* practical expression.

Benezet himself recognized this Christian motivation and gave expression to it. The opening sentence in his letter to Queen Charlotte states that he acts from "a sense of religious duty."[66] In a letter to Granville Sharp he articulates both his core motivation and his understanding of black people, whom he describes as "our neighbors, whom we are by the Gospel enjoined to love as ourselves."[67] The common sense test of our love was simply the Golden Rule, which, when applied to slavery could have no other outcome than the abolishing of such an unequal relationship. To Benezet, all arguments based on biblical prooftexts which seemed to support slavery (e.g., Paul's encouraging slaves' obedience in Eph., 6:5-8), or theological systems that appeared to work around the difficulties of slavery were demolished by the principle of love and the mutuality of the Golden Rule. Anything else was rationalization, justification of greed or an example of the power of prejudice when it facilitated financial gain.

Because the gospel made this kind of love possible, Benezet opposed anything that deterred the spread of that gospel, and in his mind nothing deterred it as effectively as slavery. In 1767 he wrote the Society for the Propagation of the Gospel, which supported slavery, stating that the slave trade and slavery were the "greatest impediment to the promulgation of the Gospel of Jesus Christ."[68] Benezet's motivation was linked to the whole of Christianity, especially to the all pervading central core of love for God and love for all humankind. As stated above, Benezet's application of his faith was common sense and practical rather than theologically complex and sophisticated. But, above all, it was his faith that drove his tireless endeavors on behalf of the slave. It was the practicality and inclusiveness of his faith that enabled him to link arms and even celebrate friendship with people of such diverse religious persuasions and vocations as the deist Benjamin Franklin, the physician Benjamin Rush, the Calvinist George Whitefield, the Anglican Granville Sharp and the founder of Methodism, John Wesley. And

---

66. Letter from Benezet to Queen Charlotte, 1783, quoted in Clarkson, *History*, Vol. 1, p. 172.

67. Benezet to Sharp, 14 May, 1772, quoted in Brookes, p. 292.

it is safe to say that it was his faith that fostered the persistence which contributed to his massive influence.

Anthony Benezet is buried in an unmarked grave, in the Friend's Burial Ground in Philadelphia, as was his desire. While we shall keep faith with his desire to avoid vanity and ostentation, it is *most* genuinely in keeping with his spirit and purpose if we can learn from his life and example how we too may influence our age with the claims of the gospel of love, touching the deepest recesses of human need with the imperatives of the Kingdom of God. Anthony Benezet is dead, but his example lives on exerting a powerful influence and motivation for those who see the injustices of society and are not willing to be cynical or passive about bringing change where human need cries for human care. In the truest spirit of Christian love and responsibility Anthony Benezet is alive.

---

68. Benezet to the S.P.G., 26 April, 1767, quoted in Brookes, p. 272. While the above focus on the common sense principles of love and mutuality are true, this was discovered by the present writer only after suspecting that there *might* be a doctrinal distinctive that fueled Benezet's singlemindedness. When it was discovered that Benezet had translated from the French and republished a tract entitled *The Plain Path to Christian Perfection*, the suspicion was fed. Perhaps Benezet had been influenced by Wesley's concept of Christian Perfection. Perhaps his emphasis on love was similar to Wesley's perspective that "Christian perfection, is neither more nor less than pure love" (John Wesley, *Letters*, Telford, Vol. VI, p. 223, To Walter Churchey, 21 Feb., 1771). The same theme is seen in another Wesley letter: "what is it [perfection] more or less than humble, gentle, patient love! (*Letters*, Vol. VII, p. 120, to Ann Loxdale, 12 April, 1782). In his *Plain Account of Christian Perfection* Wesley affirmed that we should aspire to "nothing more but more of...love" (*Works*, Vol. XI, p. 430, Jackson ed., 1872). Would it not be exciting to learn that while Benezet clearly influenced Wesley to work against slavery, Wesley was the theological influence that persuaded Benezet of the power of holiness and its social implications? After examining the book and reading Benezet's preface it became apparent that "Christian Perfection" of the title was not the equivalent of Wesley's doctrine. In fact, the book that Benezet translated from the French, according to his 1780 preface was originally written "in the German language about two hundred and fifty years ago" (*The Plain Path to Christian Perfection*, Philadelphia, 1831, preface by Benezet for an edition printed in 1780, .p. iii). The thesis of the small book is that reconciliation with God is to be found "solely by renouncing ourselves, denying the world, and following our blessed Saviour in regeneration" (subtitle, preface, p. i). Benezet's preface points out that early Christianity was characterized by humility, contrition towards God and love towards others. This was the sacrifice acceptable to God, but it was lost after the early church, and replaced by "pomp and show, strange modes of worship and confused and dark opinions" with teachers and leaders who "assumed an authority and respect from their offices" (preface, p. 4). It is only by an inward work, a purifying fire, that the "corruption and hardness of their hearts" can be changed and the "root of sin" destroyed (preface, pp. ix - x). Benezet's preface concludes with the words: "The Christian religion, is indeed the simplest thing in the whole world, and the most easy to understood, if *self* is but truly renounced" (preface, p. xii). The book then lays out in ninety-nine pages (15 chapters) ways to die to sin and to renounce the will. The flavor of the book is more reflective of a medieval mystical approach than that of John Wesley. The point of this discussion is to simply confirm that Benezet's motivation lay not in a particular doctrine, but the whole of the Christian message which he believed focused on love.

WORKS CITED

Primary Sources:

Benezet, Anthony. *The Case of our Fellow-Creatures, the Oppressed Africans, respectfully recommended to The Serious Consideration of the Legislature of Great-Britain, by the People called Quakers.* London: James Phillips, 1784.

————. *A Caution and Warning to Great-Britain, and Her Colonies, in A Short Representation of the Calamitous State of the Enslaved Negroes in the British Dominions.* Philadelphia: D. Hall, and W. Sellers, 1767 (first edition 1766).

————. *A Mite Cast into the Treasure: or, Observations on Slave-Keeping.* Philadelphia (no publisher), 1772.

————. *Observations on the Enslaving, Importing and Purchasing of Negroes with some Advice thereon extracted from the Yearly Meeting Epistle of London for the Present Year.* Germantown, 1759.

————. *A Short Account of that Part of Africa Inhabited by Negroes.* Philadelphia: W. Dunlap, 1762.

————. *Some Historical Account of Guinea, Its Situation, Produce and the General Disposition of its Inhabitants with an Inquiry into the Rise and Progress of the Slave Trade, Its Nature and Lamentable Effects.* Philadelphia: Joseph Crukshank, 1771.

Clarkson, Thomas. *The History of the Rise, Progress and Accomplishment of the Abolition of the African Slave Trade by the British Parliament,* 2 vols. London: Hurst, Rees and Orme, 1808.

Hutcheson, Francis. *A System of Moral Philosophy,* 2 vols. London: A. Millar, 1755.

Montesquieu, Charles de Secondat, Baron de. *The Spirit of Laws,* 2 vols. Trans. by Mr. Nugent, 2nd ed. London: J. Nourse & P. Vaillant, 1752.

Sharp, Granville. Letter to John Wesley, early 1774. Wesley College Library, Bristol, private collection.

Vaux, Roberts. *Memoirs of the Life of Anthony Benezet.* Philadelphia: James P. Parke, 1817.

Wesley, John. *The Letters of the Rev. John Wesley, A.M.* Edited by John Telford, standard edition, 8 vols. London: The Epworth Press, 1931.

————. *The Works of the Rev. John Wesley, A.M.*, 14 vols. Edited by Thomas Jackson, 3rd ed. London: Wesleyan Conference Office, 1872.

Secondary sources:

Anstey, Roger. *The Atlantic Slave Trade and British Abolition 1760-1810.* London: Macmillan Press Ltd., 1975.

Ayling, Stanley. *John Wesley.* London: Collins, 1979.

Baker, Frank. *The Relations Between the Society of Friends and Early Methodism.* London: Epworth Press, 1949.

Brookes, George S. *Friend Anthony Benezet.* Philadelphia: University of Pennsylvania Press, 1937.

Hoare, Prince. *Memoirs of Granville Sharp, Esq.* London: Henry Colburn and Co., 1820.

Rice, C. Duncan. *The Rise and Fall of Black Slavery.* Baton Rouge: Louisiana State University Press, 1975.

Articles:

Simon, John S. "George Washington's Library," *Wesley Historical Society Proceedings* XIII (1922) pp. 1 - 4.

Unpublished:

Brendlinger, Irv. "A Study of the Views of Major Eighteenth Century Evangelicals on Slavery and Race, With Special Reference to John Wesley." Ph.D. Thesis, University of Edinburgh, 1982.

The Indians' Friends

Quakers and Native Americans in the Seventeenth Century

JAMES D. LE SHANA

On July 24, 1683, an English subject in the New World wrote an enthusiastic letter to Lord North in which he described his experiences with the native population. He told of trade with the Indians and the purchase of land, two common objectives of Europeans at this time. "A Fair we have had, and weekly markets," he explained,

> ...to which the ancient lowly inhabitants come to sell their produce to their profit and our accommodation. I have also bought lands of the Natives, treated them largely, and settled a firm and advantageous correspondency [sic.] with them, who are a careless, merry people yet in property strict with us, though a kind [of] community among themselves.

Nothing in this passage seems particularly surprising. However, the author continued his description of the Indians in a fashion that separates him from many of his countrymen. "In counsel", he wrote, the Indians appear "so deliberate, in speech short, grave and eloquent, young and old in their several class, that I have never seen in Europe any thing more wise, cautious and dexterous." He concluded his complementary comments on the Indians by remarking, "'tis as admirable to me as it may look incredible on that side of the water." Whether he viewed them as equal in every way or not, this Englishman admired and respected the Indians.[1]

Far from standing alone, William Penn, the author of this letter to Lord North, represents a sub-group of English society often overlooked in

IOI

contemporary accounts of European and Indian relations, the Quakers. Normally, the Friends are lumped together in evaluation with the rest of the English colonizers or they are dismissed altogether as insignificant bystanders.[2] Although persecution curbed the growth of the Quaker movement after the Restoration in the 1660's, their activities were not crippled. To the contrary, this religious group reached its peak in numbers and influence in America during the colonial period, especially for the hundred years from 1660 to 1760.[3]

In their attitudes toward Native Americans, the Quakers bore similarities to other English groups involved in America, yet diverged in interesting and significant ways. Like their New England kin, Friends actively endeavored to missionize, colonize, and trade with Indians. However, they also held distinctive views of Native Americans, resulting in some unique practices and responses. Even though various individual non-Quaker examples of fair treatment and kindness may be cited, Friends as a group tended to maintain a keen appreciation and respect for the Indians and their various cultures.

The main objective of this study is to examine the relationship between Quakers and Native Americans during the second half of the seventeenth century, with a special emphasis on their missionary efforts. A secondary purpose is to add to the perspective that not all English colonizers, let alone all Europeans, thought and behaved alike. To accomplish these goals, a brief review of European contact with Indians will be followed by a more detailed analysis of Friends involvement. A survey of the Quaker interests in evange-

---

1. The term "careless" meant "care-free," connoting contentment rather than irresponsibility. For purposes of quotation in this essay, the seventeenth-century style of capitalizing and abbreviating many words has been contemporized for ease of reading. William Penn, "To Lord North," in Richard S. Dunn and Mary Maples Dunn, eds., *The Papers of William Penn*, Vol.II (Philadelphia: University of Pennsylvania Press, 1982), pp. 414-415.

2. For scholarship on European and Native American relations in Colonial America see James H. Merrell, *The Indians' New World: Catawbas and Their Neighbors from European Contact Through the Era of Removal* (Chapel Hill: The University of North Carolina Press, 1989); William Cronon, *Changes In The Land: Indians, Colonists, and the Ecology of New England* (New York: Hill and Wang, 1987); Bernard W. Sheehan, *Savagism and Civility: Indians and Englishmen in Colonial Virginia* (Cambridge: Cambridge University Press, 1980); James Axtell, *The Invasion Within: The Contest of Cultures in Colonial North America* (New York: Oxford University Press, 1985); Edward P. Dozier, *The Pueblo Indians of North America*, (Prospect Heights, Illinois: Waveland Press, Inc., 1983); Neal Salisbury, *Manitou and Providence: Indians, Europeans, and the Making of New England, 1500-1643* (New York: Oxford University Press, 1982); and Francis Jennings, *The Invasion of America: Indians, Colonialism, and the Cant of Conquest* (Chapel Hill: The University of North Carolina Press, 1975).

3. These dates are somewhat arbitrary, but are close to the last date in which a Quaker was killed in Boston by the Puritans (1661) and when some of the Friends in power in Philadelphia resigned their political positions due to hostilities with Indians in the Western territories (1756).

lism, colonization, and trade relations will intertwine with a discussion of their particular views about and treatment of Indians.

European attitudes toward Indians depended on their motives for exploring and colonizing as well as their socio-religious backgrounds. French and English examples will illustrate. The early French interest in North America and its native inhabitants focused mainly on discovering gold and other riches. As a result, their interaction with Indians proved less colonial in nature than commercial, and the prospect of wealth through fishing, trapping, and trading made up for the paucity of gold. With the founding of Quebec in 1608, Catholic missions soon followed. The French viewed religion as a valuable tool in maintaining territorial control and trade advantages with Indians. However, in order to win Christian converts, Jesuit missionaries attempted to avoid making them "Frenchmen" first. They developed "flying missions" in which the Jesuits lived with semino-madic Indian hunters and traders, learned their language, and then endeavored to replace traditional native beliefs with their own. While the Jesuits claimed success in these efforts, many Indians simply incorporated French Catholicism, with its rituals and icons, into their symbolic and pan-theistic world view.[4]

In contrast to the French, the English agenda in the New World focused on the acquisition of territory for farming and colonization. Although they valued trade, they desired to dominate both the land and the people they found on it. Many of the English viewed Indians as obstructions to colonization or else failed to consider them at all. Native Americans moved much and worked little, disqualifying them from the right to own their land. As John Cotton, the colonial minister, explained, "in a vacant soil he that taketh possession of it, and bestoweth culture and husbandry upon it, his right it is."[5] Most colonists thus rationalized the conquest of New England through disease and force, disregarding Indian ownership and claims. Native American customs and behaviors received similar rejection by most English missionaries. They believed that they first needed to civilize the "savages" before they could convert them, establishing English order and industry through Indian schools, "praying towns," and Biblical instruction. As promoters of a word-based system of Christianity, dependent upon the transmission of written and spoken ideas, they found it difficult to convert Indians without first making them linguistically and also culturally, "Englishmen." According to current scholarship, this soteriological imperative of civilizing Indians before "Christianizing" them characterized all English missionary efforts. However, this perspective ignores the contribution of Quakers.[6]

---

4. See Neal Salisbury, *Manitou and Providence*, pp. 72-80; and James Axtell, *The Invasion Within*, pp. 71-127.

5. John Cotton quoted in William Cronon, *Changes In The Land*, pp. 56-57.

The role of Quaker missionaries in European and Indian relations remains an important area of analysis commonly neglected by historians.[7] In contrast to their countrymen and women from England, the Quakers provide a glimpse of an active religious group, intent on promoting their brand of Christianity while demonstrating cultural respect and genuine kindness. One explanation for this oversight of Quakers by scholars relates to a common misperception that Friends avoid evangelism. Echoing others, historian James Axtell reasoned that "the Quakers did not believe in prose-lyting" unless by quiet example. Elton Trueblood described well this "popular conception" in which "Quakers are an exceedingly mild and harm-less people, largely given to silence, totally unaggressive, with a religion that is neither evangelical in content nor evangelistic in practice."[8] To follow this logic, if Quakers eschewed evangelism in general, they certainly would not have tried to convert Indians.

Contrary to the myth of the quiet and non-evangelistic Quaker, the evi-dence indicates that Friends in early America, especially in the seventeenth century, demonstrated great concern for the souls of others. "Whoever preaches the gospel," wrote Quaker theologian, Robert Barclay, "is really an evangelist." He also emphasized clearly the evangelistic goal of Friends when he stated in his Apology, "We desire therefore all that come among us to be proselyted." In Trueblood's words, "All tried to make converts and they tried all the time."[9] Starting with the founder of the Friends move-ment, George Fox, the Quakers attempted to evangelize a lost world. Fox experienced his own "conversion" in 1647, which led to a desire to help oth-ers spiritually. He encountered personally the "Light of Christ" and immediately began sharing with others the spiritual answers he found in

---

6. See Bernard W. Sheehan, *Savagism and Civility*, p. 116; James Axtell, *The Invasion Within*, pp. 131-135; and Charles M. Segal and David C. Stineback, *Puritans, Indians, and Man-ifest Destiny* (New York: G.P. Putnam's Sons, 1977), pp. 141-179.

7. For scholarship on colonial Quakerism see Rufus M. Jones, *The Quakers In The Ameri-can Colonies* (New York, 1911); James Bowden, *The History of the Society of Friends in America*, Vol. I and II (New York: Arno Press, 1972); Frederick B. Tolles, *Quakers and the Atlantic Culture* (New York: The Macmillan Company, 1960); Carla Gardina Pestana, *Quakers and Baptists in Colonial Massachusetts* (New York, 1991); Jonathan M. Chu, *Neighbors, Friends, or Madmen: The Puritan Adjustment to Quakerism in Seventeenth-Century Massachusetts Bay* (Westport, Conn., 1985); Barry Levy, *Quakers and the American Family: British Settlement in the Delaware Valley* (New York, 1988); and Arthur J. Worrall, *Quakers in the Colonial Northeast* (Hanover, N. H., 1980). For Quaker relations with Indians, the definitive work remains Rayner Wickersham Kelsey, *Friends and the Indians, 1655-1917* (Philadelphia: The Associated Executive Committee of Friends on Indian Affairs, 1917).

8. James Axtell, *The Invasion Within*, p. 275; D. Elton Trueblood, *The People Called Quak-ers*, (New York: Harper and Row, 1966), p. 1.

9. Robert Barclay, *An Apology For The True Christian Divinity Being An Explanation And Vindication Of The Principles And Doctrines Of The People Called Quakers* (Philadelphia: Friends' Book Store, 1908), pp. 309 and 340; and D. Elton Trueblood, *The People Called Quakers*, p. 5.

Jesus. "I was sent to turn people from darkness to the Light," he wrote in his *Journal*,

>...that they might receive Christ Jesus; for to as many as should receive Him in His Light, I saw He would give power to become the sons of God; which power I had obtained by receiving Christ.[10]

In describing his call to ministry, Fox wrote in evangelistic terms similar to other Protestant missionaries. He aspired to lead people to "receive" Christ Jesus.

Like Fox, Quaker missionaries in the New World aimed to evangelize and spread the Gospel. Expelled from Plymouth in 1657, Christopher Holder and John Copeland went toward Salem. Along the way they held meetings and won converts. As they later recalled,

>Having obtained mercy from God, and being baptized into his covenant Christ Jesus, [we] preached freely unto them the things we had seen and heard, and our hands had handled, which as an engrafted word took place in them, such as never can be rooted out.[11]

Typical of other Quaker missionaries, Holder and Copeland believed that their "hearers" soon became their "fellow-sufferers."[12] The success of many Quaker evangelistic efforts helps to account for the legislation passed against them in most of the colonies. Within 10 years of its founding, the Society of Friends in England and America grew to 50,000 adherents. From 1655 to 1662, at least sixty missionaries traveled across the Atlantic.[13] A minute from a Friends Meeting in Skipton in 1660, describes the vast spread of their missionary activities. "We have received certain information from Friends in London of the great work and service of the Lord beyond the seas," they recorded,

>...in several parts and regions, as Germany, America, Virginia, and many other places as Florence, Mantua, Palatine, Tuscany, Italy, Rome, Turkey, Jerusalem, France, Geneva, Norway, Barbados, Bermuda, Antigua, Surinam, Newfoundland, through all which Friends have passed in the service of the Lord, and divers other places, countries, islands, and nations.[14]

---

10. Rufus M. Jones, ed., *The Journal of George Fox* (Richmond, Indiana: Friends United Press, 1976), p. 102. See also Walter R. Williams, *The Rich Heritage of Quakerism* (Newberg, Oregon: The Barclay Press, 1987), p. 1.

11. James Bowden, *The History of the Society of Friends in America*, Vol. I, pp. 87-88.

12. *Ibid.*

13. Frederick B. Tolles, *Quakers and the Atlantic Culture*, p. 9.

14. Skipton Meeting Minute, quoted in Walter R. Williams, *The Rich Heritage of Quakerism*, p.60.

Quaker missionaries traveled extensively, demonstrating their commitment to the priority of preaching the gospel of Jesus Christ.

In addition to a desire to evangelize colonists, the early Friends exhibited a focused concern to win native converts. The above minute from the Skipton Meeting continued by referring to the "many nations of the Indians" in which Quakers "had service for the Lord…published His Name and declared the everlasting Gospel of peace unto them that have been afar off, that they might be brought nigh unto God." Rather than simply trying to reach Englishmen with their message, Friends attempted to proselytize Indians.[15]

When George Fox visited the colonies in 1672, he initiated a number of missionary encounters with Indians and typically reported a positive reception. On one such occasion on the eastern shore of Chesapeake Bay, Fox held an evangelistic meeting to which he invited "the Indian emperor and his kings." When his intended guests arrived, Fox recorded "two good opportunities" with them. They not only "heard the word of the Lord willingly," they also "confessed to it." Thus, Fox believed his listeners assented to the truth of his message and could become his fellow Christian laborers. "What I spoke to them," he wrote, "I desired them to speak to their people,"

> …to let them know that God was raising up His tabernacle of witness in their wilderness-country, and was setting up His standard and glorious ensign of righteousness. They carried themselves very courteously and lovingly, and inquired where the next meeting would be, saying that they would come to it.[16]

The records fail to indicate whether or not these Indians heard Fox preach again. What is certain is that many others did.

Fox's missionary trip to America lasted for two years, during which time he traveled widely and met with many Indians. Accompanied by other Quaker missionaries, he sometimes hired Indians to transport his group in their canoes and often used them as guides. He went out of his way to visit Indian encampments and enjoyed the overnight hospitality of Indian hosts. Near Rhode Island he spoke to "about a hundred" Indians, and in North Carolina he even met with "one of the Indian priests." Considering the frequency of contact he had with Indians, combined with his bold personality and compulsion to preach, it is not hard to imagine that many of them heard Fox proclaim the gospel message. He penned in his *Journal* that he and some companions "passed through many Indian towns, and over some rivers and bogs" near Delaware Bay. As they "came among the Indians" they

---

15. *Ibid.*
16. Rufus M. Jones, ed., *The Journal of George Fox*, pp. 499-500.

continually "declared the day of the Lord to them." Though Fox failed to proselytize all of his Indian hearers, he believed that many responded favorably and some became "convinced." Some of the conversions occurred in Maryland, where he met with another Indian "emperor" and "two others of the chief men" among them. "I spoke to them by an interpreter," Fox explained,

> ...they heard the Truth attentively, and were very loving. A blessed meeting this was, of great service both for convincing and for establishing in the Truth those that were convinced of it. Blessed be the Lord, who causeth His blessed Truth to spread![17]

Fox felt that at least some of his Indian listeners became Christian believers.

George Fox not only practiced Indian evangelism, he preached its importance to his fellow Friends. In his pivotal doctrinal statement to the Governor of Barbados, written at the outset of his journey to America in 1671, he noted that "Indians make up a very large part of the families in this island for whom an account will be required by Him Who comes to judge the quick and the dead, at the great day of judgment."[18] Ten years later he wrote to Quakers in Carolina, urging them to "have meetings with the Indian kings and their people, to preach the gospel of peace, of life, and of salvation to them."[19] Fox knew that many of his co-religionists traveled to America as colonists for reasons other than evangelism. In 1682 he wrote to Friends "that are gone, and are going over to plant, and make outward plantations." Yet he entreated these Quaker planters to "invite all the Indians, and their kings" and "have meetings with them." While Friends cultivated their own earthly plantations, Fox hoped that they would not neglect making "heavenly plantations" in the Indians' hearts, "and so beget them to God, that they may serve and worship him, and spread his truth abroad."[20] At least some Quakers heeded Fox's instructions. Following his visit to Virginia, Fox wrote back to them concerning encouraging news.

> I received letters giving me an account of the service some of you had with and amongst the Indian king and his council; and if you go over again to Carolina, you may inquire of Captain Batts, the governor, with whom I left

---

17. Quakers frequently used the term "convincement" for "conversion," perhaps partly because they believed that God alone can convert or change a person's heart. Rufus M. Jones, ed., *The Journal of George Fox*, pp. 482-535.

18. George Fox, "Letter to the Governor of Barbados," in Walter R. Williams, *The Rich Heritage of Quakerism*, p. 76.

19. George Fox, "To Friends in Carolina," *The Works of George Fox*, Vol. 8 (New York: AMS Press, 1975), p. 202.

20. George Fox, "An epistle to all planters, and such who are transporting themselves into foreign plantations in America," *The Works of George Fox*, Vol. 8, p. 218.

a paper to be read to the [Indian] Emperor, and his thirty kings under him of the Tuscaroras.[21]

Although the contents of Fox's "paper" to the Indians remains a matter of speculation, his letter to the Virginian Quakers demonstrates his desire for on-going Indian contacts. He wrote, not to Friends adverse to ministry with Indians, but to ones who already attempted to fill their roles as missionaries to them.

As Englishmen, some Friends might have been expected to hope for cultural change among the Indians. In a letter to George Fox in 1686, John Archdale expressed pleasure that "some of the Indians" in Carolina "are so civilized as to come into English habits" which might serve as "a good preparation for the gospel." However, a strategic plan to reduce Indians to civility never became the stated objective of Friends. In fact, some Quakers thought that English behaviors needed to change prior to Indian conversions. "If any of them [from England] come to be sea-men or travel," wrote John Bellers, "they will be as so many missionaries...their regular lives will greatly strengthen the testimony of such as shall have a ministry, whilst the prophane [sic.] and vitious [sic.] lives of our present sea-men, etc., is one of the greatest scandals and obstacles to the Indians' conversion."[22] Thomas Story, a well-traveled Quaker missionary, observed similarly the corrupting influences of English colonists who made *pretense* to religion and knowledge, and yet are worse in *practice.*" They taught Indians "immoralities," such as "drunkenness, swearing, and the like." William Penn noted the Indians' civility and sense of order, although untutored in English ways. "None speak but the aged, they having consulted the rest before," he observed in 1683. "Thus in selling me their land they ordered themselves; I must say...they are an extroordinary [sic.] people." This favorable view of Indian behavior prompted Josiah Coale to declare that he found many Indians "more sober and Christian-like" than some "Christians so-called."[23]

Rather than preaching the need to civilize Indians prior to their conversion, the message of Friends focused simply on the belief that "there is no salvation in any other name, but by the name of Jesus."[24] Viewing Indians as

---

21. George Fox quoted in James Bowden, *The History of the Society of Friends in America,* Vol. I, p. 412. For interesting accounts of other early Quaker missionaries with Indians see *A Journal of the Life of Thomas Story* (New-Castle-Upon-Tyne: Isaac Thompson & Co., 1747), p. 155; and James Dickinson, "Journal of James Dickinson," in William Evans and Thomas Evans, eds., *The Friends' Library,* Vol. XII (Philadelphia, 1848), p. 390.

22. "John Archdale to George Fox," in James Bowden, *The History of the Society of Friends in America,* Vol. I, p. 416; and Ruth A. Fry, *John Bellers, 1654-1725, Quaker, Economist and Social Reformer* (London: Cassell and Company, Ltd., 1935), pp. 151-152.

23. *A Journal of the Life of Thomas Story,* p. 155; William Penn, "To The Earl of Sunderland," Richard S. Dunn and Mary Maples Dunn, eds., *The Papers of William Penn,* Vol.II, p. 417; Josiah Coale quoted in Howard Brinton, *Friends For 300 Years,* p. 38.

"men" rather than as people who failed as "Englishmen," Quakers exhibited a belief that Christ intended the gospel message to be for all mankind. Indians stood as their spiritual peers in that they shared equally in need of the Savior. Fox explained that "Christ died for the tawnies [Indians]...as well as for you that are called white."[25] Quakers thus demonstrated both a respect for Indians and a concern for their eternal souls. It rarely seemed to occur to early Friends that Indians who converted to Christianity through Quakers might need to give up their cultural heritage.

Fox and other Quaker missionaries attempted to start new churches or "Meetings" among the colonists and desired to develop them with the Indians. However, despite the emphasis on missions and proselytizing, no Indian Quaker churches appeared and few participated in established Meetings. As late as 1700, William Penn addressed Philadelphia Friends with a long-standing concern, "that Friends ought to be very careful in discharging a good conscience" toward Indians "for the good of their souls" so that "they might as frequent as may be come to Meetings on first days." Penn hoped that the Indians would receive Christ and join the membership of the Meetings. The minuted Quaker response to Penn's request suggests at least two fundamental barriers to fulfilling his vision, intermittent proximity and language problems. First of all, Friends recorded that "when the Indians come to town" they would speak with them and try to "get a Meeting amongst them."[26] Apparently, the Quakers expected to contact the seminomadic Indians at some point for trade or other purposes, but not on a continuous basis as settled neighbors. Even friendly Indians maintained separate cultural practices and did not live with Friends. Similarly, no Quakers went to live among Indians for any length of time until the eighteenth century. The "flying missions" of the French employed no Quaker "pilots" and therefore no on-going ministry occurred with an Indian clan or tribe. Those Friends who relocated eventually to preach to Indians lived "near" them rather than "as" them or "with" them.[27] Each group thus seemed to prefer their own, familiar customs and social patterns.

Difficulties with language posed a second kind of hurdle for the conversion of Indians to Quaker Christianity. The Philadelphia Friends who answered Penn and discussed starting a Meeting with Indians reported their

24. George Fox, "To Friends In Carolina," *The Works of George Fox*, Vol. 8, p. 37.

25. George Fox, "Gospel Family Order, Being a Short Discourse Concerning The Ordering of Families, Both of Whites, Blacks, and Indians," in J. William Frost, *The Quaker Origins of Antislavery* (Norwood, Pennsylvania: Norwood Editions, 1980), p. 47.

26. "Philadelphia Monthly Meeting Minutes," in J. William Frost, *The Quaker Origins of Antislavery*, p. 73.

27. Notice Walter R. Williams, *The Rich Heritage of Quakerism*, p. 162. For a more descriptive account of some Quaker missionaries who lived and worked with the Seneca in the late eighteenth century, see Anthony F.C. Wallace, *The Death and Rebirth of the Seneca* (New York: Vintage Books, 1969).

need for "interpreters". Not everyone could speak effectively with Indians, and so they hoped that some "among Friends that can speak Indian well" would join them.[28] Certainly, Quaker Meetings without effective interpreters would hold little attraction for Indians, but a deeper problem of language relates to the transmission of complex spiritual ideas. Religion involves a set of sacred symbols or concepts, and effective communication of those ideas requires arriving at mutually understood meanings.[29] It may be that when Quakers spoke of their God, the Light of Christ, and salvation, some Indians failed to comprehend the theological abstractions. Whereas the French Jesuits, with their image-based Catholicism could more easily appeal to Indians and so produced at least the appearance of conversions, the English Quakers' non-ritualistic and word-based system of beliefs did not resonate with the Indians' spiritual framework. Those Indians that Fox "convinced" of the "truth" may have failed to fully grasp the meaning of his message or he may have misunderstood their response, confusing Indian graciousness with evangelistic success. With the help of skillful interpreters, some Indians may have understood enough of the Quakers' preaching to offer an informed response. In this case, presented with the option of jettisoning their religious and cultural traditions in favor of Friends' beliefs, even those Indians who appreciated Quakers may have rejected their religious system. Although Friends desired to proselytize Indians and treated them with kindness and respect, they simply failed to communicate clearly or persuasively the relevance and necessity of their Christ.

In common with other Europeans, colonial Quakers *attempted* to proselytize Native Americans in the late seventeenth century. They likewise pursued another English objective in the New World, colonization on land owned by Indians. The desire by Friends to acquire land and colonize appears evident almost from the beginning of the Quaker movement. Rufus Jones suggests that the concept of a Quaker colony began with George Fox. Josiah Coale, a Friend who traveled extensively among Indians in America, mentioned in a letter that Fox commissioned him to "treat with the Susquehanna Indians for the purchase of a strip of territory." Though Fox's request is not preserved, Coale's answer demonstrates that he hoped a group of Quakers would inhabit the land. "As concerning Friends buying a piece of land of the Susquehanna Indians," he responded, "I have spoken of it to them and told them what thou said concerning it, but their answer was that there is no land that is habitable or fit for situation beyond Baltimore's liberty [territory]." It is striking that Coale sent this letter in 1660, some

---

28. "Philadelphia Monthly Meeting Minutes," in J. William Frost, *The Quaker Origins of Antislavery*, p. 73.

29. See Clifford Geertz, "Ethos, World View, and the Analysis of Sacred Symbols," and "Religion As a Cultural System," in *The Interpretation of Cultures: Selected Essays* (New York: Basic Books, 1973), pp. 88-114 and 128-132.

twelve years prior to Fox's visit to America. About this same time, William Penn also turned his attention to the New World. Writing in 1681 about his new Pennsylvania territory, he recalled, "This I can say, that I had an *opening of joy* as to these parts in the year 1661, at Oxford twenty years since."[30]

Perhaps motivated by Fox's visit and impact, Quakers obtained possession of a large part of New Jersey the year after he returned to England in 1674, by a purchase made through John Fenwick and Edward Byllynge. When the province opened to settlers, the proprietors announced their purpose to "lay a foundation for after ages to understand their liberty as men and Christians, that they may not be brought into bondage but by their own consent; for we put the power in the people."[31] In contrast to Puritan norms, the Quakers thus established the right of every man to worship without interruption or molestation. This freedom extended to Indians, as well. Perhaps the most well-known and successful Quaker colony is the one established by William Penn. In exchange for a large war debt owed to his father's estate, Charles II gave Penn a large tract of land in the New World. Known as "Penn's Woods" or Pennsylvania, this land grant would be the location for a "Holy Experiment" based on religious toleration for all, including Indians. In contrast to other English settlements, this new Quaker colony rested on the conviction that "liberty of conscience...must not be denied, even by those that are most scandalized at the ill use some seem to have made of such pretenses."[32]

Almost from the moment he received his charter, Penn focused his attention on Indian affairs. His rights to the land came through the crown's claims of ownership based on conquest of the Dutch. But Penn realized the ethical problem of developing an English colony in Pennsylvania while attempting to respect the rights of the original inhabitants. On October 18, 1681, Penn dispatched a letter to the Lenni Lenape, or Delaware Indians, who lived within the bounds of his new territory. Penn opened his letter with, "My Friends," followed by words which pointed to their mutual accountability for right behavior. "There is a great God and power that hath made the world," he explained, "to whom you and I, and all people owe their being and well-being, and to whom you and I must one day give an account for all that we do in the world." It is significant that Penn consistently applied his maxims equally to the English and the Indians. They needed to "do good to one another." Penn then attempted to explain the

30. Rufus M. Jones, ed., *The Journal of George Fox*, pp. 515-516.

31. Quoted in Clifton E. Olmstead, *History of Religion in the United States* (New Jersey: Prentice-Hall, Inc., 1960), p. 113.

32. "Penn and Liberty of Conscience, 1686," in Edwin S. Gaustad, ed., *A Documentary History Of Religion In America: To the Civil War* (Grand Rapids: William B. Eerdmans Publishing Company, 1982), p. 119.

reason for his interest in their land, and his desire to maintain friendly and peaceable relations.

> Now this great God Hath been pleased to make me concerned in your part of the world, and the king of the country, where I live, hath given me a great province therein; but I desire to enjoy it *with your love and consent*, that we may always live together as neighbours and friends; else what would the great God do to us, who hath made us, not to devour and destroy one another, but to live soberly and kindly together in the world?[33]

Penn prepared well for this initial letter. He knew that the Indians held legitimate grievances against previous white colonists. "I am very sensible of the unkindness and injustice that have been too much exercised towards you by the people of these parts of the world," he empathized, "but I am not such a man." Perhaps the Indians' pain and the transgressions toward them echoed in the hearts of early Friends like Penn who also suffered at the hands of Englishmen. Guided by Quaker principles, Penn aimed to treat Native Americans better than the proprietors of other colonies. He knew he would need to earn the trust of the Indians over time, expressing his desire to "win and gain [their] love and friendship by a kind, just, and peaceable life." Not only did he believe that God would hold him accountable for his behavior toward the Indians, but he also found motivation in his "great love and regard" for the Indians as a people.[34]

Penn soon proved his effectiveness as both a gracious diplomat with the Indians and as a colonial strategist. On October 28, 1681, he sent orders with his cousin, Colonel Markham, to "buy the land of the true owners which I think is the Susquehanna people." In their dealings with the Indians, Penn and the Quakers gained a reputation for honesty and fairness. Yet Penn was no fool. He also instructed Markham to "treat speedily with the Indians for land before they are furnisht [sic.] by others with things that please them," adding that he should "take advice in this."[35] A few years later, during a personal visit to America, Penn initiated a famous Indian treaty that gained a legendary if somewhat confused status. Supposedly, he met with the Delawares under an old elm tree at the village of Schackamaxon. That he did meet with them at some time and establish a treaty around 1683 appears certain, but the exact location, date, and contents of the treaty are unclear. Benjamin West painted a huge, anachronistic picture commemorating it. Although no treaty document exists, a second significant treaty occurred in 1701 which reportedly echoed its terms. With pledges of recip-

---

33. "William Penn and the Indians, 1681," Edwin S. Gaustad, *A Documentary History Of Religion In America: To the Civil War*, pp. 123-124.

34. *Ibid.*

35. William Penn, "Additional Instructions To William Markham," in Richard S. Dunn and Mary Maples Dunn, eds., *The Papers of William Penn*, Vol.II, p. 129.

rocal good will, it also provided for fair treatment in the courts. Voltaire called it the only Indian treaty never ratified by an oath and never broken. During Penn's lifetime, this claim appears to have validity. Even as late as 1731, the Pennsylvania Governor could write of Penn's treaty saying that he "made a strong chain of friendship" with the Indians "which has been kept bright to this day."[36]

To the Iroquois, Penn was the beloved "Onas" and the Delaware called him brother "Miquon." Both names meant "feather," and since quills were used for writing they punned on his name. [37] Penn cultivated his relationship with the Indians through fair dealings and mutual trust. He attempted to learn some of the Indians' language and considered them "as the same flesh and blood with the Christians and the same as if the one body were to be divided into two parts."[38] These are not the words of the typical Englishman who viewed Native Americans as inherently inferior. Penn's combination of personal integrity, genuine respect, and proffered kindness helps to explain the great success of his Quaker experiment. In contrast to other colonies experiencing Indian warfare and outbursts of violence, Indians and Quakers in Pennsylvania shared good will for many years. According to the Pennsylvania Gazette in 1743, an Indian representative reaffirmed to the Governor that Indians continued to view the colonists in Pennsylvania as "one flesh and blood with themselves" by "virtue of the treaties subsisting." Therefore they could have "neither intention nor inclination to hurt them." By 1758, when Indian hostilities in the west became frequent, the Philadelphia Yearly Meeting could still report its "thankfulness for the peculiar favour extended and continued to our Friends and Brethren in profession, none of whom have as we have yet heard been slain nor carried into captivity."[39] The fact that friendly relations broke down eventually in the eighteenth century between the Pennsylvania government and the Delaware Indians simply underscores the effectiveness of Penn and the early Friends.[40]

---

36. Governor Patrick Gordon quoted in Francis Jennings, "Brother Miquon: Good Lord!," in Richard S. Dunn and Mary Maples Dunn, eds., *The World Of William Penn* (Philadelphia: University of Pennsylvania Press, 1986), p. 200. Quaker scholars often retell the story of Penn's treaty. For example see John Punshon, *Portrait In Grey: A Short History of the Quakers* (London: Quaker Home Service, 1986), p. 177; Elfrida Vipont, *The Story Of Quakerism: 1652-1952* (London: The Bannisdale Press, 1954), pp. 119-120; and Walter R. Williams, *The Rich Heritage of Quakerism*, p. 129.

37. See Francis Jennings, "Brother Miquon: Good Lord!," in Richard S. Dunn and Mary Maples Dunn, eds., *The World Of William Penn*, p. 198.

38. Quoted in Clifton E. Olmstead, *History of Religion in the United States* (New Jersey: Prentice-Hall, Inc., 1960), p. 116.

39. *The Pennsylvania Gazette*, Philadelphia, February 2, 1743; and "Philadelphia Yearly Meeting Minutes, 1758", in Francis Jennings, "Brother Miquon: Good Lord!," in Richard S. Dunn and Mary Maples Dunn, eds., *The World Of William Penn*, p. 207.

In addition to missionary efforts and colonization, a third major issue that commanded the attention of early Quakers in dealing with Indians, relates to trade and commerce. The great Quaker bankers of the eighteenth century, such as the Barclays, Lloyds, and Gurneys, had their roots in the textile businesses, merchant houses, trading centers, and infant industries of the seventeenth century. Quaker leaders encouraged Friends to participate diligently in commerce. Thomas Chalkley, author of one of the most widely published Quaker Journals, taught that "the tradesman and the merchant, do not understand by our Lord's Doctrine that they must neglect their calling, or grow idle in their business." Instead, they "must certainly work, and be industrious." George Fox observed that as a result of Quaker efforts, they "had more trade than any of their neighbours, and if there was any trading, they had a great part of it."[41] The detractors of Friends also noted their trading and business talents. A popular book first published in 1684 stated:

> They are generally merchants and mechanicks [sic.], and are observed to be very punctual in their dealings, men of few words in a bargain, modest and composed in their deportment, temperate in their lives and using great frugality in all things. In a word, they are singularly industrious, sparing no labour or pains to increase their wealth.[42]

Although sometimes criticized for their business proclivity, even those outside of Quakerism recognized their commercial efforts and hard work. Friends also developed a reputation for honesty and truthfulness in their business transactions. Early books of Church Discipline urged Quakers to demonstrate integrity in their commercial dealings. All those who "trade by sea or land," Friends instructed,

> ...and buy, bargain or contract beyond their abilities, and such as keep not their words, promises, or engagments [sic.] in their dealings or do not pay or satisfy their just debts according to time agreed on, these being a reproach to the truth and a manifest injury and injustice.[43]

---

40. Perhaps the most infamous case of injustice became known as the "Walking Purchase," in which the Delaware Indians lost a large tract of land to the Proprietors in 1737. See Hugh Barbour and J. William Frost, *The Quakers* (New York: Greenwood Press, 1988), pp. 126-127.

41. "A Journal, or Historical Account, of the Life, Travels, and Christian Experiences, of the Antient, Faithful Servant of Jesus Christ, Thomas Chalkley" in *A Collection of the Works of Thomas Chalkley* (Philadelphia, 1749), pp. 97-98; and George Fox quoted in Frederick B. Tolles, *Meeting House and Counting House: The Quaker Merchants of Colonial Philadelphia, 1682-1763* (New York: The Norton Library, 1963), p. 46.

42. Giovanni Paolo Marana in Frederick B. Tolles, *Meeting House and Counting House*, p. 47.

Local elders attempted to enforce these instructions through direct confrontation and brought notice of infractions to the Quaker Meetings. Fox recorded that, "people came to see Friends' honesty and truthfulness" and knew that "for conscience sake towards God, they would not cozen [sic.] and cheat them."[44]

Those people who came to trust and "deal with" Friends included the Indians.

As has been mentioned, some of the most important trade agreements between the Quakers and Indians involved the acquisition of land. When Penn made his treaties with the Delaware Indians, he secured them with gifts of European articles. These presents included customary items such as knives, axes, fishhooks, needles, blankets, stockings, and coats. By 1685, Penn calculated that his spending on exchanges with Indians already totaled £1,200 in presents and purchase money for a small section of southeastern Pennsylvania.[45] Despite the potential for lucrative earnings, Penn and other Quakers spurned trading one typical European commodity with Indians, alcohol. Penn believed that "the Dutch, Sweeds and English learned them drunkenness" in which state they "kill and burn one another." Although he knew that some natives loved rum and would readily accept it, he thought that it produced "mischief" for Indians and colonists alike. Quakers in North Carolina ordered Friends not to "barter, or exchance [sic.] directly or indirectly to the Indians rum, brandy, or any other strong liquors." They opposed selling alcohol to Indians "since the settlements of these countries," so that they would not contribute to their "abuse and hurt."[46] Although interested in trade with Indians and desirous of financial gain, early Quakers in general refused to sacrifice principles for profits. Many discovered that respect for Indians and friendly relations ensured the basis for further advantageous trade. Friends exchanged English manufactured goods for Indian furs, yielding handsome returns. Penn came to depend upon trade with Indians to defray the costs of his colonial enterprise, and in 1703 he proposed monopolizing the fur trade in lieu of taxes. His Quaker secretary, James Logan, refused even to approach the Quaker-dominated Pennsylvania Assembly with his request. "The merchants will never bear it," he flatly stated, "contrivance and management may give thee a share with the rest, but more is not to be depended upon."[47] By 1717, Logan himself became a "great dealer in furs and skins" and confided to a friend that

---

43. *The Book of Discipline for the People Called Quakers for North Carolina* (Quaker Collection, Guilford College Library, Greensboro, North Carolina: Handwritten copy, 1755), p. 16.

44. George Fox in Frederick B. Tolles, *Meeting House and Counting House*, p. 59.

45. See Francis Jennings, "Brother Miquon: Good Lord!," in Richard S. Dunn and Mary Maples Dunn, eds., *The World Of William Penn*, p. 198.

46. William Penn, "To The Earl Of Sunderland," in Richard S. Dunn and Mary Maples Dunn, eds., *The Papers of William Penn*, Vol.II, p. 416; and *The Book of Discipline for the People Called Quakers for North Carolina*, p. 17.

he "looked upon it as a particular Providence" that God "led [him] into the Indian trade."[48]

The early Quakers deserve acknowledgment as a distinctive sub-group among English colonists in their treatment of Native Americans. Contrary to the view that Friends observed Indian relations in the New World as passive bystanders, the evidence indicates that they participated as concerned Christians and active traders. During the late seventeenth century, Quakers excelled in converting their countrymen and attempted also to evangelize the Indians. While they failed to proselytize many Indians, the Friends found success in colonization and trade relations. Woven into the fabric of their dealings with the Indians were threads of respect, kindness, and honesty that seemed to separate them from at least some Europeans. Penn, and many other Quaker colonists, encountered Indians they considered "admirable," treating them with a degree of equality as "the same flesh and blood" and finding reciprocal appreciation. In contrast with the trail of treachery, condescension, and brutality left by other Europeans, colonial Quakers established a legacy of friendship toward Indians, if not Indian Friends.

47. James Logan quoted in Francis Jennings, "Brother Miquon: Good Lord!," in Richard S. Dunn and Mary Maples Dunn, eds., *The World Of William Penn*, p. 196.

48. James Logan quoted in Frederick B. Tolles, *Quakers and the Atlantic Culture*, p. 62.

Rufus Jones and Quaker Unity

HUGH BARBOUR

The Society of Friends, for Rufus Jones[1] as for Arthur Roberts,[2] remains a single movement, called by God to a special role in American Christianity and world history. Both men have also been realistically aware of human limitations and diversity. Yet they have seen God's power, shared in meetings for worship as well as in the religious experience of individuals, able to change human society and transcend human ideas and institutions.

1887, when Christ-centered Friends were brought together in Richmond by their disagreements over ministry and sacramental Ordinances, was a time of great hope among American churches. Revivals and Holiness camp meetings aroused evangelical Protestants, while New Englanders were shown the creativity of the individual human spirit by Emerson, Lowell and Thoreau. The subjective human mind was affirmed by people as diverse as William James and Mary Baker Eddy. Throughout America, faith in social progress and concern for laborers and the poor interacted in the temperance and women's rights movements, in populist parties, in settlement houses in cities, and in the "social gospel." A decade of ferment in the Student Christian Movement, centered in the Student YMCA, was climaxed by a national conference at Harvard led by Luther Wishard, and the first of the annual summer student conferences at Northfield School under Dwight L. Moody, from which grew the Student Volunteer Movement

---

1. See his initial editorial in *The Friends Review* (Vol XLVII #5, 8/24/1893) "Fore Cast;" also Diana Alten, "Rufus Jones and The American Friend, a Quest for Unity," *Quaker History* (hereafter QH) 74:1,Spring 1985, pp.41-48.

2. Arthur O. Roberts, *The Association of Evangelical Friends* (Newberg, OR: Barclay Press, 1975) p.47. He worked to prevent evangelical Friends becoming a narrow organization.

which enrolled thousands of teachers, doctors, and church leaders for Protestant foreign missions and "the evangelization of the world in this generation."[3] Moody's broad and eager spirit drew scientists such as Henry Drummond and doctors such as Wilfred Grenfell to work with evangelists and Bible scholars.

Jones reflected the self-giving optimism of this era. He shared these men's belief that all truth is God's one truth, whether biblical, historical, or scientific, that God is personal and loving and that religion is rooted in personal experience. The student YMCA at Haverford College, where Rufus Jones graduated in 1885, had begun in 1879. From 1886 to 1893 the English Quaker New Testament scholar Rendel Harris taught at Haverford. He became Jones' intimate friend, and later the Director of Woodbrooke, the Quaker college outside Birmingham.[4] Jones in his small autobiographies has less to say about their influence on him than about the Haverford professors who drew him to the writings of German mystics, and to the idealist philosophies of Kant and Plato,[5] for whom duty, the good, and the beautiful were central parts of truth.

Rufus Jones' links with the Richmond conference of 1887 were direct. That autumn he began teaching at the Friends School in Providence, RI, (later called Moses Brown School), where his cousin Augustine Jones was headmaster. In 1874 Augustine Jones, while still a lawyer at Lynn, Massachusetts, had been asked to deliver a message on "The Society of Friends" at the Disciples Church in Boston, as part of a series on churches' doctrines and history within "the Universal Church." Augustine Jones foreshadowed the Richmond Declaration of Faith in saying that "the sacrifice of Christ was both physical and spiritual" and "The Inward Light is both universal and saving"—universal because it is in every man of every capacity in the world, and saving because it has in it the power and virtue of the atonement. He stressed that Fox, like Jesus, abolished outward ceremonies, above all in worship. He gave more emphasis than was done at Richmond to "the testi-

---

3. Clarence Shedd, *Two Centuries of Student Christian Movements* (New York, 1934); Hugh Barbour, "The Origins of Phillips Brooks House at Harvard" MS for Yale program on Religion in Higher Education, 1943-44.

4. Harris gave up a professorship at the University of Leiden to accept the Woodbrooke post, which had first been offered to Rufus Jones. He became a close friend of RMJ and both had been with Rowntree on a famous hiking trip in Switzerland in 1896 where they "brainstormed" what became the "Rowntree Series" of Quaker histories. RMJ wrote on *Quakers in the American Colonies and Later Periods of Quakerism* and two prefatory volumes on *Studies in Mystical Religion* and *Spiritual Reformers in the 16th and 17th Centuries*. See Stephen Allott, *John Wilhelm Rowntree, 1868-1905*, (York, England: Sessions Book Trust, 1994).

5. Rufus M.Jones (hereafter RMJ), *The Trail of Life in College* (New York, 1929); RMJ, *Haverford College: A History and an Interpretation* (New York, 1933). pp. 57, 66-7, 94-5. Rendel Harris taught at Johns Hopkins while RMJ was a Haverford student, but their early personal contacts have not been traced. He wrote on 3/30/1895 and 10/5/96 his approval of RMJ's editorials in the early issues of *The American Friend*.

mony of the Eternal Spirit, manifested in the heart and conscience," and to Quaker education, Quakers' rejection of war and violence, and Quaker stands and work on liberty of conscience, oaths, slavery, and prison work.[6] He may have been the first Friend to call Quakers "mystics."[7] Whittier, who had proposed Augustine Jones for the speech, visited him to commend it. Sixty other Friends also wrote praises, though it was attacked as too doctrinal by James Carey Thomas of Baltimore, and as not orthodox enough by Thomas Kimber in *The Christian Worker.* [8] Augustine Jones was one of New England's representatives at Richmond in 1887. Another was Eli Jones, Rufus' uncle, who with his wife Sybil Jones had played major roles in Quaker revivals and in arousing Quaker commitment to foreign missions, notably at Ramallah, Palestine. Rufus wrote his first book in 1889 as a tribute to them. Joseph Bevan Braithwaite, the author of the Richmond Declaration, seems also to have stopped at Providence in 1887 on his way home to England.[9] Rufus had been welcomed like a young Abe Lincoln[10] on his visit the previous year in the stately homes of English Friends such as Braithwaite and the statesman John Bright. Rufus was inspired by the Richmond meeting as the first time when the "Orthodox" Yearly Meetings from the English Channel to the Pacific gathered as one.

Rufus' bonds to these men and women, and to the growing unity of Christ-centered Friends for which they worked, was perhaps the strongest reason why he kept his membership lifelong in New England Yearly Meeting, rather than transfering it to the "Orthodox" Philadelphia Yearly Meeting, which had created Haverford College, but was itself unofficially deeply divided into "Gurneyite" and "Wilburite" factions and therefore had no official ties to any other yearly meeting. Liberal Friends in the Hicksite

---

6. Augustine Jones' address was published verbatim in the Lynn *Semi-Weekly Reporter* on February 11, 1874, and as a Quaker pamphlet later that year.

7. Emerson had already done so, and Caroline Stephen, a British convinced Friend, would do so in her *Quaker Strongholds* (London, 1890) before Rufus Jones wrote about mystics, but Haverford philosophers were already leading him in the same direction.

8. Augustine Jones' manuscript autobiography, copied in typescript, is among the archives of Moses Brown School. He responded to Thomas' doubts by showing him passages in Barclay, Fox and Bates. Augustine Jones wrote frequently to Rufus throughout his life, particularly in 1904, when the Moses Brown Board forced his retirement as headmaster at the age of 68, because he fought to continue its role as a boarding school for Quaker boys and girls from rural Meetings, while many on the board wished to make it a college preparatory school, and to merge it with two other similar schools in Providence. Augustine Jones was bitter that Rufus had not supported him more actively on a recent visit to Providence.

9. Elizabeth Gray Vining, *Friend of Life: A Biography of Rufus M. Jones*, (1958, repr.Phila., 1981) p. 57, does not give her source for this statement.

10. I have not found whether D.Elton Trueblood, in writing on *The Humor of Christ* and *The Abraham Lincoln: Theologian of American Anguish* (1972) ever compared Lincoln and Jones, who both taught by humorous stories in a country drawl. See Trueblood, *While it is Day* (New York,1974).

tradition, which in 1900 formed Friends General Conference, have drawn strength from Rufus' teachings about the universal inward Light and the early history of Friends. They often forget, however, that Jones was never a Hicksite. He had contacts and friendships with individual Hicksites through the Friends Social Union and his love of golf,[11] but until World War I brought all Quakers together to support their Peace Testimony through the AFSC, Rufus Jones had few official contacts with even the Philadelphia Hicksites.

Two excellent articles in *Quaker History*[12] combine to give a balanced account of the results of Rufus Jones' call to become editor of *The Friends Review*, published in Philadelphia since 1847[13], to try to reach out through it to a wider circle of Friends. The next step was its merging in 1894 with the evangelical Quaker journal, *The Christian Worker* (based at that time in Chicago) to form *The American Friend*. Walter Malone had spoken in 1892, at the first Quinquennial conference following the Richmond one, about Friends' need for a single mission board, a single press, and a single journal,[14] for which he had Allen Jay in mind as editor, since Calvin Pritchard at *The Christian Worker* had followed David Updegraff into approving water baptism.[15] Malone had replaced Pritchard with the "more pliable" Peter W. Raidabaugh. That the journals' merger carried forward the spirit of the Richmond Conference is shown by the role of its Presiding Clerk, James Wood of New York,[16] at the meeting in New York on May 26, 1894 of Mal-

---

11. Sources here are manuscript minutebooks at Swarthmore, suggested orally by Jerry Frost.

12. Diana Alten, *loc.cit.*, and John Oliver, "J. Walter Malone: *The American Friend* and an Evangelical Quaker's Social Agenda" (*Quaker History*, 80:2, Fall, 1991), pp.63-84.

13. Letters of Isaac Sharpless, President of Haverford, to RMJ, 3/25, 4/15, 5/10, and 6/28/93 offered RMJ this position, since RMJ had edited the Haverford student paper, and discussed financing it by combining it with RMJ teaching at Haverford.

14. Oliver, *loc.cit.*, says that Walter Malone wrote Timothy Nicholson, Nov.12,1891, saying either Pritchard or Malone must leave *The Christian Worker*, alternatively, perhaps Nicholson could combine with President Mills and Allen Jay to turn *Friends Review* into an *American Friend* with Jay as editor. This may be the name's origin.

15. Malone also wrote to RMJ deploring Dougan Clark's water baptism, 9/13/94.

16. James Wood was President also of the American Bible Society, while living on his family farm at Mt.Kisco, NY, where he had introduced Southdown sheep and Angus cattle, and presided over the county agricultural society and the New York State exhibit at the 1893 Columbian Exposition in Chicago. He had also given there at the World's Parliament of Religions a presentation of *The Society of Friends and its Mission*, strikingly like Augustine Jones's, apart from a greater stress on the Spirit as Christ within us. Jones published it in *The Friends Review*, 10/19/1893, and the Friends Book and Tract Committee reprinted it in New York. He wrote long essays for *The Friends Review* , on "Irish Home Rule" (1/4/1894)—based on personal visits—and "The Pastoral Question"—based on I Cor. 12, and judiciously balanced since Wood himself believed in worship based on silence. Wood continued on the Board of *The American Friend*, and wrote articles for it. My footnote #50, below, puts these into their contexts..

one,[17] Raidabaugh,[18] Sharpless, Allen Thomas, and Rufus which arranged the merger.

The American Friend was published in Philadelphia until 1912, partly to ensure its continued support there, but Jones published letters and articles from many leading evangelical Friends,[19] explaining that he stated his own beliefs in editorials but did not judge the opinions in articles by other Friends, even when they judged each other. He accepted from the beginning frequent invitations to speak in the Quaker colleges: Earlham (on Dante), Guilford, Wilmington, Penn and Friends University,[20] and Yearly Meetings in Iowa, North Carolina, Indiana, and Kansas. In 1905 he added Whittier College, California Yearly Meeting and Oregon Friends.[21] Whenever he could he visited in the homes of evangelical Friends such as Allen Jay and John Henry Douglas. He exchanged many letters with Douglas, Calvin Pritchard, Luke Woodard, David Hadley, and others who made clear where they disagreed with him. Allen and Mahalah Jay, Timothy Nicholson, Joel Bean, and James Wood wrote to encourage him.[22]

The Richmond Conference of 1887 created no new structures, though some were suggested. Already the Associated Executive Committee of Friends on Indian affairs had been set up in 1869, while the Quaker Women's Missionary Conference which Mahalah Jay called in Indianapolis in 1888 matured into the American Friends Board of Missions after 1894. In 1887 it had been agreed to call together representatives of the doctrinally "Orthodox" Yearly Meetings at five-yearly intervals. The 1897 meeting

17. A copy of Malone's memo on the New York meeting is in RMJ's papers at Haverford Quaker Collection.

18. Raidabaugh appears as "Associate editor" on the "masthead" of the first issue of *The American Friend*, (7/19/1894; hereafter *Am.Fd.*) along with "Field Editors" Allen Jay of Richmond, J.Walter Malone of Cleveland, Stephen M. Hadley of Oskaloosa, George L. Crossman of Lynn, Mass., and Thomas Newlin of Newberg, OR, and both Philadelphia and Chicago addresses. By 1897 the Chicago address had disappeared, and Raidabaugh was only another field editor. By 1899 only Rufus Jones was listed.

19. In preparation for the discussion of the proposed Uniform Discipline in 1900-02 he invited papers on Ministry (11/1/1900) from Richard Haworth, George A. Barton, Elbert Russell, Richard H.Thomas, Andrew F. Mitchell, Edward Kelsey, and Thomas Newlin. He had also printed (5/1900) long negative statements by Esther Tuttle Pritchard and A. H. Hussey, though answering their points.

20. Vining, *op.cit.* pp.69, pp. 117-22.

21. The 1907 Five Years Meeting session heard from its Board of Education that RMJ had been asked to give a set of five lectures at Wilmington, Earlham, and Penn Colleges and Friends University. He also gave at that 1907 session a paper on "The Present Opportunity for Friends." The discussion that followed, by Rayner Kelsey, Abijah Weaver of New York, Elbert Russell, David Hadley of Western Yearly Meeting, Mabel Douglas of Oregon, Edward Grubb of London, and others, was reported in the minutes and printed in *Am. Fd.* in equally objective detail.

22. See letters in Boxes 5, 8, 10, 12 in Rufus Jones' papers at Haverford Quaker Collection.

"unlike the two former conferences, ...followed a definite, prearranged program, and its discussions were all opened by thoughtful, solid addresses:"[23] The clerk, Carey Thomas, presented on "The Theory and Practice of Quakerism" and Thomas Newlin of Oregon on "Christian Sociology." President J.J. Mills of Earlham spoke on "Qualifications for the Christian Ministry" (less than half of the Indiana Meetings had yet adopted the pastoral system). Rufus Jones spoke on "Shall there be a Central Body?" Naturally the pages of *The American Friend*, which reported the sessions fully, were also full both before and after the meetings, of essays on all these topics, but in particular, with those for and against a "uniform Discipline" to unify the Yearly Meetings. The Business Committee, with one representative from each Yearly Meeting, included Wood, Jones, Thomas, John Henry Douglas of Oregon and Allen Jay of Indiana. The committee that was asked to draw up a suggested Uniform Discipline, two per Yearly Meeting, included most of these (Mahala Jay and President Mills replacing Allen Jay) and also Emma Malone and Edgar Nicholson.[24] This committee asked Wood and Jones to draft a proposed text. In 1898 they worked intensively at Wood's farm,[25] and circulated a draft to the whole committee and others. It was then "greatly transformed," sent out again in a second draft for further revising, and late in 1899 mailed out, and also printed in the *American Friend*, for all Yearly Meetings to study before the next "Quinquennial conference" in 1902.[26] (New England first took it up, but deferred decision for a year. New York seems to have first officially adopted it.) The 1902 "Quinquennial Session" accepted the Constitution which the draft included, and thereby on its second day transformed itself into the Five Years Meeting, the federation now called Friends United Meeting. For various reasons, London, Dublin, and Philadelphia Meetings never fully accepted this Discipline and affiliation,[27] and Ohio did not yield over water baptism. The other "Orthodox" Yearly Meetings used or included the Discipline in their Books of Faith and Practice for the next half century, and most at once joined Five Years Meeting.

Rufus Jones had hoped for a sharing of purposes, programs, love and friendship among all Quakers, while he expected some doctrinal disagreements. He had written on "The Unity of the Church" (6/13/1901), as Ohio Friends began plans to publish a rival *Evangelical Friend:*[28]

---

23. *Am.Fd.*, 10/28/1897, p.1005.

24. *Am.Fd.*,11/4/1897.

25. During 1898, Sallie Coutant Jones, Rufus' wife, was dying of tuberculosis at Saranac Lake, further north in New York State. Letters to and from him were mainly about her.

26. *Am. Fd.*, 12/14/1899.

27. Elbert Russell, *History of Quakerism* (New York, 1942) pp.493-5.

28. Malone finally started this publication in 1905, and meanwhile issued *The Soul Winner.*

It has been the mission of the present writer to work for peace and unity, and to promote the spiritual power of this branch of the Church.... Our one possibility of being a people of God lay in union, not of opinion, but of heart and purpose. We have toiled and struggled and prayed for this end. ...This AMERICAN FRIEND has been a standing monument of union and of Christian fellowship and brotherhood. It has been open at all times for everyone who has a message for the church, ...and the truth has gained immensely by it.... . *What is true can be shown to be true*, and there is nothing in our faith which needs any shield against the light.

Unity in program, however, was no easier than unity in doctrine. Already in 1901, *The American Friend* carried Mahalah Jay's report on the new mission in Gibara, Cuba, and Dr. George DeVol's report on arriving at Nanking, China, along with Rufus' report on the Mohonk international arbitration conference called by the Quaker Smileys. But Cuba was at first the only mission field directly under the Board of Missions of the Five Years Meeting, whose other functions of sharing news, mission candidates, and funds just continued Friends' more informal earlier customs. Quakers shared in a national Ecumenical Missions Conference in 1900, Wood participated in the 1910 international one at Edinburgh, and Rufus Jones addressed the First Missionary Conference of Friends at Richmond in 1906, linking missions to the Discipline.[29] He printed news from mission fields in almost every edition of *The American Friend*, such as Theophilus and Fareda Waldmeieer's letter of thanks to the Philadelphia committee supporting his Lebanon Hospital for the Insane (7/30/1897) and Martha Hadley's letter of 8/9/1899 from Kotzebue, Alaska; but Jones did not visit Latin America, nor Asia until 1926 and 1932.[30]

From 1902 to 1907 Jones' personal correspondance and the messages sent to *The American Friend* were again much filled with distrust of the new institutions by evangelical Friends such as Edward Mott of Oregon, David Hadley of Indiana, and John Henry Douglas, retired to California. The attack was partly aimed at the Haverford summer schools which brought young Friends together to study the Bible and Quaker history; the attack on

29. In 1907, Charles Tebbetts of California replaced Mahalah Jay as Secretary. (Christina M. Jones, *American Friends in World Missions*, (Elgin, IL: 1946) Ch.III. After 1902, work in China continued under Ohio, Alaska and later Guatemala under California YM, Bolivia under Oregon, and Japan under Philadelphia. In 1905 Western Yearly Meeting transferred Mexican work, between 1907 and 1912 Iowa's Jamaican work, Ohio's East Africa Industrial Mission, and in 1918, New England's Ramallah schools were transferred to Five Years Meeting's care (*ibid.* Chs.III, XII) .

30. Rufus Jones' love and scholarship were largely limited to Christian mystics; he seldom wrote about Asian religions, and though he visited Gandhi in 1926, he may never have shared in Zen meditation until his visit to Japan in 1932. On the other hand, though he also printed news of home missions, for instance among Native Americans, he also does not seem to have visited Friends' Oklahoma Indian churches.

its reading list by Esther Tuttle Pritchard and Jones' defense of scholarship "done in profound loyalty to Christ" were printed in *The American Friend*.[31] Some evangelicals targeted Thomas Newlin at Pacific College, and Earlham College, whose Bible professor, Elbert Russell, a Hoosier farm boy, was asked by President Mills to stay on after his graduating from Earlham, to replace Dougan Clark, who had been baptized. Russell was given time out to study Hebrew at Moody Bible Institute in Chicago, and after two more years at the University of Chicago returned in 1903 teaching the historical settings of the Bible writers.[32] Allen Jay, staunchly evangelical, had rebuilt North Carolina Yearly Meeting after the Civil War and had been Superintendent of Earlham from 1881 to 1887. In 1907 he wrote to Rufus Jones:[33]

> I lived four years with William P. Pinkham at Earlham College. He is made of the material that Martyrs are made of. He is working for almost nothing, and will continue to do so; for he verily believes he is doing God's service. Edward Mott is built on the same style... . And on top of all this is the desire of Ohio Yearly Meeting and all of its sympathizers from Ohio to California, to see Earlham College chastised and Indiana Yearly Meeting, which has stood in their way, humiliated and driven to the wall so they can carry out their revolutionary schemes... . President Kelly, who knows Mott well, ...says it is a deep and well laid plan... . I don't believe the strongest and best man in the Quaker Church today can sit in the office in Philadelphia and edit a paper that is going to win this fight with E[vangelical] F[riends]...It is not well written articles on Christian Philosophy that we need. They are attending Quarterly Meetings, Conferences, and public occasions of all kinds, writing private letters and reaching Friends in every way. I note thy proposition to talk over matters when thee comes to Earlham. I fear it will be too late to do much good.

To James Wood, a fellow veteran of the Richmond Conference, Allen Jay wrote a cover letter:

> I fear you in the East do not realize the battle that is on in these Yearly Meetings. Too long we have folded our hands and said it will blow over... . With a zeal born of fanaticism they are resolved to run *The American Friend* out of existence, and drive the Board of Trustees to turn Elbert Russell and some others out of the Earlham Faculty.

---

31. "Friends have not encouraged real thought on these high themes among the rank and file of the membership... . Deeper thought and more first-hand knowledge of these matters will deepen our grasp of truth, promote our spiritual life, and increase our power" (3/14/1901).

32. Hugh Barbour and J.William Frost, *The Quakers* (Richmond, IN: Friends United Press,1994) p.363.

33. Jay to Jones 1/16/1907; to Wood 1/4/07, both in Box 10 of Rufus Jones' papers, Haverford. The best discussion of this crisis is Thomas Hamm, *The Transformation of American Quakerism* (Bloomington, IN: Indiana University Press, 1988) Ch.VII.

In the end, Newlin was driven from Pacific College, but Russell, though under repeated attack, stayed at Earlham until he resigned in 1915 over a clash with President Kelly.[34] In a vain effort at conciliation, Rufus Jones turned over the editorship of *The American Friend* to Herman Newman, and in 1912 to S. Edgar Nicholson, at which time it was put under charge of the Five Years Meeting and published at its new office building in Richmond. The Five Years Meeting of 1902 had also abolished Quaker "birthright" membership, which was felt to undercut the need for individual conversion or commitment,[35] and in 1912 voted to join the Federal (now the National) Council of Churches.

The charges of "unsoundness" and "modernism" against Rufus Jones and the colleges had deeper roots than rivalry for power and leadership, or even rejection of evolution and "higher criticism" of the Bible. Denial of the Virgin Birth (a charge leveled against even the famous non-Quakers Briggs and Fosdick in New York), and of the immediate Second Coming of Christ, a more vital issue for many Friends, do not appear as central charges against Jones. He never minimized evil in individual hearts or society, trusting in God's power to overcome it; but Jones had no doctrine of Original Sin.[36] His vital doctrine of Christ's Atonement was based on God's love, not God's justice. Though he had accepted Christ at a revival as a teenager, his highest religious experiences came unexpectedly, by no decision of his own, from God's grace and loving presence. For Jones, anyone who had known the presence and power of God working within, provided he or she tried constantly to be a disciple of Christ, could be accepted as a Quaker, or at least as a "wider Quaker"[37] or a mystic. The central clash between Jones and his accusers was over Holiness. All agreed it was a central Quaker doctrine, but for Jones sanctification was a lifelong process of self-examination and self-opening to God.[38]

The greatest evangelical Friends, such as Everett Cattell and Arthur Roberts have always understood growth in grace, the disciplines of inner cleansing, and learning how to be guided by the Spirit.[39] Yet many of the

34. Opal Thornburg, *Earlham, the Story of the College,1847-1962* (Richmond,1962) pp.262-3.

35. Ohio and California Yearly Meetings later wished to go back to listing Associate Members. The membership statistics for these years depended on such factors, but may have in any case made evangelical Friends feel vulnerable by comparison to expanding churches. In the figures for 1899 and 1900 (after which Jones did not print them in *Am.Fd.*) the gains in west-coast Yearly Meetings did not equal the losses in Western, Iowa and Kansas.

36. Wilmer A. Cooper, "Rufus M. Jones and the Contemporary Quaker View of Man," Ph.D. thesis, Vanderbilt University, 1956). Like Fox (for whom the main issue was predestination) Jones rejected Calvinism, accusing even Robert Barclay of being misled by it.

37. The "Wider Quaker Fellowship" was begun after World War I for the sake of Christian pacifists and loyal members of other churches, notably in Europe.

38. See Jones' editorial "Ye are Called to an Holy Life" in *Am. Fd.*, 10/18/1894.

leaders in Ohio, Iowa, Oregon, Kansas, and California Yearly Meetings had shared in interchurch revivals and camp meetings, and had gone through a sudden moment of total sanctification, a "baptism of the Holy Spirit," a "second blessing" months or years after their conversion (their accepting their need for the Atonement). They felt infused by power for love and purity, and felt anyone who had not experienced instant total Holiness should not claim to have the Light or the Spirit within him. Luke Woodard and evangelical Friends had made this a precondition of recognition for ministers, elders, and missionaries in New York Yearly Meeting as early as 1875. Kansas and Oregon leaders wished all Friends to be as strict. Because of this experience they felt closer to "Holiness churches" such as the Nazarenes and Wesleyan Methodists than they did to Quakers who had not experienced immediate Holiness. Jones showed that Fox had understood lifelong growth in sanctification as he did, but for Dougan Clark "the kind of holiness somebody had two hundred years ago" was irrelevant.[40] Evangelical Friends, however, were stopped short by the Ohio Friend Levi Lupton, who like the Pentecostalists could claim that the ultimate and decisive mark of the Spirit was "speaking in tongues."[41]

The evangelical Friends therefore fell back on two doctrinal statements that all Yearly Meetings within Five Years Meeting had accepted, Braithwaite's long 1887 "Declaration of Faith" and the letter sent by Fox and his mission party in 1671 to prove their orthodoxy to the Governor of Barbados.[42] The Uniform Discipline, though printed with these two documents, placed more centrally a short declaration written mainly by Rufus Jones. Various Friends and yearly meetings had asked that the status of the older statements be established. A committee named by the Five Years Meeting of 1907 reported back in 1912 that "these documents are historic statements of belief, approved by the Five Years Meeting in 1902, ...and approved again at this time, 1912, but they are not to be regarded as constituting a creed." A motion to strike out the last phrase failed by a 65 to 69 vote,[43] but the conflict continued. In 1922, in face of epistles from Oregon and Kansas Yearly Meetings, Jones as chairman of the Business Committee felt he had won harmony when he agreed that "the clause has been widely misunderstood in at least two directions [and] should now be eliminated."[44] Kansas and Ore-

39. Everett Lewis Cattell, *The Spirit of Holiness*, (Kansas City: Beacon Hill Press, 1977), esp. Chs.1, 2 & 4. Arthur O. Roberts, *Through Flaming Sword*, (Portland, OR: Barclay Press, 1959, pp.63-72, *Move Over, Elijah* (Newberg, OR: Barclay Press, 1967) Ch.6, and many poems in the "Love" and "Listen" sections of *Listen to the Lord* (same,1974).

40. Clark,"The Society of Friends and Holiness" in *The Christian Worker* 1/14/1886. When "Holiness evangelicals" speak of ecumenical ties, they mean fellowship with Holiness Christians, whereas RMJ meant by it the traditional Christian churches.

41. Thomas Hamm, *Transformation*, pp. 169-70.

42. It also was intended to prove that the Quakers would not stir up slaves to rebellion.

43. *Minutes of the Five Years Meeting 1912 Indianapolis, Indiana* p.50.

gon Friends, however, were not so easily satisfied. The faith statements were not used to exclude publications or missionaries they regarded as unsound. Moreover the effort to create a Friends Forward Movement with a large United Budget to support Quaker missions and colleges, as other denominations were then doing, failed badly. It had aimed at a centralization that seemed to threaten the projects and power of local evangelical leaders. Oregon Yearly Meeting in 1926 and Kansas in 1937 voted to leave Five Years Meeting.[45]

Rufus Jones' heartbreaks over the disunity of Christ-centered Friends were, happily for him, balanced by other bonds and programs which developed for him in the same years. He made during his life seventeen trips to England,[46] where at this time all Friends worshipped out of unprogrammed silence, but were basically Christ-centered and had had no Hicksite-Orthodox Separation.[47] British Friends were fully part of the processes of intervisiting that led to the Richmond Conference and the Five Years Meeting, but some, such as William Jones and Rufus' friend Henry Stanley Newman made a point of visiting Hicksite as well as Orthodox Meetings.[48] Jones did not have to create "the transatlantic Quaker community,"[49] and unlike his Cadbury in-laws had no English cousins in his Maine family, but he read the same books on science, psychology, and philosophy as those his age in Britain, Germany, and France, mostly written by authors as devotedly Christian as he. He learned biology from Thomas Battey, "spiritual guide and illuminative preacher," a science student under Agassiz, and Gray, Rufus' predecessor at Oakwood and his teacher at Providence:

He courageously and fearlessly faced the facts of science as they broke upon the world in the nineteenth century, and he not only kept his own

44. *Minutes of the Five Years Meeting of the Friends in America held in Richmond 1922...* p.119. "Thomas K. Brown of Philadelphia was gratified to see Friends concerned as to how much they might yield in the interests of harmony rather than determined to make no concessions. ...The feeling of the meeting was well expressed in the singing of 'Blest Be The Tie that Binds' and the Doxology" (p.120).

45. Ohio Yearly Meeting (now Evangelical Friends Church—Eastern Region) and the evangelical majority within Nebraska Yearly Meeting, which became Rocky Mountain, later joined the Evangelical Friends Alliance, too. Central Yearly Meeting, a splinter from Indiana in 1922, chose total isolation but has a mission in Bolivia. See David Holden, *Friends Divided* (Richmond, IN: Friends United Press, 1988) Ch.17.

46. Data from Mary Hoxie Jones, 1995.

47. They had lately become more aware than most American "Orthodox" of their common bonds with Hicksite Yearly Meetings: see Edwin C.Bronner,*"The Other Branch:" London Yearly Meeting and the Hicksites, 1827-1912,* (London: Friends Hist.Soc. 1975), especially on British reactions to Joel Bean's treatment.

48. Edwin Bronner is the master historian of this material. Some British Friends were not as highly honored at home as in America (e.g. Stanley Pumphrey and Walter Robson).

49. See Frederick B.Tolles, *Quakers and the Atlantic Culture* (New York, 1960) and *James Logan and the Culture of Provincial America* (New York, 1953).

faith, but he led his students on into a deeper faith than they had before they came to school.[50]

Jones found in the younger British Friends the same openness to the wider world of prayer and learning. Though British Friends had been led by doctrinal conservatives like Joseph Bevan Braithwaite and had disowned David Duncan and his liberal manchester circle about 1858,[51] new Quaker books and ideas had led the young English Friends to meet at Manchester in 1895, between Jones' first two trips to England. They kept the same high truth standards he demanded of himself, for instance in Rufus' accuracy about the history of Christian mysticism;[52] in his first days at *The Friends Review* Jones printed his own essay on mystics (10/12/1893) and Joseph Bevan Braithwaite's on Quaker history (10/29/93). Though he soon found it better to present his historical discoveries in scholarly books and lectures at seminaries,[53] Rufus had published similar pieces by James Wood[54] and Augustine Jones.[55]

Rufus Jones' friendships with young English Quakers such as John Wilhelm Rowntree and William, son of Joseph Bevan Braithwaite, were a delight of his life.[56] In an important step for the unity of Quakerism, he worked with these men on a program to revive the Society of Friends by uniting it with its own past through a series of histories, later nicknamed

---

50. RMJ: "Thomas J. Battey," eulogy in *Am. Fd,.* 8/13/1931, reprinted in *Moses Brown Alumni Bulletin*, April, 1932.

51. See Bronner, *Other Branch*, pp. 30ff.

52. His M.A. thesis Harvard under J.H. Thayer in 1900 was on the "life in Christ" mysticism of St. Paul and St. John. I am among the scholars who have challenged RMJ's assertions about the direct links he thought he had found between European mystics and the earliest Quakers, because of the complexity of Fox's "thought-world" of "spiritual puritanism," but his factual knowledge of the history of European Christian mysticism is impressive.

53. Apart from single lectures and annual sermons, for instance at Harvard, he gave series of "big-name" lectures at Yale, Columbia, Vanderbilt, Southern California and Southern Methodist Universities and Oberlin and Rochester Seminaries; most were then published.

54. From James Wood, besides the speech at the World Parliament of Religions, an essay on "The Pastoral Question," and the report on Irish Home Rule in *The Friends Review*, Rufus put in *Am.Fd.* Wood's report from London Yearly Meeting on "Correspondence between the Yearly Meetings" (8/2/1894), which included their mutual reception of certificates of membership and ministers' credentials. Wood agreed that "it is best for those who agree in doctrine to be associated in church fellowship" and was uneasy that London Yearly Meeting proposed to correspond with all bodies calling themselves Friends, but "the first concern for this body is sincere obedience to the will of Christ." *Am.Fd.* on 8/20/1894 included Wood's essay "What Makes a Friend," and on 3/28/1901 Jones ran Wood's essay on "Biblical Research" which said that "conclusions should not be accepted unless they are confirmed by the consensus of Christian Scholarship [which] can alone understand and properly weigh the evidence. ...The writer frankly admits his inability to weigh the evidence in these matters."

On 8/15/1901 *Am. Fd.* printed a short answer by Wood, as chairman of the Committee on Uniform Discipline "in the absence of the Editor" justifying "the Article of Belief in the Uniform Discipline."

"the Rowntree Series," of which William Braithwaite's are unequaled for readability and accuracy.

This group also began in 1897 a series of summer schools or conferences, four years before a similar program was begun at Haverford, drawing young Friends together for study, worship, Bible study, and discussion. This series drew working-class as well as university Quakers and non-Friends: British Quakers undertook a major program of adult education. By 1902 the summer schools had also led to the founding of a year-round Quaker study center at Woodbrooke, the mansion donated by George Cadbury the chocolate maker, affiliated to the University of Birmingham. Its board offered the headship to Rufus, but he, despite a summer visit with his new bride Elizabeth Cadbury Jones, deferred decision until after the Five Years Meeting session of 1902, when he decided American Quaker needs were more crucial.[57] Only in 1930 were American Friends able to start a similar school, Pendle Hill, near Swarthmore, named, like Rufus' Maine summer home, for the site of George Fox's vision of "a great people to be gathered." Jones was invited by the disappointed British to lecture in England most summers, and gave the first (and was the only person invited for a second) of the Swarthmore Lectures at London Yearly Meeting. Rufus Jones' greatest influence on Quaker unity was thus less through institutions such as the Five Years Meeting, than through the widely dynamic influence of his vision of Friends as a movement based on direct inward experience of God. Yet the unity of all Friends was seen more easily by British than by American Quakers.

Two of the most important programs that unified twentieth century Friends were bound to involve Rufus Jones, although his role in starting them is still being studied.[58] In response to World War I, and the pressures that were drawing America into it, a Friends National Peace Committee including all Quaker branches wrote a "Message from the Society of Friends" on their shared peace testimony. Four American Friends joined the British Friends Ambulance Unit, and seven the War Victims Relief Committee. As soon as America declared war, on April 6, 1917, Rufus Jones and younger Friends began a training unit for similar workers at Haverford, drawing funds and volunteers from Friends General Conference, Philadelphia Yearly Meeting (Orthdox) and Five Years Meeting. The coordinators

---

55. Augustine Jones wrote for *The Friends Review* on 1/2/1894 about Jacob's Well and spiritual worship, on (2/1/)1894 on "The Great Inspired Confession" of Peter at Caesarea Philippi, where he had largely visited, and a historical essay on "Nicholas Upsall" for *Am.Fd.* 3/14/1901; for local printing on "George Fox in New England."

56. This aspect of his life has been beautifully covered in Vining's biography. See also Edwin Bronner, *op. cit.* p.41 etc.

57. See Vining's biography of RMJ and Stephen Allott's of John Wilhelm Rowntree.

58. Jerry William Frost's article "'Our Deeds Carry our Message': The Early History of the American Friends Service Committee" in *Quaker History* (Vol.81#1, Spring 1992) may be the nucleus of a future book.

of this work asked Rufus Jones to chair what then became the American Friends Service Committee.

The wartime program in France, and the reconstruction and feeding programs in France, Germany, Poland, and Russia after the war are a well and often told story, important in this paper mainly because Orthodox and Hicksite Friends worked side by side, and learned to trust each other. However, Rufus Jones was kept busy in trips to Washington and France. In the years after World War I, he was seen more rarely than earlier in Richmond or the midwest except for Five Years Meeting sessions (which he never missed) or university lectures.[59] He remained a patriarchal figure in his own Yearly Meeting of Friends for New England, whose sessions he attended every year from 1940.[60] Rufus Jones encouraged plans for the reunion in 1945 of all five groups of Meetings in New England: the "Wilburite" and "Gurneyite" Yearly Meetings of Friends and the college-city Meetings in Providence, Cambridge and the Connecticut Valley. He visited them all, but was not on structural planning committees.[61] He was asked to give the congratulatory speech for the "wedding celebration" in 1945.[62] He did much less to help the reunion of the Philadelphia and New York Hicksite and Orthodox Yearly Meetings, entrenched behind generations of mutual distrust. In each case Young Friends and some local Meetings united first. (In New York Yearly Meeting local Meetings in Farmington and "All Friends" (New Jersey) Quarters led the way).[63]

The second new program, growing out of the war work, was the first Friends World Conference in London in 1920, to which all Quakers from

---

59. RMJ, *A Service of Love in War Time* (New York, 1920); and see Frost, *loc.cit.*; Vining, *op.cit.*, Chs. XV & XVI.

60. In 1940 he "brought the thought of the [Yearly] Meeting back to church extension" (1940 *Minutes*, p.27) but asked to be released from the World Consultation Committee; in 1942 he "spoke of his interest in the new Monthly Meetings under the American Friends Fellowship Council;" in 1942 he urged them to collect and catalog the papers of Moses Brown; in 1943 Passmore Elkinton reported that the American Friends Fellowship Council "originated from a concern of Rufus Jones as he returned from a trip around the world" (1943 *Minutes* p.13).

61. It is hard to find evidence of Rufus Jones' role in the Committees or discussions within the ("Gurneyite") Yearly Meeting of Friends for New England. He does not seem to have formally attended the "Wilburite" Conservative New England Yearly Meeting in Westerly until he was welcomed there in 1944 (1944 *Minutes*, p.8). Rufus Jones and Henry Perry then reported on the AFSC's decision to continue administering Civilian Public Service Camps despite disagreement about compromises thereby forced on conscientious objectors by the government. By 1944, the Wilburites' clerk, Henry Perry, and his Yearly Meeting "Committee on Relations with Other Meetings" who had already reported in 1933 that "the time has come for the unity of all the established groups of Friends in New England," had been meeting with the Connecticut Valley Association Friends for two years, and the plans were complete for the legal changes that would be needed in all five groups. The college-city Meetings later persuaded the Yearly Meeting to join also Friends General Conference. RMJ had hoped such double memberships would unify Friends. Data recommended to me by Elizabeth Cazden.

all countries were invited. Again, the young Friends pioneered, also meeting internationally in 1920, and in 1929 nationally in connection with a conference Passmore Elkinton called of all American Friends. In 1937, the America Friends Fellowship Council, growing out of the AFSC committee Elkinton chaired, called a second world conference, at Swarthmore College, asking Rufus Jones to preside. From this and its European parallel grew the Friends World Committee for Consultation.[64] By funding intervisitation, recognizing and linking Yearly Meetings, and setting up conferences it has helped Friends from many continents and cultures become friends and understand each others often varied and divergent forms of worship and of loyalty to God, Jesus, and the Bible. Even less than Rufus Jones has it tried to delimit the forms of religious experience or doctrine that should be called Quaker. That kind of spiritual discernment, as Rufus Jones and Arthur Roberts witness, can come where experience of God's love and of the depths of evil and suffering meet in the Cross of Christ.

---

62. 1945 *Minutes* of the united New England Yearly Meeting, p. 45. See also Daisy Newman, *A Procession of Friends* (Garden City, 1972). He also brought from the Executive Committee of Five Years Meeting, an invitation for the newly united Yearly Meeting to join as a whole, which was immediately accepted, but caused a defection of some Rhode Island Friends who were unhappy to hear that "the Discipline of the Five Years Meeting is now undergoing substantial revision. It is understood that the Discipline as revised will be accepted by the united Yearly Meeting with reservation of the right to adapt it to the needs of the subordinate Meetings." (1944 *Minutes* of New England Yearly Meeting (Wilburite)).

63. Barbour, Densmore, Moger, Sorel, VanWagner, and Worrall *Quaker Crosscurrents:* (Syracuse Univ.Press, 1994), Ch.XV (largely by Alson Van Wagner).

64. Friends World Committee for Consultation (FWCC) was begun in Europe in 1937. The American Friends Fellowship Council was merged into FWCC's America section only in 1954 (each, for instance, asked independently for support by New England Yearly Meeting in 1945. Herbert Hadley's detailed history of FWCC, *Friends World Wide* (London, 1991) Ch.1, unlike Elkinton, assigns no major role to Rufus Jones in either organization, though he was chairman of AFSC from 1935 to 1944 and presiding clerk of the Five Years Meeting session in 1935.

Quaker Interpretation

The Nature of Mysticism

And the Sources of Religious Insight in the Journal of George Fox

GAYLE BEEBE

As a definitive work of the Society of Friends, the *Journal of George Fox* has set the tone and tenor for the Society's understanding of one's experience of God or the ultimately Real.[1] Various interpretations of Fox have been offered, but a consistent theme in all interpretations has been Fox's emphasis on the necessity of an experimental or experiential understanding of one's encounter with God. A result of this consistent emphasis has been a trend Fox started himself: since one's experience of God is the touchstone of religious faith, the role or importance of religious texts, religious communities and religious doctrines must play a secondary role in one's apprehension of the ultimately Real. Because Fox emphasized the primacy of the Spirit, or the "light of Christ within," over any other religious authority the interpretive tendency has often treated his work as a call for radical individualism in religious experience. But this is simply not the case.[2]

George Fox did emphasize the responsibility each individual possesses to seek God. Fox did not, however, believe this search took place apart from others or apart from the necessary input of religious texts.[3] God calls us to

---

1. By ultimately Real I mean the highest being or state to which each religion's adherents are inclined to aspire. I am indebted to John Hick's definition as outlined in *An Interpretation of Religion*, for this designation.

2. In the epilogue to *The Rich Heritage of Quakerism*, Paul Anderson offers a helpful summary of changes in scholarly opinion since the 1950's which substantiate this thesis. See *The Rich Heritage of Quakerism* (Newberg, OR: Barclay Press, 1987), pp. 254 ff.

be in prayer, but also calls us to join together in worship and good works, as Fox's own life testifies. As the Society developed under the guidance of George Fox, a greater emphasis was laid on the role of corporate guidance over individual guidance, on the Spirit that never leads contrary to Scripture, and on replacing or modifying those doctrines which seem contrary to Scripture, not simply discarding or ignoring their valuable role in guiding one's religious quest.[4]

Combined with an emphasis on the individual aspect of his thought, other more recent interpretations have looked for parallels between Fox's understanding of religious experience and the understanding of religious experience found in the major religions of the world.[5] Most of these attempts, however, have tended to diminish the role played by both cultural currents in seventeenth-century England and historical developments in the Christian church in Fox's understanding of the religious life.[6]

It is true that Fox emphasized a return to "Primitive Christianity," which he identified as New Testament, first-century Christianity as found in the Bible. But this emphasis should not sidetrack us from the very clear contextual nature of his thought. That is to say, while Fox may not have returned to "Primitive Christianity" as he claimed, he nonetheless provided a unique contribution to a part of the Christian mystical tradition which began as early as the twelfth-century in Europe and England.

As a result, in approaching a sensitive treatment of Fox's *Journal* it will be necessary to demonstrate that Fox was part of a broader community of interpretation that had emerged in England. In demonstrating this connection, it will also be necessary to show how Fox's understanding of religious experience included the role of religious texts, the importance of religious doctrines and the specific structure of religious communities, all of which place his thought in a specific religious tradition. Although efforts to find the common ground of religious experience across religious traditions is necessary, in Fox's case it is quite artificial and forces one to find the lowest

---

3. One of several examples that could be cited is Fox's "Letter to the Governor of Barbados," as reprinted in *Faith and Practice*, Southwest Yearly Meeting, 1988.

4. Russell, Elbert. *A History of Quakerism*. Richmond, IN: Friends United Press, 1973 (reprint from 1945 edition); Barclay, Robert. *An Apology for the True Christian Divinity*. Richmond, IN: Friends United Press, 1978 (reprint). Both books give extensive coverage to this point.

5. Gracia-Fay, Ellwood. "The Proclamation of Paradise: George Fox as Mystic and Prophet," Summer, 1991. Gracia-Fay's paper is a helpful treatment of George Fox and for the most part I agree with her analysis. My main point of disagreement concerns the suggestion that Fox combines personal communion mysticism and ontological union mysticism in his thought. He does believe in union, but it is clearly the "unio mystica" union of the Christian tradition, and not the ontological union of transpersonal monism, as my paper will try to demonstrate.

6. Latourette, Kenneth Scott. *A History of Christianity*, Volume II. San Francisco: Harper and Row, Publishers, Inc., 1953, 1975, pp. 797-835.

common denominator in order to defend this position.[7] There are parallel ideas and even similar phrases, but Fox consistently worked within a Christian framework and envisioned the outcome of the religious life to be one which led not only to personal communion with God, but also to union with God through the witness and work of Jesus Christ.

Consequently, in order to do Fox's understanding justice we must see that he was not only a part of his English religious context, but also a part of the Augustinian-Franciscan synthesis provided by Bonaventure and mediated into England by the Cambridge Platonists and others. Clearly, distinctions such as "personal communion" and "ontological union" are useful in considering Fox's thought.[8] But these distinctions remain accurate only to the extent they are modified to reflect Fox's own personal understanding and application.

For example, to suggest Fox's understanding of ontological union and Shankara's understanding of ontological union are similar or even compatible grossly misrepresents the distinct differences between both lines of thought.[9] Fox never believed union with God meant merging into God or a universal spirit, nor did he believe it was something accomplished without Jesus Christ.

Therefore, in proceeding with this treatment, it will be necessary to contrast Fox's understanding of the nature of religious experience with the prevailing tendency to see religious experience as an individual and autonomous category unto itself. Coupled with this consideration will be the need to show that religious experiences, although similar in their pre-reflective states, are not similar when interpreted across religious traditions, but differ according to the conditioning of consciousness each religious tradition provides. Finally, it will be necessary to show the way in which the major currents moving in Fox's own personal context influenced his own unique synthesis which emerged.

Towards a Working Definition of Mystical Experience

Attempting to define mystical experience is as varied as it is complex. The word, "mysticism," is a derivative of the Greek term, "Muein," which

---

7. For example, in the first one-hundred pages of Fox's *Journal*, there are at least 148 direct references or allusions to the Christian Bible as well as Fox's personal admission that he came to an understanding of God's love through the mediation of Jesus Christ.

8. I am indebted to the definitions offered by John Hutchison for this point. Mysticism of "personal communion" is typified as leading to immediate communion with the religious object while the mysticism of ontological union is typified as absorption into this object. Hutchison, John A. *Paths of Faith*. New York: McGraw-Hill Book Company, 1969, pp. 510-512.

9. Shankara's *Crest-Jewel of Discrimination*. Translated with an Introduction by Swami Prabhacananda and Christopher Isherwood. Hollywood, CA: Vedanta Press, 1946.

means "to remain silent."[10] Originally, it pertained specifically to the Greek Mystery Religions and included the acquisition of special knowledge leading to mystical insight. As early as 1899, W.R. Inge, offered as many as 26 different definitions of mysticism in an appendix to his definitive work, but summarized his study by suggesting that, "true mysticism is the attempt to realize, in thought and feeling, the immanence of the temporal in the eternal, and of the eternal in the temporal."[11] Evelyn Underhill, writing twelve years later suggested that mysticism is "the expression of the innate tendency of the human spirit towards complete harmony with the transcendental order..."[12] Ernst Troeltsch, identified mysticism as the primacy of direct or immediate religious experience.[13] And Rufus Jones, making his own original contribution to the discussion, defined mysticism as, "...the type of religion which puts the emphasis on immediate awareness of relation with God, on direct and intimate consciousness of the Divine presence. It is religion in its most acute, intense, and living stage."[14] More recently, mysticism has come to mean the sense of immediacy that ensues when religious documents and religious experience emphasize such immediacy.[15]

Beginning with William James and his landmark work, *The Varieties of Religious Experience*, an effort to define and identify religious experience has dominated the agendas of philosopher and theologian alike. Within this treatise, James himself considers various types of religious experience, including legitimate and pathological forms, as well as an extensive treatment of mysticism which has set the tone for much of the discussion in the English-speaking world. Of central significance for our purpose is the attempt James makes to identify four common elements native to all mystical experiences: ineffability, noetic, transiency, and passivity.[16]

Ineffability is essential to mystical experience and expresses the inability of language and concept to articulate this state or experience adequately.[17] A noetic quality is also an essential ingredient in defining mystical experience and is defined by its ability to enlarge one's perspective, alter one's conscious

---

10. Louis Dupre, "Mysticism," p. 245, *Encyclopedia of Religion*, Vol. #10. Edited by Mircea Eliade. New York: Macmillan Pub. Co., 1987.

11. Inge, William Ralph. *Christian Mysticism*. London: Menthuen Pub. Co., 1899, p. 335.

12. Underhill, Evelyn. *Mysticism*. 1911.

13. Troeltsch, Ernst. *The Social Teaching of the Christian Churches*, Vol. I, II.

14. Jones, Rufus. *Studies in Mystical Religion*. New York: MacMillan and Co., Limited, 1923, p. XV.

15. Mysticism and Religious Traditions. Edited by Stephen Katz. New York: Oxford Univ. Press, 1983.

16. James, William. *The Varieties of Religious Experience*. New York: Mentor Books, 1958 edition, pp. 292-293.

17. James, pp. 292-293. As early as Schleiermacher's *On Religion* (1799), Schleiermacher is noting the difference between one's intuition of the infinite, and the inevitable necessity yet difficulty of placing this intuition within a specific religious tradition in order to understand it.

awareness or in some way shift a person's outlook from one point-of-view to another.[18] Transiency is a third element of mystical experience and James indicates that this is not essential, but often seems present when one describes a mystical experience—i.e. the state comes and goes; it does not linger.[19] Passivity indicates that the individual does not produce the mystical encounter, but through discipline one can prepare for it.[20]

The impact of James' work is impossible to overestimate. Although other prominent works either accompanied or followed him, no single work cast such a long shadow over the discussion in the twentieth-century. The most significant effect of his work is the impact it has had in defining the parameters of the discussion. The way people have understood, interpreted, and approached mysticism and religious experience have followed largely the categories James first established.

Of critical significance is the effect his focus on the individual nature of religious experience has had in diminishing the role and importance of religious communities and traditions. Although James captured a vital part of the mystical life in emphasizing the individual, he diminished the importance of the process of preparation which often precluded such individual experiences.

In virtually every major religious tradition an emphasis is placed on the importance of preparation to realize the desired goal or state of that specific religion. In each context, a variety of paths of preparation are offered in order to help the individual realize or encounter the ultimately Real. These are not done apart from a communal context, but are interpreted to the individual through the traditions and the history of one's community. Some may pursue this state by the path of knowledge through rational dialectic, others may pursue this state through moral deeds, while still others may pursue this state through ascetic practices. Even Amazon tribes advocate special modes of preparation, utilizing the mind altering capacities of certain drugs in order to reach their desired goal. This is all to say there is a

---

18. James, p. 293. John Hick discusses this sort of change or transformation as a change from self-centeredness to reality-centeredness. *An Interpretation of Religion*. New Haven , CN: Yale University Press, 1989.

19. James, 293.

20. James, p. 293. Bertrand Russell, in *Mysticism and Logic and Other Essays*, notes four areas he considers typical of mystical experience. First, is insights based on intuition over reason, sense and analysis. Reality, therefore, lies behind the world of appearance. Second, all reality is unified. Third, the temporal dimension of reality is denied. And fourth, all evil is mere appearance. Besides failing to offer cogent examples that substantiate his thesis, Russell also ignores the possibility of an experience interpreted mystically which re-orders one's life. Consequently, although a valuable essay for its discussion of the motive behind mysticism and science, it is not satisfactory in providing explanatory power for a wide array of experiences and phenomena.

strong emphasis in all religious traditions that preparation can be a useful tool in one's apprehension or experience of the ultimately Real.[21]

In Christianity, choosing the Christian mystical path will in some way include the person or being of Jesus Christ. In Advaita Vedanta, one's complete absorption into Brahman will result from the corporate preparation of text and religious community. In Zen Buddhism as depicted by Shibayana's *A Flower Does Not Talk*, or by Suzuki in *The Manual of Zen Buddhism*, the goal of emptiness is informed by the religious texts as well as by the values re-enforced by the structure of the monastic community. In the case of the Apostle Paul, even his mystical encounter with God on the road to Damascus (Acts 9) is clearly set within the communal and historical perimeters of his Jewish heritage.[22]

This cursory glance at various traditions is meant to suggest that the dominant element in mysticism is not the uniqueness of individual experience spread across various religious traditions, but the uniqueness of mystical experience within each religious tradition. Mystical experience, although possessing unique qualities and effects, is not a separate, autonomous category of human experience, but in each religion contains a specific understanding and structure concerning how one experiences a state of ultimate Reality as defined by that religion.

In a helpful article on the role each religious context plays on its own understanding of mystical experience, Robert Gimello writes,

> Mysticism is inextricably bound up with, dependent upon and usually subservient to the deeper beliefs and values of the traditions, cultures, and historical milieux (sic) which harbour it. As it is intricately related to those beliefs and values, so must it vary according to them.[23]

Elsewhere, Gimello argues that it is not only impossible, but also quite artificial to try to reduce the variety of mystical experiences to a vital common core.[24] By contrast, all religious traditions illustrate that mystical experiences within their tradition have specific structures formed by con-

---

21. Within the Christian tradition this is a pivotal part in all mystical literature. For George Fox, his nearly five-year quest, culminating in the experience of Christ addressing him directly, was a direct result of his arduous preparation. Elsewhere, in Pascal's *Pensees*, Pascal offers advice to the reader who is having trouble believing in God by suggesting that they should change their habits so that they can develop a dispositional state that will lead them to God. Middlesex, England: Penguin Books, (Krailsheimer edition, 1965, fragment 149).

22. Segal, Alan F. *Paul the Convert: The Apostolate and Apostasy of Saul the Pharisee*. New Haven: Yale Univ. Press, 1990. Segal makes a provocative case that Paul's conversion is closely contained within his Jewish community.

23. Robert M. Gimello, "Mysticism in Its Contexts," p. 63, *Mysticism and Religious Traditions*, Edited by Steven T. Katz. New York: Oxford University Press, 1983.

24. Ibid., p. 62.

cepts, beliefs, values and expectations built into the very fabric of a specific religious tradition.[25]

Combined with the specific understanding of mysticism as mediated by various religious traditions is the belief that no religious experience gains cognitive meaning without some form of mediation. This is a difficult part of the argument since many attempts to explain religious experience have sought to do so by reducing religious experience to a naturalistic explanation.[26] Without digressing too far, however, it is important to note that as early as Schleiermacher, pre-reflective experience which acquires cognitive meaning was being argued. Despite various criticisms of this line of argument,[27] there are plenty of sources to support the notion that we have experiences which go beyond our capacity to understand them. These experiences become intelligible when set within a religious context which can interpret them.

Earlier, it was noted that James had included "immediacy" as one of the four elements distinguishing mysticism.[28] This emphasis, however, captures only the initial experience and not the whole event. The whole event would include why humans have this experience, why humans refer this experience to a higher power, what experiences and habits predispose one to such an experience, and what makes one feel the need for such experiences. It is in the pre-immediate anticipation of and post-immediate reflection upon mystical experience that so many other dimensions of knowledge and understanding come into play.

Hans Penner amplifies this point when he writes,

> If mystical experiences have any significance it will be necessary to locate these experiences within the set of relations which mediate them.[29]

This is not to say that one does not have an experience they interpret as "immediate." Such an interpretation of "immediacy," however, typically comes through categories and dispositions either already existent in the person or as mediated out of the social context of which the person is a part. This is not to deny various forms of epistemology, most notably Hegelian epistemology, which suggest that through the tension and interaction of a variety of inner and outer forces new understanding comes to the human.[30] Actually, this position is built on such an epistemology. A person

25. Ibid., pp. 60-65.

26. Ludwig Feuerbach's *Essence of Christianity* is perhaps the finest attempt since it incorporates a systematic effort to reduce all aspects of religion (experience, dogma, text formation, community of faith, et. al.) to a naturalistic explanation.

27. Wayne Proudfoot's *Religious Experience*, Berkeley, CA: The University of California Press, 1985, is one notable example.

28. James, *Varieties*, pp. 292-293.

29. Hans Penner, "The Mystical Illusion," p. 98, *Katz*, loc. cit.

must have an experience which needs further understanding. Such a need results in consultation with past knowledge and drives the human to discover new knowledge in order to understand a dimension of reality introduced through religious experience.

To illustrate further, consider two examples from Western religious traditions, one from the Hebrew Scriptures, the other from the Christian Scriptures. In I Samuel 3, Eli and Samuel are in the private quarters of the Temple, almost asleep, when Samuel hears a voice he interprets as Eli's. Three times he hears the voice believing each time that it is Eli's. From the text it is apparent that Samuel has not yet acquired the categories to hear this voice as originating in God. Subsequent to the third encounter, however, Eli realizes that the voice is coming from God, although there is no indication that he has ever heard the voice himself.[31] Nevertheless, he gives Samuel specific instructions regarding how he should respond. Eventually, Samuel hears the voice again and because of Eli's tutoring is able to enlarge his perception and come to a more complete understanding of God.

What is unique in this story is not the manner in which Samuel's experience is alike or different from other mystical experiences, but the way in which Samuel's perception of God is changed. This understanding of religious experience was part of the communal context within which Samuel had his own religious experience. Consequently, Samuel's understanding of this experience, even though the experience was temporal and passive, but not ineffable, became noetic only after Eli's assistance in helping Samuel become aware of God.

A second illustration, taken from the life of the Apostle Paul, augments this point. In Acts 9, Paul has a mystical encounter with God which fundamentally re-orders his life and his understanding of the Absolute or ultimately Real.[32] Traveling to Damascus to further his campaign against the first Christians, Paul is blinded by a light and hears a voice telling him to change his ways and come to a new understanding of God.

This experience does fit all four categories of James' definition, but the important element beyond these categories is that this experience fits entirely within the religious context of which Paul was a part.[33] This experi-

---

30. Hegel, G. W. F. *Phenomenology of Spirit*. Oxford University Press, 1977 edition.

31. Since this incident is largely descriptive it is sometimes neglected as a legitimate source of religious insight. In an unpublished paper. "The Epistemology of Religious Experience," I have argued for the epistemic value of such an experience similar to the epistemic criteria found in Pascal's *Pensees*. It is more than merely a will-to-believe, as is often thought, but includes the role of human need in the development of legitimate epistemic criteria.

32. Revised Standard Version of the Bible, 1946, 1952, 1971, 1973, Acts 9.

33. See Alan Segal, in chapters one and two of *Paul the Convert*, argues this point convincingly. Also, John Hutchison, *Paths of Faith*, New York: McGraw Hill Book Company, 1969, amplifies this point when he defines an Old Testament prophet as one who hears the word of God and does it.

ence did not lead Paul off in an entirely unknown direction, but altered his understanding of the timetable of God and the value of non-Jews in God's ultimate purposes.[34]

Both examples are cited in order to suggest that within specific religious traditions, mystical experiences are understood and interpreted along lines compatible with that religious tradition. Both examples emphasize the perceptual shift that must occur in order to see reality accurately as defined by their religious tradition. In neither case could the established conceptual apparatus handle the new experience, but through a perceptual shift new conceptions were created which could bring illumination and understanding to these new experiences.

The efforts in recent years to find a common core to mystical experience is part of a larger project to account for the varieties of religious traditions found throughout the world. Although the explanatory hypothesis offered by John Hick[35] and others has been useful, it has often sublimated certain unique claims made by specific religions in order to achieve its purpose.[36] In the process, the unique features of a specific religion and the unique experiences of the Absolute or the ultimately Real chronicled and encouraged by each religion have been sacrificed in order to find points of contact compatible across religious lines.

Echoing this point, Steven Katz observes,

> The Christian experience of unio mystica (mystical union) fulfilled in Christ is not the Buddhist experience of nirvana. The Buddhist is 'nirvanized' i.e. becomes a new ontic reality in which there is no place for either individual souls or a transcendent Divine Being...Karma not grace governs the movement of the historic-transcendental situation and necessity rather than a benevolent will provides the causal power.[37]

Robert Corrington amplifies this point when he makes an excellent case for the epistemological role played by one's relation to their community. It is within one's communities that signs and symbols are appropriated, reviewed and either rejected or embraced which facilitate an individual's acquisition of knowledge. Subsequently, signs and symbols play an indispensable role in one's understanding and interpretation of their lived experience. In moving cross-culturally, one comes to realize that signs and symbols must be modified if even rudimentary understanding will occur.

34. To an extent, Early Christianity was a form of Mystical Judaism, but became a distinct religion of its own as it moved beyond its Judaic borders.

35. Hick, op. cit.

36. *Toward a Universal Theology of Religion*, edited by Leonard Swidler and *No Other Name?* by Paul Knitter are two of several other sources which substantiate this observation.

37. Steven Katz, "The 'Conservative' Character of Mystical Experience," pp. 40-41, *Katz*, op. cit.

Nevertheless, the cross-cultural context becomes a new embodiment of community within which new signs and symbols can emerge.[38]

This is not to deny the reality of the individual dimension in religious experience. It is simply an attempt to show that there is more to religious experience than an individual's experience of it. The community of context does make an impact and must be factored in if one's understanding of religious experience is to be comprehensive and accurate. In the next section, a demonstration of the context within which George Fox had his religious experience will be attempted.

Sources of Religious Insight in the Religious Context of Seventeenth-Century England

Around 529 C.E., the Academy in Athens closed its doors and the first Benedictine monastery opened its doors signifying a shift in emphasis that would dominate the Christian world.[39] This shift would come to have a marked influence not only on the religious life of England, but also on the understanding and experiences of George Fox. Several individuals played a role in this transition including Bernard of Clairvaux, Bonaventure, Meister Eckhart and Francis of Assisi.[40]

Francis' impact was particularly significant as it shifted the emphasis of Christian mysticism away from its neo-platonic influences and back towards the Biblical tradition of the Hebrew prophets.[41]

Eventually, George Fox incorporated much of this mystical tradition into his own thought. Of particular significance, was the Franciscan emphasis on an itinerant ministry, a willingness to suffer at the hands of the authorities, an understanding of the true church as those whose life exemplifies the life of Christ, and a recognition that union with God was possible only through the mediating role of Jesus Christ.[42] All of these themes were central to Fox's ministry, but all were not at odds with the dominant religious culture of seventeenth-century England as is commonly thought. Clearly, the Church of England and its understanding of the nature of the religious life held sway. But the dominant religious culture did not prevent the incursion of several other themes into its religious and cultural life. Paramount among these incursions was an understanding of the religious life

---

38. Corrington, Robert S. *The Community of Interpreters.* Macon, GA: Mercer University Press, 1987.

39. "Benedict," in *The Encyclopedia of Religion.* Vol. II. Edited by Mircea Eliade.

40. Hutchison, op. cit., p. 511.

41. Of particular impact was Francis' desire to cultivate a devotion to the earthly, human example of Jesus Christ. Francis did not reject Augustine's understanding of the inner Christ as teacher, but instead, amplified this teaching in order to include the outer witness of Jesus' life as recorded in the Gospels.

42. H.P. Owen, loc. cit.

which emphasized unity with God through Jesus Christ. Although ostracized for this position, Fox's declaration of this thought was new neither in Christianity nor in England itself.

As early as Origen the understanding of 'unio mystica' included a focus on the soul as the bride of Christ.[43] Augustine modified Origen and found in Christ the Logos as the interior teacher of wisdom.[44] This interior guide was the foundation of knowledge and supplied the mind with what it needed to know and understand. "Jesus alone," began Augustine, "teaches me anything who sets before my eyes, or one of my other bodily senses, or my mind, the things which I desire to know."[45]

Eventually, George Fox would modify Augustine to emphasize the "light of Christ Within" which leads into all truth. But this inner light always followed the Biblical Jesus. Understanding was governed by this inner light, but the reality of applying this inner understanding in outward form was governed by the Biblical Jesus.[46]

This emphasis by Fox was not new to him, but included a stream of thought beginning as early as the twelfth-century. Bernard McGinn provides a helpful discussion of this development when he identifies four primary issues which developed between the twelfth- and the sixteenth-century which became characteristic of Christian mysticism.[47] McGinn notes that the new understanding of union with God which began to emerge in the twelfth-century was based on a new understanding of the role of love and knowledge in the mystical life. Of particular significance was the emphasis on love and knowledge as not only critical to realizing this union, but also as an integral part of the experience itself.

McGinn continues by noting the way in which these unique developments led to a specific understanding of union within Christian mysticism. Specifically, the Christian understanding of union was not an ontological union of essence or substance, but an effective, functional union of willing and loving.[48]

Bonaventure, as an heir of this development, systematized Francis' insight in such works as *The Soul's Journey Into God* and *The Tree of Life*. The

---

43. Louis Dupre, "Mysticism," p. 252. *Encyclopedia of Religion*. Edited by Mircea Eliade. op. cit.

44. Bernard McGinn, "Love, Knowledge and Unio Mystica in the Western Christian Tradition," pp. 59-87. *Mystical Union and Monotheism: An Ecumenical Dialogue*. Edited by Moshe Idel and Bernard McGinn. New York: MacMillan Publishing Company, 1989.

45. Augustine, "The Teacher," p. 31. *Philosophy in the Middle Ages*. Translated texts edited by Hyman and Walsh. Indianapolis: Hackett Publishing Company, 1973.

46. *Journal of George Fox*, Edited by John L. Nickalls. Philadelphia: Religious Society of Friends, 1985, pp. 33-35.

47. Idel and McGinn, op. cit., p. 61.

48. Idel and McGinn, op. cit., p. 63.

Tree of Life, for example, was a series of meditations from the life of Christ and reflected a Franciscan-type devotion to the historical Jesus.

Clearly, there are other sources of influence, but this Augustinian-Fran-ciscan-Bonaventure influence entered the English context through such works as *The Cloud of Unknowing* and the Cambridge Platonists.[49]

Other sources, such as Jacob Boehme's, *The Way to Christ*, would enter through the Cambridge Platonists, but the intellectual and spiritual heritage would be marked by a clear understanding of two mystical traditions: the personal communion tradition of the Hebrew prophets and the union with God through Jesus Christ of St. Francis. This latter form of union was not synonymous with ontological union since the Christian context always retained a sense of separation between the Creator and the creature. This distinction was retained by Fox, as well, and represented a unique under-standing of union mediated by Jesus Christ.[50]

H. P. Owen extends this point when he writes,

> Christian mysticism has always been Christocentric. Through Christ, union with God and a knowledge of divine things is attained.[51]

Elsewhere, Owen elaborates, observing,

> ...mystical experience...is (meant to lead to) the perfection of charity and not, as in the case with other mystics, a mysterious means of acquiring transcendental knowledge.[52]

Owen summarizes his own treatment of Christian mysticism by noting two tendencies of mysticism in England: first, they (English mystics) believed that what dogma and Scripture described as possible was in fact attainable experientially. And second, the truth determined by Scripture and dogma was meant to give focus to one's religious quest. Both tendencies became powerful forces in Fox's thought and identified the way in which he came to approach his own religious journey.

Before moving on to a consideration of Fox's own thought a brief com-ment on Jacob Boehme is important. There is no doubt that Jacob Boehme influenced George Fox. How extensive this influence was, however, is hard to determine since Fox never footnotes his sources. Clear evidence is appar-

---

49. I cite *The Cloud of Unknowing* since it resembles Fox's own thought so closely. Of par-ticular interest is the emphasis on desire which leads to an immediate experience of Christ. This line of thought is echoed in Fox when the culmination of his own desire leads to an imme-diate experience of Jesus Christ (p. 11, elsewhere). *The Cloud of Unknowing*. Edited with an Introduction by James Walsh, S.J. New York: Paulist Press, 1981.

50. H. P. Owen, op. cit., p. 159, *Katz,*, op. cit.

51. H. P. Owen, op. cit., p. 158, *Katz*, op. cit.

52. Owen, p. 159.

ent in the use of identical or slightly modified phrases. Both borrow extensively from images found in the Johannine literature. Both use the phrase, "the light which lighteth every man," or slight modifications of it, to describe their understanding of the role of Jesus Christ. Both emphasize the importance of following the light within.[53] Both emphasize the role of human initiative in seeking God.[54]

Secondary references include the fact that followers of Boehme eventually identified with the Quaker movement.[55] Further evidence is found in the fact that in 1647, John Sparrow translated one of Boehme's most popular works, *The Way to Christ*, into English,[56] and by 1661, had translated a major portion of his entire corpus. Of course, the role played by the Cambridge Platonists in introducing Boehme's work into England cannot be ignored either. Louis Bouyer has noted that such themes as the inner rational light, the significance of the Bible, the role of the Biblical Jesus, the emphasis on the Church as the bride of Christ, and the importance of obedience to the Biblical witness of Jesus are all important themes which developed at this time in part because of the influence of Boehme on the Cambridge Platonists.[57] Of course, close parallels with Fox's own religious thought are striking. All of this is meant to illustrate that although Fox did not refer to Boehme personally, Boehme's influence was pervasive in the culture and Fox, whether knowingly or not, reflected many of Boehme's themes in his own writings.

Evidence of the Sources in the Journal of George Fox

Throughout the *Journal* of George Fox the various sources noted above are evident. From the beginning, the emphasis of identity with the historical Christ is apparent. Fox, at the beginning of his religious quest, notes,

And then I saw how Christ was tempted...and how Satan...laid snares for me and baits to draw me to commit some sin,...[58]

Elsewhere, Fox emphasizes the importance of following Christ's historical example by refusing to honor social customs which were against the designs of God. In one telling example, Fox, believing God alone deserves

53. Boehme, Jacob. *The Signature of all Things*. Translated by Clifford Bax. New York: E. P. Dutton and Co., p. X, no printing date is given, but it was originally released in 1621.

54. Boehme, Jacob. *The Way to Christ*. Translated by Peter Erb. New York: Paulist Press, 1978, p. 15. Fox, George. *Journal*. p. 11.

55. *Christian Spirituality*. Edited by Frank N. Magill and Ian P. McGreal. San Francisco: Harper and Row, Publishers, 1988, p. 273.

56. Boehme, *The Way to Christ*, p. 2.

57. Bouyer, Louis. *A History of Christian Spirituality III: Orthodox Spirituality and Anglican Spirituality*. New York: The Seabury Press, 1982, pp. 134-166.

58. Fox, p. 4.

honor and respect, refused to doff his cap as custom required. Defending his action, Fox exclaimed,

> But Christ tells us, "how can ye believe, who receive honour one of another, and seek not the honour that cometh from God only?"[59]

Later, when extolling the witness and testimony of Jesus and Scripture as sufficient for belief, Fox argued,

> And so I directed people to their teacher, Christ Jesus their saviour,...and so did set up Christ in the hearts of the people.

A corollary to the Franciscan emphasis on the historical Jesus is an emphasis on an itinerant ministry and the sufferings incurred as a result of such a ministry. For much of Fox's life the Quaker movement was officially outlawed. Much like Christianity in its first four centuries, waves of persecution against Quakers ebbed and flowed according to the attitudes of different rulers. Not until 1689, two years before Fox's death, with passage of the Act of Toleration,[60] were Quakers able to gain legal status in English society.

Throughout his ministry, Fox encountered serious persecution at the hands of his detractors. A perceived threat to the social and religious order of his day, Fox became a target for some of the most persistent and pernicious torment in seventeenth-century England. As early as 1649, Fox was imprisoned for his refusal to honor the specific precepts of England's state religion.[61] Upon his release, Fox challenged his accusers and a long and difficult period in which Quakers suffered severe and terrible misfortunes at the hands of the English legal system ensued.[62]

Other examples abound including a stoning by the citizens of Lancaster (120), a complete and thorough beating by the constables and citizens of Ulverston (127-128), and a deliberate miscarriage of justice in Fox's trial upon a return trip through Lancaster (133-134.) All of these examples illustrate the extent to which Fox and the Early Quakers suffered for their religious faith.

A second element in the *Journal* is the significance that the Bible played in Fox's own understanding of religious experience. As noted above, in the first one-hundred pages of the *Journal*, there are at least 148 direct references or allusions to the Christian Bible.[63] Fox consistently used the Bible to

---

59. Fox, p. 37.
60. Russell, Elbert. *The History of Quakerism*. Richmond, IN: Friends United Press, 1979, pp. 3, 186, 189.
61. Fox, p. 62.
62. Fox, pp. 66-72.
63. Fox, 1-100.

gain insight into the realities of life and to show the relevance of the religious life to these realities.[64] In every instance, Jesus was the key who, as inward teacher, unlocked the hidden mysteries of life and granted one noetic insight into these mysteries. Defending his position, Fox explained, "...how by Jesus, the opener of the door by his heavenly key, the entrance was given."[65] Even when interpreting the Old Testament, Fox believed Christ was the key to understanding stories and themes of ancient Israel.[66] His emphasis enlarged the allegorical interpretation of Scripture and included the role Christ played in bringing understanding to the religious seeker.

The difficulty for Fox, however, was getting people beyond the objective text of Scripture to capture the spirit of God, which is love, that is present in Scripture. For Fox, this meant the spirit of Scripture must be exalted over the text of Scripture.[67] Inevitably, this heightened the spirit of conflict between Fox and the religious authorities. Following the example of Francis, Boehme and the Apostle Paul, Fox consistently showed how the Bible illustrated the true nature and purpose of the religious life. As the movement gained momentum, Fox amplified the importance of Scripture, citing the Hebrew prophets to illustrate how God wanted us to live and the writings of John to illustrate how God wanted us to love.[68] Even Fox's challenge to the ruling government was based on Scripture.[69]

The third and perhaps most significant element in his thought is the role he ascribes to Christ as the inner teacher. Following the example of Augustine, Fox identified Christ as the inward teacher who alone could bring insight. In developing this treatment of Christ, Fox used two phrases interchangeably. One was the "light of Christ within." The other, a reference to "Christ as teacher." Both embodied the Augustinian ideal and stood apart from either Locke's understanding of the "light of reason,"[70] or Descartes' understanding of the "light of nature."[71]

As early as 1647, Fox began to co-mingle references to the Holy Spirit with the divine light of Christ evident in all things.[72] His intent was to direct people to the light within, which is Christ, who can teach one all things.[73]

---

64. Fox, 13.

65. Fox, 13-14.

66. Fox, 32.

67. Fox, 40.

68. Fox, 186-87, 236, 243.

69. Fox, 220.

70. Locke, John. *An Essay Concerning Human Understanding*. Abridged by Richard Taylor. Garden City, NY: Anchor Books, Anchor Press/Doubleday, 1974, pp. 123-125.

71. Descartes, Rene. *Meditations on First Philosophy* Translated with an Introduction by Laurence J. Lafleur. Indianapolis, IN: Bobbs-Merrill Educational Publishing, 1951, 1960, pp. 37-39, 41-50. Originally published in 1641.

72. Fox, 15.

Whether or not Fox believed this light could literally teach a person every-thing, thereby rejecting all academic endeavor as some Quakers claim, it is clear that Fox believed this light was sufficient to teach a person all they needed to know about the religious life.

When confronting priests in Mansfield, for example, Fox rebuked their ambitions for human learning by asking, "...if they had not a teacher within them...[who could answer their needs and questions]..."[74] Believing that Christ as teacher was the sole criterion for gaining wisdom and understand-ing of God, Fox rejected all religious traditions, exclaiming,

> ...I was [sent] to bring people off from all the world's religions, which are vain, that they might know the pure religion, and might visit the fatherless, the widows and the strangers, and keep themselves from the spots of the world...and turn people to the inward light...by which all might know their salvation.[75]

Later when addressing the religious leaders in Ratcliffe and a congrega-tion in Malton, Fox synthesized Augustine and Francis by first directing people to their inner teacher and then admonishing the people to live an outward, obedient life after the example of Jesus.[76]

Fox's contention with the religious establishment heightened with his teachings of Christ as the inward and sufficient teacher. Criticizing the min-istry of the professional clergy, Fox urged that people follow, "the true teacher [and not these] hirelings such as teach for fleece and prey upon the people..."[77] His only desire was to see people come to an awareness of the spirit of God in themselves, by which they could know God, apprehend Christ, understand Scripture and enjoy heavenly fellowship in the spirit.[78]

Throughout his ministry Fox sought to direct people to the inward Christ. This incessant desire and drive was born out of his own religious quest and his personal, experiential discovery of Christ's satisfaction of his inner need. Writing after nearly four years of his own religious quest, Fox exclaimed,

---

73. Fox, 20.

74. Fox, 20.

75. Fox, 35. I do not wish to explore this extensively, but two items emerge from this quote, the first regards Fox's possible attitude towards other religions. Since there is no evi-dence he encountered any religions other than Roman Catholicism, Anglicanism, or Calvinism this is sheer conjecture. Nevertheless, it does seem clear that in whatever context, Fox would have emphasized the hidden presence of Christ and would have embraced a position similar to Karl Rahner's in our own time. The second item is simply an observation that Fox believed the primary goal of religion was soteriological in much the same manner John Hick, op. cit., has argued.

76. Fox, 82-85.

77. Fox, 149.

78. Fox, 155.

And when all my hopes in them and in all men were gone, so that I had nothing outwardly to help me, nor could tell what to do, then Oh then, I heard a voice which said, 'there is one, even Christ Jesus, that can speak to thy condition,' and when I heard it my heart did leap for joy.[79]

This discovery of Fox's cemented his own sense of the need for the human to desire God in order to discover the significance of Christ for the religious life. This element of desire was an important ingredient in Fox's focus on the role of Christ. He took the admonition to seek God literally and believed this search would culminate in the experience of the presence mediated by Jesus Christ.[80] Fox did not want to receive mediated knowledge, but wanted and believed Christ alone could bring him into union with the spirit of God and believed people's desire to experience God often became sidetracked by all sorts of superstitious ceremonies.[81]

A fourth element in Fox's thought is the clear suspicion of religious practices and religious traditions. This is an unfortunate theme in Fox's thought and represents one of the most significant oversights of his *Journal*. Fox's suspicion of religious tradition and ritual entirely sidestepped the religious traditions and rituals he quickly prescribed for the new sect. He completely rejected the Roman Catholic traditions [p. 78], and consistently challenged the traditions of the Church of England and even in some cases the dissenting groups in England itself.[82] In all cases, Fox justified his teaching by reference to Scripture, but this did little to soften his dismissal of the valuable role tradition and discipline could play in the religious life.[83]

In addition, so much of Fox's own thought was informed by the rituals and traditions which had governed his earlier life. Clearly, he felt they had impeded his access to an experiential understanding of God. But in rejecting the significance of religious tradition, Fox failed to see the significant and important role they could play in facilitating one's search for God. Instead, Fox offered his own definition of the true church and the people who make up the true church. Following the tradition of the English mystics, Fox suggested that the true church was,

...the pillar and ground of Truth, made up of living stones,...a spiritual household of which Christ was the head.[84]

All of this helped accelerate his rejection of churchly authorities and further alienated him from the cultural mainstream.

---

79. Fox, 11. cf. 69.
80. Fox, 11-12.
81. Fox, 87.
82. Fox, 47, 113, 1844, 417.
83. Fox, 184, et. al..
84. Fox, 24.

In some circles, these very cultural conditions have been used to provide a sociological explanation for religious experience. In particular, Stephen Kent has argued that the Quaker movement emerged because of the sociological deprivation to which it was subjected.[85] Although one can concur with Kent's emphasis on the role sociological conditions can play in one's understanding of mystical experience, he entirely ignores both the religious contributions made to this context and the possibility and even validity of religious experience discovered by George Fox.

A fifth element in Fox's thought is the noetic quality akin to William James which Fox finds in religious experience. As early as 1647, Fox realized that following the light of Christ would consistently lead to new insights.[86] This knowledge was acquired as one learns to love God and this love for God brings one to a deeper union with God in Jesus Christ. This perceptual shift does not occur easily or often, but is gained by one who is committed to the light and subsequently acquires illumination of the truth of God through this light.

In seeking to augment this perspective, Fox utilized the life and witness of the Apostle Paul. Noting that Paul had been raised in the outward law of his Jewish heritage, Fox went on to suggest that his convincement on the road to Damascus had changed Paul's entire life and ministry. His absorption into the spirit of Christ had caused Paul to see life in a new way.[87] Fox does not explore this observation further, nor does he note that much of what Paul perceived in a new way was simply an outcropping or fulfillment of his own religious tradition. Nevertheless, this perceptual re-ordering was critical for Fox and for his belief about what an encounter with God and guidance by the light of Christ would accomplish.

A sixth and final element in Fox is his acknowledgment that the law of the Spirit is actually the pure love of God.[88] This perception by Fox, gained during the period of his own religious awakening, shaped much of his later emphasis in ethics. Pacifism was not a retreat from society, but the active love of God capable of engineering peace throughout the world.[89] Prison reform was not the latest crusading notion of a social activist, but the active love of God restoring human dignity to all of God's creation.[90] Honesty in business was not the accidental product of social upbringing, but the outworking of God's love to live all of life with integrity.[91]

---

85. Stephen A. Kent, "Mysticism, Quakerism, and Relative Deprivation: A Sociological Reply to R. A. Naulty," *Religion* (1989) 19, pp. 157-178.

86. Fox, 16, etc. al.

87. Fox, 22.

88. Fox, 16.

89. Fox, 197.

90. Fox, 19, 42-46

91. Fox, 169-170

In each case, Fox saw in the endless love of God the satisfaction for all human need and the ultimate pattern for human living. At times, his identification with the suffering and rejection of Christ became distorted, but these distortions were due in part to his greater desire to help people see the infinite love of Christ which conquers suffering.[92] Fox believed the ultimate goal of life was to exemplify this love and as such believed proper teaching in any context was teaching which led people to understand this love. To love one's neighbor, in Fox's mind, was to learn what it meant to love oneself and to hurt one's neighbor was to discover that you were in fact hurting yourself.[93]

The parallels with Martin Buber's *I And Thou* are striking. Like Buber, Fox believed that one comes to a proper understanding of God by understanding and participating in human relationships. Clearly, this is a pattern found in most forms of 'personal communion' mysticism, but beyond defining it as a certain type it represents Fox's implicit acknowledgment of the role of the religious community. His correctives to radical individualism in religion emerged gradually and developed mostly in reaction to the Ranters and other fringe groups he encountered. Although he recognized and emphasized the role of individual responsibility, he always did so in relation to the communal context of which he was part. Elsewhere, Fox emphasizes the significance of Christ as the mediator of this love and the way by which humans become open to this love. He also noted, however, the way humans often ran from this love and the unquenched desire which inevitably led them back to his love. Ultimately, Fox believed this love was the spirit which united humans with the Spirit of God.

This emphasis was more than just an individual learning how to enter active service of God. It was the cornerstone of society, the spirit by which Fox, and later William Penn, believed all elements of life should be governed. It was unique not because it was a new insight or even an entirely original synthesis, but because it was applied across such broad domains of society and culture. Trade and commerce, war and peace, justice and social relations, education and prison reform and care for the poor were only a few of the areas touched by Fox's life and teaching. Later, new accents would emerge as other members of the Society assumed leadership, but always with the belief that to apply the pure love of God to social relations was to experience God's pure love itself.

Conclusion

Throughout the *Journal* Fox's disarming frankness often causes one to overlook his connection with a legacy that preceded him. His own reliance

---

92. Fox, 68, et. al.
93. Fox, 28.

on the spirit for guidance and his frequent use of the Bible make it appear that these two elements alone were sufficient for understanding the development of his thought. Nevertheless, this paper has attempted to show the underlying reliance Fox had on sources other than himself and God.

Religious texts, religious doctrines and the religious community all played a pivotal role for Fox. Of particular importance were the writings of the Gospel of John whose emphasis on love and whose effort to establish a community based on love were critical. Fox also absorbed a theme from John and echoed in Boehme that heaven and hell were not modes of eternity in the life to come, but states of existence experienced presently. The Bible was, for Fox, a source of primary insight into the nature and reality of God and the nature and reality of the religious life. It was also Fox's favorite weapon when defending his point of view against the numerous detractors in seventeenth-century England.

Religious doctrines played an important role as well, although Fox often appeared to diminish this role. In one notable exchange, Fox rejected the legitimacy of the Ranters because they believed that God's substance was changeable. Fox could not accept a God who could change and could not accept any group as legitimate who taught such a position. Another example is his acceptance of the legitimacy of the canon of Scripture. Unlike Luther, who wanted to discard books like the epistle of James, Fox never challenged the legitimacy of the traditional canon. Even in his treatment of the Old Testament he never digressed into discussing the possible incompatibilities between the God of the Old Testament and the God of love of the New Testament. In fact, to a large extent, the only differences Fox had with Orthodox Christianity are the ones Robert Barclay outlined in his defense of the Quaker interpretation of the Christian faith.[94]

The religious community was extremely important to Fox and the role he played in forming various communities of faith throughout England played an indispensable role in the growth and survival of the Quaker movement. To a certain extent, Fox's understanding of how one experiences God could be considered as a form of social mysticism since he placed such a heavy emphasis on the role played by the gathered community in one's encounter with God. It was in one's relation to another human that one gained insight into their relation with God. In fact, Fox's emphasis on the way in which one comes to understand God in community foreshadows Hegel's later emphasis on the Absolute coming to an understanding and manifestation of itself in the religious community.[95]

Fox's thought, moreover, was clearly contextualized within a Christian framework. When he emphasized the role of community it was the Chris-

---

94. *Barclay*, op. cit.
95. Hegel, G.W.F. *Lectures on the Philosophy of Religion*, Translated and edited by Peter C. Hodgson, Berkeley, CA: University of California Press, 1983, pp. 470-489.

tian community he envisioned. One can only speculate as to how he would handle the reality of world religions, as is noted above. Anything which stifled the human spirit coming to an understanding of the ultimately Real would be condemned by Fox. Most likely, he would make allowance for the existence of world religions by emphasizing the light of Christ hidden throughout the world as noted by Paul in Romans 1. But this remains sheer conjecture.

On the importance of religious experience, Fox would have no equal. Religious experience, or mystical experience, was for Fox the paramount experience of life. Such an experience ushered in the peace that comes from the pure love of God. Such experience could not be engineered, but it could be prepared for if one understood the nature of the religious quest. The religious quest was a rigorous journey which often alienated one from the mainstream of society. Beginning with the Hebrew prophets and flowing through Jesus Christ, the first disciples, the Early Church, Francis, Luther, Boehme, and others, Fox had ample evidence that the religious journey often alienated you from your own cultural context. Nevertheless, Fox advocated this approach in religion since it was the only one which could bring an individual into fellowship with God.

Although Fox used terms like "salvation" sparingly, he clearly believed the religious quest was salvific in nature. The only measure of a religion was its ability to bring the human into fellowship with the love of God. The soteriological nature of Fox's thought focused on the peace experienced and the insight gained. The human's understanding of their experience of this love became the final criterion in one's experience of true religion. Later, when exposed to a broader culture than seventeenth-century England, this insight would not withstand the onslaught of individual authority in religious interpretation. Nevertheless, Fox insisted on the centrality of Christ in mediating this new state.

Fox seemed at times to border on the bizarre in his religious quest. Visually reliving the martyrdom of one-thousand residents in Lichfield was only one example of many visions and premonitions which informed his religious quest. He was not a religious lunatic or even a psychologically unstable person, as some have claimed, but was driven by a need to identify with the experiences of Jesus Christ. In suffering, in joy, in insight, in gaining insight, in gaining access to God and even coming to understand one's true relation to God were for Fox all a part of his quest to follow the example of Christ.

The life of Christ formed the central metaphysical key to Fox's system. Through his life and through one's experience of his guiding light one discovered the sufficiency of Christ leading one to the fullness of love experienced in God. His emphasis on the sufficiency of Christ as inward teacher and his focus on the historic events of Christ's life, however, led Fox and others into several abuses which embarrassed the Society. Most notable among these episodes was James Naylor's enactment of Christ's triumphal entry in which women stood by the side of the road giving praise as Naylor rode by on a donkey. The incident deeply angered Fox and gained Naylor the punishment of a heretic. But its long term effect was to help Fox and others realize the danger inherent in overemphasizing the individual nature of the religious quest. Gradually, such events helped the Society develop a stronger sense of the corporate nature of the religious life and helped them form a theology of religious experience which would allow the Society to endure.

Fox's deep resistance to religious tradition is one of the most puzzling parts of his thought. Unlike many other religious mystics, Fox did not easily accept the religious traditions and doctrines of his religious context. To an extent he exemplified the "protestant principle" at its finest in repeatedly reforming the nature of religious doctrine and its ability to influence the religious life based on his own authority and interpretation. But this did not always serve the Society well and allowed a seed of suspicion to enter the Society which has never been eradicated. Robert Barclay helped to correct this tendency partially, but the authority and influence of Fox has prevented its removal entirely.

Finally, the majesty of love formed the pinnacle of Fox's thought. The Spirit of God was the spirit of love and as such formed the foundation of personal ethics, social concerns, communal relations and economic commerce. To love and to live life with love was to work to bring the abstract principle of God's love into concrete reality. Fox never wearied of making this emphasis. He believed that if individuals could have an authentic encounter with the spirit of love then all concerns in civil society were solvable. The idea of two independent spheres of life living alongside one another, as Augustine had argued in *The City of God* and the Calvinists of Fox's time made popular, found no reception with Fox. Life was a single piece and one was to live life at all times as a single piece.

Fox had his flaws, but they were no more significant than the flaws of other great mortals. His emphases at times were extreme, but only because the circumstances of his time were extreme. He was caught in the flux of revolutionary times and sought to find a calming influence in the love of God. There were many streams of life and thought which flowed into Fox and out of his unique synthesis came an understanding of mystical experience which launched a new movement in religious history. The uniqueness of these insights would at times wane, but the clarity and authority with which he expressed these insights have made an enduring contribution to our understanding of religious experience.

WORKS CITED

Almond, Philip, C. *Mystical Experience and Religious Doctrine*. New York: Mouton Publishers, 1982.

Augustine. *On Christian Doctrine*. Translated by D. W. Robertson, Jr. Indianapolis: Bobbs-Merrill Educational Publishing, 1958.

Barclay, Robert. *An Apology for the True Christian Divinity*. Richmond, IN: Friends United Press, 1978. (Reprint)

The Rule of St. Benedict in English. Edited by Timothy Fry, O.S.B. Collegeville, MN: The Liturgical Press, 1982.

The Bhagavad-Gita. Translated by Barbara Stoler Miller. New York: Bantam Books, 1986.

The Confessions of Jacob Boehme. Compiled and edited by W. Scott Palmer. New York: Harper and Brother, Pub., 1954.

Boehme, Jacob. *The Signature of All Things*. Translated with an introduction by Clifford Bax. New York: E. P. Dutton and Co.

Boehme, Jacob. *The Way to Christ*. New York: Paulist Press, 1978.

Bouyer, Louis. *A History of Christian Spirituality Vol. III: Orthodox Spirituality and Protestant and Anglican Spirituality*. New York: The Seabury Press, 1982.

Brann, Eva T. H. *The World of the Imagination*. Savage, MD: Rowman and Littlefield Pub., Inc., 1991.

The Cloud of the Unknowing. Edited with an introduction by James Walsh, S.J. New York: Paulist Press, 1981.

Cherian, M.A. *Advaita Vedanta and Madhyamika Buddhism: Eastern Religions in Western Thought*. Great Britain: M.A. Cherian, 1988.

Chris.tian Spirituality. Edited by Frank N. Magill and Ian P. McGreal. San Francisco: Harper and Row, Publishers, 1988.

Corrington, Robert S. *The Community of. Interpreters* Macon, GA: Mercer University Press, 1987.

Descartes, Rene. *Meditations on First Philosophy*. Translated with an Introduction by Laurence J. Lafleur. Indianapolis, IN: Bobbs-Merrill Educational Publishing Co., 1951, 1960. Originally published in 1641.

The Drunken Universe: An Anthology of Persian Sufi Poetry. Translated with commentary by Peter Lamborn Wilson and Nasrollah Pourjavady. Grand Rapids: Phanes Press, 1987.

Meister Eckhart: A Modern Translation. Translated with an introduction by Raymond Bernard Blakney. New York: Harper and Row, Pub., 1941.

Evans, G. R. *The Language and Logic of the Bible: The Earlier Middle Ages*. New York: Cambridge University Press, 1984.

Feuerbach, Ludwig. *The Essence of Christianity*. San Francisco: Harper and Row, Pub. Inc., 1957. Originally published in 1841.

Journal of George Fox. edited by John L. Nickalls. Introduction by Henry J. Cadbury. Philadelphia: Religious Society of Friends, 1985.

Fox, Matthew. *Breakthrough: Meister Eckhart's Creation Spirituality in New Translation.* Garden City, NY: Image Books, 1980.

German Mystical Writings. Translated and edited by Karen J. Campbell. New York: Continuum, 1991.

Hegel, G.W.F. *Lectures on the Philosophy of Religion.* Translated and edited by Peter C. Hodgson. Berkeley, CA: University of California Press, 1988.

Hegel, G.W.F. *Phenomenology of Spirit.* Translated by A.V. Miller. New York: Oxford University Press, 1977.

Herbert, George. *The Temple.* Edited by John N. Wall, Jr. New York: Paulist Press, 1981.

Hick, John. *An Interpretation of Religion.* New Haven, CN: Yale University Press, 1989.

Hutchison, John A. *The Paths of Faith.* New York: McGraw-Hill Book Co., 1969.

The Spiritual Exercises of St. Ignatius Loyola. Translated and edited by Lewis Delmage, S.J. Boston: Daughters of St. Paul, 1978.

Inge, William Ralph. *Christian Mysticism.* London: Methuen Pub. Co., 1899.

James, William. *The Varieties of Religious Experience.* New York: Mentor Books, 1958. Reprint of the 1901-02 Gifford Lectures.

The Mystical Doctrine of St. John of the Cross. Translated and edited by R. H. J. Steuart. London: Sheed and Ward, 1934.

Johnston, William. *Christian Mysticism Today.* San Francisco: Harper and Row, Pub., 1984.

Johnston, William. *Still Point: Reflection on Zen and Christian Mysticism.* New York: Fordham University Press, 1970.

Jones, Rufus. *Studies in Mystical Religion.* New York: The MacMillan Co., 1923.

King, Ursula. *Towards a New Mysticism.* New York: The Seabury Press, 1981.

Stephen A. Kent, "Mysticism, Quakerism, and Relative Deprivation: A Sociological Reply to R. A. Naulty," *Religion* (1989) 19, 157-178.

Latourette, Kenneth Scott. *A History of Christianity, Volume II.* San Francisco: Harper and Row, Publishers, Inc., 1953, 1975.

Kohn, Livia. *Early Chinese Mysticism.* Princeton: Princeton University Press, 1992.

Locke, John. *An Essay Concerning Human Understanding.* Abridged by Richard Taylor. Garden City, NY: Anchor Books, Anchor Press/Doubleday, 1974.

Louth, Andrew. *The Origins of the Christian Mystical Tradition.* Oxford: Clarendon Press, 1981.

McGinn, Bernard. *The Foundations of Mysticism.* New York: The Crossroad Pub. Co., 1991.

"Mystical Union," *Encyclopedia of Religion,* edited by Mircea Eliade, New York: MacMillan Publishing Co., 1987, pp. 239-245.

"Mysticism," *Encyclopedia of Religion,,* edited by Mircea Eliade, op. cit., pp. 245-261.

Mysticism and Philosophical Analysis. Edited by Steven T. Katz. New York: Oxford University Press, 1978.

Mysticism and Religious Traditions. Edited by Steven T. Katz. New York: Oxford University Press, 1983.

Mystical Union and Monotheism: An Ecumenical Dialogue. Edited by Moshe Idel and Bernard McGinn. New York: MacMillan Pub. Co., 1989.

Niebuhr, Richard H. *The Meaning of Revelation.* New York: MacMillan Publishing Co., 1941.

On Sharing Religious Experience. Edited by Hendrik M. Vroom, et.al. Grand Rapids, William B. Eerdmans Publishing Co., 1992.

Otto, Rudolf. *The Idea of the Holy.* Translated by John W. Harvey. New York: Oxford University Press, 1958. Originally published in 1923.

Otto, Rudolf. *Mysticism East and West.* Wheaton, Ill.: The Theosophical Publishing House, 1932, 1987.

Parrinder, Geoffrey. *Mysticism in the World's Religions.* New York: Oxford University Press, 1976.

Pascal, Blaise. *Pensees.* Translated with an Introduction by Thomas Krailsheimer. Middlesex, Eng: Penguin, 1965.

Philosophy in the Middle Ages. Articles translated by Arthur Hyman and James J. Walsh. Indianapolis: Hackett Pub. Co., 1973.

Pre-Reformation English Spirituality. Edited and introduced by James Walsh, Í.J. New York: Fordham University Press,

Proudfoot, Wayne. *Religious Experience.* Berkeley, CA: The University of California Press, 1985.

Revised Standard Version of the Bible, 1946, 1952, 1971, 1973.

Religions and the Truth. Edited by Hendrik M. Vroom. Grand Rapids: William B. Eerdmans Pub. Co., 1989.

Russell, Bertrand. *Mysticism and Logic and Other Essays.* New York: Longmans, Green and Co., 1917, 1925.

Russell, Elbert. *The History of Quakerism.* Richmond, IN: Friends United Press, 1979.

Schleiermacher, Friedrich. *On Religion.* Translated by Richard Crouter. New York: Cambridge University Press, 1988. Originally published in 1799.

Segal, Alan F. *Paul the Convert: The Apostolate and Apostasy of Saul the Pharisee.* New Haven, CN: Yale University Press, 1990.

Shankara's Crest-Jewel of Discrimination. Translated by Swami Prabhavananda and Christopher Isherwood. Hollywood: Vedanta Press, 1947, 1978.

Smart, Ninian. *The Religious Experience of Mankind.* New York: Scribner and Sons, 1969.

Sontag, Frederick. *Love Beyond Pain: Mysticism Within Christianity.* New York: Paulist Press, 1977.

The Study of Spirituality. Edited by Jones, Wainwright and Yarnold. New York: Oxford University Press, 1986.

Toward a Universal Theology of Religion. Edited by Leonard Swidler. New York: Orbis Books, 1987.

Troeltsch, Ernst. *The Social Teaching of the Christian Churches.* Translated by Olive
    Wyon. London: Allen and Unwin, 1931.

Underhill, Evelyn. *Mysticism.* New York: Doubleday, 1911, 1990.

Wieman, Henry N. *Methods of Private Religious Living.* New York: The MacMillan
    Co., 1929.

Thy Obedience Is Perfect Freedom

1994 Indiana Yearly Meeting of Friends Quaker Lecture

T. CANBY JONES

I have gone through quite an inward exercise to come up with the organizing concept for this lecture. I daresay the Yearly Meeting Planning Committee was very pleased to find William Penn paraphrasing Jesus' words in Matthew 10:8, "Freely you have received, freely give," when they chose the theme for this Yearly Meeting, "As we have freely received from Christ, let us freely give." My first leading was to title this talk, "Thy Obedience Is Perfect Freedom." But that wonderful phrase is not from Scripture. It sure sounds like it should be, doesn't it? It must be from some one of my great spiritual friends and mentors from the Church through the ages, such as St. Augustine, *The Imitation of Christ*, or Jean Nicholas Grou. In any case that's the theme of this talk, "Thy Obedience Is Perfect Freedom."

In this talk I plan to examine freedom and obedience in Scripture, in George Fox, Thomas R. Kelly, William Penn; interpreting each with my own leadings and attempts to understand the relationship between freedom and obedience.

Freedom

Here are some Scriptures on what it means to be free:[1]

Deuteronomy 5:6:

---

1. All quotations from the Bible are from the Revised Standard Version with the exception of two. One is from the King James Version, the other from the New English Bible.

I am the Lord your God, who brought you out of the land of Egypt, out of the house of bondage.

Isaiah 58:6-9:
Is not this the fast that I choose: to loose the bonds of wickedness, to undo the thongs of the yoke, to let the oppressed go free, and to break every yoke? Is it not to share your bread with the hungry, and bring the homeless poor into your house; when you see the naked, to cover him, and not to hide yourself from your own flesh? Then shall your light break forth like the dawn, and your healing shall spring up speedily; your righteousness shall go before you, the glory of the Lord shall be your rear guard. Then you shall call, and the Lord will answer; you shall cry, and he will say, Here I am.

John 8:32 and 36:
And you will know the truth, and the truth will make you free. ...If the Son makes you free, you will be free indeed.

Galatians 3:28:
There is neither Jew nor Greek, there is neither slave nor free, there is neither male nor female; for you are all one in Christ Jesus.

Galatians 5:1:
For freedom Christ has set us free: stand fast therefore, and do not submit again to a yoke of slavery.

Concerning Deuteronomy 5:6 George Fox loved to ask, "Have you been brought out of your own Egypt, out of the house of bondage?"[2] What does God's deliverance of his people from slavery in Egypt mean to us? Do we see it as the source of our freedom? If we do not, can we claim to be spiritual children of Abraham and heirs according to the promise? I love to make a litany of the Ten Commandments, Deuteronomy 5:7-21, using this marvelous verse six as a prelude to each commandment. For example: "I am the Lord your God, who brought you out of the land of Egypt, out of the house of bondage. You shall have no other gods before me." Or, repeat the same sixth verse before "You shall not kill," "Neither shall you commit adultery," or "Neither shall you steal." Such repetition of verse six reminds me of my delivery from my own slavery in Egypt and that Christ has set me free. Out of gratitude for my liberation I don't *want* to do any of those things. From onerous requirements the Ten Commandments are transformed into counsels of life!

Concerning Isaiah 58:6-9 whenever George Fox was asked about fasting he always said Friends believe in the "true fast" as described in this

---

2. T. C. Jones, *The Power of the Lord Is Over All: The Pastoral Letters of George Fox* (Richmond IN: Friends United Press, 1989), 572 p. Ltr. #352, p. 365.

marvelous Scripture.[3] After doing all those works of mercy we are promised that our light will break forth and the Lord will not only answer our prayers but manifest himself to us with a "Here I am." Try substituting the word *freedom* or the word *obedience* for the word *fast* in verse six. How do they sound?

We come to the big ones in John 8:32 and 36. Know the truth and it shall make you free. Pilate asked Jesus, "What is truth?" He should have asked him, "Are *you* the truth?" Truth is not a "what" or a "thing" but something alive which we can know. In its highest form truth is a "who," a person, and we know who that person is. Both George Fox and Thomas Kelly go to town on this Scripture so I won't say more here. How about verse 36? "If the Son makes you free, you will be free indeed!" Not only free but we will hear the voice of our Teacher behind us saying, "This is the way, walk ye in it." (Isaiah 30:21).

Galatians 3:28 destroys the hierarchical distinction between Jew and Greek, races, tribes or nations. Gender discrimination or oppression becomes impossible. Slaves become free persons. Why? Because we are all one and all are set free by the unifying love of Christ Jesus.

Galatians 5:1 repeats the assurance that we have been liberated to freedom and calls us to stand fast, no matter what, in the integrity of that love-covenant relationship and to refuse to descend again into bondage.

George Fox

Now hear what dear George Fox has to say about true freedom for God's free men and free women. In 1668 George wrote this letter, number 260, telling how Truth makes us free.

> Dear Friends: if the Truth makes you free, then are you free indeed? So then, there are none made free men but by Truth. All that are free men, they are made free by the Truth. They are God's free men. They are Free citizens. They are freeholders of an everlasting inheritance and free [in] an everlasting Kingdom. They are free heirs of salvation. They are free [in] the heavenly city Jerusalem, which is from above. And they are free [in] the Power of an endless Life, which was before death was.
>
> So, they are not captives. They are not bondsmen. They are not servants, nor slaves. But, mark, free men and free women. And what has made them free men and free women, but Truth? For, if the Truth has made you free, then you are free indeed.
>
> So, free to worship God in Spirit and in Truth...to serve the Lord God in the Spirit and in the new life...and to be members of the True Church, Gospel Fellowship and Power of God, which was before the devil was.

---

3. Jones, *op. cit.* Ltr. 167, (1658) p. 127 & Ltr. 230, p. 188.

So, stand fast in the Liberty wherewith Christ has made you free, free from the devil, dragon, serpent and all slavery and servitude. For free men do walk in their freedom. It is the Truth that makes them free and so to triumph in Glory... .

So, it is plain, none are free but by the Truth and all in the Truth are free men.

All out of the Truth are slaves in old Adam, slaves to sin and Satan... and to their own self-righteousness...serving diverse lusts, ...serving the desires of their own minds. So, as slaves are kept in bondage. All in prison, all in the bonds of death and jaws of death; for [those] who are out of the Truth are not free men. ...

But Truth makes free from all these, free from the hypocrite's hope, which perishes and free from Nebuchadnezzar's fury. It makes free from the wild heifer's nature, from the dog, swine, horse, viper, cockatrice and serpent's nature, from the spider and his web, and from the oak and cedar, the bramble and briar, bear and lion. The Truth makes free men from all these and brings man and woman into the image of God. And so, if the Truth makes you free then are you free indeed.

And the Truth is Christ and Christ is the Truth...by which you come to be free men of the world which has no end.[4]

Oh, George, you speak so beautifully and powerfully about Truth making us free. What else can we say?

Thomas Kelly

Now let's look at an unpublished sermon of Thomas R. Kelly entitled, "Ye Shall Know the Truth" to see what we can learn from him about Truth making us free. This sermon was almost certainly first delivered in 1932 probably on Fourth of July Sunday. I express my thanks to Ronald Rembert, Associate Professor of Philosophy at Wilmington College, for bringing this and twenty-one other sermons of Thomas Kelly to light. Kelly's first point is that we live in an age in which "the general assumption seems to be that freedom is the normal state of men, and *restraint* is a violation of his nature." If that was true in 1932 it is even more true in this age of "If it feels good, do it." Or, "Don't tell me what to do. I'll do what is right in my own eyes." Freedom is believed to be living with no restraint whatever.

Tom Kelly then takes pains to show that such freedom never exists. We are in fact *slaves* to instincts, the rules of parents, the laws of nature and mathematics, laws of courtesy, fair play, the laws of the state and the laws of

---

4. Jones, *op. cit.* Ltr. 260 (1668), 1 p. 231-232.

God. "No," Tom Kelly goes on, "It seems clear to me that we are not born free, but that we are born in chains, and only gradually and progressively do we achieve freedom. Freedom is a task, not a gift, a goal, not a full possession." "When we submit to laws," he continues, "we *obtain* real freedom. Laws do not *diminish* our freedom. They are our *means to* freedom." A bit later Kelly says, "It's a great day when a person realizes that the real way to liberty is through the law. And it is a greater day when we begin to impose laws upon ourselves in order to be free."

Notice Tom's last sentence: "It's a greater day when we begin to impose laws upon ourselves." That's the moment when the freedom of obedience is born.

Kelly then interprets Jesus saying, "The truth shall make you free," by saying:

> No life is free, no nation is free, no civilization is free, until it has built itself upon the eternal nature and pattern of things, and of God. This vast order is the Truth, fragments of which we call laws. Voluntary, free submission to this cosmic order, loyal devotion to it, passionate enthusiasm for its embodiment in the ways of men, these are the sound bases of freedom. Truth-seekers are freedom makers. The deepest citizenship we can know is devotion to truth. ...Democracy is founded upon the faith that the quest and vision of truth is in every heart.

Kelly was fascinated by Eugene Millikan's recent discovery of cosmic rays. He uses cosmic rays as a parable for God's almost imperceptible divine drift or wind. He says of it:

> In this world there is a cosmic drift—a direction along which the winds of God blow across the plains of man. God's will, God's law, God's purpose and truth is the world's true order. That man and that nation is free which lines itself up with the winds of God. ... That wind is Love, and Truth. It is the cosmic order. Truth made living in love. ... This is the Truth *and the Truth shall make you free.*[5]

Do we really believe in Truth with a capital "T" that brings life, order, direction and unity to all things? If we do, we will know what it means to be free. Here's a lovely word from dear George Fox about it. "So in the Fear of God live, spread the Truth abroad and set the Truth over all...in which you have Unity. So my Love is to you all."[6]

---

5. Thomas R. Kelly, unpublished sermon [1932] "The Truth Shall Make You Free" (Haverford College, Quaker Collection).

6. Jones, *op. cit.* Letter #224 (1662), p. 183.

William Penn

Now we turn to see what we can learn from William Penn about freedom. I have used the Everyman Edition of *The Peace of Europe, The Fruits of Solitude and Other Writings*, by William Penn, edited by Edwin Bronner and published 1993, as my main source. I have found that Penn was most concerned about liberty and freedom of conscience to worship and obey God in whatever way or form we may be led to by the Holy Spirit.

In his essay of 1670, *The Great Case of Liberty and Conscience*, William Penn defines liberty of conscience as "the free and uninterrupted exercise of our consciences, in that way of worship, we are most clearly persuaded, God requires us to serve him in."[7] In chapter III Penn marshals an impressive list of scriptures which support freedom of worship and oppose coercion in religious matters. Historic evidence confirms the fact that the struggles of Friends, Mennonites and Brethren to establish the practice of voluntarism in matters of religious faith succeeded through their suffering and witness and made such freedom one of the cornerstones of democracy wherever it is now found in our world. The Conventicle and Quaker Acts of the British Parliament of 1661 and 1662 made it illegal for more than five persons to worship anywhere in Britain except in a Church of England house or liturgy. Quaker Meeting Houses were locked, destroyed, and Friends arrested when they met for worship outside of them or on their rubble in contravention of those laws. Elsewhere in this same essay Penn states: "Force may make an hypocrite; it is faith grounded upon knowledge, and consent that makes a Christian."[8]

The exciting essay by Penn in this book is his account of being tried in court in 1670 together with William Mead for having held a meeting for worship and preached outside the locked Quaker Meeting House on Gracechurch Street in London. Talk about "standing fast and refusing to submit again to the yoke of slavery"! Penn and Mead did so in dramatic fashion in their trial. The court accused them of unlawful assembly and creating a tumult and an uproar by their preaching. Penn, of course, had studied law at the Inns of Court. Penn demanded a fair trial, which the judge granted. Penn then demanded to know under what statute he was being tried. The judge, court recorder and mayor all spluttered and said "Common Law." Penn wanted to know what provision of the Common Law and the judge could not answer. The judge, court recorder and mayor all severely told the jury that they *had to* return a verdict of guilty. After deliberation the jury returned and said William Mead was innocent of the charge and that William Penn was "guilty of speaking in Gracechurch Street." That verdict

---

7. William Penn, *The Peace of Europe, Some Fruits of Solitude*, etc. F.E. Edwin Bronner (Rutland, VT: Tuttle),1993. pp. 155-56.

8. *Ibid.*, p. 167.

represented no punishable offense and in effect meant "not guilty." Twice the judge sequestered the jury "without meat, drink, fire, and tobacco" until they returned a "guilty" verdict. Penn kept loudly objecting to this process citing English law and the *Magna Charta* to the contrary. Furious with the jury and with Penn and Mead, the judge ordered the two prisoners locked up in the "dock." Apparently this was a cell in the courtroom with which to control obstreperous prisoners. It must have been open at the top because Penn could hear all the proceedings from inside it and kept shouting out his objections to the proceedings during the trial. The court still refused to accept it. The judge brought the jurors one by one to the stand to try to pressure each one to change his verdict. Each one stood fast and refused to do so. From his place in the dock Penn urged the jury that "their verdict should be free, and not compelled." He further denied that Friends made a tumult in Gracechurch Street but that it was those "that interrupted us. The jury cannot be so ignorant as to think that we met there with a design to disturb the civil peace, since...we were by force of arms kept out of our lawful house, and met as near in the street, as the soldiers would give us leave." Penn followed with his most forceful statement, "The agreement of twelve men is a verdict in law...I require the Clerk of the Peace to record it...And if the Jury bring another verdict contrary to this, I affirm they are perjured men in the law. (And looking upon the Jury, said), you are Englishmen, mind your privilege, give not away your right." The final verdict of the jury both for Penn as well as Mead was, "Not guilty." As most of you know, this trial established once and for all the right of juries in English law to make free and uncoerced verdicts.[9]

What kind of freedom have we here observed? Obviously, the freedom to speak Truth to power. In an unjust situation we must stand fast and not "submit again to the yoke of slavery." Are Quakers quarried of prophetic flint? Penn sure proved it in this case. In Letter 35 (1653)[10] George Fox shouts, "Stand up, you prophets of the Lord, for the Truth upon the earth." I love it when the unjust get told off and Truth triumphs. That is a victory in the Lamb's War which we are all called to fight.

What have we learned thus far about freedom? First, that God sets people free from bondage, whether actual in Egypt, the southern United States or the Soviet Union and from our inner slavery to ourselves and to our sin. Second, freedom means loosing the bonds of wickedness and letting the oppressed go free both in an outward and social sense and in an inward and personal sense. Third, freedom means a lifelong commitment to and knowledge of Truth. We are made free by practicing it. Our central Quaker testimony of "integrity" is a fruit of it. Obviously we know who the Truth is

---

9. *Ibid.*, pp. 147-151.
10. Jones, *op. cit.* Letter 35 (1653), p. 27.

and joyfully confess that it is the Son who makes us free indeed. Fourth, our free exercise of Truth destroys our ability to think small and to limit the grace, choice or compassion of God to genders, races or classes of people, "for we are all one in Christ Jesus." There is no limit to his love! Fifth, from Thomas Kelly we learn that freedom is a task and a goal toward which we struggle to discover that God's law pervades the universe and that it's a great day when we learn to interiorize those laws by inner discipline within ourselves. True freedom begins and ends in such inner discipline. Always respond to the winds of God. "That wind is Love, and Truth. It is the cosmic order. Truth made living in Love...This is the Truth [which] shall make you free." Finally from William Penn we have learned how tough and persistent freedom and the fight for it must be. Stand fast in the Truth! Fight for it with all the weapons of the Spirit, and the Lamb shall have the victory!

Obedience

I think that freedom is born of inner discipline committed to following and practicing living Truth. Inner discipline, in turn, is born of holy obedience, obedience to the voice of the Teacher within which it is our labor as Friends to bring all persons to be taught by.

So who wants obedience? And what is it? A very unpopular concept in our "self gratification" society. Rebellion and seeing how much you can get away with are norms for too many in our day. The claim that inner discipline or obedience to law leads to freedom is a flat contradiction to many ears. Webster's dictionary is of little help. It defines *obedient* as "submissive to the restraint, control or command of authority...subject, subservient."

We begin redeeming this term by looking at the Latin root of *obedience*. The verb to obey in Latin is *oboedire*. It means to give ear, hearken, listen to, obey, be subject to or serve. The verb is a compound of the preposition *ob*, which means before or in front of, with *audire*, which means to hear, listen to, learn from, hear with approval or to heed. Obedience then means to stand before someone listening with assent and approval and action.

The explosive fact about this root definition of obedience is that it is the central message of the Bible. The Bible's primary call and concern is that we should hear and obey the voice of Yahweh, the voice of the Lord. God's constant appeal in Scripture is that we appear before Him, listen and then carry out what we hear Him calling us to do. Jesus was in the habit of ending his important pronouncements with the words, "If you have ears, then hear!" Standing before the One Who Is, hearing, gladly accepting and doing what is asked; this is the meaning of free obedience.

I therefore define obedience as hearing God's voice and doing what He says. He calls us to renew humanity, restore the earth and live with one another in justice. Put very simply, obedience means doing God's will before our own. Such obedience is neither slavish nor coerced by externally imposed authority. It is courageous, prophetic and free. In Thomas Kelly's words, "its joys are unspeakable, its peace profound, its simplicity that of a trusting child."[11]

Obedience defies theoretical definition because to obey is to act. To obey means to do. Followers of Jesus and lovers of Torah are known best not by what they profess in words but by what they accomplish. Free obedience is a form of action.

As in the case of freedom it is time now to look at a very few select Scriptures that express obedience and disobedience.

Jeremiah 7:22-29:
For in the day that I brought them out of the land of Egypt...this command I gave them, "Obey my voice, and I will be your God, and you shall be my people; and walk in all the way that I command you, that it may be well with you." But they did not obey or incline their ear, but walked in their own counsels and the stubbornness of their evil hearts, and went backward and not forward. From the day that your fathers came out of the land of Egypt to this day, I have persistently sent all my servants the prophets to them, day after day; yet they did not listen to me, or incline their ear, but stiffened their neck. They did worse than their fathers.
So you shall speak all these words to them, but they will not listen to you. You shall call to them, but they will not answer you. And you shall say to them, "This is the nation that did not obey the voice of the Lord their God, and did not accept discipline; truth has perished; it is cut off from their lips.
"Cut off your hair and cast it away; raise a lamentation on the bare heights, for the Lord has rejected and forsaken the generation of his wrath."

What terrible words of judgment on our disobedient nation! Will we turn and listen? Notice how God, through the mouth of his prophet, begins by repeating His everlasting love covenant with His people: "Obey my voice, and I will be your God, and you shall be my people." But like us, they refuse to listen and stiffen their necks and refuse to obey. Therefore they (and we) incur the terrible judgment, "this is the nation that did not obey the voice of the Lord their God, and did not accept discipline; truth has perished... ."

The three Scriptures I want to share from the New Testament all demonstrate the obedience of Jesus.

Luke 22:41-44:
And he withdrew from them about a stone's throw, and knelt down and prayed. "Father, if thou are willing, remove this cup from me; nevertheless not my will, but thine, be done." And there appeared to him an angel from heaven, strengthening him. And being in an agony he prayed more ear-

11. Thomas R. Kelly, *A Testament of Devotion* (New York: Harper, 1941), p. 54.

nestly; and his sweat became like great drops of blood falling down upon the ground.

The word *agony* became a Christian word and is defined by this scene. Notice that one of my two definitions of holy obedience is: "Doing God's will instead of our own." This scene of our Lord in agony to obey is the source of the definition.

The Letter to the Hebrews interprets this scene.

Hebrews 5:7-8:
Because of his humble submission his prayer was heard: Son though he was he learned obedience in the school of suffering, and, once perfected became the source of eternal salvation for all who obey him. (NEB)

When we consider the agony he endured in order to obey, what else can we do but gladly obey not only His commandments but His faintest nudge or whisper? What a promise at the end of that passage. Whew!

Having taught Scripture for over thirty years there are dozens of passages that I love to meditate on and quote, but Philippians 2:5-11 is one of my most frequent favorites. For our purpose I quote only verses five through eight.

Philippians 2:5-8:
Have this mind among yourselves, which you have in Christ Jesus, who though he was in the form of God, did not count equality with God a thing to be grasped, but emptied himself, taking the form of a servant, being born in the likeness of men. And being found in human form he humbled himself and became obedient unto death, even death on a cross.

We are constantly called into God's presence and with loving attention: we are asked freely and willingly to do what He says. This is free obedience.

Verse two of Whittier's hymn, "Dear Lord and Father of Mankind," beautifully describes such obedience:

In simple trust like theirs who heard,
Beside the Syrian sea,
The gracious calling of the Lord,
Let us like them, without a word
Rise up and follow thee.

Again we are all called to empty ourselves of self, pour out our lives in service to others and obey God regardless of cost, even unto death. Jesus not only paid the price for us, His inward voice and power enable us to do likewise. Such is the nature of free obedience.

Fruits of Obedience

There are at least four qualities of or fruits of free obedience which we will now examine. They are humility, purity of heart, covenanting together and taking the form of a servant.

I define humility as seeing God in all events and having such a complete awareness of God that we lose all consciousness of self. Psalm 34 expresses it, "I will bless the Lord at all times; his praise shall continually be in my mouth." Nothing can happen in the life of a humble person in which they do not see the hand of God either in blessing or correction. I once took a class to visit a Trappist monastery. We were told of a choir monk whose byword was *"Dominus est!"* "It is the Lord!" No matter what happened to him, good or bad, beautiful or tragic he always responded *"Dominus est!"* After thirty years of silence and serving as a novice master in that Iowa monastery, the brother received a letter from the Minister General of the order asking him to go to Indonesia to be a novice master of a new monastery being founded there. His response was *"Dominus est!"* "It is the Lord!" And he was ready to go. Seeing the Lord in all events, blessing Him at all times, this constitutes true humility.

There are many types of false humility, most of them forms of inverted pride. I will list a few types. There is the "Uriah Heep type," proudly confessing the lowliness of one's position. There is the "door-mat type," which expects, even enjoys, being run over by everybody. There is the "co-dependent type" in which a person depends totally on others to define and defend his or her personhood. There is also the "I resign because I can't make a difference type." Each of these illustrates a Thomas Kelly dictum. "Oh, how slick and weasel-like is self pride."[12]

But humility has great strength. Seeing nothing of self but the power of God in all events, we are not affected by what other people or the polls may say. With the clear discernment born of a life of prayer we are emboldened to stand for Truth no matter what. Humble prophets of God join with Paul in shouting, "The weapons of our warfare are not worldly but have divine power to destroy strongholds." (2 Cor. 10:4).

Paradoxically humility involves a kind of pride as well as self-effacement. Dag Hammarskjöld, in his book, *Markings*, describes this paradox. He says:

Except in faith, nobody is humble. The mask of weakness or of Phariseeism is not the naked face of humility. And, except in faith, nobody is proud. The vanity displayed in all its varieties by the spiritually immature is not pride. To be, in faith, both humble and proud: that is, to live, to know that in God I am nothing, but that God is in me.[13]

---

12. *Ibid.*, p. 62.
13. Dag Hammarskjöld, *Markings* (New York: Knopf, 1964), p. 92.

The other half of humility, to which Hammarskjöld points is confidence in the power of God to carry out His purposes. In Psalm 37:5 we read, "Commit your way to the Lord; trust in him, and he will act." Such trust breeds great confidence that the power of God will conquer all evil. So the humble take pride in the power of God aware that they can do nothing without Him. In the process we become meek, God-blinded, humble.

Jean Nicholas Grou in his *Manual for Interior Souls*, expresses this paradox:

> By resigning ourselves entirely to God and leaving all our interests in His hands, we can *give* ourselves. And when this gift is made entirely and irrevocably…He will give us…that perfect humility which is so deep, so generous, so peaceful, so unchanging, which on the one hand makes us, as sinners, less than nothing, and on the other hand, raises us above the world, above the devil, above ourselves, and makes us great with the greatness of God. This humility is an infused humility; it grows in proportion to our temptations, our sufferings, and our humiliations. We have it, but we do not know that we have it… .[14]

Another characteristic of humility is a remarkable buoyancy and resilience. Since we no longer feel vulnerable or insecure we bounce back quickly from failure, insult, humiliation and even persecution. Insults roll off the person who has crucified self like balls of water bouncing off a hot griddle. Jesus' most difficult yet most glorious beatitude says it, "Blessed are you when men revile you and persecute you and utter all kinds of evil against you falsely on my account. Rejoice and be glad for your reward is great in heaven." (Matt. 5:11-12). I find it really difficult to act out this beatitude. Do you? Yet each time we find the grace to forgive an insult, love an enemy or see humiliation as God's gift, the miracle of exceeding joy occurs.

A further characteristic of humble persons is their childlike simplicity. Old corroded persons, set in their way like you and me are the ones Jesus had in mind when he said, "Verily I say unto you, Whosoever shall not receive the kingdom of God as a little child, he shall not enter therein." (Mk. 10:15 KJV). Such persons wear no masks of self-deception. Authentic and simple trust in God shines through every attitude and deed. Without words humble persons radiate the presence of God. We can see at a glance the fulfillment in their lives of Psalm 34:5, "Look to him, and be radiant!"

Perhaps the most delightful characteristic of humility is its ability to laugh. Humility is slightly crazy. You hunger for it. You long for it. But it's like chasing a frog. You sneak up on it and pounce, and it's gone. It's even more like chasing a loon. The loon dives and you paddle your canoe madly in the direction you think he's going to come up, and pop! He comes up sev-

---

14. Jean Nicholas Grou, *Manual for Interior Souls* (London: Burns & Oates, 1955), p. 141.

enty feet away in a direction you never dreamed of. Maybe that's why loons laugh! Humility is like that, elusive. The moment you think you've achieved it you find you have come up with pride instead. Or humility can turn on you, when you intentionally pursue it and say, "Now look, didn't you make a fool of yourself?" But that's the way it is with anything that is alive. The closer you come to its essence or the center of its life the harder it is to define precisely what you have found. A person who is blind to all else but the living word and power of God is vibrantly alive, like an artesian well pouring forth an endless supply of life-giving water.

Before he committed himself to a life of voluntary poverty and free obedience to God, St. Francis of Assisi was known as a great practical joker and a lover of laughter. He carried over this same spirit into his new life in God. There is something insecure or even sick about over-serious commitment to any cause. One gets too much involved in the success of the venture to risk ridicule. The ability you then lack most is the ability to hang loose and laugh at yourself. The humble person is saved by humor. Life is such fun, and we are its fools. The Lord would have us enjoy it as fools for His sake!

Thomas Kelly expresses the spirit of such laughter in this unforgettable passage: "I'd rather be a jolly St. Francis hymning his canticle to the sun than a dour old sobersides Quaker whose diet would appear to have been spiritual persimmons." Like Thomas Kelly in his own life we should learn to laugh at ourselves and our foibles "with the rich hearty abandon of the wind on the open prairie."[15]

The next major quality of free obedience we need to consider is purity of heart. This means a hunger for freedom from sin, a hunger and thirst for righteousness, a longing for purity of intention, the power to obey, clear guidance, and assurance that the good we attempt to do will bear fruit.

The moral degradation of the people of our world and their psychopathic addiction to violence, inter-tribal genocide and a host of other sins beggars description. Appropriate to our situation is the lament of Jeremiah:

> Be appalled, O heavens, at this, be shocked, be utterly desolate, says the Lord, for my people have committed two evils: they have forsaken me, the fountain of living waters, and hewed out cisterns for themselves, broken cisterns, that can hold no water (2:12-13).

Facing the enormity of our own sin and our inescapable responsibility for the sins in our own nation and in the world, persons committed to hear and obey God in all events, hunger to be pure as He is pure with all the energy of their souls. Thomas Kelly expresses this burning hunger:

---

15. Thomas R. Kelly, *Testament, op. cit.* p. 97 & E.M. Root describing Kelly's laugh, *ibid.*, p. 7.

> One burns for complete innocency and holiness of personal life. No man
> can look on God and live, live in his own faults, live in the shadow of the
> least self-deceit, live in harm toward his least creatures.... The blinding
> purity of God in Christ, how captivating, how alluring, how compelling it
> is! The pure in heart shall see God? More, they who see God shall cry out
> to become pure in heart, even as He is pure, with all the energy of their
> souls.[16]

Such purity and righteousness is not achieved in our own strength even
though we must "work out our own salvation with fear and trembling."
(Phil. 2:12). Purity of heart means to will one thing, God's will above our
own. We read in both Leviticus and in First Peter God's command, "Be ye
holy as I the Lord your God am holy." Before we cringe at our inability to
heed this command we hear another word from Leviticus chapter 22. It
promises, "I will be hallowed among the people of Israel; I am the Lord who
hallows you..." (22:32). The rest of the Philippians passage quoted above
fulfills the same promise, "For God is at work in you, both to will and to
work for his good pleasure." (Phil. 2:13). God intends for us, fallen creatures that we are, the gift of holiness and innocency of life.

Purity of heart is another way of expressing those difficult words of
Jesus with which he concludes the commandment that we are to love enemies, namely, "You therefore must be perfect, as your heavenly Father is
perfect." (Matt. 5:48). In the light of the fallible, fallen sin-filled performance of human beings and the fact that Jesus "knew what was in man,"
how could He call us to perfection? "Come on, Jesus, be reasonable!" Isn't
that our reaction to His challenge to us to be perfect?

A major reason we have a problem with perfection, I believe, is because
of our mechanical, abstract concept of perfection. We think of perfection as
one hundred percent absolute, static purity to which nothing can be added
and to which no further development is possible. In science and mechanics
such abstract goals are logical and serve as goals to work toward but
mechanical, electronic or scientific perfection is unattainable.

But human beings are no mere mechanisms. We are organisms with
clear limitations. We are divinely created, divinely purposed, Spirit-inhab-
ited organisms. Reborn persons are really something to get excited about,
even if they cannot achieve mechanical perfection. Such abstract perfection
was never God's intent for us anyway. An organic, growing spiritual kind of
human perfection or purity of heart is made possible through the gift of
God's grace by which He hallows us His human creatures. When the Lord
hallows us He instills in us both a standard of purity and righteousness
toward which we strive and grants us the grace to live in that condition of
free obedience. George Fox got very hot under the collar toward those who

---

16. *Ibid.*, pp. 65-66.

"roared it up for the power of sin in this life." He firmly believed that it was the work of Christ to restore us as humans to the image of God we possessed in the Garden of Eden before the Fall. Here's how he expressed it:

> But now Christ was come to redeem, translate, convert, and regenerate man...up into the light, life, and image, and likeness of God again as man and woman were in before they fell. ...And Christ saith, "Be ye perfect even as my heavenly father is perfect," for he who was perfect comes to make man and woman perfect again and bring them again to the state God made them in; so he is the maker up of the breach and peace betwixt God and man. ...But I told them Christ was come freely, who hath perfected forever by one offering all them that are sanctified, and renews them up in the image of God.... And this, Christ the heavenly man has done freely. And therefore all are to look unto him, and all that have received him are to walk in him, the life, the substance, the first and the last, the rock of ages and the foundation of many generations.[17]

Dynamic perfection or purity of heart springs from purity of intention. In the words of James Nayler, "As it bears no evil in itself, so it conceives none in thoughts to any other." Purity of intention is characterized by growth. Because it is not mechanical, purity of intention is something we learn by experience and grow up into. We grow by practice, by long agonizing experience. We try, we fail, we try again until we develop a skill. Like Brother Lawrence if we fail we spend no time in self-recrimination but breathe a simple prayer, "This is what I am except thou aid me," and get with the task of freely obeying Him. Jean Nicholas Grou states that "Purity of intention is having God alone as our object free from all self-interest."[18]

Purity of intention results in pure love for God, love for His children and an everlasting love unfeigned. Without deceit or dissimulation the love of God flows through us and we accept and love other persons as God loves them with no "ifs," "ands" or "buts." We no longer love others for the love we will receive in return. We love for love alone out of the inexpressible gratitude we have to God who first loved us and gave Himself for us.

Purity of heart also instills in us the power to obey. The atoning death of our Lord Jesus did not just *impute* righteousness to humanity; it *imparted* righteousness to us. The same Power which raised Jesus from the dead raises us from enslaved disobedience into active free obedience and to keeping of His commandments. Again George Fox has a wonderful word about this:

---

17. George Fox. *Journal*, J.L. Nickalls ed. (Cambridge University Press), 1952. pp. 367-368.

18. J. N. Grou, *Spiritual Maxims* (Springfield, IL: Templegate Press, 1961). #7, p. 78.

And God is equal and righteous, and commands nothing but what is equal and just, and measurable, and reasonable, according to that which men may perform; and such as he gives the law to, he gives power...and ability...and they were then to love God with their strength, and their souls, and their neighbors as themselves.[19]

In another place George Fox celebrates the sense of fulfillment we experience as we seek to live in purity of heart and to be perfect as Jesus called us to be. George says:

And the Ministry of Christ is for the perfecting of the Saints, till that all come to the measure of the stature of the fullness of Christ, to a perfect man...praises to the Lord forever, who hath sent forth his son in the likeness of sinful flesh, to condemn sin in the flesh, that in him we might be made the righteousness of God.[20]

Out of free individual obedience, humility and purity of heart grows group commitment or covenanting together. There is serious doubt whether isolated individuals can sustain free obedience without group support. Commitment together means joining the family of Christ, living in blessed community, a mutual experience of confession, worship, disciplines, a radical caring for one another and a going forth to witness and serve. In such a fellowship we share the astonishment of early Friend Francis Howgill, when he said:

The Kingdom of Heaven did gather us and catch us all, as in a net, and his heavenly power at one time drew many hundreds to land. We came to know a place to stand in and what to wait in; and the Lord appeared daily to us, to our astonishment, amazement and great admiration, insomuch that we often said to one another with great joy of heart: "What, is the Kingdom of God come to be with men? And will he take up his tabernacle among the sons of men, as he did of old? ..."[21]

At Sinai God having brought Israel out of Egypt pledged to be their God, to love them, to dwell with and guide them and be faithful to them forever. The people responded, "The Lord our God we will serve, and his voice we will obey." (Josh. 24:24). Such was the love covenant between them.

In the New Testament God expresses his covenant through the spiritual Israel, a household of God which brings into being a new humanity. It is a

---

19. George Fox, *The Great Mystery & Collected Works*. Vol. III (Philadelphia & New York M.T.G. Groul, 1831), p. 538. "In answer to Henry Foreside."

20. George Fox. *A Paper Sent Forth into the World & C.* (London: G. Calvert, 1652), p. 7.

21. Francis Howgill, in *Christian Faith & Practice in the Experience of the Society of Friends* (London: London Yearly Meeting), 1960. 15 chapters, 677 selections.

spiritual kingdom of priests promised in Exodus 19:6 and realized in the radical caring fellowship of the New Testament church. The nature of this covenant group is powerfully expressed in two Scripture passages. In the first one Peter calls us to be built into:

> A spiritual house...a holy priesthood, to offer spiritual sacrifices acceptable to God through Jesus Christ...a chosen race, a royal priesthood, a holy nation, God's own people, that you may declare the wonderful deeds of him who called you out of darkness into his marvelous light (I Pet. 2:5, 9).

In Colossians Paul describes the quality of life in the covenant fellowship:

> Put on then, as God's chosen ones, holy and beloved, compassion, kindness, lowliness, meekness and patience, forbearing one another and, if one has a complaint against another, forgiving each other as the Lord has forgiven you, so you also must forgive. And above all these put on love which binds everything together in perfect harmony. And let the peace of Christ rule in your hearts, to which indeed you were called in the one body. And be thankful. Let the word of Christ dwell in you richly, as you teach and admonish one another in all wisdom, and as you sing psalms and hymns and spiritual songs with thankfulness in your hearts to God. And whatever you do, in word or deed, do everything in the name of the Lord Jesus, giving thanks to God the Father through him.

Our covenanting together results in radical caring, creative worship, mutual discipline and leads us out in witness and service.

Free obedience issues in humility, purity of heart, commitment to one another and service. Service is closely connected to humility. The one who sees God in all the events of life will live not to serve oneself but others. That quality of humility which causes us to become instruments of purpose larger than ourselves, in which we lose all consciousness of self, is the chief source of our service to God and our fellow human beings.

Covenanting together in community also results in service. Jesus sent out both twelve and seventy to witness and to serve. They preached the immediate coming of the Kingdom of God; they challenged people to enter it. They healed the sick and cast out evil spirits. They returned to Jesus jubilant. Jesus exulted that he saw the power of Satan failing as a result of their witness and service. (Lk. 10:1-12, 17-20)

We have previously examined the great self-emptying Scripture Philippians 2:5-11 to show Jesus' humility. We now stress that it also emphasizes his taking on the form of a *servant*. His chief act of service was becoming obedient unto death on the cross, but he also met personal needs in dozens of other ways. In Mark 10:43-45 he tells us: "Whoever would be great among you must be your servant and whoever would be first among you must be the slave of all. For the Son of man came not to be served but to serve, and to give his life as a ransom for many." What should this mean for us? It means that we must become the willing slaves of all and to serve with no thought of reward as he served. In the Gospel of John Jesus' final great sign, demonstrating who he is, is his washing his disciples' feet. He concludes the event by saying, "If I then, your Lord and Teacher, have washed your feet, you also ought to wash one another's feet." (Jn. 13:14). Jesus' humble action calls us to wash the feet of all humankind even as he has done.

In addition Jesus' whole life acted out the role of the suffering servant of mankind prefigured by the prophet Isaiah. In I Peter we find the clearest command that we should follow Jesus' steps into this kind of service.

> For to this you have been called, because Christ also suffered for you, leaving you an example, that you should follow in his steps. He committed no sin; no guile was found on his lips. When he was reviled, he did not revile in return; when he suffered, he did not threaten; but trusted to him who judges justly. He himself bore our sins in his body on the tree, that we might die to sin and live to righteousness. By his wounds you have been healed (I Pet. 2:21-24).

In the light of these Scriptures real service can mean many things. It means we must suffer on behalf of others. It means we must follow in Jesus' steps, always seeking to act with redemptive love. Conscious of his forgiveness for our wrongdoing, we must seek in some measure to bear the sins and violence of others thereby through grace of our Lord bringing the hostility to an end.

Like the twelve and the seventy whom Jesus sent out, service means in the first place preaching the good news that God has begun the fulfillment of his promise that the reign and rule of God has begun. Calling for repentance we minister to the deep spiritual hunger of all. We are also called to heal the sick, feed the hungry, give drink to the thirsty, clothe the naked, offer hospitality to the homeless and visit the widows and fatherless in their need—these commands of our Lord reflecting the true fast called for in Isaiah 58, fill out the picture of what it means to serve.

Living to serve others and not ourselves also means faithfulness to the Christian peace testimony, the practice of nonviolent resistance to evil. It is inconceivable that the humble servant of Christ who seeks to freely obey him in all things, who has found purity of heart and who asks for no right save to serve the needs of others should sanction or participate in war or violence in any form.

For example, in 1536 four survivors of a Spanish expedition to Florida arrived on foot in Mexico after eight years of travel, during which time these former soldiers had become faith healers of the diseases of the hundreds of Indian tribes they had passed through on their way. The first signs of white men they came across were burned and empty Indian villages destroyed by Spanish slave catchers. The first group of Spaniards they encountered were such slavers. The slavers wanted, of course, to enslave the Indians who had accompanied the Florida survivors. Alvar Nuñez, one of the survivors, relates the incident:

> They had their interpreters make a fine speech. He told our Indians that we were as a matter of fact Christians too, but had gone astray for a long while, and were people of no luck and little heart. But the Christians on horseback were real Christians, and the lords of the land to be obeyed and served. Our Indians considered this point of view. They answered that the real Christians apparently lied, that we could not possibly be Christians. For we appeared out of the sunrise, they out of the sunset; we cured the sick, while they killed even the healthy; we went naked and barefoot, while they wore clothes, and rode on horseback and stuck people with lances; we asked for nothing and gave away all we were given, while they never gave anybody anything and had no other aim than to steal.[22]

Rarely does the contrast between the nature of the true servant of Christ and the nominal Christian hypocrite get so sharply defined.

A humility which is self-effacing and yet exhibits assurance and boldness derived from the greatness of the One who involves us in His tasks; a purity of heart which is not only aware of the filth of humanity, but also hungers and thirsts for righteousness and finds, through grace, that a life of dynamic and free obedience is possible here and now; a commitment together in voluntary covenant with people of God who care radically for one another and witness gladly to others; plus the deep desire not to be served but to serve, meeting the spiritual and physical needs of others by methods consistent with the spirit and example of the one who came to wash the feet of all humanity—these are the fruits of free obedience.

Free obedience, then, means hearing God's voice, doing what God says and doing God's will before our own. Set free from bondage, we commit ourselves to liberating others. Within the limitless love of God's bountiful care we learn that doing the Truth makes us free. With inner discipline we learn to stand fast for Truth. Prompted by Christ, our Teacher within, and in process of being perfected toward our full potential as children of God, we exhibit the fruits of free obedience.

Put succinctly, obedience means to hear, to heed and to act upon the instruction of true authority. To do so voluntarily, from inner constraint and without coercion is free obedience. As we practice it we thankfully confess, "Thy obedience is perfect freedom!"

---

22. Haniel Long, Tr., *Interlinear to Cabeza de Vaca* (Santa Fe: Writer's Editions, 1939), pp. 35-36.

Christ Is Still the Answer

DEAN FREIDAY

Perhaps one of the most significant developments among American Friends during this last century was the 1970 St. Louis Conference. Uniquely among Quaker conferences, "official" delegates were appointed by all the yearly meetings of Friends in the U. S. and Canada. The appointees of two yearly meetings were unable to attend for health or other last-minute emergencies, but no yearly meeting boycotted the Conference. In accordance with Friends' principles, the group could not legislate, but position papers were presented for FUM, FGC, and (the then) EFA.

A highlight of that gathering was the address given by Everett L. Cattell[1] on behalf of Evangelical Friends and calling for Quaker unity under the lordship of Jesus Christ. For many who were present this address had a lasting impact. In a sense a 1986 article by Arthur O. Roberts was a suggestion of the possible ways in which Cattell's proposals might be implemented.[2]

At St. Louis cordial dialogue occurred across what had previously been barriers. So much common ground was expressed that a Faith & Life Movement was established, along with a Faith & Life Panel to look at significant theological issues. The Panel did much by correspondence and met regularly once a year for ten years. A series of regional conferences was held

---

1. "A New Approach for Friends," pp. 32-44 in *What Future for Friends? Report of the St. Louis Conference: A Gathering of Concerned Friends.* October 5-7, 1970, published at the request of the Conference (Philadelphia, Friends World Committee for Consultation [the then "American Section"], [1971]) vi + 58 pages.

2. "Paths Toward a Quaker Future" *Friends Journal* (March 1, 1987). The article also appeared in *Quaker Life* and *Evangelical Friend* Further page citations are from the *Friends Journal* edition.

under the Movement in the interest of involving Friends on the meeting benches and not just their "leadership," pastoral or otherwise.

Yet, in spite of genuine enthusiasm for closer relations between the Quaker varieties and much conferencing and particularly discussion of the Roberts article,[3] no structural changes appear to have resulted. This is especially unfortunate in view of the condition of the world, the role that Quakers working together might have, and the possible input, from the reconsideration by all varieties of Quakers, of the essence of early Quakerism. Cattell's thesis and Roberts' proposals deserve renewed consideration.

In this paper we will take a look at our "World," particularly the North American portion, the place of Quakers in it, and the proposals made by these two authors. A quarter of a century after St. Louis several questions remain:

Where were Friends then in relation to each other?

What was their situation in relation to the cultural context?

Where did we go from there, and where are we today?

Did we take Everett Cattell's advice, and what has happened in relation to Arthur Roberts' "paths?"

I. Friends in Relation to Each Other

One of the remarkable things about St. Louis was that while the "call" had dared to address only "the Friends Church," it was heeded by the unprogrammed as well as programmed Friends. The proposal was to seek "under the guidance of the Holy Spirit...a workable, challenging, and cooperative means whereby the Friends Church can be an active, enthusiastic, Christ-centered, and Spirit-directed force in this day of revolution."[4]

Everett Cattell, the keynote speaker for the Evangelical Friends, stressed that the central reality that we needed to face was the Lordship of Christ, being "measured by nothing less than the full stature of Christ" (Eph 4:13 NEB):

> This Lordship of Christ is a great center for illumination. This is the inner light we seek. The light at one and the same time illuminates the loving and forgiving heart of the God who is the Father of our Lord Jesus Christ, and as well the corruption and evil of our own hearts, of men [and women] around us, and of the whole kingdom of this world in which we live and in which we feel so much at home until we see Jesus. ...
>
> All of us are creatures of our cultures far more than we realize and liberation into the Kingdom of God is extremely difficult.[5]

---

3. *Ibid.*
4. From the Introduction, p. v of the St. Louis Report (cited in fn 1).
5. *What Future...* , p. 41.

In the 26 years since then it has gotten even more difficult. We were aware then of a neo-paganism that flourished for a time and still has some echoes. The real "flash in the pan," however, whose very title assured it a widespread journalistic hearing, was the "death of God theology." It lasted barely a decade. By 1970 it was already being succeeded by other forms of "secular theology" or antitheology. New Ageism, which has been troublesome for some current Quaker groups (as well as mainstream churches) had not yet arrived.

Yet in spite of these and other attacks on belief, and although most traditional denominations continue to be in a sorry state of declining membership, shrinking attendance, and financial difficulties there is a widespread hunger for guidance beyond the human. It is still embryonic and has yet to penetrate in any depth either church structures or the structures of society. But some ideas, such as "character," as it involves truthfulness and integrity, are making some comeback. While it is obvious that "the whole picture" involves a large number of interacting factors, it is very difficult to analyze them and to come to grips with them.

II. Our Cultural Context

In struggling with the broad picture of our present world and its religious significance, Dr. Susan E. Davies, a United Church of Christ theologian has said:

> The rules our predecessors knew, the ways of common life we inherited, which made sense as recently as ten years ago, have fallen away.... We are left to discover the new duties these new occasions demand.
>
> We are living through a cultural paradigm shift so vast we cannot yet grasp it.... More people are refugees and homeless than at any other time in the 20th century. Massive human tragedy co-exists with...the wonder of an increasingly non-racial South Africa.
>
> The worlds we have known both within and outside the church...are altering before our very eyes, engendering complex responses of frustration, exhaustion, deeply rooted rage...[but also] a persistent determined hope. [Yet] "all our theological buckets leak," as Luther Smith of Candler School of Theology has said.
>
> The time has come for us to confess that none of us in the broader Christian community carries the fullness of God's vision and purpose for the world. None of us, no matter how ancient or new, no matter how well-established or crumbling or surging on the wings of the Spirit; none of us alone embodies fully the presence and purpose of Christ's people on earth. All of us have a partial testimony. We are merely the branches on the vine, not the vine itself.... We have all been grafted into God's purposes, and our particular fruits...are gifts of God for the world, and not for our own continuation.[6]

If this appraisal fits the huge mainstream constituencies, how much more it applies to our 300,000 members, divided four ways in terms of doctrine, and attempting to bring Witness to countries all over the world!

No one needs to be told that the U.S., in particular, needs restoration of community-agreed-upon ethical principles. A survey on values by—believe it or not—that "patron saint" of the Elderly, the American Association of Retired Persons subheaded its "Feedback" on that survey:[7] "America is headed straight to hell, figuratively and literally, unless it changes course soon." And "not one person disputed the premise that American society is decaying." Those surveyed suggested that individuals need "to take a stand for the basic virtues...like integrity, responsibility and selflessness...that have been out of fashion." The article concluded "society's salvation may well rest on each individual's willingness to exert a positive influence on others..."

One person, who by no means denies the foundational role of faith on religious values, Stephen R. Covey, has translated the Gospel into secular terms. He speaks of seven personal habits that are not the keys to "success" or "wealth," but which characterize "highly effective people," people who influence other people toward restoration of community and ethical values. Without being gimmicky, Covey avoids religious terminology altogether. The Golden Rule and other Christian precepts become roughly: if you wish to be understood, begin by trying to understand the other person. This and the other six "habits" that he enunciates have successfully turned specific corporate structures from competition to cooperation and mutual responsibility. And community life in Columbus, Ohio, has been revitalized.[8]

Much thought that is both realistic and creative is being heard on public television. "Peggy Noonan on Values" was a series of one-on-one interviews. It had very constructive comments on the role of religion. Noonan herself stated that "politicians can't really get to our deepest problems, which are largely spiritual ones." Here, the richness of the discussion by a professor of social philosophy; a "left-wing-intellectual-devout Christian-single mother-artist" and others, can only be randomly sampled.

Bill Moyers, of Baptist background, pointed out that religion must have a part in the civil debate because it is "a source of values and ideas...the means by which we try to make sense" of the world and "form our lives in the midst of chaos." Fr. John Neuhaus corroborated. One of the clearest

---

6. In a sermon, "The Shapes We Take While We Wait," delivered at the Minneapolis meeting of NCCC-USA Faith & Order, March 18,1995, here in abridged form and used with the author's permission.

7. *Modern Maturity* (Nov-Dec. 1995):12-14.

8. Stephen R. Covey. *Seven Habits of Highly Effective People: Restoring the Character Ethic* (New York: Simon & Schuster, 1989). Covey, a Mormon, makes no effort to hide the Christian derivative of his "habits."

analyses on this point was by Michael Lerner, editor of "the liberal Jewish magazine *Tikkun*," who said: "We have gone overboard in arguing for separation of church and state." We've said "that the whole area of values, the whole area of spiritual sensitivity and commitment can't even be discussed in the public arena." And people are under "a cloud of suspicion if they so much as suggest that their ideas...stem from a religious commitment."[9]

These secular approaches and analyses by no means detract from the focus on Christ as still the answer for Quakers. They are supplemental attempts to bridge the gap between market-economy, and media and other detracting cultural factors. They represent some small beginnings at efforts to restore a national ethical synthesis, reclaim the victims of the drug culture (largely children) and instill some agreed-upon "values." We will have to ignore the political distortion that the word *values* has taken until a better generalizing word comes along. But whatever the distortions, religion in general, Christianity in America, and Quakers in particular have to "mind the store," while others distort the debate by substituting overemphasized individual "rights," or false values.

Other clues as to what is happening have come from widely different sources, and they pertain to both the childhood and adult portions of the age spectrum. A non-Quaker visitor to our meeting at Manasquan (NJ) was prompted by the Spirit of Christ to speak of North America as having become an "adolescent culture." Many adults are reluctant to accept responsibility or to be accountable to anybody or anything, she said. Individual rights, too, have triumphed over the give and take that make for genuine community and which require consideration of the common good as well as individual interests.

For these *adolescent adults* marriage, if an option at all, is merely a substitute for long-term living-together. Any offspring who result are a by-product rather than being regarded as the central purpose of such relations. To say that is not to deny the genuine love of many a single-parent who struggles against almost overwhelming economic and societal odds to provide as normal a parenthood for their children as possible.

Nevertheless, the tendency is for marriages to fall apart under the slightest stress or hardship. Multi-generational families are becoming rarer

---

9. The Noonan interviews were in a three-part series aired on Public Television (in NJ on WNET-13 February 10, 17, 24, 1995). In them also Stanley Crouch warned that the problems affecting the black community, whether it is family breakdown, drugs, or teenage pregnancy "tends to be the metaphor for the national future" and eventually becomes everyone's problem. Another Afro-American, Shelby Steele, warned that in casting everything in terms of rights, whether ethnic, feminist, or whatever, tends to "Balkanize our society rather than integrate it." Daniel Patrick Moynihan, a New York Senator who grew up on Manhattan's West Side, raised the question whether "all abuses of freedom [may] make Americans impatient with freedom itself." Ironically, we are producing a society divided along class lines, "with a dependent population and a population resentful of the dependent population."

and rarer. "Traditional families" of father, mother, and children had shrunk to 40 percent in England in 1992.[10] In the U.S. it had slipped even further. For 1990 such families constituted only 19 percent of all households.

This lack of family structure does away with a major part of the protected environment in which children can gradually learn to cope with the realities which face them. Concomitantly "the age of childhood...characterized by innocence, play and learning has shrunk to a span of only a few years. From halfway through the years of primary school the young person today enters the phase of the *adult-child*."[11]

Some of the specific causes for these changes which surround the adult-child and which bring on this "early adulthood" are spelled out in a consultative report on children and the churches, already cited, and which has been published by the Council of Churches in Britain and Ireland (CCBI).

Television, the CCBI report points out, has been not only a "key instrument in bringing about the erosion of childhood," but it represents a return to the supremacy of "image" over "word." In the Medieval era, in particular, church-buildings were not only centers for hearing, but they constituted great storybooks in stone, mosaic, and stained glass. They conveyed pictorially the Gospel and its biblical antecedents, as well as heroic exemplars of the faith, to congregants who for the most part could not read.

With Gutenberg, the printed word became supreme, and thinking was expressed in verbal propositions or theses. The entire thrust of learning shifted toward reduction of illiteracy and the accumulation of knowledge. Thought was transmitted from generation to generation via the printed word.

We still have not come to grips with the electronic revolution and all of the implications of the return to image supremacy—in a different and all-pervasive way. "Learning" in its broadest connotation no longer consists of occasionally viewing a few pictures in a church building, as in the earlier period of image supremacy, but of being barraged almost endlessly by a flood of images. The consequences cannot be overestimated. The pity is that in spite of the potential of the image for enlarging horizons, by and large the trend is toward "superficiality and trivialization. The quick fix of the sound bite, with its simplistic message, is a perverse influence in society." And with the accompanying "decline in literacy may come a decline in the capacity for reasoning."[12]

---

10. *Unfinished Business: Children and the Churches*, third in a series of studies by the Consultative Group on Ministry Among Children of the Council of Churches of Britain and Ireland (CCBI). It was published in 1994 or 1995 (London: CCBI Publications), viii + 80 pages, here §1.7, p. 7. Janet Scott, Head of Religious Studies Department, Homerton College, Cambridge, was the Quaker member of the CGMC.

11. CGMC, *op. cit.* §1.1, p. 4.

12. *Ibid.*, §1.3, p. 5.

Then, too, playtime provided the child with an opportunity to make "sense of the world in that necessary mingling of fantasy and reality which constitutes play. While the media are also able to mix fantasy and reality, for them it is coupled with the power to manipulate, and viewing is passive and tends to be solitary."

"The impact of the immediate and the simplistic and the view that if you see something, then that is how it must be, create a dangerous kind of fantasy world." And where "computer games channel the child's imagination in particular ways...[and] encourage violence, they are a cause for concern." While the CCBI Report's comment that "The churches must promote a different lifestyle and challenge these values" is addressed to the area of "commercialism, consumerism, and market forces,"[13] it could equally well be applied to almost all of our secular surroundings.

A primary concern must be for children, who by themselves are powerless and yet are "on the front-line" so to speak in the battle against a culture which is inimical to their well-being:

> In response to the implications of the incarnation of Jesus Christ, the churches have an unavoidable duty to attempt to be in touch with the experiences and lives of children today. Primarily, the churches must set an example of listening to children, their hopes and their fears. There are dangers everywhere for children: child abuse (within and outside the family), environmental hazards and accidents, and street crime. The churches must recognize that children are vulnerable and in need of protection, and must speak out and act on their behalf.[14]

This is not just a call for social activism:

> Whilst attempting to be a Christian conscience within society, the churches must also reclaim the numinous, and witness to the presence and power of God. Implicit in this is the challenge to the Church to recognize how children learn, and how they learn about God. In a world of many different beliefs it is important that children are given the opportunity to explore belief in God for themselves and what it means for them.[15]

It should be the mission of all churches and all Friends not only to evangelize in general, but to develop a particular form of evangelism adapted to children. For Friends, who have always emphasized a relational ecclesiology, the opening sentence of the Evangelism and Children section of the CCBI report is directly pertinent:

---

13. *Ibid.*, §2.3, p. 15.
14. *Ibid.*, §2.2, p. 15.
15. *Ibid.*, §2.5, p. 15.

Faith in the God who is revealed in Jesus Christ through the Holy Spirit is expressed in personal relationship with God and with others.[16]

We need to emphasize *and practice* "such a vision of life, faith and the world as will fascinate children enough to win their allegiance to Christ" and enable them to both learn about faith and to "participate freely in it." Children should, "at least in part, discover the Gospel for themselves through experiences and encounters rather than" simply verbally.[17] Friends have better than a passing score for involving children and giving them a sense of ownership in their meetings and churches, but are we doing as well in getting across the specific thrusts of Quaker beliefs?

III. Returning to Friends

It isn't enough to sketch some parameters for evangelization and action for the whole Christian Church. What is our particular role, and are we making progress in doing some things together? We need to look again at Everett Cattell's St. Louis advice for Friends, and also ponder the paths toward a Quaker future outlined by Arthur O. Roberts. We need also to review the significance of the Faith & Life Movement and the Faith & Life Panel which were set up following St. Louis. Were they merely passing phenomena, or did they evoke unrealized implications which are still relevant if we are to move closer together?

Everett Cattell characterized what we had been trying to do prior to St. Louis as a *synthetic approach* composed of certain organizational steps. FGC was organized in 1900-1902 "around special concerns" rather than constituting a uniting of Yearly Meetings. FUM (then Five Years Meeting) had hoped to become more of "a legislative body with binding powers," than it became and FUM remains "in reality a federation because of the heterogeneity of its elements."[18] Cattell asked if "the basis of our efforts had not been too synthetic, too artificial, too much putting together of things which do not belong together in any natural sense."[19]

He uses the word "realignment" seven times, but not in the sense of redividing as it has been used more recently. Everett Cattell suggested that it could mean a "setting for a *symbiotic* approach...a new way of living side by side but preserving our differences with greater integrity than at present." He continues:

But could it be that a still better thing could happen? That we all bow low before our common Lord and Saviour Jesus Christ. That we acknowledge

---

16. *Ibid.*, §2.29, p. 23.
17. *Ibid.*, ¶2.32, (ii), p. 25.
18. *What Future...* , p. 33.
19. *What Future...* , p. 34.

him openly and unapologetically.... That we then take the time and the patience to work out from the center, under the guidance of the Holy Spirit, and with truly and utterly humbled and surrendered hearts, the meaning of that Lordship, in *a new system* of bringing men [and women] to Christ, a new system of cleansing our hearts and the whole circle of our personalities, a new system of lifestyle demanded by Christ in a pagan culture full of injustice and evil and exploitation, and a new system of labor to bring elements of society in line with the Kingdom of God, without losing hope when rebuffed, and assured by the faith that the King himself will complete His Kingdom in his own day.[20]

Elsewhere he states specifically[21] that he was appealing "to all Quakers... [those at St. Louis, at least] to make a fresh systems approach to the revival of primitive Quakerism." He goes on to say that honesty requires us to ask some hard questions of the "humanists or naturalists or syncretists or what have you" that are among us.

IV. A Few Queries for Quakers Individually and Corporately

[1] Are we on the "cutting edge" or "like a ship without a rudder"? For nearly 300 years Quakers have definitely been on the "cutting edge" of Christianity. Not only did they pioneer great reforms in the social structure—women's rights and abolition of slavery, just to name two areas out of a possible half dozen or more. They were also an *experiential reformation.* Barclay's Doctrine of Perfection was adopted bodily by John Wesley with only minor editing to update obsolete words or remove some excess verbiage. It is now regarded as the showpiece of *Methodist* doctrine!

We tend to be unaware of our direct or indirect spiritual descendants. Hannah Whitall Smith (1832-1911), a Philadelphia Quaker who joined the Plymouth Brethren, provided the Holiness Movement with its enduring classic, *The Christian's Secret of a Happy Life*, in 1875. Her collected works are still in print. The Apostolic Church developed out of the Holiness Movement, and out of that blossomed Pentecostalism. Perhaps these are "the great people to be gathered" envisioned by George Fox. There are now nearly 500 million Pentecostals and charismatics worldwide, and a recent Pentecostal merger in the U.S. created the largest single denomination in the U.S. with about 50 million members.

[2] In reference to reaching a hurting world with the love of Christ, are we "part of the solution or part of the problem"? The needs that have been outlined above are of colossal proportions, and only a few of them have been touched upon. Quakers of all varieties are at work in complementary ways. There is great zeal for evangelizing in terms that are well adapted to

20. *What Future...* , p. 44.
21. *What Future...* , p. 39.

particular mission fields coupled with readiness to adapt to new situations. Bolivia's altiplano, e.g., had been badly neglected or abandoned by all other Christians. Through coupling situation-improving with proclamation by Evangelical Friends, Bolivia has seen new life. Add to this kind of commitment that of other varieties of Friends with specialized areas of competence and if we work together on behalf of a common Lord, Quakers will definitely be "part of the solution."

In some regions, Friends of all varieties are again experiencing genuine "seeking," the kind that is a complement to "finding." Others seem committed to standing pat on a provincial understanding of Quakerism and belligerently undermining attempts to reformulate a genuine Quakerism for today's world.

[3] Are we prioritizing our central callings, rather than idolizing our particular strategies and structures? Ritualizing is not supposed to be part of Quakerism, but force of habit can cause us repeatedly to "just do something" because it has always been done that way. Are we simply being busy at make-work, a kind of treadmill activity? Or is it the business of our lives to implement the things that Jesus lived and died for?

[4] Are we first and foremost attending to the leadings of Christ, as opposed to "keeping up with the Joneses" out of some sort of spiritual insecurity? Do we adopt practices like Sacraments simply because the church down the street has them, or because some new members would like to bring them in? Actually we do a disservice to those who have high regard for Sacraments where we do so. Our witness is now regarded constructively by the wider church as a contribution to true sacramentality.

Are we adopting "church-growth techniques" merely because they have built Crystal Cathedrals or whopping-big drive-in congregations? Shouldn't we, instead, be proper stewards of the Truth we have received from the Lord?

[5] Are we picking up the gimmicks of lukewarm (Rev. 3:16) Protestantism—non-controversial preaching or messages; non-involvement in justice issues or advocacy; making worship entertaining; developing programs to help seniors, in particular, but members in general kill time with diversions such as bus trips, museum visits, restaurant parties?

[6] In our meetings and churches do we accept our share of the responsibilities, or do we expect the pastor or a handful of committed Friends to carry the whole load? We are stereotyped when we are called a "do-it-yourself religion," or it's said that "you can believe anything and be a Quaker." But we need to remember that we are being called, gathered, and sent. We are not without purpose, and watering down statements of faith by some provide evidence to support such charges.

[7] Is Christ the dynamic Lord of our lives, not just a notional tenet of faith? Are we really ready to accept the Lordship of Christ as Everett Cattell

asked? Do we attempt to meet today's questions in awareness of the truth that Christ is still the answer—leading us to lives of greater sanctification/ holiness and ready to exemplify his love both personally and through our church/meeting structures?

[8] Are we willing to link hands as Friends, subordinating our wills to Christ's and seeking to discern what it is that he would have us do?

If we are, let's find a way to "get with it!"

Arthur Roberts has said that "if our differences are addressed through faith, they will lead to renewed spiritual vigor." In his summary, he gives some tentative and partial conclusions. At that point he picks out the positive contributions (as well as, elsewhere, some negative drawbacks) that each of his seven paths could make: (1) Perspective from the "restorationists" (= Everett Cattell's "revival of primitive Quakerism"). (2) Spontaneity under the Spirit's leadings from charismatic Friends. (3) While he sees mysticism as "a scenic route," it can also offer "a good complement to the lives of the saints." (4) Universalism (if not connected to the universal mission of Jesus Christ), however, "will be a dead-end road if followed very long." (5) Fundamentalism "is a detour." Those traveling that route face "a fork in the road," and the way "leading back to the Quaker highway will be less well marked." (6) Liberalism "embodies Gospel principles." It has been "chastened by events of recent decades, and is recovering confidence in Christian transcendence, including the biblical witness. In stretches it now runs parallel with evangelicalism." (7) Evangelicalism, Arthur Roberts says:

> is an alternate route—I prefer it. Its three lanes–proclamation, fellowship, and service–are now open. Forced to show distinction from fundamentalism, it may soon merge with an equally chastened liberalism. This will be a relief to many Friends, I think. At that time, designated signs may be replaced. Perhaps "Christocentric"; or simply "Quaker," will suffice to indicate that we are people of the Christian Way.[22]

Arthur Roberts, here, has added some incisive definition to the purifying difference the Lordship of Christ could make for all parts of the Quaker spectrum. At the heart of the *Evangel*, the "good news," is Christ—the great role model and source of direction for liberals and conservatives alike. New structures and new strategies will not solve anything by themselves. As Everett Cattell reminds us, the true divisions between Friends are not the result of using or not using pastors and structured worship. These have ceased to be problems for many Friends.

The central issue is the willingness to attend to and follow the direct leadership of Christ. Doing so was the great discovery of the early Quakers.

---

22. On p. 17 of the *Friends Journal* version of Arthur Roberts, "Paths Toward a Quaker Future" (March 1, 1987). 2/7/1996 D. F.

Discerning His will for them caused them to travel halfway around the world (often on foot and through wilderness) to proclaim the good news wherever they went and to "publish" truth at home as well. Often it was done at the cost of imprisonment or the distraint of all their worldly goods. That witness and the message that the world desperately needs now is that Christ is still the answer.

What Future for Evangelical Friends?

CHARLES MYLANDER

When John Wooden was coach of UCLA's basketball team he taught his players who scored a basket to honor the teammate who passed the ball to him. While running back down the floor the scoring player pointed to the one who gave the assist or set the pick. Since those now-famous days you can often see basketball players pointing to a teammate, giving credit for setting them up to score. In this book many of us are pointing in honor to Dr. Arthur O. Roberts, our professor who again and again gave us an assist that made a significant difference in our lives.

When I was first approached about writing a chapter, one thought popped into my mind. Over and over Arthur Roberts used to talk about "a Friends Church—evangelical in nature and worldwide in scope." Some of us caught his dream and to this day we pursue his vision. Dreams never come true just like the man with the original vision pictured. But some do come true in a form that is clearly recognizable. This one is in progress, still in the making.

I would like to divide the chapter into three major headings, *Theology, Vision* and *Strategy*.

Theology

As we look at a Friends Church that is "evangelical in nature," it immediately suggests the stark reality, known well by Arthur Roberts, that not all Friends are evangelical. All Friends do hold their earliest history in common. To this day many share similar testimonies, distinctives and a unique way of conducting business. Theologically, then, what essential beliefs make a Friend evangelical? Three heartfelt convictions distinguish evangelical Friends from others.

- Evangelical Friends hold to the centrality of Jesus Christ including His exclusive claims as the only way of salvation.
- Evangelical Friends hold to the authority of scripture, including its teaching on sexual issues.
- Evangelical Friends hold to the unity of Friends faith including receiving into membership only those who know Jesus Christ as Lord and Savior.

The Chair Analogy

Compare evangelical Friends focus on Christ and His authority to a chair with a seat, four legs and a back. The seat of the chair is Christ Himself. Responding to Christ's light and grace, we trust Him as Lord, Savior and coming King. The seat of the chair is what supports us. We put the weight of our lives on the centrality of Jesus Christ.

He is the pre-existent One, God the Son
who was incarnated Jesus of Nazareth,
lived a sinless life,
died on Calvary's cross,
rose bodily from the tomb,
ascended to the right hand of the Father,
was seated with Him in the heavenly realms
and is present in our lives as Lord, Savior, Teacher and Friend.

Compare our evangelical Friends view of revelation and authority to the four legs of a chair. Think of them as

the Holy Spirit of God,
the written word of God,
the powerful and personal works of God, and
the faithful people of God.

The four legs are all part of the same chair. What the Holy Spirit teaches is the same truth as what the prophets and apostles taught in the written words of scripture. God's mighty works confirm this truth and God's faithful people give witness to it in their hearts and with their lips. In other words, God's truth is all one.

The back of the chair is *tradition*. All Christian movements have their unique distinctives and traditions which they value. Most often these are interpretations of scripture and developments of historical theology. It's quite possible to sit on a chair without a back on it. However, the back brings much comfort and a feeling of security. This may well be why chairs outsell stools. So with Friends our unique history, testimonies and traditions give us support and stability. We value them.

The most comfortable part of a chair is its padding. It's also the most attractive. In this analogy the padding on the Friends chair is personal *experience*. I love holy-ground experiences, the times when a person meets God in a life-changing way. I love to share my own and to hear about other people's personal experiences with Christ.

Whenever we brag on a chair, it's almost always because of the beauty and the comfort, and not because of the quality of the frame. When we talk about Christ and the uniqueness of Friends we most often speak of our experiences with our living Lord and His people. Yet most of us would not want a chair that's all padding. Nor can we justify a faith that is all experience but is not supported by the seat of Christ Himself and the solid legs of God's Holy Spirit, God's written word, God's mighty works and God's faithful people.

With the chair analogy in mind, let's take a look at the three core convictions.

- Evangelical Friends hold to the centrality of Jesus Christ including His exclusive claims as the only way of salvation.

Our Lord Jesus Christ is absolutely believable when He says, "I am the way and the truth and the life. No one comes to the Father except through me." (John 14:6 NIV) We believe that there is salvation in no other name under heaven because no one else ever lived a sinless life, died as a perfect sacrifice for sin and rose from the dead to give us a living hope forever. The exclusive claims of Jesus Christ as the only way to the heavenly Father are a scandal to some today.

Unacceptable Universalism

Robert Barclay in his well-known *Apology* has rightly shown how the light of Christ gives a universal offer of salvation, even to those who have not yet heard the name of Jesus.[1] However, he denies (and so do we) a universal experience of salvation.

> Indeed, the name *Jesus* signifies the saviour who will free them from the sin and the iniquity in their hearts.
>
> I confess that there is no other name by which to be saved. But salvation does not lie in the literal knowledge of that name, but in the experience of

1. Dean Freiday, ed., *Barclay's Apology in Modern English*, pp. 112-124.

what it signifies. Those who merely know his name, without any real experience of its meaning, are not saved by it. But those who know the meaning
and have experienced his power can be saved without knowing his name.

This is why God has raised faithful witnesses and evangelists in our age to
preach again his everlasting gospel. It is their task to help all become aware
of the light within themselves and to know Christ in them.[2]

A world of difference exists between what Friends originally taught and
the universalist Quakers of today. A universal offer of salvation (a la Barclay
and the scriptures) says that all who received the inward light of Christ will
believe and trust in Him. When and if they hear His name and gospel
authentically proclaimed, they will recognize and receive *Jesus* as their light.
But the false teaching of universalism claims salvation for all who are sincere
believers in any religious experience, even if they bypass the Christ of the
scriptures.

With hearts full of love and truth we evangelical Friends reject any system that bypasses putting one's full weight of faith for salvation upon the
seat of the chair, our Lord Jesus Christ. We can no longer tolerate the heresy of universalism, the false teaching that all people will go to heaven
whether or not they trust in Jesus Christ and His saving light.

The second core conviction is this:

• Evangelical Friends hold to the authority of scripture, including
   its teaching on sexual issues.

Some Friends try to reinterpret or disagree with the scriptures when it
comes to both heterosexual and homosexual behavior outside of marriage.
God's Holy Spirit is the one who enlightens us, leads us and witnesses
within our hearts that we belong to the Lord Jesus. The Spirit is the One
who reminds us what Jesus taught and empowers us to obey Him. He is the
One who inspired the scriptures. He never contradicts today by continuing
revelation what He inspired in the written word of God centuries ago.

Some Friends groups polarize when the revealed truth of scripture con-
flicts with current thinking on sexual issues. Some liberal Quakers take
pride in the practicing homosexuals in their Meetings. Some even "bless"
same sex unions of two men or two women. (Some scholars have tried to
reinterpret the scriptures on these issues but without success. Evangelical
scholars, and many others, believe that scriptural teaching is undeniably
clear that homosexual activity is forbidden.)

---

2. *Ibid.*, Pp. 113, 123.

From our earliest days we evangelical Friends have considered the scriptures as authoritative when it comes to disputes over our faith and practice. Robert Barclay wrote concerning the scriptures,

> We consider them the only proper outward judge of controversies among Christians. Whatever doctrine is contrary to their testimony may properly be rejected as false. We are very willing for all of our own doctrines and practices to be tried by them. We have never refused to honor them as the judge and test for any disputes we have had on matters of doctrine. We are even willing to allow this to be stated as a positive maxim: Anything which anyone may do while claiming to be led by the Spirit, which is contrary to the scriptures, may be considered as a delusion of the devil. We never claim the Spirit's leading as a cover for anything that is evil. Since every evil contradicts the scriptures, it must also be contrary to the Spirit from which they came. The motions of the Spirit can never contradict one another, although they sometimes appear to do so in the blind eyes of the natural man.[3]

We evangelical Friends reject the teaching that homosexual activity or heterosexual acts outside of marriage are acceptable. While we welcome into our churches those with a homosexual orientation, we reject homosexual activity as sinful and displeasing to our God and Savior, Jesus Christ. We do the same for premarital or extramarital sex.

Turn your attention now to the third core conviction.

- Evangelical Friends hold to the unity of Friends faith including receiving into membership only those who know Jesus Christ as Lord and Savior.

Some Friends have claimed a mystical experience that either contradicts or is in no way related to our Lord Jesus Christ whom we worship as Creator, Savior and living Lord.

A few have even involved themselves in goddess worship, new age practices, or wicca (a form of witchcraft). We evangelical Friends reject this kind of idolatry and must renounce it as a counterfeit to true Christianity and a distortion of authentic Friends teachings.

Some Friends take into membership Hindus, Buddhists, Jews, new age practitioners, and others who openly reject Jesus Christ. They teach or imply that all sincere religious seekers are heaven-bound. We can only say with tears that the lies of universalism have replaced the truth of a universal offer of salvation through Jesus Christ and His light. When we call for a Friends Church that is evangelical in nature, we base it on the centrality of

---

3. *Ibid.*, p. 60.

Jesus Christ, including the unity of Friends faith which must be exclusively Christian.

Vision

A Friends Church that is "evangelical in nature" speaks of theology; one that is "worldwide in scope" calls for vision. The purpose of evangelical Friends today is to fulfill the Great Commission (Matt. 28:16-20) in the spirit of the Great Commandment (Mark 12:28-31). Evangelical Friends exist to make more and better friends of our Lord Jesus Christ. Our passion is for everyone in every culture to know Jesus and to know Him better. Our intent is to penetrate the cultures around us, whether at home or abroad, with the life-changing gospel and loving acts of service in the name of Christ.

Our goal is to multiply family, followers and friends of Christ. To be more explicit, we intend to multiply *redeemed* family, *devoted* followers and *intimate* friends of our Lord Jesus Christ. We are commissioned to disciple the nations, all the ethnic groups of the world. Making disciples means bringing people into living union with Christ. It includes teaching them to learn from the Lord Jesus and obey His commands, in short, to become the apprentices of Jesus. The Holy Spirit who moved the first Christians and early Friends will compel us to fulfill our part of this worldwide vision.

While we do not pretend to be the only expression of the Body of Christ, we are one Holy Spirit-formed incarnation of His Church. Our intent is to plant evangelical Friends churches in recognized Yearly Meetings throughout the world. We envision each evangelical Yearly Meeting fulfilling three essential functions. In short, the three are *church, school* and *mission.*

The first essential function is *church.* We envision healthy evangelical Friends churches that grow and reproduce. Where we are falling short is in reproduction. We cannot pretend to fulfill the Great Commission if we nurture our present churches only. All evangelical Friends must support a great church-planting movement if we are to fulfill our part of the Great Commission. We intend to plant churches that practice intimacy with Christ (Great Commandment) and disciple-making evangelism with Christ (Great Commission). "Worldwide in scope" means we will multiply throughout our own people groups, and beyond.

The second essential function is *school.* We envision effective means of training evangelists, pastors, elders, teachers, and other workers. Their task is to build up evangelical Friends churches. We build them up when we teach them obedient intimacy with Christ and church-multiplying evangelism. We can do no less if we are to obey everything that Jesus commanded us. Nowhere in the world, Friends included, does the church prosper without adequate training for its workers and leaders. Only God calls and ordains, but we must enlist and equip those whom He taps on the shoulder and thrusts into the harvest.

The third essential function is *mission*. We envision every evangelical Yearly Meeting in every part of the world with an effective Missions Board. The task of this Board is to send national missionaries supported by their own people. Such mobilization will happen as the national Mission Boards lift the vision of penetrating other cultures, languages and people groups with the gospel as understood by evangelical Friends. Even a moment's thought makes it clear that we will never have a Friends Church that is worldwide in scope if we only focus on our present few churches. We must step outside of ourselves and take the gospel to other people groups who will hear and respond to the good news.

If we can use an analogy from sports, we must have a forceful offense and a powerful defense. Our offense is the Great Commission, to disciple the ethnic groups of the world. Our defense is the Great Commandment, to love God with all our heart, soul, mind and strength and to love our neighbors as ourselves. Our offense is powerful intercessory prayer. Our defense is winning in spiritual warfare. Our offense is church-planting evangelism. Our defense is discipleship that includes intimacy with Christ and obedience to His commands. Our offense is church growth. Our defense is church health.

We envision an aggressive offense that raises up churches and people who practice love and step outside of themselves to spread in word and deed the greatest message of all, Christ's redeeming love. Living communion with Christ and life-changing evangelism walk hand in hand. We envision a powerful defense that teaches our people to conquer the devil, the flesh and the world. All our good intentions will come to nothing if we ignore the enemies of the spiritual life in Christ. All evangelical Friends need to understand freedom in Christ, and need to live in its power. Once again may it be said of us, in the words of George Fox, "the power of the Lord is over all."

Strategy

It is compelling to speak with Arthur Roberts of "a Friends Church that is evangelical in nature and worldwide in scope." But if we only speak and never act, the dreams will never come into reality. We must turn theology into practice and vision into strategy if we are to obey our Lord. Yet there is always a danger in writing about strategy. While our theology and vision seldom change, our strategy often will. When we think and write strategically, it is always with the understanding that it may change tomorrow.

International Thrust

The brightest spots on the evangelical Friends globe are outside the United States. What do we see emerging among evangelical Friends? We see an international, Christ-proclaiming, Scripture-authoritative, leadership-respecting Friends Church that values Biblical standards and clearly stated beliefs. This movement speaks the biblical language of today's Friends who see themselves as evangelical Protestants. More and more it is doing business, setting an agenda, and creating an identity. Regional alliances of Evangelical Friends International are already under way in Latin America, Africa and Asia. Ron Stansell, Director of the Evangelical Friends International Council reported on the progress at the 1996 meeting of Evangelical Friends International / North America.

> We can indeed claim there now exists a "Friends Church evangelical in nature and worldwide in scope." Asian Friends know each other. Central American Quakers have personal friendships with South American Quakers. Each Regional conference has been marked by much learning about neighboring Friends, prayer, inspiration and drawing of strength from peers. Furthermore, cross-cultural missionary work is happening by Friends in all three Regions. Guatemalan, Honduran and Salvadoran Friends have formed a consortium to support a missionary in Nicaragua. Bolivian Friends are serving in Peru. Burundi Friends have ministered in Zaire and nurtured new churches there as well as loaning preachers to Rwanda. In Asia, Taiwanese Friends are supporting a Chinese investment of time, interest, and finances in Indonesia and Nepal as well as on mainland China.[4]

The growth and health of evangelical Friends churches is most encouraging. Evangelical Friends Mission, a commission of Evangelical Friends International has launched several new mission fields, especially among unreached people groups. A church-planting movement is evident at least on every continent. New Yearly Meetings and mission fields are growing and older ones are beginning to send their own national missionaries.

Both on the international scene and within the United States we need to implement the "thirty-fold principle." In a famous parable Jesus taught that seed that fell on good ground would bear fruit—thirty, sixty or even a hundred times more than what was planted (Mark 4:8, 20). Apply Jesus' principle to our Yearly Meetings.

Suppose that in its lifetime, one Yearly Meeting planted five others around the world. This is not unthinkable in this day of receptivity and rapid communication. Then suppose that each of these Yearly Meetings were taught to plant five other evangelical Yearly Meetings. The result would be thirty Yearly Meetings. Reproducing chains soon break down without constant effort and fresh starts. *However, workable strategies that mul-*

---

4. Ron Stansell, written report to the Coordinating Council of Evangelical Friends International/North America, Twin Rocks Conference Center, Rockaway Beach, Oregon, January 7, 1996.

tiply Yearly Meetings produce far more than no realistic goals at all. The important principle of multiplication means that every Yearly Meeting must intend to reproduce itself again and again. It will never happen if we never try.

Discipleship Training

We will multiply evangelical Friends churches at home and abroad only when we adequately train our people. Biblical ignorance is a fact of modern life, a reality far different from the days of George Fox and William Penn. We must equip our people on at least three levels.

On the *personal level* our strategy is to lead new Christians and immature believers to maturity in Christ. Most of our churches are woefully inadequate in giving our people a comprehensive plan to master the basics of Christian living. What we need is both a quality two-year course and a delivery system for our people to use it. It will take good teaching, systematic organization and motivational leadership—and one thing more, prayer. Most of all it will take personal models of the Christian life who are examples to follow.

On the *ministry level* our strategy is to teach all of our people to dedicate themselves to Christ, enjoy their spiritual wealth and use their spiritual gifts. Ministry and stewardship become a way of life for those who live in communion with Christ. As we listen to the Lord, hear His voice and capture His heart of love, we will step outside of ourselves. He invites us to join Him in His work, and we must adjust our lives and obey. What we need are a variety of courses and training, on a non-academic level that equip evangelical Friends to use their gifts, talents and strengths.

On the *professional level* our strategy is to educate and equip our God-called leaders and discerning followers with the best we can offer. First-rate academics and on-site apprenticeships increasingly walk hand in hand. Every ministry student needs an apprenticeship in the essential life of a biblical saint and the practical roles of prophet, priest and king. Saints are men and women of God who live in constant communion with Christ. Prophets are communicators; priests are people builders and kings are leaders. How can we feed Jesus' sheep if we have poorly equipped shepherds?

National Strategy

Within the United States a strategic move might be to create one Yearly Meeting that is evangelical in nature and nationwide in scope. We no longer live in the horse and buggy days. With airlines, phones, FAX machines, computers, e-mail and continual new breakthroughs in communication technology, it is easy for us to communicate anywhere in the nation. In fact it's much easier than it was for our ancestors to communicate within regional Yearly Meetings. Our failure to build one Yearly Meeting nationwide has led to provincial thinking and no effective national strategy. Our outreach is limited by the horse and buggy boundaries of our Yearly Meeting founders.

Whether or not we form a single evangelical Yearly Meeting, the first and foremost strategic step for evangelical Friends in the United States is simply to redraw our boundaries. *Our new boundaries must include all of the United States, not just the states where Yearly Meetings in Evangelical Friends International now exist.* In all probability this implies that every Yearly Meeting must set a high priority on planting a new Yearly Meeting, or a new district of their present Yearly Meeting in states adjacent to their present boundaries. In many states we have few if any evangelical Friends Churches.

Church Health, Growth and Planting

If we are to fill the United States with evangelical Friends Churches then we must give priority to church health, growth and planting. What are the marks of a healthy church? While many exist, essential qualities include becoming

- missions-minded,
- church-planting,
- financially-free,
- quality-based,
- splendor-displaying.

A brief explanation will make these terms clear. *Missions-minded* churches invest their time and energy in fulfilling the Great Commission around the world. *Church-planting* churches do the same within the United States. Church planting is widely recognized as the most effective form of evangelism when measured by the standard of lasting results. *Financially-free* churches operate in a way that they pay their bills on time and do not take on debt for non-capital items. They avoid debt overload and foolish speculation with their limited resources.

Quality-based means churches that preach the scriptures and practice the spiritual disciplines that lead to intimacy with Christ. Living communion is a way of life for them; they pray and obey. In addition it means that everything is done with excellence. Shoddiness and mediocrity are out, and high standards in preaching, pastoral care, facilities, people-touching ministries are in. *Splendor-displaying* means evangelical Friends who radiate the love, joy, peace, kindness and presence of the living Lord Jesus. What happens in splendor-displaying churches cannot be explained in human terms alone; it is divinely supernatural.

When it comes to church growth our strategy is to manage activity rather than results. We intend to teach pastors and workers to listen to the living Christ, discern His work around them, and join Him in His activity. Faithfulness in evangelism, discipleship and assimilating new people are visible examples of His work. High morale, compelling vision and continuing momentum are invisible gifts from the Holy Spirit. It takes excellence in leadership, both paid and volunteer to stimulate the kinds of activity that Christ uses for both health and growth.

When it comes to church planting much has been learned in recent years. The technology has improved and the cost decreased. The success rate of new churches has skyrocketed. The survival rate has moved dramatically upward. The greatest need at the moment is for visionary sponsoring churches and church-planters. In short, we need people called by God to launch new evangelical Friends Churches.

Prayer Power

An evangelical Friends worldwide movement of church health, growth and planting with godly, equipped leaders is a big order. It will never happen without a Spirit-inspired prayer movement. Just as prayer precedes revival, so also prayer precedes church health, growth and planting. Without prayer we will never build a strong offense.

Prayer is a primary means of overcoming the devil, the flesh and the world. Our evangelical Friends churches will never penetrate the spiritual darkness around us if we depend only on human resources, however good. Christ designed His church as a body to be connected to one Head. Without Christ's grace, truth, love, power and righteousness, our people will search for satisfaction of their inner longings elsewhere. Christ has already given all we need, but prayer brings us into awareness of our riches and of their Giver. Without prayer we will never build a strong defense.

Prayer gives us both humility and confidence. We begin to understand our weaknesses and our strengths. We begin to appreciate what we have to learn from others, and what we have to contribute. Without prayer we are doomed to mediocrity or isolation. Only prayer will turn us from a memory into a movement.

What Will It Take?

What will it take to keep the momentum going toward "a Friends Church that is evangelical in nature and worldwide in scope"?
- The inspiration and guidance of the Holy Spirit
- A determination to live under the authority of Scripture
- An obedient response to God's works around us
- A few God-called, Spirit-inspired leaders and many equipped, discerning followers
- A deep conviction that our Lord Jesus Christ is leading evangelical Friends churches into better days ahead.

Let us be wise enough to move confidently and carefully ahead. We must have good theology, vision and strategy. But we must have something more. We must have an active passion for people. We must feed our Lord's sheep, care for His flock and seek the wandering and the lost. Without a broken heart for the hurts of people we will miss the compassion of the Lord Jesus. We follow the Suffering Servant who laid down His life for His own, and for His enemies. Only as we humbly follow Jesus, taking up our crosses, will we attain unto resurrection!

Some Reflections on Quakers and the Evangelical Spirit

JOHN PUNSHON

I suppose that Arthur Roberts was the first evangelical Friend I ever met. On what was probably the third day of my very first visit to the United States, I flew out to Oregon to meet him and visit George Fox College. I had been teaching at Woodbrooke, the English Quaker study center, for a couple of years, and I was beginning to get an inkling that there were many Friends in the world who were not like us. I wanted to get as far away from London Yearly Meeting as I possibly could, and Northwest Yearly Meeting seemed to be the place.

Arthur met me at Portland airport, entertained me to fruit pie on the way back to Newberg and seemed more interested in my attitude to the cultivation of filberts than the soundness of my doctrine. I remember that, as it happened, the then yearly meeting clerk was also eating in the pie shop and I wondered whether the Quakers were *everywhere* in the Willamette Valley. I spent a memorable few days with the Robertses learning a lot about Quakerism that I didn't know and being inducted into the mysteries of football (American style).

These things were a considerable advantage to me when I came back to the United States to teach for a period of some years. I come from an island, and in Quaker terms we are, well, *insular*. So as I began to move among Friends of a different persuasion and heritage from what I was accustomed to, I had to come to terms with the fact that evangelical Friends are a clear theological and organizational majority within the worldwide Society of Friends.

I wish I had known more about evangelical Quakerism, and earlier than I did. I wish that evangelical Friends had taken more trouble to find me. I could have done with their help in trying to place myself in the Quaker spectrum. In England I probably count as a conservative liberal. In America I might just pass as a reformed evangelical. Why else do I feel at home in the pastoral tradition? The answer is probably that in America I have been put back in touch with a part of the heritage of Britain Yearly Meeting which that body ignores, but which is vital to a comprehensive understanding of what being a Friend means.

The Origin of My Interest

I grew up as a Friend in Ratcliff and Barking Monthly Meeting, the area of which stretches from the neighborhood of the Tower of London, along the north bank of the River Thames down to its estuary some forty miles to the east. It is a very old monthly meeting—more comparable to America's quarterly meetings, I should explain, because it is a grouping of a number of "Preparative" or local meetings. One of these was Wanstead, which I still think of as my home meeting, though at present I belong to First Friends, Richmond, Indiana.

I mention this because Friends moved their meeting to Wanstead in 1870, since population changes required them to move away from the place where they had met earlier, in what was originally the village of Plaistow. A number of Friends lived round about that village, including the eminent physician and Clerk of London Yearly Meeting, John Fothergill, and a little later, Joseph Fry and his wife Elizabeth Fry (nee Gurney). The children of Wanstead meeting used to slide along the benches in the meeting house so that they could have the proud boast that they had once sat (though they could not be specific as to where) on the same seat as the great Elizabeth Fry. Indeed, my wife and I were married sitting on the Elders' bench in this meeting.

So my Quaker life began as a member of the same meeting that Elizabeth Fry had belonged to before me. It is a source of quiet satisfaction and modest pride to Ratcliff and Barking Friends that one of their number was such an adornment to the Society, as well as being a social reformer of the front rank. But I did not grasp what was involved in all this till some time later, when I had to sort through the books of two meetings that were closing down, and I encountered what must have been a pair of classical nineteenth-century Quaker libraries.

Nostalgic pride gave way to something else as I catalogued those books. It struck me that London Yearly Meeting in the very recent past had been part of the Orthodox, or evangelical Quaker world, not the theologically liberal one. When I read the Discipline of my yearly meeting there was very little indication that this had been so. The question was then inescapable.

Was Elizabeth Fry anything more than this figure of nostalgic pride, or were her religious principles something that led to what she had done, and might they still hold good today?

I guess my awareness of, and concern for, evangelical Quakerism stems from that experience. From being a new Friend inspired by the Quaker story and the Quaker way of life, I began to be drawn to the theological foundations of that life. I found that in the past these principles had been rather different from what I had been given to understand was the essence of Quakerism, and there was another kind of Quaker answer to my life-questions which had to do with the meaning of the scriptures and the work of Jesus Christ in addition to His teaching.

I have found myself traveling down that road, and as the years go by I have been increasingly interested in the tradition my own yearly meeting gave up. It is not quite the same as the American variety, because we developed neither the pastoral system nor holiness discipleship, but preserved silent waiting and evangelical principles throughout the nineteenth century. It might be thought that evangelical Quakerism necessarily requires a pastoral system, but historically, that is not so.

So having come to the United States I have been brought face to face with aspects of Quakerism that my own yearly meeting no longer expresses, but which are alive and well here. I have faced challenges to my Christian faith and my understanding of Quakerism that I have not encountered before.

There are perhaps three questions, or areas of importance to consider. First, there is the academic question. Until recently there has not been a great deal of interest in Evangelical Quakerism as a phenomenon, though I hope others will now come along and begin to cultivate the ground so admirably broken by Thomas Hamm. I am very struck, for example, by the sheer diversity of Evangelical Quakerism, and I would like to see some theorizing about it.

Then for me, and I suspect many other Friends too, there is the personal question of what it means to be both an evangelical and a Quaker. On the one hand, there are different kinds of evangelicalism, not all compatible with one another below the most general level. On the other, there are competing versions of what fundamental Quaker principles are. One of the facts of life seems to me to be that we are under constant pressure to define ourselves in relation to the extremes, and are pulled this way and that by strongly-held, but not necessarily strong opinions. I would also like to be able to state some of the ways in which it is possible for individuals to adopt evangelical positions that are at the same time informed by fundamental Quaker values and beliefs—in so far as these things diverge, a point which is itself at issue.

In the third place there is the "future of Quakerism" question. There are certain matters in which the whole Church needs the ministry of the Society of Friends, just as Friends themselves are not self-sufficient, and in their turn need the ministry of other Christians. In other words, there is a distinctive Quaker understanding of the gospel which needs constantly to be heard. But as a matter of history, that understanding has been overlaid by evangelical and liberal theologies of various sorts, and the question of the future of Quakerism is usually approached in terms of what we are to make of the apparently fundamental division between the two. However, my own feeling is that this is a false distinction, and we need a much deeper appreciation of the ways in which early Quakerism was understood and misunderstood at the time of our separations in the last century. We need to learn that Evangelical Quakerism was not born on the American Frontier.

So it matters to think about Quaker evangelicalism from the standpoint of Quaker history and theology, because these are the things that ultimately give us our character. But there are also reasons which I also find of interest and importance personally. For example, I have to reconcile two things, and I find many evangelicals in a similar position to me. I am firmly convinced, for example, of the need for Christian social action. But on the other hand I am equally convinced of the priority of the gospel. There can be no conversion of society without transformed individuals, and that comes first. I have the feeling that the biblical perspective on the human condition and its needs is being forgotten in the quest for contemporary relevance. The evangelical insistence on scriptural standards for belief and conduct has never been more needed.

However, as I have just remarked, there are different kinds of evangelicalism, some differentiated by their values and practices, others by particular doctrinal emphases. One aspect of evangelical Christianity which is not really appreciated by outsiders is that it is a very broad church comprising a rich variety of viewpoints. But we are always, as I have said, challenged at the extremes, and it seems to me that what we need today is a strong *Christian* humanism (which is what I conceive real evangelicalism to be) as against the defensiveness of the fundamentalist temperament. While the one seems to me to be highly compatible with the Quaker heritage, the other, I would think, is not.

Indeed, to take this thought further, I recall the words of Joseph John Gurney, that Quakerism is "the religion of our Lord and Savior Jesus Christ, without diminution, without addition, and without compromise." Nowadays there are difficulties with this formulation. What counts as diminution, addition, or compromise? There are some subtle points there I am not as confident about as Joseph John Gurney was. Nevertheless, in the doctrines proclaimed by the Society of Friends, I see the truth of the gospel of Jesus Christ in a fuller form than I find elsewhere.

Hence, I am coming to think it is possible to take a stand on a set of principles that is both Quaker and evangelical, and possibly this is the best prospect we have for Quaker renewal. I say "coming to think," because this is the matter I am trying to test out. I want therefore to look at what the evangelical values are, to see what we might say were the essential characteristics of Quakerism, to look at the relationships between the two, and then draw some conclusions from history, and to see where we are today.

What Are the Evangelical Values?

Now I know that the correct formulation of doctrine is an important evangelical preoccupation, but Christians have to be concerned with the effects as well as the content of belief. As it has come down to us, the evangelical movement is a continuation of the profound spiritual forces generated by the Reformation. It takes a variety of forms, and is more diverse than many people are prepared—or willing—to give it credit for. It is normally thought of as a fairly rigid and doctrinaire movement, and there is that side to it. But what is sometimes overlooked is that it is essentially a religion of experience, and should be understood primarily as that.

I have to say also that I do not see evangelical values as separate from the values of the rest of the Church. Difference of opinion among Christians is one of the facts of life and has to be handled carefully. It should always be conducted charitably, too, and we need the humility to be able to recognise when we are wrong. But at the same time, there are matters of principle over which we need to have Luther's courage and say, "Here I stand, I can do no other."

The relationship of evangelicals to other Christians in such matters is sometimes a matter of principle like this, and that is why we have the National Association of Evangelicals as well as the National Council of Christian Churches. But the separatism of some evangelicals works against their own best interests. The evangelical values are essential for the health of the rest of the Church, and represent the base lines of Christianity to which the rest of Christianity always, sooner or later, returns. The reasons are not theological or doctrinal, but it is because these values represent how people really are and what Christianity ultimately represents.

First, therefore, we must understand that the evangelical faith is essentially a matter of personal experience. Many people locate the truth of Christianity in its ethical teaching, and there is much there that is of great value to the world beyond the Church. But that is not the essence of the thing. Prior to the good works comes the commitment. Prior to the discipleship comes the counting of the cost. In order to endure to the end, we need a power that goes beyond the unredeemed human condition. That can only come, says the gospel, and the evangelical faith, by conversion, and an experience of the transforming power of Jesus Christ. Christianity is not following the rules, it is following Christ. People think evangelicalism is primarily about belief, but it is really about a relationship.

The second value of evangelicalism is its insistence on the primacy of scripture as a guide to life and the source of authority about doctrine in the Christian community. This is part of the scandal it causes in a lot of religious circles. Apart from its assertions about inspiration and infallibility there is a general point to be made about fidelity to the written Word. We are separated from the earthly life of Christ by about two thousand years. We live in a highly self-confident age and there are many people who think that the best clue to the meaning of scripture is to be found in the results of the most recent scholarship. The consequence of this is a tendency for many people to trust books about the Bible rather than the Bible itself. We need evangelicals to challenge this preoccupation with the wisdom of the age in the name of the "wisdom from on high" (James 3:17).

The third value is related to this challenge to the automatic assumptions of the age. There is an important sense in which the presentation of the gospel must be changed as the circumstances in which it is preached change. Indeed, we can see that process at work in Paul's sermon on the Areopagus in Acts. The culture of the age must be engaged with understanding. But that is a high risk strategy, and it sometimes happens that apologists for the Christian faith go beyond a sympathetic understanding of the assumptions of the world and instead adopt them. Rather than seeing the ills of contemporary life as malfunction, the evangelical mind sees them as the result of deliberate self-centered choices which it makes sense to see as "sin." It follows from this that instead of damage limitation and repair in the quest for meaning and authentic existence, the evangelical faith is a standing testimony to the possibility of personal liberation and transformation.

The Essential Characteristics of Quakerism

Let us turn now to Quakerism, the other half of our heritage. There is some difference of opinion about how we should define Quakerism in order to talk about it, but I shall follow Wilmer Cooper's line of thought that there is a central theological tradition coming down to us from the past which is not the formal basis of either the liberal or the evangelical branch of Quakerism, but states certain positions which we find ourselves unable to escape from unless we wish to sever any connection with our past. There are evangelical and liberal Friends who would be quite happy to make that escape, but I am not one of them, because I am convinced of the truth of much of the central, or as it has been called, "normative" Quaker tradition. What follows is not a complete account of that tradition, but I hope it expresses the main outlines.

Naturally, the main principle is that saving knowledge of God comes from personal experience and not intellectual processes. George Fox and the other Friends were very outspoken, and often overstated their case—but in this they were undoubtedly right. There is, of course, no other way to read either the gospel account of the words of Jesus or the New Testament letters. We are invited into a living relationship with Christ. We have to pick up our cross ourselves, and we do that with our hearts and not our heads. It takes repentance, love, commitment and perseverance, and those things come from within. Quaker preaching was originally intended to awaken these virtues rather than to teach a scheme of salvation, since the scheme was seen naturally to follow the experience, since it was a precondition of it. In any case, the early Quaker message was proclaimed in an almost exclusively Christian culture.

This means, therefore, in the second place, that our knowledge of Christ comes through His presence with us in His Spirit. However, this is not simply a matter of personal and subjective experience. The Holy Spirit descended upon the Church as a body and therefore there are necessarily two dimensions to our experience of the Spirit. We are called out of the world as individuals, and into the body of the Christ. Perhaps the most significant consequence of this is the silent meeting and the open worship that we so often fail to understand *theologically* nowadays. The traditional spirituality of Quakerism is specifically designed for us to still the clamor of our own minds and to turn within, away from outward ceremonies and distractions, so that we can hear the still, small voice of God, so that He who dwells in the high and holy place may come to dwell with those of the humble and the contrite heart (Isaiah 57:15). That is how the way of the Lord is prepared. It is on such as these that the Spirit will fall.

Now the third feature of the tradition is a theological generalization that fits these claims into the story told by the Bible. This story is sometimes called "salvation history." It is seen as a record of the actions of God in the ordinary course of human history, and has a period of preparation and fulfillment. So when we look at the Old and New Testaments we see that each is essential to the story, but there are significant differences between them which we can resolve in a variety of ways. For example, the 53rd chapter of Isaiah and the crucifixion narratives can clearly be seen as prophecy and fulfillment. But there are several interpretative keys which we can use, and one of them is provided in Jeremiah 31, where a prophetic outline of the New Covenant (which was then in the future) is laid out, and in Hebrews 9 which Joseph John Gurney himself interpreted to show that the New Covenant was to be entirely inward and spiritual.

Fourthly, what we know as the Quaker "distinctives" necessarily follow from this. Our traditional—and contemporary—disuse of the ordinances flows from these principles. Far from teaching that these things are unnecessary to the Christian, we can see how they are an essential, but a real, and inward one. The apparent commands to practice the ordinances derive their meaning from their theological context. They do not create that context and are perfectly capable of more than one interpretation without going outside the confines of scripture.

Moreover it is these things that have produced the church we are—one which has historically been willing to take the risk of relying on the Holy Spirit, and to this day makes that a reality by rejecting voting in the Lord's work in reliance on guidance from above; a church which recognises God can call anyone to the ministry without ordination and formal recognition, which has no clergy and has had women ministers for 300 years; a church which is known by the world as one which places a high value on simplicity and honesty, and is willing to pay the price of resisting coercion in matters of conscience.

Quakerism is known in the world through the achievements of those who have followed this tradition. We live openly because no part of life is hidden from God's purposes, demands or grace, and we produce a John Woolman. We recognise that what we follow is not a teaching but a person, so we find and carry his cross. Thus we produce a Levi Coffin. Our testimonies have led inevitably to respect for the individuals, no matter how degraded, as children of God, so we have produced people like Elizabeth Fry. And we must not forget that in the life and work of William Penn, we have helped the world to build political freedom, rejecting all that is narrow-minded, authoritarian and of a persecuting disposition.

Quakerism and Evangelicalism

So now let us look at our Quakerism and our evangelicalism side by side. In many walks of life one comes across people who are satisfied with the way things are now, and who do not think very much about the past. They like to close the book, to get to the destination, just to sit outside on a summer evening. On the other hand, when we are considering the state of the gospel in the world, or "the prospering of Truth" as the old Quaker jargon used to have it, I think that attitude is inadequate. We all have our own special call, and as scripture reminds us, we do not all have the same ministry. This applies to churches as well as people. We have particular gifts, and we have to discern what they are before we can use them.

Quakerism began as a great revival of evangelism in the seventeenth century. Quite what the historical circumstances were that caused it, we can debate. The main outlines are clear, but the details are fuzzy, and I have played my part in that debate. However, what we need to register is that the early Quakers had a well-developed theology which was in the Armenian and not the Reformed tradition. They were bitterly hostile to the proposition that Jesus did not die for us all, but only for the elect. They also said it was a poor gospel that saved us from the consequences of sin but could not save us from sin itself. Their faith was born in the century of the European religious wars, and they retreated into a quiet seclusion when a more rational secular public mood developed, partly as a response to this un-Christian carnage.

In the eighteenth century there was another great revival of personal faith stemming from the preaching of John Wesley and his fellow laborers. It is to them that we really owe the evangelical faith in the form in which we have received it, and we can see, with the perspective time gives us, how they carried forward the great themes of the Reformation. As the century wore on, all the churches were affected by the Awakening, including the Society of Friends. It is as if there were a great welling-up of religious enthusiasm into all parts of the Church. Perhaps Wesley was the inspiration, but in fact the ground was prepared. People were ready to hear the message.

Here we return to the point about identity and historical perspective. The historical and theological roots of Quakerism were in some ways closer to the Reformation experience than those of Wesley and his followers. Wesley encountered opposition, but not persecution. He had to push at the door, but he did not have to assault the drawbridge of a castle. So his communities took a different form from the Quaker meetings of the time. In some ways they were comparable, but in others they were not. Quakerism accommodated itself to the Great Awakening rather awkwardly. It had a past, and a character, and that was going to influence how it responded to the new enthusiasm.

Over a period of some decades, evangelical ideas spread in the Society of Friends. They made greater progress in England than America, perhaps, but had an appeal in part because they offered to many a return to experience from a religion that had become highly formal. Evangelical ideas were problematic for Quakers because they were almost necessarily in tension with sectarian Christianity. This is why Quakerism as a whole has had difficulties with evangelicalism, paralleled, I might add, elsewhere. Friends by the end of the eighteenth century were already highly distinctive and dependent on tradition, and probably too small in numbers to contain strong differences of opinion.

As everybody knows, the tensions that built up after the Revolutionary War reached a head in Philadelphia in 1827 when the so-called "Hicksites" separated from the so-called "Orthodox." In the intervening years most of the Orthodox yearly meetings have matured into the pastoral, or evangelical tradition represented by Friends United Meeting and Evangelical Friends International, while the Hicksite tradition has become liberal, and is represented to a considerable degree by the yearly meetings which are part of the Friends General Conference.

So if we review our history, we find that our lineage leads back to one or other of the sides in 1827. It is difficult to be dispassionate about them, and something inside us tugs at our understanding and encourages us to support "our" side in these controversies. This attitude has served us ill, in my submission, and it is time we had a look at these controversies without regarding the protagonists like baseball teams. I have two provocative comments to make. I am afraid that the Orthodox party look pretty unpleasant to me and I don't think I would have liked them. On the other hand, I incline to their opinions against the Hicksites, so the awful possibility arises that you can be nice and wrong and nasty and right.

The second thing is that we dare not take them at face value. In squabbling over who were the real Quakers they resorted to little more than proof-texting from Barclay, Penn and Fox. The theological battle, it seems to me, was never really joined. The substance of their argument was about three matters which continue to exercise the Society of Friends: the nature of the Inward Light, the manner of the Atonement, and the authority of scripture. Let us now look at these matters in general and in detail.

The Emergence of Evangelical Quakerism

In the first place it should be emphasized that the Orthodox of the last century were concerned as much with their Quakerism as their evangelicalism. They did not see a difference between the two, and I wish more contemporary evangelical Friends shared their opinion. Though evangelical in theology, they worshipped in silence, a practice they did not abandon for another half-century. There was no question of the pastorate because they had a strict doctrine of spirit-led ministry, preaching and prayer. In addition, they maintained the testimonies, both theological and ethical, with memorable strictness. That is why in the debates of the times they sought to ground their own claims in Quaker precedent and the teachings of scripture equally.

But they had problems with the authority of scripture. The evangelical position is that there is no appeal from scripture to any other authority, whether it be reason, tradition or the Church. The traditional Quaker position, as stated by Robert Barclay was apparently the opposite of this. Since the scriptures were given forth by the Spirit, he said, it is the Spirit which was the Christian's ultimate authority and not the scriptures. On the surface, these positions look irreconcilable, and if Barclay's doctrine of scripture is one of the fundamentals of Quakerism, then the case is made. Evangelical Quakerism is a hybrid and not the real thing.

But is this inference unavoidable? There are reasons to doubt it. In spite of all the qualifications, the early Quakers accepted fully the authority of scripture in settling doctrinal controversy, and appealed to it constantly. They knew their Bibles so well that the very first historian of Quakerism, the Dutchman Gerard Croese, said that if the whole Bible were lost, it could be reconstituted from the writings of George Fox. It can be argued that the early Friends were just as jealous of the truths of scripture as their evangelical descendants. So to say that early Quakerism had a defective doctrine of scripture is to avoid the complexity of the theology involved.

Moreover, the strict evangelical position is also problematical. To assert that scripture is our ultimate authority is easily done, but questions arise when we seek to give some account of precisely how. For example, there is a difference between understanding scripture and understanding it *savingly*. Where does that difference lie? Then again, we need to know how we can get guidance in circumstances not directly addressed in the text. How can we account for the fact that people draw divergent lessons from this same text? Then there is the consideration that we know from experience that God answers our prayers and guides us through life without apparently referring us to the sacred text every time we raise our hearts in prayer. I think we would agree that without the prior inspiration of the Living Word in our hearts, a teachable spirit and the support of a community of faith, we shall not understand the truth of the Written Word before our eyes.

The early Quakers put this in scriptural terms. Christ describes himself as the Light of the World (John 9:5), and he promises to be with his followers in Spirit, leading them into all the truth (John 16:13). In the earliest books of the New Testament we find Christians called "Children of Light" (Ephesians 5:8). With what I would describe as orthodoxy, the early Quakers said that there must be *something* which you bring to the scriptures that will assure you of right understanding and divine guidance. That they called the Light of Christ Within.

This is as good an answer as any, in fact, because it gives a realistic explanation for what we know. We are saved because of our faith. Something deep in our souls answers the call of God through the preaching of the gospel. In the words of "Amazing Grace," "I once was blind, but now I see." But the Light does not just bring us to repentance and grace, it sustains and sanctifies us in a living, active way. We can read about it in the scripture, but it lives in our hearts, and it guides us though life, charting our course through unfamiliar waters. We come to it in prayer.

Now in 1827 nobody was in the mood to think dispassionately about these things. The Hicksite group recognised that the Light was the living presence of Christ within. But they upset the balance by giving primacy to the Light and then making it a principle not of discernment, but of understanding and interpretation. The Light became a principle of selection. On the other hand, the Orthodox had become highly suspicious of the doctrine of Light. Scripture was a necessary check on personal enthusiasm. But it was not necessary to deny the spirit-led discipleship of which the scripture itself eloquently speaks, but that was the direction in which they were drawn.

At issue was the whole question of religious authority and in what sense scriptural authority is exerted. The Orthodox mistook their own reading of scripture for its correct interpretation. The Hicksites thought that because scripture was being wrongly interpreted, the principle of authority itself was open to doubt. As soon as you look at their written documents you find a tangled confusion of argument, in which both sides appeal to the original Quaker tradition. Quite genuinely, each party could look to part of that tradition in its support, but in fact a debate about a contemporary issue was going on under the guise of an argument about historical precedents. The underlying question was where we find authority. Is it scripture alone? Is it the Inward Light alone? Or is it a combination of both that is stronger than either?

This unwillingness to accept the scriptural warrant for the doctrine of the Light had fateful consequences, because in time it led to a reworking of the doctrine of the atonement among Orthodox Friends and the acceptance of the reformed theology of justification and sanctification. It is there, rather than in the doctrine of scripture, in my view, that the Rubicon was crossed, and evangelical Quakerism found its port of entry into the wider evangelical world.

Or perhaps one should rather say that this was the means by which the wider evangelicalism entered the Society of Friends. Acceptance of different doctrines will necessarily lead to a different style of preaching and discipleship, and in due course Friends found themselves receptive to both Wesleyan spirituality and pastoral system. It has also led to an attenuation of Quaker doctrine on the nature of the New Covenant, the inwardness of the ordinances and a weakening of the traditional doctrine of the ministry. It has led moreover to the lowering of obstacles to change at the time of the revivals and the influence of the Prophetic and Bible School movements in the Society of Friends.

The consequence seems to me to be that there are two forms of evangelical faith in the Society of Friends, the older version which preserves the ancient theology of Quakerism on an evangelical foundation, and a newer version for which current developments are more important than the tradition. I would characterize the former as evangelical Quakerism and the latter as Quaker evangelicalism. This is more than a distinction of words.

So Where Do We Find Ourselves Today?

While these changes have been taking place in the evangelical branch of Quakerism, similar processes have been at work in the non-evangelical branch. This is usually described as "liberal," but one must be careful with terminology because both branches display considerable diversity and are equally open to thoughtless and uninformed criticism. The relationships between them in the past has been successively hostile, tolerant and appreciative, at any rate at the official level, but there are various indications that a new *modus vivendi* is being worked out.

In the first place, arising out of genealogy, perhaps, but certainly out of an appreciation of the past, there seems to be a deepening interest in many Friends in what their heritage has been. This is less a revival of interest in the theology or spirituality of the Quaker past as a sense of identity and belonging. People are interested, sometimes, to my mind to the point of excruciating boredom, with the whole Quaker thing—thee's and thou's and bonnets and all. There is a romance associated with Quakerism, and people fall for it.

However, there is also a deepening interest in the spirituality of Quakerism as a particular, unique and challenging form of Christian discipleship, notably the holding of silent worship in the name of Jesus, and the adoption of the testimonies as a way of righteousness rather than political statement. This is clearly noticeable among liberal Friends, and perhaps it illustrates a point that everybody comes to when they begin to take Quakerism seriously. When immigrants come to a new country they settle down and work hard and try to fit in as best they can. Their children have to get ahead and assimilate, leaving the culture of the old country behind. But then the grandchildren come and talk to their grandparents, and often find something powerful in their elderly words. So they turn to their parents and say, "Why have you kept us from our heritage?"

A little over a hundred years ago the Society of Friends, Hicksite and Orthodox together, emerged from their traditional seclusion and each took a different theological path. Now I find Friends, often convinced Friends, measuring what they know against the past, and finding it wanting. They know where they want to go, but need a guide for the route. One of the conclusions I would like to draw is that evangelicals are often better placed than others to appreciate the theology which underlies the typical experiences of Quakerism, and could have a great deal to say to the searchers for the real thing.

The realignment controversy, which still rumbles on like thunder in some places, is an illustration of the fundamental choices that many people seem to be ready to make. One does not have to take a view on that controversy to understand what is at issue. My pennyworth of comment is that there are many people outside the evangelical yearly meetings who are disillusioned with a form of religion that is so open that it seems unable to provide clear guidance in the things that really matter. Identity comes from the past and what we believe, and there is no escape from that. To assert a clear faith is not to indicate that one has closed one's mind, but to show that one has an identity and is able to ask fundamental questions with a sense of security. Many Quakers are looking for this kind of security, this kind of faith, this kind of identity. And where is it to be found? In many places, of course, but I want to suggest that the evangelical tradition has an important role, if it would only adopt it, in nourishing these green shoots. But that means choosing to value the heritage—to be evangelical Quakers.

So What Have Evangelical Friends to Say?

In conclusion, I would like to ask what the message of evangelical Quakerism might be for today. If my analysis is anywhere near the truth, there is still a viable and important form of Quakerism, evangelical in inspiration, which can pose important questions, and suggest important answers for other parts of both the Quaker and the Christian worlds. There are also some questions it needs to ask itself.

To begin with, what do evangelical Quakers have to say to themselves? First, I think, they need a long hard look at the pastoral system. The mission-based yearly meetings outside the United States are showing encouraging growth, but at home, many Quaker congregations are small and in rural areas, where the population itself is declining. It is difficult to find the pastor's salary, let alone health insurance and pension plan, and this leads to part-time service, the unattractiveness of the pastorate as a career option or vocation, and the appointment of non-Quaker pastors.

There are yearly meetings in which the average age of the pastorate is so advanced that there is no telling where the next generation will come from. Moreover the system, if such it can be called, was superimposed on the traditional structure of Quaker church government, so that the pastor has neither the authority nor the position of pastors of other denominations. The effective use of our pastoral resources seems to me to be one of the most pressing questions that face us. The importance of these challenges should not be underestimated; but nor should they be seen as insurmountable.

The positive side is clear to me. Evangelical Friends enjoy considerable agreement on doctrine and the basics of the faith. There is a faintly puzzled air in some ecumenical Quaker gatherings, encouraged by the form in which they are arranged. Deep questions are put, but there seems to be more interest in the questions than concern at finding satisfactory answers to them. Perhaps the reason that evangelicals do not show up en masse for these gatherings is that they by and large do not need to debate matters of doctrine. They know where they stand. In addition to this, and perhaps the consequence of it, is a structure of meetings and yearly meetings that is corporate yet not over-centralised, with a very good track record of both evangelism and witness.

But Friends need a vision of themselves as a church that goes beyond the usual statistics of conversions made or money raised for missions. These things flow from the activities of inspired people. The great opportunity for Evangelical Quakerism, it seems to me, is to find the vision nestling in its tradition, which is waiting to be rediscovered. In one sense, all movements of renewal are a return to an earlier vitality. Institutions can never be revived, but people can, and are.

Second, what can evangelicals say to the liberal branch of Quakerism? To begin with, it is necessary to note that while many Friends in that tradition have relinquished any connection with historical Christianity, there are still many others who do see themselves as Christians, and maintain the faith in circumstances of considerable difficulty. Explicit, corporate Christian commitment is no longer a reality in many meetings, and there is a great variety of opinion among Christian Friends. Some are content with this state of affairs, but others are not.

Evangelicals, if they could take thought about how to do it, might be of considerable service in these circumstances. I discern a deep and often unarticulated unease with that kind of Christianity in which the historical-critical method controls doctrine rather than the other way round. I meet Friends who are beginning to realise that if the substance of the faith changes as intellectual fashions change, there can be no everlasting gospel. I meet Friends who, often to their own great surprise, are beginning to realise that "modern thought" does not make it easier to hear the gospel, but rather the reverse. In these circumstances the common ground of Quakerism might facilitate a message that otherwise would not be heard.

Third, what can evangelical Quakers say to other evangelicals? I guess I have to say that this is where the distinction I drew between Quaker evangelicals and evangelical Quakers shows up. There are three matters of Quaker doctrine which make a very great deal of theological sense and depend on our essentially Reformation ecclesiology. They are the inward reality of the ordinances, the governance of the church without ordination, and the spiritual equality of women, particularly in the ministry. These are not separated ideas, each to be supported by its separate line of proof texts, but things that go to the root of our understanding of Christ and His covenant with us.

Like any other branch of the Church, evangelicals can be seduced by power, influence and popularity. There are ways of preaching the gospel consistent with the simplicity of Christ and there are ways that are not. There are ways of governing Christ's people that are consistent with His example; there are those that are not. Evangelical Friends can have a great mission still in proclaiming the truth to churches and Christians departing from the apostolic simplicity, beginning to make ceremony a substitute for sincerity, and misreading the New Testament to exclude women from the ministry.

During the last century, the main group of evangelical Quakers in the United States came to be known as the "Gurneyites." They were not all of one mind, and they made their mistakes, some of them pretty drastic. But among themselves they protected the memory and the vision of the man from whom they were named. Joseph John Gurney had a vision of Quaker Christianity as a way of life which is as close as one can ever come to the intentions of Christ for his followers. The evangelical tradition within the Society of Friends has much to be proud of, and much to say.

Word and World

The Mother Tongue: Acquiring Language and Being Human

REBECCA THOMAS ANKENY

One of my favorite Far Sides shows a spider on an analyst's couch, saying, "It's the same dream night after night...I walk out on my web, and suddenly a foot sticks—and then another foot sticks, and another, and another, and another... ." Gary Larsen's spider expresses the impression that people who are fascinated by language have: language is like a web. I spin it out thinking that I have it under control, and suddenly it seems I am caught in the system of words. I open my mouth to speak, and suddenly words appear or disappear, the wrong words come, or unintentional double meanings embarrass me like slipping on a banana peel. Or I get entangled in what I'm trying to express or in the associations of words with each other. Language helps us get what we want. However, we are caught in it also, tantalized by and yet separated from what we most deeply desire.

Jacques Lacan, French psychoanalyst, has thought and written about the relationship of language to the human being. I will tell this as if it were a story about Lacan himself.[1]

The infant Jacques began without any defined center of self, no sense of difference between himself and other, and direct access to reality, particularly the body of his mother.[2] This pre-Oedipal stage Lacan later came to

---

1. This information on Lacan comes out of Terry Eagleton's *Literary Theory: An Introduction* (Minneapolis: U of Minn Press, 1983). See also *Jacques Lacan* by Anika Lemaire, translated by David Macey (London: Routledge & Kegan Paul, 1977).

2. Terry Eagleton, *Literary Theory, An Introduction* (Minneapolis: U of Minn Press, 1983), p. 164.

call "the imaginary" state of being. In this state of being, baby Jacques knew really only two terms, himself and the other, his mother, who represented external reality for him.[3] Within this "imaginary" state of being, little Jacques first began to develop an ego, an integrated self-image, as his mother and the mirror reflected back to him a unified image of himself.[4] Lacan later came to call this the "mirror" stage, and it is basically narcissistic. In this reflected image, the child Jacques saw a self which was himself but at the same time unified in a way alien from his experience of himself and the world.[5] The small child before the mirror was "a kind of 'signifier'—something capable of bestowing meaning—and...the image the child [saw was] a kind of 'signified,' or the meaning of the child."[6] Jacques perceived no gap "between signifier and signified, subject and world," between himself and his image.[7]

The dyadic relationship with his mother and his residence in the imaginary state of being were disrupted for little Jacques by the entrance of his father into his perception. His father did not allow Jacques unlimited access to his mother,[8] and therefore Father signified the arrival of Law, first understood as the social taboo on incest with the mother and then as the representative of "the wider familial and social network" of which Jacques was a part.[9] Jacques' desire for his mother was driven underground and became the unconscious.[10]

Jacques' new perception of his father forced him into awareness that "one term or subject is what it is only by excluding another."[11] The father signified Jacques' first awareness of sexual distinctions.[12] This first discovery of sexual difference occurred at about the same time (around three years old) that Jacques was discovering language itself, discovering that "a sign has meaning only by dint of its difference from other signs, and...that a sign presupposes the *absence* of the object it signifies. ...[A]ll language...substitutes itself for some direct, wordless possession of the object itself."[13] The child Jacques learned that his own identity was "constituted by [his] relations of difference and similarity to the other subjects [his mother and father] around [him]."[14]

---

3. Eagleton, p. 165.
4. Eagleton, p. 164.
5. Eagleton, p. 165.
6. Eagleton, p. 166.
7. Eagleton, p. 166.
8. Oddly enough, the implication is that the mother would allow such access if not prohibited by the father. This seems to place the mother in a position of entire passivity.
9. Eagleton, p. 165.
10. Eagleton, p. 165.
11. Eagleton, p. 166.
12. Eagleton, p. 165.
13. Eagleton, p. 166.

Little Jacques then moved from the imaginary state of being into what Lacan later came to call "the symbolic order." Unfortunately, Jacques was permanently split between the conscious ego and the unconscious, which was the desire his father's presence forced him to repress. Jacques learned to substitute the empty world of language for direct access to reality, particularly to the now prohibited body of the mother. He found language to be empty because it was "just an endless process of difference and absence: instead of being able to possess anything in its fullness, the child...now simply [moved] from one signifier to another, along a linguistic chain which is potentially infinite."[15] His entry into language meant that he was severed from what Lacan came to call the "real."[16] The loss of access to the mother's body left "a gap at the very center of his being" which little Jacques tried to fill with other objects. However, he was "never able to recover the pure (if fictive) self-identity and self-completion which he [had known] in the imaginary."[17] In order to use language, little Jacques worked hard to contain its sliding and evasiveness, "provisionally nailing down words onto meanings."[18]

When he grew up Jacques Lacan came to write the following: Language is never entirely under our control, but instead is what internally divides us.[19] Language, parents, and the symbolic order are not synonymous, but they are intimately allied: they pre-exist us, they assign us *our* places, they bring us into being and then outrun our grasp. These, together with the unconscious, are the Other, the object of our desire which at the same time generates our desire because we "are caught up in linguistic, sexual and social relations."[20] Lacan implies that language is a sign of our initiation into the symbolic order which includes culture and family, but he emphasizes that it also divides us from ourselves, others, and the world, and that it is ultimately unable to fulfill our desire for connectedness.

A very different picture of what it means when a child acquires language emerges in the writings of neurologist Dr. Oliver Sacks. Sacks became interested in deafness and the deaf with especial focus on the place language plays in the development of the human being. In his 1989 book *Seeing Voices*, Dr. Sacks describes his understanding of the relationship between the human being and language. Again, here is the story of that relationship as if it were his own.

---

14. Eagleton, p. 167.
15. Eagleton, p. 167.
16. Eagleton, p. 168.
17. Eagleton, p. 168.
18. "[F]or Lacan all our discourse is in a sense a slip of the tongue; if the process of language is as slippery and ambiguous as he suggests, we can never mean precisely what we say and never say precisely what we mean" (Eagleton, p. 169).
19. Eagleton, p. 169.
20. Eagleton, p. 174.

The infant Oliver began with his own independent experience of the world arrived at through the senses,[21] all of which worked normally. As a hearing infant, Oliver's first language use, first communication, was between his mother and himself.[22] Little Oliver was able to acquire language at all because "grammatical potential is present...in every child's brain" (47, note).[23] However, he could never have acquired language in isolation, as is evidenced by the plight of the prelingually deaf who are not exposed to language of any kind in the crucial period from birth until five years.[24] The child Oliver's innate ability to use language was activated by many transactions with other people, though at first mostly his mother, who already possessed linguistic power and competence.[25] Oliver's mother, and most of the others who talked with him, were a step ahead; the infant Oliver could not "move into, or conceive of, the next stage ahead except through its being occupied and communicated to him by his mother."[26] The child's independent sensory experience of the world correlated with and confirmed the mother's language and in turn, was given meaning by it. It was his mother's language, internalized by Oliver, that allowed him "to move from sensation into 'sense,' to ascend from a perceptual into a conceptual world."[27]

The ability to name gave the child Oliver the feeling of a kind of ownership.[28] He gained the ability to question and developed "an active and questing disposition in the mind," not "spontaneously...or directly from the impact of experience," but from the communicative exchange; it required *dialogue*, in particular the complex dialogue of mother and child.[29] Oliver's mother had "[a] terrible power...to communicate with her child properly or not; ...[she could] introduce a 'generalized reflection of reality,' a conceptual world that [would] give coherence and meaning to life, and challenge the mind and emotions of the child, or [she could] leave everything at the level of the ungeneralized, the unquestioned, at something almost below the

---

21. Oliver Sacks, *Seeing Voices* (New York: Quality Paperback Book Club Edition, 1990), p. 62.

22. Sacks does not exclude fathers or other persons who are caregivers during infancy from performing this function.

23. Sacks, p. 47, note.

24. Sacks, p. 83. Dr. Kathleen Kleiner, a colleague of mine in psychology specializing in infant development, tells me that children have significant pre-natal exposure to language, also.

25. Sacks, 25.

26. Sacks, p. 63.

27. Sacks, p. 63. Noam Chomsky writes: "We cannot avoid being struck by the enormous disparity between knowledge and experience, in the case of language, between the generative grammar that expresses the linguistic competence of the native speaker and the meager and degenerate data [to which he is exposed] on the basis of which he has constructed this grammar for himself" (quoted in Sacks, p. 83).

28. Sacks, p. 49.

29. Sacks, p. 66.

animal level of the perceptual."[30] Furthermore, from dialogue, external and social, Oliver moved to monologue, inner speech, in order to become himself, to think. "[O]ur real language, our real identity, lies in inner speech, in that ceaseless stream and generation of meaning that constitutes the individual mind."[31] Because Oliver learned language at the appropriate time,[32] he was able to "enter fully into [the] human estate and culture, communicate freely with [his] fellows, acquire and share information."[33]

When Oliver grew up, he studied the phenomenon of deafness and wrote the following:

> The study of the deaf shows us that much of what is distinctively human in us—our capacities for language, for thought, for communication, and culture—do not develop automatically in us, are not just biological functions, but are, equally, social and historical in origin; that they are a *gift*—the most wonderful of gifts—from one generation to another. We see that Culture is as crucial as Nature.[34]

His understanding of the function of language for human beings became this: The human being without language is alienated from self, from others, from culture; without questions, without metaphors, without propositions, without past or future, without imagination. Language connects us to ourselves, to others, to culture. He writes:

> Language arises—biologically—from below, from the irrepressible need of the human individual to think and communicate. But it is also generated, and transmitted—culturally—from above, a living and urgent embodiment of the history, the world-views, the images and passions of a people.[35]

But he still longed for a primal language, like that envisioned by the eighteenth-century Romantic Jean Jacques Rousseau:

> a primordial or original human language, in which everything has its true and natural name; a language so concrete, so particular, that it can catch the

---

30. Sacks, p. 67.
31. Sacks, p. 74.
32. Sacks adds: "But then, suddenly, and in the most dramatic way, the developing child becomes open to language, becomes able to construct a grammar from the utterances of his parents. He shows a spectacular ability, a genius for language, between the ages of twenty-one and thirty-six months..., and then a diminishing capacity, which ends at childhood's end (roughly at the age of twelve or thirteen)" (Sacks, pp. 83-84).
33. Sacks, pp. 8-9. He continues:"[T]o be defective in language, for a human being, is one of the most desperate of calamities, for it is only through language that we enter fully into our human estate and culture, communicate freely with our fellows, acquire and share information."
34. Sacks, p. xiii.
35. Sacks, p. 125.

essence, the "itness," of everything; so spontaneous that it expresses all emotion directly; and so transparent that it is incapable of any evasion or deception. Such a language would be without (and indeed would have no need for) logic, grammar, metaphor, or abstractions—it would be a language not mediate, a symbolic expression of thought and feeling, but, almost magically, an *im*mediate one. Perhaps the thought of such a language—a language of the heart, a language of perfect transparency and lucidity, a language that can say everything, without ever deceiving or entangling us (Wittgenstein often spoke of the bewitchment of language), a language as pure and profound as music—is a universal fantasy.[36]

Sacks explored the language of Sign perhaps in the hope that this would be that universal language, but it was not. Even though he emphasizes the way language connects us and helps us express ourselves, his desires for direct communion and absolute clarity remained frustrated by language.

These modern writers articulate the double nature of language that philosophers and writers have discussed since the Enlightenment—the perceptions that language is how we put ourselves together and connect with others, and that language divides us from ourselves and keeps us from connecting with others. George MacDonald, among many others, thought about how language both conveys and evades meaning and connection, and gave his thinking fictional representation in his novel *Sir Gibbie* (1879) and non-fictional expression in an essay "A Sketch of Individual Development." The novel emphasizes the need we have for language in order to be connected to ourselves, others, and the world. The essay explores the emptiness of language and recognizes what deconstructionists in our century have pointed out: if we assume that language has any real meaning, we are also making the assumption, whether we are aware of it or not, that God exists.

Gibbie is a poverty-stricken orphan; MacDonald also makes him mute, thereby placing his acquisition of language in the foreground.[37] Gibbie's mother died soon after his birth, so he never had that simultaneous exposure to love and language Sacks points to as typical. Gibbie's only parent was an alcoholic cobbler called Sir George Galbraith, who had inherited a baronetcy but no property, and who provided nothing like Lacan's "Law" for his son. Little Gibbie spent his early childhood destitute, uneducated, and very rarely spoken to. When his father died, Gibbie inherited the title, but it meant nothing to him or to anyone around him. Gibbie's muteness caused others to consider him half-witted, especially because he combined muteness with entire innocence, a lack of curiosity, and a non-discriminating love for humanity. He could communicate only through facial expression, and he

---

36. Sacks, p. 16, note.

37. For my earlier discussion of MacDonald, see *"That Rare Thing, A True Reader:" Authors, Readers, and Texts in the Fiction of George MacDonald"* (Diss. U of Oregon, 1986. Ann Arbor: UMI, 1986. 8622480).

was always smiling. Though MacDonald says that Gibbie was in "the kingdom of heaven," he also says that "Gibbie by no means belonged to the higher order, was as yet, indeed, not much better than a very blessed little animal."[38] Though his moment to moment existence satisfied him, his fragmentary and incoherent areas of knowledge left him at the mercy of the moment and with no way to make himself understood. Gibbie witnessed the murder of a sailor friend, and all at once became aware of evil. He began to question and doubt what he had always taken for granted, and his fragmentary existence no longer satisfied him. At the age of eight, Gibbie understood language when its referent was before his eyes. His understanding, however, was like that of a dog to whom the word "sit" refers always to its performing the action, but who never will know when it is "sitting pretty." Language was literal for Gibbie. He misinterpreted three of the four texts he heard, all of which were metaphorical or ideal, and he had no idea that he could associate any of them with words in a book.

Because Gibbie had only his face with which to express himself, he could express only present feeling and that inexactly.[39] Gibbie's speechlessness confined him to the small world of the present and visible. He could not make known his invisible world. He could communicate neither his history nor his thoughts, and consequently was mostly unaware that he had a history or thoughts. The fear and doubt Gibbie experienced after witnessing violence made him aware of loneliness and of his speechlessness. He could respond to violence only by running away, and one cannot run away forever. Furthermore, his inability to exert the power of language invited others to abuse their power, and he discovered this unfortunate human tendency wherever there are humans.

Alone in the country, he hid in the barn at the Mains farm. He played brownie to the housekeeper there by doing her chores before she woke, and he helped Donal Grant herd the cows. Donal read poetry to him in the fields. The laird whipped Gibbie for vagrancy and impersonating a brownie. Gibbie was, of course, unable to explain himself. He ran away again, this

---

38. George MacDonald, *Sir Gibbie* (New York: A.L. Burt, n.d.), p. 6.

39. MacDonald writes in "The Imagination: Its Function and Culture" in *The Imagination and Other Essays* (Boston: Lothrop, n.d.): "[F]or how shall two agree together what name they shall give to a thought or a feeling? How shall the one show the other that which is invisible? True, he can unveil the mind's construction in the face—that living, eternally changeful symbol which God has hung in front of the unseen spirit—but that without words reaches only to the expression of present feeling. To attempt to employ it alone for the conveyance of the intellectual or the historical would constantly mislead; while the expression of feeling itself would be misinterpreted, especially with regard to cause and object: the dumb show would be worse than dumb.

But let a man become aware of some new movement within him. Loneliness comes with it, for he would share his mind with his friend, and he cannot; he is shut up in speechlessness" (p. 7).

time to the mountain, and there found Janet Grant, Donal's mother. Janet taught Gibbie to read and write. One of his first literate acts was to identify himself as Sir Gibbie Galbraith. When some years later a wealthy relative of his died, the minister of Gibbie's parish traced him and took him back to the city to inherit. The minister hoped that Gibbie would be unable to assert himself, leaving the minister in charge of Gibbie's money. However, because Gibbie was able to write to make his wishes known, he took control of his fortune when he turned twenty-one, set up a center for reclaiming destitute and fallen women, bought the estate of the laird who whipped him, and married the laird's daughter. Participating in language by means of literacy made it possible for Gibbie to take his place in society and to turn the tables on those who ignored, oppressed, or exploited him.

Like the deaf children studied by Oliver Sacks, Gibbie dramatizes the extent to which language works to bridge the gulf isolating one human from another. He also shows how necessary it is to participate in language to one's survival in human society as an acknowledged human being. Mac-Donald identifies the patterns of language that communicate the past and the ideal with narrative and metaphor, respectively. Gibbie lacks the ability to perceive that fragments can relate to each other in such a way as to make a meaningful whole as they do in narrative; he also lacks the ability to abstract a quality from two unlike things so that they can be compared in metaphor. He does not think and cannot express himself in the ways Mac-Donald considers the work of the imagination. Oliver Sacks writes about similar limitations in children who were prelingually deaf, though Gibbie is not deaf, only mute. Gibbie's learning the metaphoric ability to see resemblances between apparently unlike things, for instance, between flowers and humans, signals the waking of Gibbie's imagination. MacDonald sees this waking as a necessary occurrence if Gibbie is to participate fully in language and to take his place as a complete human. MacDonald elsewhere represents the ability to see "some form, aspect, or movement of nature, some relation between its forms, or between such and himself which resembles the state or motion within" a person as prerequisite to the ability to use language at all.[40]

When he runs away, Gibbie finds he is not at home in the natural universe. For Gibbie the city is "friendliness, comfort, home"! Nature is "emptiness—the abode of the things, not beings."[41] Gibbie is a materialist, and the material universe gives him no welcome. He needs metaphor before he can turn the material world into his home. The light of the sunrise reminds him of the dead sailor's eyes and teeth and "the red burst from his throat."[42] Although he makes a dreadful comparison between sunrise and a

---

40. MacDonald, "The Imagination: Its Function and Culture," p. 8.
41. MacDonald, *Sir Gibbie*, p. 57.
42. MacDonald, *Sir Gibbie*, p. 56.

slit throat, as Gibbie abstracts the quality of red from both sunrise and blood he begins to think in terms of metaphor. A few weeks later Gibbie has become "greatly reconciled to the loneliness of nature and no more afraid of her solitary presence."[43] The word "presence" signifies a distinct change in Gibbie's relationship to nature, from finding nature impersonal to thinking of nature as a presence. In part this arises from his desperate longing for people, and it moves Gibbie to discover analogies between nature and the human being. This awareness of emptiness in Nature at first sounds similar to Jacques Lacan's idea that the world of language is empty, but the order is backwards. Lacan suggests that being denied direct access to reality precipitates the child into the empty world of language; MacDonald suggests that being denied access to language places a child in the empty world of nature. Gibbie's new ability to use metaphor begins to turn what is into what it is not in order to relate nature to himself. This story suggests that an essential step toward participating in language is understanding that language does not always mean what it says. The connecting of Gibbie's literal-mindedness with his illiteracy suggests that one must be aware of the artificiality of language before one can use it effectively. To recognize artifice is to recognize conventional patterns.

Let's return to that early point in the story when Gibbie comes from the city to the Mains' farm, before he learns to read. His acquaintance with the herd-boy Donal Grant is significant because it is his first friendship with a reader. Gibbie has never heard a narrative, and has as yet no concept of literature at all, but that is about to change, as Donal opens to Gibbie the possibility of connections between spoken words and the miracle of narrative, and between spoken words and words written in books.

> "Can ye read, cratur?" asked Donal.
>> Gibbie shook his head.
> "Canna ye speyk, man?"
> Again Gibbie shook his head.
> "Can ye hear?"
> Gibbie burst out laughing. He knew that he heard better than other people.
> "Hearken till this, than," said Donal.
> He took his book from the grass and read, in a chant, or rather in a lilt, the Danish ballad of Chyld Dyring, as translated by Sir Walter Scott. Gibbie's eyes grew wider and wider as he listened; their pupils dilated, and his lips parted: it seemed as if his soul were looking out of doors and windows at once—but a puzzled soul that understood nothing of what it saw. Yet plainly, either the sounds, or the thought-matter vaguely operative beyond the line where intelligence begins, or, it may be, the sparkle of individual word or phrase islanded in a chaos of rhythmic motion, wrought somehow

43. MacDonald, *Sir Gibbie*, p. 65.

upon him, for his attention was fixed as by a spell. When Donal ceased, he remained open-mouthed and motionless for a time; then, drawing himself slidingly over the grass to Donal's feet, he raised his head and peeped above his knees at the book. A moment only he gazed, and drew back with a hungry sigh: he had seen nothing in the book like what Donal had been drawing from it—as if one should look into the well of which he had just drunk and see there nothing but dry pebbles and sand! The wind blew gentle, the sun shone bright, all nature closed softly round the two, and the soul whose bright children they were, was nearer than the one to the other, nearer than the sun or wind or daisy or Chyld Dyring. To his amazement, Donal saw the tears gathering in Gibbie's eyes. ...The child in whom neither cold nor hunger nor nakedness nor loneliness could move a throb of self-pity, was moved to tears that a loveliness, to him strange and unintelligible, had passed away, and he had no power to call it back.

"Wad ye like to hear't again?" asked Donal, more than half-understanding him instinctively.

Gibbie's face answered with a flash, and Donal read the poem again, and Gibbie's delight returned greater than before, for now something like a dawn began to appear among the cloudy words. Donal read it a third time, and closed the book, for it was almost the hour for driving the cattle home. He had never yet seen, and perhaps never again did see, such a look of thankful devotion on human countenance as met his lifted eyes.[44]

Perhaps it is the concept of completeness as well as the story itself that Gibbie seeks to grasp as he hears the ballad a second and third time. His apparent enchantment—note the connection of magic and song—is also a coming awake to the possibilities of language, reversing the usual connotations of "enchantment." Language itself reverses our ordinary differentiation of its uses when we realize that the etymological root of "spell" is a word meaning both discourse and tale, and "spell" is associated both with magic and with the way letters combine to form words as well. Gibbie has never come under the spell of language until this moment, and has therefore not yet become fully human.

Shortly after this passage, the narrator states that "it is impossible for me to say" how much of the ballad Gibbie understands, yet he pinpoints this moment as the beginning of Gibbie's awakening to the knowledge of himself as a self. This move towards self-consciousness is neither an unfortunate necessity nor a fortunate fall, but instead it signifies Gibbie's transition into a higher life without loss of his goodness. When he can recognize narrative, Gibbie gains a way to comprehend his own history as well, which means that he begins to know himself as a self.[45]

It is no accident that MacDonald chooses poetry for Gibbie to hear; MacDonald considers poetry to be essential language. "[P]oetry is the

---

44. MacDonald, *Sir Gibbie*, pp. 96-97.

source of all the language that belongs to the inner world, whether it be of passion or of metaphysics, of psychology or of aspiration," MacDonald writes in "The Imagination."[46] Gibbie is nearing his entry into the kingdom of imagination that perceives an invisible and inner world and describes it in narrative and metaphor. MacDonald dramatizes a further necessary move toward literacy in the associating of words with books. This may be why Donal does not simply sing Gibbie a Scots ballad from memory. As incredible as it seems to Gibbie, Donal draws the lovely succession of sounds, words, images, and events that make up the ballad he hears out of a book filled with what are to Gibbie arbitrarily shaped and meaninglessly grouped black marks. The phenomenon seems nothing short of miraculous. This scene suggests that the narrative and the book which we often consider ordinary parts of our lives are in fact near-miracles.

Gibbie has never before heard the whole of any text and has therefore not known that such a miracle as a complete story exists. The ballad alerts him to the possibility that a beautiful whole can be constructed out of fragments; a belief in that possibility provides a necessary hope to those who are learning to read and to those who are learning to live. Perhaps this hope for wholeness is again similar to Jacques Lacan's idea of desire for the Other. However, the explicit difference between the two is that MacDonald links the possibility of wholeness to the existence of a Soul imminent in the world, nearer than nature or the ballad to Donal and Gibbie, nearer to each of them than they are to each other. In other words, MacDonald finds the beautiful whole made possible by the existence of God. He presents the reading of the ballad—standing in for the entire use of language—as a sacrament, because it is evidence to him of the nearness of God.

---

45. Immediately following the incident related above, the narrator remarks: "Certainly it was the beginning of much. But the waking up of a human soul to know itself in the mirror of its thoughts and feelings, its loves and delights, oppresses me with so heavy a sense of marvel and inexplicable mystery that when I imagine myself such as Gibbie then was, I cannot imagine myself coming awake. ... When, by slow filmy unveilings, life grew clearer to Gibbie and he not only knew, but knew that he knew, his thoughts always went back to that day in the meadow with Donal Grant as the beginning of his knowledge of beautiful things in the world of man.... . But when or how the change in him began, the turn of the balance, the first push toward life of the evermore invisible germ—of that he remained, much as he wondered, often as he searched his consciousness, as ignorant to the last as I am now" (pp. 97-98).

MacDonald calls this the second birth in his essay, "A Sketch of Individual Development," this change from a simple awareness to a consciousness that includes awareness of self and other. Now, in the terms MacDonald uses in the "Sketch" (p. 45), Gibbie begins "a higher life" and the possibility of "real life...life with a share in its own existence" opens to him. It takes place for Gibbie much later in his life than is normal.

46. MacDonald, "The Imagination: Its Function and Culture," p. 9.

I want to give George MacDonald the last word in this discussion for several reasons. First, his awareness of the duplicity of language predates moderns by a century or so. (Of course, other writers noted this as well even earlier.) Second, though he differs from many modern theoreticians by believing in a Creator, he shares with them the assumption that any meaningfulness in the universe depends absolutely on the existence of that Creator.

In his essay, "A Sketch of Individual Development" (written sometime prior to 1883), MacDonald outlines his ideas of how a person changes in understanding of both nature and poetry. This essay has even greater applicability if we see that nature stands in for objective reality, and poetry stands in for the symbolic system of which language is a part.

Though this sketch may be based on MacDonald's personal experiences—both as a child and as a parent—it labels itself as a work of the imagination, necessarily so, since part of what it describes lies outside the memory. The essay also includes awareness that it describes only one of several types of human beings and that it leaves out some details of the development of that one type (48, 68).[47] Following our method used for Sacks and Lacan, we will tell the story as if George MacDonald were the central character in it.

The infant George's first awareness of the world encompassed only himself and his mother as an extension of himself. In this first consciousness, every need was met by a loving minister. As little George grew, he became conscious of a wider world apart from him which did not concern itself with him as its center. This movement from consciousness to self-consciousness, an awareness of the difference between self and other, MacDonald later came to call a "second birth." Little George based his relationship to this external world on his "fancies, desires, preferences," and he began to see objects outside himself as "lovely, desirable, good, or ugly, hateful, bad."[48] When he acted on his emotions toward and thoughts about this separate world, George on occasion met with opposition from his mother.[49] This brought about what he came later to call a third birth, the birth of his desire and also of his conscience, which he found sided with his mother. George then knew that the self he was conscious of was capable of action, that it could be divided between desire and conscience, and that he had to choose what to do.

Later on, when George went to school, he encountered the force of public opinion. He discovered that public opinion could be at odds with his

47. MacDonald, "A Sketch of Individual Development," in *The Imagination and Other Essays* (Boston: Lothrop, n.d.), pp. 48, 68.

48. MacDonald, "A Sketch of Individual Development," pp. 45-46.

49. This contrasts with Lacan's idea that it is the Father who brings Law, or opposition to desire, into the child's awareness.

conscience. The choice to do what is right regardless of desire as well as consequence MacDonald later came to call a fourth birth, the development of the real Will. This birth took years as an adult to complete, perhaps a whole lifetime.

Because MacDonald was a poet, he discussed the relationship of the human to language in terms of the relationship of the human to poetry. To return to our narrative, the adult George went through several phases in evaluating the meaningfulness of language. First, as an idealist, he thought that meaning is inherent in nature and in words. His encounter with the scientific world view shocked him into materialism, which he called "soulless Law." He then believed that nature and words had only the meanings he read into them. His falling in love gave him an intuitive sense of the grand unity of nature, of which he was a part, but he saw that nature itself was in conflict between a "rush for death, a panic flight into the moveless silence... the tumultuous conflict of forces rushing, and fighting as they rush, into the arms of eternal negation" and "vitality, revealed in growth, itself an unending resurrection."[50] As he began to see correspondences between apparently unrelated natural laws, he renewed his vision of the oneness of the universe and began to hope that this oneness was evidence of a Creator God. He also began to understand that in order for a poem or any other written text to mean anything, it must have behind it an author; and in order for that human author to mean anything, the human must have behind him or her a greater Author. George could not believe that the products of human thought mean anything when he was not sure that the human being means anything.

At this point, George heard the gospel story. His skepticism about words made it difficult to believe this story. But he noticed that the central character Jesus said that if a person would understand the words, that person would first need to obey them. The existence of God may be suggested by the universe, as the existence of an author is suggested by the presence of a text. But God can be known not through language or nature, but only by doing, by experiment, by experience. So George tried to obey what he thought the texts said, and he came to define truth not as a statement but as a person, the Author of nature and of human beings.

Epilogue

Jacques Lacan presents language as a sign of loss; its acquisition takes place as a result of losing access to the mother because of the intervention of the father. It reminds us always of that loss even while it makes possible our awareness of self and connection to others. Oliver Sacks describes language as a sign of gain; its acquisition takes place in loving exchange between

---

50. MacDonald, "A Sketch of Individual Development," p. 57.

mother and child and makes possible the child's awareness of self and connection to others. However, he longs also for a more direct, more immediate means of communication. George MacDonald's character Gibbie begins with loss—mother, father, speech, friend. He acquires two substitute mothers: Nature teaches him metaphoric thinking, and Janet Grant teaches him to write and read. He also acquires a substitute father and a friend in Donal Grant, who introduces him to narrative. Metaphor and narrative combined with literacy make it possible for him to identify himself and to connect with other people. However, in his non-fiction, George MacDonald shows that language is only as meaningful as nature or the human being. If they mean nothing, language is also empty of meaning. And nature and the human being can be meaningful only if there is a Creator behind them that makes them so. Whether we recognize it as such or not, the use of language is an act of faith.

All three writers recognize the human condition as one of longing for wholeness, for integrity, for connectedness, for communion. This longing is well expressed in a poem by Walt Whitman, 19th-century American Quaker poet who celebrated connectedness in his *Song of Myself*, but dramatized his ultimate sense of isolation in the final incomplete sentence of his poem, "A Noiseless Patient Spider:"

> A noiseless patient spider,
> I mark'd where on a little promontory it stood isolated,
> Mark'd how to explore the vacant vast surrounding,
> It launch'd forth filament, filament, filament, out of itself,
> Ever unreeling them, ever tirelessly speeding them.
>
> And you O my soul where you stand,
> Surrounded, detached, in measureless oceans of space,
> Ceaselessly musing, venturing, throwing, seeking the spheres to connect them,
> Till the bridge you will need be form'd, till the ductile anchor hold,
> Till the gossamer thread you fling catch somewhere, O my soul.

WORKS CITED

Ankeny, Rebecca Thomas. "That Rare Thing, A True Reader:" Authors, Readers, and Texts in the Fiction of George MacDonald" Diss. U of Oregon, 1986. Ann Arbor: UMI, 1986. 8622480.

Eagleton, Terry. *Literary Theory, An Introduction.* Minneapolis: U of Minn Press, 1983.

Lemaire, Anika. *Jacques Lacan.* Trans. David Macey. London: Routledge and Kegan Paul, 1970, 1977.

MacDonald, George. *Sir Gibbie.* 1879. New York: A. L. Burt, n.d.

"A Sketch of Individual Development." *The Imagination and Other Essays.* Boston: Lothrop, n.d. 43-76.

Sacks, Oliver. *Seeing Voices.* 1989, 1990. New York: Quality Paperback Book Club Edition, 1990.

The Anti-Theatrical Prejudice and the Quakers

A Late Twentieth Century Perspective

MICHAEL P. GRAVES

Quakers are remembered generally for their historical efforts to end slavery, reform prisons, improve the plight of the mentally ill, and other humanitarian goals. They are also recognized for their contributions to science, the industrial revolution, reform of banking and insistence on ethical business practices. However, they are not noted for their contributions to the arts, which are in fact minimal. With regard to the theatre, early Quakers would probably be numbered among Jonas Barish's "legions of hard-shelled, mole-eyed fanatics" who occasionally have filled the ranks of theatre-bashers (*The Anti-theatrical Prejudice*, 2) . Seventeenth-century Quakers were, after all, characteristic radical Puritans in this regard.

Today's Quakers are considerably less "hard-shelled" and "mole-eyed" and there are signs on both sides of the Atlantic that the Society of Friends has made progress toward making peace with the theatre. Indeed, one could argue that the situation has changed radically in the last three hundred fifty years, but there remains an ambiguity at best, an antipathy at worst, between Quaker thought and the theatre. This topic is too broad to be encompassed within the limits of this essay, which can merely open doors slightly to a subject that should be treated in more depth at another time and place. Accordingly, this essay will only survey and illustrate the changes in Quaker position toward the theatre and suggest some of their implications. Specifically, it will attempt two things: (1) to sketch historically the development of Quaker attitudes toward the theatre prior to the 1960's, and (2) to document some of the changes in attitude since 1960.

I

The Early Quaker Experience. Frederick Nicholson has written an excellent brief history of the gradual change of attitude toward the arts, including the theatre, among British Quakers (*Quakers and the Arts*). Unfortunately, there is no equivalent study of American Quaker attitudes,[1] but the history of American Quaker "liberalization" of attitudes toward the arts during the first two hundred years essentially parallels—although lags behind—that of our British counterparts. Developing on the fringes of mid seventeenth century radical Puritanism, Quakerism became for a period of time the fastest growing English sect. The essential Quaker message was that the Inward Light of Christ enlightens every person and that all can attend to that Light—manifested directly to individuals—and thus attain salvation without recourse to church tradition, creed, sacrament, clergy or even the Bible. They believed they were experiencing a revival of "primitive Christianity."[2] In their zeal to effect their apocalyptic vision they "cleaned house," so to speak, and reduced the Christian experience to what they saw as its essence. Nicholson observed: "...they announced the immanence of the Kingdom of Heaven and the immanence of the Day of the Lord.... Time was short; all energy, all faculties, had to be concentrated on this mission; nothing that seemed to stand in the way of Righteousness could be tolerated. 'I was moved,' said [George] Fox, 'to cry out against all sorts of music, and against the mountebanks playing tricks on their stages; for *they burthened the pure life*, and stirred up the people's vanity'" (*Quakers and the Arts*, 2, emphasis Nicholson's). Fox's view captured two of the early Quakers' objections to theatre: (1) that it was not truthful—it played tricks, and (2) that it represented at best a means of diversion from attaining the "pure life" of ethical and moral behavior and at worst, an inducement to corrupt behavior.

Fox's view was not unique. Space does not permit an extensive review of early Quaker writings on the subject, but in passing let me note that Robert Barclay, the most important early Quaker intellectual, roundly condemned the theatre in his influential *Apology for the True Christian Divinity*, first published in English in 1678. In Proposition Fifteen, he asserted: "...these games, sports, plays, dancing, comedies, &c. do naturally tend to draw men from God's fear, to make them forget heaven, death, and judgment, to foster

---

1. Bacon (*The Quiet Rebels*) devotes seven pages of a chapter to "Quakers and the Arts," 162-168.

2. For an excellent scholarly treatment of the earliest years, which situates Quakerism in the ranks of radical Puritanism, see Barbour, *The Quakers in Puritan England*.New Haven:Yale University Press, 1964. See also items by Barbour and Roberts, Bauman, Braithwaite, and Creasey in the "List of Works Consulted."

lust, vanity, and wantonness…" (343). Even the sophisticated and courtly, William Penn, queried: "How many plays did Jesus Christ and His Apostles recreate themselves at? What poets, romances, comedies, and the like did the Apostles and Saints make, or use to pass away their time withal? I know, they did all redeem their time, to avoid foolish talking, vain jesting, profane babblings, and fabulous stories."[3] Barclay and Penn, of course, were writing in the notorious era of Restoration drama, and their views do not necessitate a rejection of all theatrical endeavor, but that is precisely how they were interpreted by their contemporaries and later Quakers, and the influence of these writers was enormous.

Eighteenth and Nineteenth Century Quaker Attitudes. The earliest Quakers' eighteenth century successors largely relinquished efforts to evangelize and reform the world, turning instead quietly inward in an epoch characterized by the development of "testimonies" that marked Quakers as "peculiar" people. A part of their "peculiarity," in addition to the well-known plain speech and Quaker gray, included rejection of games, sport, theatre and, in general, anything undertaken for the purpose of pleasure alone.[4]

There are numerous examples of Quaker writings that reflect the antitheatrical prejudice throughout the eighteenth and nineteenth centuries on both sides of the Atlantic. An interesting instance not noted in the secondary literature is the *Remonstrance…against the Erection of a Theatre* by Bristol Monthly Meeting (England) in 1764. The document presents the standard Quaker objections to the theatre: promotion of vanity, disorder, lewdness, folly, intemperance, and debauchery; encouragement of wildness and idleness; injury to the light of religion; authority of magistrates weakened by a corruption of manners; and the influence of actors held as generally injurious to youth. What appears to be a new argument surfaces in the document tying the traditional Quaker position against theatre—that it is a time-wasting diversion—to the new concerns of the rising industrial revolution, Bristol being a major commercial city. The *Remonstrance* counsels: "It is well known that Commerce, under the Divine Blessings, is the great Support of this City. The chief Sinews of Commerce are Frugality and Industry. How much then does it behove [sic] to check the Growth of Profusion and Idleness, by discouraging dissolute Recreations, of which the Performers are a dead Weight on the Industry of the Community" (1).

Another illustration of the persistent negative teaching against theatre among eighteenth and nineteenth century Quakers, together with threat of "disownment" (the Quaker equivalent of excommunication) for theatre attendees, is discovered in perusal of books of discipline, also published as "Faith and Practice," or sometimes edited, collected and published in part

3. *No Cross, No Crown*, 1682. Quoted in Nicholson, 7.
4. See the works by Bauman and Braithwaite in the "List of Works Consulted" for good descriptions of the progression of Quakers toward "quietism."

as "Christian Advices." For example, the 1866 *Discipline* of Western Yearly Meeting (Indiana) advised:

> ...to watch carefully over the youth...to prevent them by affectionate counsel and brotherly admonition, from frequenting stage-plays, horse-races, music, dancing, and other vain sports and amusements...it being abundantly obvious, that those practices have a tendency to alienate the mind from the counsel of divine wisdom—and to foster those impure dispositions which lead to debauchery and wickedness. If, therefore, any of our members fall into any of these practices, and cannot be prevailed with by private labor to decline them, the Monthly Meetings to which they belong should be informed thereof, and if they cannot be reclaimed by further labor, should proceed to disown them (66-67).

Changes in British Quaker Attitudes. Even as the Western Yearly Meeting document found print, a movement was gaining ground that would call into question the attitude of blanket rejection of the fine and performing arts among Friends. Nicholson credits two essays published in 1859 with initiating the turn-around among English Quakers. Both John Stephenson Rowntree and Thomas Hancock endeavored to account for the decline in influence and numbers of nineteenth century Quakers, and both laid some of the blame on the old Quaker antagonism toward the arts. Nicholson noted that the "two essays, with their keen criticism of Quaker deficiencies, initiated a grand debate within the Society of Friends" (91). Matters generally move slowly among Friends, and it was not until 1895—thirty-six years later—after decades of grass roots Quaker accommodation to changes in contemporary British culture (e.g., the influence of the Adult School Movement, the relaxation of Quaker antipathy toward music, and the virtual disappearance of the Quaker distinct pattern of speech and costume), that English Quakers finally held a conference where the place of the arts became the essential part of the agenda. Nicholson points out that eventually, in the first quarter of the twentieth century, Quakers eliminated their objections to acting, partly due to the effective work of a Birmingham Quaker, Wilfred F. Southall, who toured and lectured about Palestine accompanied by twenty-four amateur actors posing as Biblical characters (99).

At length, the 1925 *Discipline* of the London Yearly Meeting gave "official" recognition to the creative arts (105). Nicholson compares the 1925 *Discipline* with the image of an early nineteenth century Quaker found in Thomas Clarkson's famous book of 1806, *A Portraiture of Quakerism*:

> To the Quaker of 1806 the drama is unacceptable because it "occasions an extraordinary excitement of the mind," and stage-plays "hold out false morals." In 1925 dramatic art is "one by which performers and spectators alike may gain a truer insight into human life, a deeper appreciation of its

meaning, and wider sympathy with mankind." In 1806 acting was an accomplishment of the Prince of Darkness. Friends of 1925, however, are advised to exercise "due discrimination," perform or watch drama in "appropriate conditions" and "make a careful choice to support good plays."There is also repeated the warning of the danger of "personating the character of others," for even in 1925 "we need to remember the possibilities of injury to the actor's personality which may arise from constantly representing the character of other persons" (108-109).

Changes in American Quaker Attitudes. On the other side of the Atlantic, American Quakers, although partially influenced by the writings and events of London Yearly Meeting, faced somewhat different circumstances and their narrative of change differs from the British account. We must bear in mind that in America, Quakerism was rent by schism for both doctrinal and socio-economic reasons, and that the very vastness of the geography mitigated against frequent contact.[5] For these reasons, American Quakerism is not characterized by one voice, one Yearly Meeting, one chain of events. To further complicate the tale, the holiness revivals of the late nineteenth century, which swept through the Midwest, had a profound effect on American Quakerism, but virtually no effect on English Friends. The revivals produced, if anything, a stricter emphasis on self-examination and holy living, but also held out hope to many unchurched and non-Quaker seekers for salvation. As a result the ranks of Quakers in the Midwest swelled to the point where the traditional nonpastoral elder system could not meet the needs of the new converts. Thus several yearly meetings adopted a system of full time paid (or "released") pastors.[6]

Another circumstance that distinguished American from British Quakerism during the nineteenth century related to their differing systems of education. In both England and America, Quakers established their own primary and secondary schools. However, in America, Quakers went further and established colleges. Eventually, these centers of intellectual ferment and cultural scrutiny would play a role in the story of American Quakerism's accommodation to theatre.[7]

I noted above that there is no equivalent to Nicholson's study with respect to American Quakers' relationship to the arts, and this essay can do

---

5. A brief description of the results of schism on the face of Quakerism in North America can be found in Bronner, *American Quakers Today*, 11-31. See also Frost and Barbour, 169-182, and 234-36. The latter includes a chart of the "separations," including yearly meeting membership figures through 1982. For a reasonably contemporary description of typical worship patterns among the various Friends groups in North America, see Hall, *Quaker Worship in North America*.

6. For an account of the effects of revivalism on nineteenth century Quakerism see Williams, *The Rich Heritage of Quakerism*,192-201. See also Frost and Barbour, 203-218.

7. Frost and Barbour, 241-42.

little more than indicate the preliminary results of some potentially fruitful avenues of investigation, one of which is a perusal of books of discipline issued by yearly meetings in America. The *Christian Advices Issued by The Yearly Meeting of Friends Held in Philadelphia*, published in 1859, the same year as the Rowntree and Hancock lectures in England, repeats a section published in the earlier 1808 discipline, which had included this caution:

> As our time passeth swiftly away, and our delight ought to be in the law of the Lord, it is advised that a watchful care be exercised over our youth and others in membership, to prevent their going to stage-plays, horse-races, music, dancing, or any such vain sports and pasttimes.... And as we are not only accountable for our substance, but also for our time, let them be employed in fulfilling our respective religious and social duties, remembering the injunction, "Work while it is called today, for the night cometh wherein no man can work" (45).

The situation had not changed appreciably by 1908—one hundred years later—when Friends in Pennsylvania, New Jersey and Delaware issued *Principles of Quakerism*, which included the following passage:

> Friends believe that Christians should not go to see theatrical performances, first, because acting is essentially demoralizing to the actors. The fact that some men and women of the stage accept and follow the ordinary laws of morality, in no way weakens this objection. The demoralizing effect of the whole atmosphere and surroundings of stage life is recognized by many of those engaged in it.... Secondly, Friends are opposed to theatre-going because of its effect on those who go. Everybody condemns bad plays, but who shall say where the line shall be drawn? Most of the plays patronized by the better class of people contain passages which are objectionable from the point of view of strict morality. Add to this the unwholesome artificial mental excitement produced by watching plays, and the questionable associations into which play-going leads, and it becomes sufficiently evident that the practice is adverse to spiritual growth (194-195).

My own survey of American Quaker disciplines published prior to 1900 indicates that the majority of them either carried warnings about the theatre or strong admonitions to lead a circumspect life that excluded sports, wagers, tobacco, strong drink and stage plays, all of these activities linked in the same passage. The 1895 *Discipline* of the newly-formed Oregon Yearly Meeting is typical: "Guard watchfully against...such companionship, indulgences and recreations as will interfere with your growth in grace. Avoid such places as are low and demoralizing in their tendency, and all gambling, lotteries, theaters, the use of tobacco, intoxicating liquors, and all other practices of a hurtful or sinful tendency" (59). However, when the *Discipline* was revised in 1924, it included no direct mention of "theatre," but did include, in another section, the following Query 5: "Are you careful to avoid all places and amusements inconsistent with a Christian character; and do you observe true moderation in all things?" (81). Clearly, there was a modification of outlook toward theatre which had moved from blanket condemnation to an emphasis on individual judgment based upon a moral framework and upon moderation. By 1931 D. Elton Trueblood could write: "At one time Friends went so far as to oppose the arts in private life, but that time is happily past. Friends now go freely to concerts and theater performances..." (*Problems of Quakerism*, 62).

II

It is one thing to allow attendance at the theatre, according to the dictates of one's conscience; it is quite another to *encourage* attendance or *develop* within Quaker circles people who will serve the theatre and/or the church as playwrights, actors or directors. In other words, there is a marked difference between guardedly partaking as spectators and participating as artists. Yet this is what has begun to occur among English and American Friends since about 1960. In 1969, Margaret Bacon wrote somewhat enthusiastically regarding the Quaker anti-theatrical bias: "...this prejudice has disappeared as completely as snow in summer" (*The Quiet Rebels*, 168).

There are four substantial signs of the process of change with respect to theatre among Quakers. One sign is the development of a philosophical and theological dialogue among Friends about the arts sparked by the presentation of three notable Swarthmore Lectures among British Friends and continued with the publication of several other essays. Another sign is a list of practical theatre endeavors which Quakers have initiated on both sides of the Atlantic. A third sign is the emergence of Quaker playwrights and performers. The final sign is the beginning of substantial attitudinal change in the approach of Yearly Meetings and local meetings and churches toward the arts in general and theatre in particular.

The Intellectual Dialogue. The intellectual dialogue began with Kenneth C. Barnes' 1960 Swarthmore Lecture, *The Creative Imagination*, in which he explored the act of creativity in both science and poetry and argued implicitly against didacticism in art. He observed: "...in any activity that is in the nature of a discovery we cannot know in advance what the discovery will be, for this would be to make an absurdity of the whole process" (26). Later he asserted: "If we have faith in the unity of God and Truth we should have the courage to follow where truth leads" (27). Fifteen years later Barnes wrote with regard to Friends and the arts: "What should be said to Friends in particular? Certainly that they should release themselves finally and completely from the mistaken view that gaiety in living, in form and colour and conduct, is touched with sin. Also from any thought that the arts are on the circumference of the activity of the spirit. They are at the centre" (*A Vast*

Bundle of Opportunities, 118). Here was a respected Quaker scientist and artist joining the argument about the arts at its very core. Barnes continued his thinking and writing on the arts with the publication of *Integrity and the Arts* in 1984.

In 1978 J. Ormerod Greenwood presented a Swarthmore Lecture published as *Signs of Life*, in which he argued essentially that denying the range of experience found in the arts involves a denial of part of oneself. He also presented a positive image of "ephemeral art," thus implying a concept of "art" and "artist" that is intentionally not elitist and more inclusive in scope. His view tended to move toward what might be called a Quaker view of the arts, which for theatre would mean a concept incorporating more reliance on improvisation and the widespread involvement of non-professionals. Greenwood's wholesale affirmation of the arts has caused Quakers in England to dialogue seriously about the "dark side" of art, a topic which moves full circle to some of the core objections voiced by the seventeenth century Quaker writers (Benner, "Art and so on," 233).

Laurence Lerner's 1984 Swarthmore Lecture, *The Two Cinnas*, a sophisticatedly beautiful piece of writing dealing with the impulse to achieve political objectives counterpoised with the artistic impulse, argued that the artist is a kind of prophet: "What the poet can do for us here is to warn, to warn much more vividly and unforgettably than any of us can" (36). Lerner's view of the artist was more limiting than Greenwood's and seemed to call for a special recognition of the artist as prophet among Friends.

The Swarthmore Lectures by Barnes, Greenwood and Lerner, and a number of articles in *The Friends' Quarterly* and *Quaker Monthly*, indicate a healthy acceptance of art, including theatre, by British Quakers as well as an attempt to dialogue about and come to grips with the relationship of the arts to Quaker belief.

In America the output of learned essays and presentations is not as great or as well known among Friends. A survey of the major American Quaker periodicals—*Evangelical Friend*, *Quaker Life*, and *Friends Journal*—revealed no recent articles addressing the issues raised by British Quakers. One issue of the American intellectual journal, *Quaker Religious Thought*, did address the subject of Friends and the arts. It included essays by Candida Palmer and Chris Downing that spoke to some of the issues raised by the British writers, such as Downing's consideration of didacticism and its place ("Friends' Relation to the Arts," 28, ff.). Palmer made a strong case for the need for community among Friends with respect for the arts, a community that would make "Quaker art" possible, an art that not only universally reflects human aspiration, achievement and failure, but also reflects the unique Quaker vision. Downing, on the other hand, argued for an art that "doesn't simply confirm us in our prior prejudices" (Downing, 29). This is not a frivolous issue among Quakers, who have been intensely practical and occasionally didactic in their practice of spirituality. It is not surprising that many of the Quaker efforts at indigenous theatre have tended to manifest a distinctly practical and didactic hue. We turn now to a sampling of these experiments.

Quaker Strides in Theatrical Performance and Experiment. As interesting and provocative as the new dialogue on the arts has been among Friends, it is perhaps not as visible as the strides actually made by Quakers in theatrical performance. In Britain, 1978 saw the beginnings of "The Leaveners," a London Yearly Meeting sanctioned youth theatre that employs street theatre, music, masks, dance, clowning, processional, improvisation, etc., to put together shows that are performed during the summer and are sometimes taken on tours. The eighteen year history of the venture has been evaluated with generally glowing praise for its accomplishments (Marsh, "The Leaveners—An Appraisal").

Another British Quaker project, The Peace Action Caravan, launched in 1979, a year after The Leaveners, developed a street theatre program that was taken to schools and colleges in order to raise consciousness about world peace issues, particularly concerning nuclear disarmament (Pyper, "Witnessing for Peace," 596-597). British Quakers have also developed programs such as "Questabout" and "Dramaquest," that use dramatic techniques such as involving young people in role-playing about Quaker history, thought and current social problems.[8]

In America, one of the most visible signs of a Quaker rapprochement with theatre is seen in the curricula and outreach of the Quaker Colleges. Most of the colleges have drama or theatre departments, and some have traveling theatre troupes.[9] Let me note programs at three of the most conservative colleges on the list of eleven, institutions most closely tied to their regional yearly meetings, places where one might expect the appearance of vestigial traditional Quaker objections toward theatre. Barclay College, Havilland, Kansas, maintains a drama troupe that has "provided a unique ministry to the churches through the dramatization of Biblical and ethical themes" (*Barclay College Catalog*, 1992-94, 28). The *Catalog* describes the troupe as "A performance group that employs plays, skits, readings, and

---

8. See articles by Davison and Anderson on these topics in the List of Works Consulted.See also Darlene R. Graves, "User-Friendly Theatre," for a detailed description of the British Quaker Theatrical experience considered against a backdrop of the implications of Quaker spirituality on the nature of theatre.

9. A look at the catalogs of several Quaker colleges reveals that there are theatre majors, minors, traveling troupes and/or extra-curricular programs in theatre at Barclay College, Earlham College, Friends University, George Fox College, Guilford College, Haverford College, Malone College, Swarthmore College, Whittier College, William Penn College, and Wilmington College.Earlham College (Richmond, Indiana) offers twenty-three courses combining theatre or dance while Guilford College (Greensboro, North Carolina) lists twenty-eight theatre courses taught by three full time faculty members.

other dramatic forms to share God's love" (60). And yes, Barclay College takes its name from Robert Barclay, the early Quaker writer who had asserted that theatre "naturally tend[s] to draw men from God's fear"!

In Newberg, Oregon, George Fox College has for nearly three decades fielded a theatre troupe variously known as "Friendship Seven," "Inter-Mission," and "George Fox College Players," that has toured regionally and nationally with programs that included set plays, music and improvised drama. During the period 1973-1987, the George Fox College drama group, then known as "Inter-Mission," employed improvisational drama rather than set plays as the bulk of their touring material. Today, George Fox University continues the tradition of touring drama and maintains a rich offering of traditional on-campus theatre performances in addition to regular music theatre productions. The 1995-96 *George Fox College Catalog* includes a course called "Theatre As Ministry," the description of which calls to mind some early Quaker concerns about theatre and refocuses them within the context of ministry: "A consideration of theatre skills as tools for meeting human needs in essentially nontheatrical environments. Focus on drama as a service medium rather than as strictly an entertainment vehicle" (92). Fox, Penn and Barclay would be pleased.

Similarly, Malone College, Canton, Ohio, has also developed a respectable program in drama and was, until recent years, the location each summer of the Christians in Theatre Arts (CITA) conference. Malone College's *Academic Catalog 1995-96* lists a Theatre Concentration within the Communication Arts major and describes among its six theatre courses, an offering called "Christian Drama," a part of which deals with a concern that students "understand the unique problems of producing religious dramas in non-theatrical environments" (78).

Clearly, these conservative Quaker colleges, representing geographically diverse yearly meetings, have discovered ways to develop curriculum and activities in theatre that blend evangelical Quaker concerns with the performing arts.

The Emergence of Quaker Playwrights and Performers. Quakers have also begun to witness the emergence of a small number of writers and performers who have experimented with a variety of theatrical forms and performances styles. The improvisational theatre work of Leaveners and Inter-Mission have already been noted. In addition to these innovations, I should like to focus briefly on the contributions of four additional Quaker theatrical innovators.

Arthur O. Roberts, Professor-at-Large at George Fox College, teamed with composer David Miller, to produce two musical dramas. The first, *Children of the Light*, a moving and lively depiction of the earliest years of the Quaker movement, was performed initially to enthusiastic audiences at Bauman Auditorium, George Fox College, February 12 and 13, 1983, and at the sessions of Northwest Yearly Meeting July 24, 1983. Between two and three thousand people attended these performances.[10] Roberts and Miller combined their talents again six years later to write and produce a sophisticated and prophetic musical drama on the life of Jonah, *Jonah ben Amittai*, which premiered at Reedwood Friends Church, Portland, Oregon, February 25 and 26, 1989.[11]

On the "representational" end of the theatrical scale, William C. Kashatus, a teacher at William Penn Charter School in Philadelphia, has been performing "living history" for more than a decade. His Quaker Living History Series includes a choice of three twenty minute one-person performances based upon an interweaving of journal entries and other surviving primary source materials from the lives of George Fox (*Walking in the Light with George Fox*), Nathaniel Wetherill (*Nathaniel Wetherill's Conflict of Conviction*) and Levi Coffin (*President of the Underground Railroad*). As a professional historian as well as an accomplished actor, Kashatus strives to "present the people and events of the past as honestly and as accurately as possible. This involves integrating *their* own words and *their* own experiences, taken from letters, diaries, journals, or speeches, into the performance itself."[12]

Another Quaker innovator, Rich Swingle, has been performing one-person shows with Quaker themes. His *A Clear Leading*, based on incidents in John Woolman's life, has delighted audiences across America and was featured at the John Woolman Forum sponsored by the Center for Peace Learning of George Fox College, and will be performed at The Lamb's Little Theatre in New York City in 1996. Swingle is a serious playwright and actor whose latest program features the characters Gideon, Lazarus, Jeremiah, St. Patrick, and Jonah—all "people that heard God's voice and responded in different ways" (Swingle. E-mail to the author. 5 April, 1996). Swingle adds: "I talk about what that process is all about, bringing these folk to the stage to show what is was like for them." Swingle also employs a form of "sociodrama" in his performances which reaches back into the roots of

---

10. David Miller was also the musical director; Richard Benham the stage director; and Joseph Gilmore acted as production supervisor. Lee Whitcomb played the lead role of George Fox in each of these performances. A number of audio tapes were subsequently sold, and the little song, "The People not the Steeple is the Church," has been used at Quaker youth gatherings. *Children of the Light* was also performed in readers theatre style before a gathering of the Friends Association for Higher Education, at Friends University, Wichita, Kansas, in June, 1984.

11. Benjamin Dobbeck directed the production and Richard Zeller played the title role.

12. Taken from Kashatus' descriptive brochure, *Dr. K's Living History Programs*. Emphasis in original. William Kashatus also performs an American Living History Series, which includes such characters as Tom Paine and Abraham Lincoln, and conducts National Historical Park Tours. He may be contacted at Dr. K's Living History Programs, 3461 West Queen Lane, Philadelphia, PA19129.

Quaker thought and culture. On this topic he remarks: "I believe this process of bringing people up on stage to experience issues, rather than being lectured, is particularly valuable in dealing with issues of conflict resolution."[13]

These recent examples of Quakers who have experimented with various theatrical forms hopefully hint at a growing edge of involvement by Quakers in theatre beyond the threshold of mere attendance.

The Beginnings of Change in Yearly Meeting Attitude. There are other signs of Quaker rapprochement with theatre, but none so dramatic as the recent developments in Northwest Yearly Meeting, formerly Oregon Yearly Meeting. We noted earlier that Oregon Yearly Meeting changed from a blanket rejection of theatre in its 1895 *Discipline* as "low and demoralizing," to a position in the 1924 *Discipline* for the individual to take responsibility to observe "true moderation." New language was added to the 1970 *Discipline* to "encourage wholesome recreation and discourage those amusements which debase or foster the debasement of the body as the temple of God" (12). By 1975, a novel organizational scheme was adopted that created a new yearly meeting committee dealing with music and the arts operating under the Spiritual Life Board. The new committee was "responsible in the realm of both vocal and instrumental music, their composition, drama, radio and television, arts and crafts, and other creative activities by and for the church" (*Constitution and Discipline*, 46). Here, at last, was a proactive and organized effort to make the arts, including theatre, an active feature of the life of local Quaker meetings in the Pacific Northwest. There has since been no repudiation of the effort. On the contrary, the 1987 *Discipline*, now known as *Faith and Practice*, reported yet another organizational change that further enhanced the position of the arts. The change involved inaugurating a list of "commissions" at the yearly meeting level, including a "Commission of Fine Arts" with the following responsibilities: to offer "guidance to the local churches in vocal and instrumental music, in poetry and drama, in the visual arts and crafts, and in other creative activities by and for the church" (70).

With such an open policy toward the arts, it is not surprising that local meetings in the Pacific Northwest have begun to experiment with theatrical performance as a part of worship. For example, 2nd Street Community Church, an extension ministry of Newberg Friends Church (Oregon), is an example of a local meeting that habitually and intentionally incorporates

---

13. Swingle has also written a play, *I Come and Go at His Command*, about Mary Dyer, one of four Quakers hanged by Puritans on Boston Common (1660). Another of his plays, *Big Fish Little Worm*, is a twenty minute one-person drama that tells the story of Jonah.Swingle often follows this play by a "hot seat," where he as author/performer answers questions from the audience in character. Swingle may be contacted at 130 West 44th Street, New York, NY 10036-4078.

drama into the worship life of the meeting. A drama ministry team regularly meets to develop and rehearse dramatic vignettes to be presented in meeting for worship and to provide a dramatic entré for the pastor's sermon topic.[14]

Apparently, at least in Northwest Yearly Meeting, theatre no longer "burthen[s] the pure life, and stirr[s] up the people's vanity" as had so troubled George Fox in the seventeenth century, or perhaps this is a sign that Quaker ranks are being thinned of the more vocal "hard-shelled, mole-eyed fanatics" whose thin skin refuses to tolerate greasepaint.

Conclusion

I trust this survey of the changes in Quaker attitudes toward theatre has indicated something of the sea change accomplished by Quakers over the past three and one half centuries. However, the history of the anti-theatrical prejudice among Quakers is still being written. Although the blanket condemnation of theatre is no longer present among Quakers to any appreciable degree, there persists a core of distrust despite the changes.

I mentioned at the outset of this essay that there remains an ambiguity at best, an antipathy at worst, between Quaker thought and the theatre. The ambiguity or antipathy surface from time to time in print and in rump sessions at Quaker colleges and at yearly meeting sessions. The points of tension, for example, revolve around the basic question about whether art is possible without conflict, and to what extent a sect that has placed considerable emphasis on peacemaking and achieving decision by consensus can participate in and employ a medium where conflict is the stuff of plot. Another perennial topic involves an updated phrasing of the "work for the night is coming" argument of three centuries past: whether Christians should work directly in the arena of social action or indirectly in the arena of the arts, or both. In other words, is the theatre a waste of time that might be better spent in missions or social work? Should Quakers' main theatrical concern be with "theatre as ministry" or "theatre in nontheatrical environments"? A related question is: if a Quaker decides to work in the arts, to what extent should the art be didactic? This type of question is still seriously posed, and, given Quaker roots, is entirely appropriate.

Another interesting topic that is beginning to surface among Quakers is the idea that Friends may have a particular, perhaps unique, gateway to theatre implied by the Quaker approach to Christian spirituality, which stresses the immediate revelation of God. For example, it may be that a theology of immediate revelation naturally leads to improvisational theatre just as it naturally led early Quakers to impromptu preaching. The Leaveners in

---

14. For more information on this drama ministry program, contact Pastor David Conant, 2nd Street Community Church, 2nd & College Streets, Newberg, OR 97132.

England, and Inter-Mission in the United States, have to an extent operated on this principle. However, if each actor is a potential playwright under direct inspiration, what place would a director hold in such a system? How would consensus operate on stage?[15]

These are among the serious and significant questions that are suggested by this survey. Space does not permit their discussion here. For now, I will conclude with this observation: the Quakers have made remarkable progress in accommodating themselves to the theatre. If the next thirty years produces as much growth in the employment of theatre among Quakers as the last thirty, Friends will be hard pressed not to come to grips, self-consciously and forcefully, with the tensions that arise from the interrelationships among their history, their theological assumptions, and their current practice with regard to theatre.

WORKS CITED

Anderson, John. "What is 'Dramaquest'?" *Quaker Monthly.* 65-11 (1986): 222-225.

Bacon, Margaret H. *The Quiet Rebels: The Story of Quakers in America.* New York: Basic Books, 1969.

Barbour, Hugh. *The Quakers in Puritan England.* New Haven: Yale University Press, 1964.

Barbour, Hugh and J. W. Frost. *The Quakers.* New York: Greenwood Press, 1988.

Barbour, Hugh and Arthur O. Roberts, eds. *Early Quaker Writings, 1650-1700.* Grand Rapids, MI: William B. Eerdmans Company, 1973.

Barclay, Robert. *An Apology for the True Christian Divinity...* 13th ed. Manchester, England: William Irwin, 1869. First Published in English in 1678.

Bauman, Richard. "Aspects of Quaker Rhetoric." *Quarterly Journal of Speech* 56 (1970): 67-74.

————. *Let Your Words Be Few: Symbolism of Speaking and Silence Among Seventeenth-Century Quakers.* Cambridge: UP, 1983.

Barnes, Kenneth C. *A Vast Bundle of Opportunities: An Exploration of Creativity in Personal Life and Community.* London: George Allen & Unwin, 1975.

————. "Integrity—in Quakerism and the Arts." *Quaker Monthly.* 62-6 (1983): 125-128.

————. "Integrity—in Quakerism and the Arts (2)." *Quaker Monthly.* 62-7 (1983): 148-152.

————. *Integrity in the Arts.* York, England: William Sessions, 1984.

————. *The Creative Imagination.* Swarthmore Lecture, 1960. London: George Allen & Unwin, 1960.

---

15. Some of the implications of Quaker theology relevant to theatre have been addressed in a provocative and entertaining way by Darlene R. Graves in "User-Friendly Theatre."

Barish, Jonas. *The Anti-theatrical Prejudice.* Berkeley, CA: University of California, 1981.

Benner, John. "Art and So On." *Quaker Monthly.* 59-12 (1980): 233-236.

Blamires, David. "Traditional Quakers Challenged." *Quaker Monthly.* 57-9 (1978): 161-164.

Book of Discipline of New York Yearly Meeting of the Religious Society of Friends, General Conference Affiliation. Rev. ed. New York: Knickerbocker, 1930.

Book of Discipline of Ohio Yearly Meeting of the Friends Church. Rev. ed. Damascus, Ohio, 1968.

Braithwaite, William C. *The Beginnings of Quakerism.* Ed. Henry J. Cadbury. 2nd ed. Cambridge: University Press, 1959.

————. *The Second Period of Quakerism.* Ed. Henry J. Cadbury. 2nd ed. Cambridge: University Press, 1961.

Christian Advices Issued by the Yearly Meeting of Friends Held in Philadelphia. Philadelphia: Friends' Book Store, 1859.

Clarkson, Thomas. *A Portraiture of Quakerism.* 3 vols. London: Longman, Hurst, 1806.

Constitution and Discipline of Northwest Yearly Meeting of Friends Church. Newberg, OR: Barclay, 1975.

Coren, Pamela. "Quakers and the Arts—Again." *Quaker Monthly.* 67-7 (1988): 150-151.

Creasey, Maurice A. "'Inward' and 'Outward'; A Study in Early Quaker Language." *Journal of the Friends Historical Society [Supplement]* 30: 1-24.

Davison, Alec. "Effervescence from the Leaveners." *The Friends' Quarterly.* 23 (1984): 243-248.

————. "Questabout takes to the Road." *Quaker Monthly.* 63-4 (1984): 66-68.

————. "Take a Look at Young Friends: The Leaveners." *Quaker Monthly.* 62-5 (1983): 100.

The Discipline of Iowa Yearly Meeting of the Society of Friends. Rev. ed. West Branch, IA, 1914.

The Discipline of Oregon Yearly Meeting of Friends Church. Newberg, OR: Newberg Graphic, 1895.

Discipline of Oregon Yearly Meeting of Friends Church. Newberg, OR, 1924.

Downing, Chris. "Friends' Relation to the Arts: Some Further Preliminary Reflections." *Quaker Religious Thought.* 14 (1972-73): 27-37.

Eddington, Paul. "Actor and Friend." *Quaker Monthly.* 59-1 (1980): 14-16.

Eichenberg, Fritz. *Art and Faith.* A Pendle Hill Pamphlet. N. p., n. d.

Eversley, Ruth. "Living with the Quaker Peace Action Caravan." *Quaker Monthly.* 62-1 (1983): 12-15.

Faith and Practice: A Book of Christian Discipline of Northwest Yearly Meeting of Friends Church. Newberg, OR: Barclay, 1987.

Faith and Practice: Book of Discipline of the North Carolina Yearly Meeting (Conservative) of the Religious Society of Friends. Rev. ed. N. p., 1983.

Faith and Practice of New England Yearly Meeting of Friends , A Book of Christian Discipline. Cambridge, MA: Cambridge University Press, 1930.

Faith and Practice of New England Yearly Meeting of Friends (Book of Discipline). N. p.: New England Yearly Meeting of Friends, 1985.

"Fires of Levana." *Quaker Monthly.* 61-4 (1982): 76.

Foreman, Connie. "'A Senior Citizen' at Her First Yearly Meeting." *Quaker Monthly.* 57-11 (1978): 204-206.

Foster, Richard. "How Liberating are the Liberal Arts?" *Evangelical Friend.* Jan/Feb, 1988: 8-10.

Gilderdale, Alan. "The Position of the Artist in the Society of Friends." *The Friends' Quarterly.* 19 (1976): 325-330.

Graves, Darlene R. "User-Friendly Theatre: The Implications of Quaker Theology on Non-Traditional Dramatic Performance," a paper presented at the annual meeting of the Speech Communication Association, November 21, 1995, San Antonio, Texas.

Greenwood, J. Ormerod. *Signs of Life: Art and Religious Experience.* Swarthmore Lecture, 1978. London: Quaker Home Service, 1978.

———. "The Power to Celebrate." *Quaker Monthly.* 63-1 (1984): 21-24.

Hall, Francis B, ed. *Quaker Worship in North America.* Richmond, IN: Friends United Press, n.d.

Hancock, Thomas. *The Peculium: An Endeavour to Throw Light on Some of the Causes of the Decline of the Society of Friends, Especially in Regard to its Original Claim of Being the Peculiar People of God.* London: Smith & Elder, 1859.

Holden, John. "The Necessity of Art." *Quaker Monthly.* 59-5 (1980): 89-91.

Holtom, Pleasaunce. "Young Makers." *Quaker Monthly.* 55-1 (1976): 1-4.

Jerome, Judson. *Candle in the Straw.* In *Religious Theatre*, No. 1, Fall 1964. Reprinted and obtainable from Friends World Committee, 152-A North 15 Street, Philadelphia, PA 19102.

Jewell, Vicki. "The *Golden Eye* at Newcastle." *Quaker Monthly.* 58-12 (1979): 234-235.

Kashatus, William C. *Dr. K's Living History Programs.* A descriptive brochure.

Lesses, Katherine. "Art and Integration." *The Friends' Quarterly.* 21 (1979): 128-137.

Lerner, Laurence. *The Two Cinnas: Quakerism, Revolution and Poetry.* Swarthmore Lecture, 1984. London: Quaker Home Service, 1984.

Marsh, John. "The Leaveners—An Appraisal." *The Friends' Quarterly.* 25 (1988): 56-61.

Marsh, Winifred. "Quaker Fellowship of the Arts—Born 1954, Still Going Strong!" *Quaker Monthly.* 60-9 (1981): 188-190.

Nicholson, Frederick J. *Quakers and the Arts: A Survey of Attitudes of British Friends to the Creative Arts from the Seventeenth to the Twentieth Century.* London: Friends Home Service Committee, 1968.

Palmer, Candida. "Cultural Impedimenta Old and New in Friends' Relation to the Arts: Some Preliminary Reflections." *Quaker Religious Thought*. 14 (1972-73): 2-26.

Penn, William. *No Cross, No Crown*. London, 1682.

Principles of Quakerism: A Collection of Essays. Issued by the representatives of the Religious Society of Friends for Pennsylvania, New Jersey and Delaware. Philadelphia, 1908.

Pyper, Hugh. "Witnessing for Peace: The Drama of Peace." *The Friends' Quarterly*. 22 (1982): 596-598.

Remonstrance...for the Welfare of our City...against the Erection of a Theatre. Birmingham, England, 1764. Broadside No. 146, Bevan Naish Collection, v. 3006, Woodbrooke College, Birmingham, England.

Rowntree, John Stephenson. *Quakerism: Past and Present*. London: Smith & Elder, 1859.

Rules of Discipline of the Yearly Meeting of Friends of North Carolina. Woodland, NC, 1908.

Sharman, Alison. "Leaven and Fire." *Quaker Monthly*. 61-12 (1982): 249-250.

Shepherd, Jack. *Makepeace Daly's Street Theatre*. London: Quaker Home Service, 1986.

Swingle, Rich. E-mail to the author. 5 April, 1996.

The Discipline of the Society of Friends of Western Yearly Meeting. Rev. 1865. Indianapolis: Douglass & Conner, 1866.

The Discipline of the Society of Friends of Western Yearly Meeting. Richmond, IN: Nicholson, 1881.

"The Leaveners Rise Again." *Quaker Monthly*. 58-6 (1983): 110.

Trueblood, D. Elton. *Problems of Quakerism*. Philadelphia: The Young Friends Movement, 1931.

Vellacott, Richard. "A Quaker Holiday Pilgrimage." *Quaker Monthly*. 63-5 (1984): 93-97.

Wright, Luella M. *The Literary Life of the Early Friends, 1650-1725*. New York: Columbia U Press, 1932.

Whittle, Peter. "A Quaker Demo." *Quaker Monthly*. 57-12 (1978): 234-236.

Windle, Barbara. "Lerner Meets Laurence Meets Lerner." *Quaker Monthly*. 63-8 (1984): 153-156.

A Nature Nudge

Rediscover the Outdoors around You

GARY K. FAWVER

For a number of years now, I have believed that informal and formal outdoor experiences built on a biblical knowledge base can be beneficial and should be purposely pursued throughout one's life. My intentions for a vocational ministry in the outdoors have been to reconnect people with the natural realm, to assist them in rediscovering the outdoors. In support of that, I conducted an action research project (as part of my D.Min. studies) to demonstrate the benefits of God's natural world, the outdoors, in the lives of a select group of people through a five-day "immersion" in that outdoor environment. The outdoor setting became the mechanism to develop physical and emotional well being in the participants. This setting was used also as a means of providing spiritual growth in both individuals and the group through Bible study, worship, and contemplation. I wanted to determine if it was possible, in a relatively short period of time, to enhance people's perceptions about the outdoors and increase their outdoor ministry effectiveness. I hoped, as a result of this experience, to encourage people, from professionals—camp leaders and church workers, college and seminary professors—to parents and interested individuals to recognize the benefits of and make intentional use of the outdoors.

Americans and the Outdoors

Americans, in increasing numbers, are seeking to be related to the outdoors and the things of nature. As never before, people are doing a variety of things from spilling into the outdoors, to buying pets and growing plants and flowers. Hundreds of millions of dollars are spent annually on recreational gear, cabins at the beach or mountain and motor homes. People generally recognize it is good to go outdoors and benefit from taking part in outdoor activities. According to the President's Commission on Americans Outdoors (PCAO), eighty percent of Americans are outdoor enthusiasts and find pleasure being outside.[1] Reasons such as catharsis, enjoyment, getting or keeping in shape, and feeling good are magnets that attract vast numbers of Americans to the outdoor setting.

Few people would dispute the statement that fresh air and sunshine are good for them. I have certainly felt that the cumulative impact on me of a lifetime of outdoor experiences and outdoor ministry has been significant. My parents sent me outside to play as a child, and when I came in my cheeks were red, I ate with a hearty appetite and slept well at night. The years I did professional backpacking, I developed strong leg muscles, increased my lung capacity and overall physical endurance. During times when my job was stressful, a week at an ocean cabin brought emotional calm and a new focus on life. During the twenty years I directed retreats at Tilikum, people, as they were leaving, would often say how relaxed they felt and how much the beautiful surroundings had helped them. What joy children sense as they catch frogs or crayfish along a lake shore, and a Sunday afternoon picnic in the park is much more enjoyable, mosquitoes and all, than the same meal in the kitchen.

How do we know this? Largely by intuition, I suppose, through our own outdoor experiences, the stories we tell and the reports we get from others. One of the researchers in this field, Richard C. Knopf, said that the literature on people-nature relations is largely intuitive. Very few people have determined, through careful research, particularly from a Christian perspective, the specific benefits of and motivations for taking part in outdoor activities.

Benefits from Being in the Outdoors: The Literature

The value of this action research project rests on the contribution it makes to my understanding of the benefits of the outdoors and how well people are motivated to be involved in the natural environment.

How do people relate to the outdoors? What are the benefits to people as they spend time outside? Just how does nature seem to soothe the body and spirit? These are questions I began asking about twelve years ago. Every so often I would read articles in the popular press like the one in *US News & World Report* that tells of the studies done on the physical and psychological benefits of nature on prisoners, hospital patients, homeowners, and office

---

1. Donna Breitenstein and Alan Ewert, "Health Benefits of Outdoor Recreation: Implications for Health Education." *Health Education* 21 (January/February 1990), 16.

workers. Patients who had gallbladder surgery recovered faster when they had a view of trees through their hospital window than when they looked out on a brick wall. And office workers with windows have more enthusiasm for their jobs. Bit by bit I was becoming convinced that for Christians and non-Christians alike, God has built into His out-of-doors resources which can restore us in body and spirit and that anecdotal reports of the benefits of the outdoors could probably be supported by scientific research.[2] To gain a general understanding, I began reviewing the literature in the field. Richard C. Knopf, one of the leading researchers in the field of natural environmental studies, was especially helpful in directing me to the significant people and summaries of studies in the field. In the book *Environmental Handbook*, Knopf wrote the chapter titled: "Human Behavior, Cognition, and Affect in the Natural Environment." It is a lengthy evaluative review of the literature on outdoor research. Knopf states:

> The literature on people-nature relations is largely intuitive. Most of its tenets have not been subjected to validation through the scientific process. Our purpose here is to transcend these disciplinary lines and sort through the accumulating maze of detail in an attempt to extract themes, principles, and concepts of value in constructing theoretical perspectives on how people relate to nature.[3]

Knopf examines the various studies on the relations between people and nature in various disciplines: forestry, leisure sciences, sociology, environmental psychology, economics, geography and marketing. He believes the data make clear that people are oriented to nature, they find it important, and they seem to like it.[4] He concludes that the meanings people

---

2. In the November 30, 1992 issue of *US News & World Report*, the feature article was called "Living with Nature" (p. 57). The writer suggested that there is an affinity among humans for the natural world, springing from our evolutionary past. (Perhaps it exists as proof of the reality of Romans 1!) "Within New York's Metropolitan Museum of Art is a Chinese garden rich with plant life and the soothing murmur of falling water. Visitors love to linger under the trees for a few meditative moments...Even in the midst of one of the world's great art collections, nature has a magnetic hold on the human psyche...The psyche's love of natural scenes can even have a powerful healing effect on the human body. Ulrich (an environmental psychologist) found that patients who had gallbladder surgery, for instance, recovered faster and needed fewer strong painkillers when they had a view of trees through their hospital window than when they looked out on a brick wall. Similarly, prison inmates suffered fewer stress-related illnesses such as upset stomachs and headaches if they could see trees from their cells." p. 57. Rachel Kaplan, an environmental psychologist at the university of Michigan surveyed 1,200 office workers. The workers with windows that look out on nature had more enthusiasm for their jobs.For the Christian, a relationship with our Father, in our Father's land ought to have even greater effects.

3. Richard C. Knopf, "Human Behavior, Cognition, and Affect in the Natural Environment," in Daniel Stokols and Irwin Altman, eds., *Handbook of Environmental Psychology* (Toronto: John Wiley & Sons, 1987).

attach to nature and the goals they pursue are fluid and individualistic, but the data also suggest that certain goals recur more than others. These goals relate to the four broad themes of escape or the quest for tranquillity, social reinforcement, competence building, and aesthetic enjoyment.[5] In this study I tried to determine whether the participants in my program view the outdoors in similar ways.

Researchers suggest that nature often emerges as a symbol of spirituality. Knopf traces the studies of several individuals in 1976 and 1983, who show that nature plays a pervasive role throughout the religious writings of diverse cultures. It is understandable, in my judgment, for people to attach rich meaning to nature, because it displays their original rootedness in God. Whether they are aware of it or not, when people are in awe of a natural phenomenon like a sunset or they desire to care for creation, is it not an innate response to the Creators' original instructions? When individuals destroy nature or are fearful of it or superstitious about it, perhaps the layers of cultural influence have built up so deeply that there is no longer any godly influence. I believe that anyone can benefit from contact with creation, but those who have a biblical knowledge base of nature and creation have tapped into the source of their affinity for the outdoors. The layers of cultural influence can affect Christian and non-Christian alike, and therefore one of the suppositions of this research project is that people must be periodically reconnected to the outdoors. Informal and formal outdoor experiences should be purposefully pursued with intentionality throughout one's life. If not there is the likelihood that our technologically filled lives will insulate us against nature.

An important document in my research was the one prepared for the President's Commission on Americans Outdoors. Established in 1985 under Ronald Reagan, the Commission published its report two years later, describing the "essential need for providing every citizen with the opportunity for outdoor experiences."[6] In the volume *A Literature Review*, experts representing several disciplines wrote a series of ten papers for the Commission on the values, benefits and consequences of public provision and use of outdoor recreation opportunities. As a whole, the papers help document the conclusion that outdoor recreation is tremendously beneficial to American citizens personally in a wide variety of ways. One paper which was particularly helpful was "Probable Personal Benefits of Outdoor Recreation." Written by B. L. Driver, pioneer in this field of research, and Perry J. Brown, another noted researcher, the paper states that over 100 empirical studies from over 100,000 recreationists have been conducted. These stud-

---

4. Ibid., 801.
5. Ibid.
6. President's Commission on Americas Outdoors (PCAO). *A Literature Review*. (Washington, DC: US. Govt. Printing Office, 1987).

ies attempt to measure how outdoor users perceive benefits from the outdoors and what motivates them to use the outdoors. The writers of this paper summarized their findings by suggesting that most studies generally conclude the perceived benefits to fall into four themes very closely paralleling those of Richard Knopf: scenic appreciation, physical health, stress mediation, and learning.[7] I asked myself once more, what benefits from the outdoors will my participants perceive?

Setting Up the Tilikum Experience

Between 1984 and 1993, I taught the course "The Christian and the Outdoors" three times at George Fox College. Between thirty-five and forty students took this course, which was designed to establish a biblical foundation for outdoor ministries. Students explored a wide variety of outdoor activities to be used by individuals, families, church groups, Christian camps, and other organizations. The only disadvantage was that the course was conducted primarily in the classroom. I longed for an intensive outdoor exposure for my students! That opportunity presented itself in this action research project. This project was conducted in May, 1995 at Tilikum, a retreat center owned by George Fox College, and of which I was founder and director for nearly twenty years. Nineteen individuals comprised the sample for the study; the core group was students who enrolled in a May Term class called "Rediscover the Outdoors."

The program was built on five foundational beliefs about the relation of God to the natural world and our relationship to both:

1. There is a biblical view of creation.
2. Even as the person and work of God is revealed in the Scripture, His creative works are visible in the world.
3. The biblical view of creation has been perverted by heretical and cultic philosophical thinking, which has led humankind to continually turn its attention away from the biblical world of nature.
4. God's handiwork of creation does not ordinarily lead people to Him. One does not discover a personal God by looking at nature.
5. Christ can lead His followers to a consideration of nature, its significance, and their place in it.

My goals for this project were four-fold:

1. To take a group of individuals and, by "immersing" them in a variety of outdoor experiences, document the benefits to those individuals and the group.
2. To establish a biblical view of the outdoors—key Scriptures about God,

---

7. B.L. Driver and Perry J. Brown. "Probable Personal Benefits of Outdoor Recreation." in President's Commission on Americans Outdoors (PCAO). *A Literature Review* (Washington DC: US. Govt. Printing Office, 1987). pp. 63-70.

Christ, and humankind and their relationship to the created order, which thereby give validation for any Christian ministry/activity that relates to the outdoors.

3. To provide participants with printed resources that they can use for their own benefit and with others.

4. To develop a course for college/seminary which will open the doors for individuals to possibilities in outdoor ministries (broader than, but including camps and retreats).

Since this course was being conducted outside of the classroom, my purpose was to involve the participants as much as possible in direct, purposeful experiences. I wanted to minimize the traditional lecture method of teaching and create an experience that utilized all the senses in the learning process.

This type of research, action or applied research, is often used in an educational setting to develop new approaches with direct application to that setting. It is empirical in the sense that it relies heavily on actual observation and behavioral data. Since it lacks scientific rigor, however, it was necessary to establish evaluation criteria, determine measurement techniques, and find other means of acquiring useful feedback.

Program Activity Units

Eight program activity units formed the core of the experience, all of which I believed to be crucial to the success of the program. The units included: group building, sensory intensifying experiences, group worship, quiet times alone, leader's teaching times, participant teaching/learning sessions, pre/post-testing, and journaling. Five of them will be discussed here.

Following the first meal, we went outside for an hour of *group building games*. Experience has shown me that the proper use of relational and physical activities speeds up the process whereby a small group develops a sense of trust. We progressed, therefore, through a variety of ice breaker / acquaintance / de-inhibitizer activities. I believe the participants became acquainted and felt comfortable with each other more quickly than if they had merely sat down and shared some information about themselves.

On the cover of the resources handbook, "Rediscovering The Outdoors," which each participant received, was Job 37:14, "Listen to this Job; stop and consider God's wonders." A unique and important way to do this is through the use of the *five senses*. It is necessary to stay alert to what the early Celtic Christians called 'tuning the five-stringed harp,' keeping each of our five senses alert to the fact of God and His surrounding presence. Not only is God's natural creation incredible, but "we are fearfully and wonderfully made" (Psalm 139:14), and it is through the senses that we are able to appreciate that creation. Unfortunately we often become so immune to the sights and sounds of nature that it takes a special emphasis on using our senses to bring us back to a recognition of nature's beauty. Therefore one of my purposes for the week was to nudge the participants into a new awareness of nature through the senses. Monday, the first full day, became sensory awareness day. In two hour blocks I led the group through a series of exercises called "Wonders of God's World." One method of heightening one sense is to restrict another. So eye patches were used by one member of each two-person team while their partners led them on a "touching nature" excursion. Then the partners switched. That evening during the fifteen minute block journalling assignment, students made comments such as this:

> I had never experienced touching the outdoors to the same degree as I did today and that was one of the activities I enjoyed most. When I felt a maple leaf I saw it in my mind's eye. I even caught myself wondering whether or not it was green.

One of the goals for this experience was to nudge the participants into a renewed awareness of nature around them; therefore, I wasn't surprised to read journal comments such as:

> "I've realized that unless I specifically think about what's around me I don't fully appreciate the beauty."

> "I take my senses for granted too often."

> "Today I noticed many little things that sometimes go unnoticed by me."

Perhaps this comment can serve as a summary of the students' feelings toward this valuable part of the program:

> Likewise, our exercises today demonstrated the multi-sensory expressions of nature. We are being bombarded with sounds, scenes, smells, textures and flavors from God's creation. Our exercises enabled me to focus on the various aspects of nature's attempts to reach out to me.

Thomas Merton, a twentieth-century Trappist monk, developed the concept of "natural contemplation" from the Greek Fathers, suggesting that we can have a true appreciation of nature and an awareness of God's presence in all of creation. Merton used the camera as a tool for contemplating nature. The aperture of the camera, he said, was the opening to his heart. He tried to see objects in nature in a way that allowed them to reveal their hidden dimension.[8] Intrigued with Merton's concept, I gave each participant a twenty-four exposure disposable camera, and they were told to walk

---

8. This idea was presented in Simsic, Wayne, *Praying With Thomas Merton* (Winona, Minnesota: Saint Mary's Press, 1994). p. 80.

around the property for three hours using the camera whenever they wanted to concentrate on an object or scene. I suggested that their purpose in using the camera was not so much artistic as it was prayerful (expressing gratitude for God's beautiful creation). I encouraged them not to become frustrated if the pictures were not "beautiful." I intended this to be a follow-up of the sensory experiences the day before. It turned out to be one of the highlight experiences of the week. The pictures were developed during the afternoon, and that evening, for over two hours, the students arranged their pictures into a personal artistic collage on posterboard. Then these nineteen works of art were displayed in the meeting room for all to see. It served as a reminder of their quest that day to capture a bit of God's creation in the Tilikum landscape. Here is one representative journal comment about this activity:

> Especially moving was the coming together to share pictures and stories of taking the pictures. People's faith and their understanding of God seems affirmed and encouraged in the sharing. I enjoyed watching the other students as they creatively used the pictures to make a statement visually about their experiences.

In my many years of Christian camping, I have taken part in many *worship experiences* at camps. Sometimes they happened around a campfire, but generally they were in a chapel and for all appearances were like any church service back home. I am convinced that particularly at a camp site and during almost any time of the year, there is a beauty in creation that should become the means to draw participants' worship to the Lord of beauty. Well planned and directed worship services can allow all the sense gates to be opened to receive God's good gifts.

I had prepared a series of worship experiences, complete enough that a worship leadership team could pick them up and, with just a few minutes of thoughtful planning, could lead a group in meaningful worship. The Friday service, "Come Outdoors With Jesus," seemed to be particularly well received. Participants were sent outside for half an hour just prior to the service. They were asked to make a list of the things of nature they saw around the camp that they recalled Christ mentioning in the Gospels. During the time of worship they shared a list of twenty-one things they had observed. As we talked, it became very clear to them that people in our society are unfamiliar with natural things like tending vineyards (John 15) and caring for sheep (John 10). They recognized that Christians must come to understand the natural world so they can grasp the parallel principles of the spiritual world. One participant made this very perceptive comment:

> Jesus used the natural settings to affirm His creative work and to give seekers tangible examples for spiritual lessons. Christ likewise used creation-

nature to help His followers retain His teachings because nature engaged the disciples' senses. It points out to me the importance of experience in learning and understanding spiritual truth.

Most people are not normally comfortable with *silence* or, for that matter, even being by themselves and not talking. Society's symbols are background music or compact radios with earphones which wrap us in a blanket of sound. Christians have tended to equate spirituality with how much they "do" for God. Often silence is seen as doing nothing and nonproductive, but I have found that in life "doing" must be counterbalanced by an emphasis on "being"—being with God.

It is important to take advantage of the outdoor environment and a calm, relaxed pace in learning to experience the benefits of being by oneself in quiet solitude. During the week therefore, I included a teaching time on the importance and benefits of listening to God. I concluded the session with an assignment for the participants to go outside, find a quiet spot, and, while by themselves, enter into three five-minute periods of self-guided silence. One participant wrote of this:

> The greatest insight I've learned this week is to listen. My heart is sad to think of how much I've shut out. I fill my head with thoughts—busy, worrisome thoughts. But when I centered down and just shut up I was able to listen and hear.

During the week I provided two opportunities for the students to be given an assignment, do some reflection and preparation, and then make a presentation to the entire group. The first of these two *student teaching/ learning* sessions considered the biblical foundation which forms the basis for outdoor ministries. I assigned each student one set of the seventeen key scriptural principles about God and His creation. In their own words, they were to share the principle, chose one or two key supporting scriptures, and state why they believed the principle to be important. The presentation session lasted over two hours with a break in the middle, and I was impressed with the clarity of the presentations, the attentive listening of the other participants, and the constructive comments and questions from many of them. One student wrote:

> The first insight that I would like to comment on is the personal discovery of how important nature was to Christ's teaching and the volume of material concerning nature that is present in the Gospels.

Assessment

I attempted to assess the value of this research project by: evaluating the accumulated findings of how fully my stated goals were met, how the results from this experience matched the findings of other researchers through the data drawn from participant pre- and post-experience inventories, a content analysis of participant journals, and comments by a participant observer. The results of this assessment were positive, as I anticipated, and therefore I was most encouraged.

In what ways were my *goals* met? First a biblical view of the outdoors was set forth. Second, the handbook, "Rediscovering the Outdoors," written for this experience became a resource the participants used during the week. I hope they will use it for their continued personal growth and as a resource with others. It has now been printed and is the textbook in my college course, "The Christian and the Outdoors." For some years I have wanted to develop an out-of-classroom course for college/seminary that would open to individuals the possibilities in outdoor ministries by giving them direct participation in a variety of outdoor experiences. After having conducted this course, I now believe it can be used by other leaders and in other outdoor locations.

One way to determine the benefits to participants from being in the outdoor program for five days was to compare how the results from this experience matched the findings of other researchers through the data drawn from participant *pre- and post-experience inventories.*

The primary purpose for the first two pre-experience surveys was to gather information on participants' prior outdoor experiences as well as to obtain a narrative on each person's knowledge of and attitudes about the outdoors. I assumed that, even though any George Fox College student could enroll for this course of his/her own free choice, people would self select who already had an affinity for the outdoors. My assumption was correct. All nineteen students, for instance, indicated they make a practice of walking in the woods, on the beach and around their homes. All of the participants had photographed nature. Only one person in the group had never attended a summer camp, only two had never served as a camp counselor, and all of them, prior to this week, had gone into the outdoors for spiritual reasons, eleven doing so regularly. I believe that I can assume my participants came to Tilikum open to and even anticipating a positive spiritually experience. This would support the research done by McDonald and Schreyer, which suggests that the actual environment can play a greater role in affording spiritual experience based on the meaning the individual brings to that place.

I prepared one objective *measurement tool* for my participants. I designed it to measure the factors motivating them to use the outdoors as they came into this program and to determine how the five-day program changed their perceptions of the benefits of the outdoors. Richard Knopf gave examples of several exit surveys used by the Forest Service as they had attempted to determine how types of experiences either add to or detract from the level of satisfaction people would receive from participating in outdoor activities like hiking, overnight camping, mountain climbing, photography, and nature study. To Knopf's list of twenty types of experiences, such as getting out of doors, learning new skills, being with friends, experiencing solitude, and taking risks, I added ten others to create a list of thirty items. This survey, "Reasons For Participating in Outdoor Activities" (RPOA), used the same Likert scale for scoring as the Forest Service survey. Since I wanted to learn if students' perceptions of outdoor benefits changed during the week, I administered the survey before and after. How did the benefits perceived by the Tilikum students correspond with the summary Knopf includes? The content of the Forest Service research when compared to results from the RPOA instrument suggests significant convergent validity.

I found that changes occured in one particular area which are consistent with what I predicted. Knopf called it "the quest for tranquility." During the week participants noted changes in areas we would describe as renewal and refreshment. Of the 30, the following items were rated the highest—pursuing tranquility, developing a sense of well being, having the mind move at a slower pace, and being renewed/refreshed. All but four of the participants had just completed a stressful week of final exams. Their exposure to the outdoors appears to have been beneficial.

Another way for me to measure the experience was by doing a content analysis of the students' *personal journals*. In order to provide structure for the journal writing, I designated two fifteen-minute periods each day for journaling and gave the students a specific item to respond to each time. This was extremely helpful evaluative information. The students' responses to experiences they had earlier each day confirmed the data drawn from the pre- and post-experience inventories. Students experienced *physical and emotional restoration*. Here is a representative entry :

> The week before this week was finals week and just last Sunday I was thinking about not even coming to this class and dropping May Term. Even though I really wanted to take this class, I was just tired of all the pressure and thought of studying. But coming here I have totally relaxed and have gotten away from it all. It's so nice because I've been learning and not even realizing it. And I have found that this week my contact with creation has re-created me.

The participants valued the opportunities to *share in this experience with their peers*, their friends.

> It is probably the discovery of nature together, the sharing of experiences that makes something meaningful. What is the use of even thinking about how to hold a newt, unless you are showing someone how? What is the

point of saying, "There is a swallow's nest," if no one is there to look? The full richness of nature is not really enjoyed until several share it.

In the book *Benefits of Leisure* and the chapter "Spiritual Benefits of Leisure Participation and Leisure Settings," McDonald and Schreyer suggest that it is impossible to operationalize or scientifically measure spirituality. They feel it may, as well, be unnecessary and counterproductive. "The consequences of spiritual benefit are real to the individual, and it is their manifestation that lends credibility and reality to the concept of spiritual benefit."[9] Journal entries given by Tilikum participants convinced me of the *spiritual benefits* of the experience:

> I believe that I'm discovering how nature is an incredible window to my soul. As I take time to quietly and thoughtfully observe nature I discover truths about myself. The other side of this window is that nature is also a window to God's heart. Nature, for a Christian, allows us to see God—His creativity, His love, His power—in a very concrete way.

Throughout the week, in personal comments and journal entries, students, expressed a renewed *appreciation of God's creation*. That appreciation was expressed very well in this journal entry:

> Finally, I love the wonderful shades of green we saw, the musical sounds we heard and the engaging flavors we tasted. Nature, through its textures, scents, songs, and scenes, is crying out to us to be experienced. It is a true loss if we were to pass through life without enjoying God's creative expressions.

One common theme kept appearing although stated in different ways. Participants acknowledged often *taking the outdoors for granted* and not taking enough time to really "see" nature. Comments read like this: "I think that I've taken the outdoors for granted too much. It is so easy for me to just stay inside and vegetate rather than go outside and experience God's creation." It is significant that eighteen of the nineteen participants came to Tilikum with a history of involvement in the outdoors. The Outdoor Activities Preference Study inventory showed that the students participated frequently in a variety of outdoor activities. And yet even people with an inclination toward the outdoors find it necessary to rediscover the joys and significance of that involvement in the outdoors. This supported my contention that contact with the outdoors must be intentional and continual.

When I began planning the five-day experience, I asked one of the students who had enrolled for the course if she would fill the role of *participant observer*. As she and I met throughout the winter and spring, she provided

---

helpful feedback as plans developed. Since she was the only participant who knew the program details and schedule, I came to depend on her for more in-depth feedback during the week than the other participants could offer. Her post-experience written report was helpful in assessing the week.

What can I conclude from this action research project? It *is* possible to reconnect people to the natural environment and to demonstrate the benefits of God's natural world in the lives of a select group of people through a five-day intensive exposure to the outdoor environment. This program, which utilized a beautiful outdoor environment and was built around the resources of the handbook "Rediscovering the Outdoors," can be taken by others—from camp leaders and church workers, college and seminary professors, to parents and interested individuals—and be used to enhance theirs and others' perceptions about the outdoors.

Poems

ED HIGGINS

Astrobiography

I have this friend in science
who tells me how he learned
astrophysics. It goes something
like this: You first lean so closely into
the source of things that
distant stars, whole galaxies,
collapse as if into the eye
of a great storm called God.
And what is important then
is how long you can hold your own
eye open to the center of mystery—
which is your lens—
as if you'd just discovered
some incomprehensible
petroglyph in a dark cave
somewhere under France maybe
only you have no light
but your own imagination
and the ocean called language.
Then as if the universe itself
were lethal oxygen
you breathe wonder in
                   slowly

at the speed of lightheadedness.

Of Light

Light's labor
is to tell darkness back,
push it toward eternity's edge—

although much darkness slips back
through, grieving the hearts
of all who must live here.

Like lead, darkness weighs
nearly as much as gold.

But light's feel
is the alchemy of love
falling in bright color,

as stars sometimes do,
back to earth's gravity.

There turned to chemical
(even among fireflies)
it burns gold-like

attracting more love still,
across open fields,

against night's threshold.

Galaxies

I have been there
up   to the Milky Way   and further
under winter and summer's night sky

loneliness like the ascent of whales rising
or the dead's silent waiting

urged up, up to where   a door   there
phosphorescence or glitter   both and neither

milt of God

nebulae charted into fate by the always cautious
or those curious to set the darkness
                                        visible

formed as readable sign
improbable blue-white luminesce

or else these may be dead souls waiting
hurled   everywhere   gathered in astral gowns

we are all here
                        they say
a billion billion eyes   watchers out

God's swirling light
the mystery alone so focused.

For the children
of Dunblane, Scotland

"Evil visted us yesterday
and we don't know why."
            —Dunblane school principal

The faint breath
of knowing
others' loss.

Dumb to one another
if even
asked:

When will we ever wear out
that old shoe
evil

that fits so well?

Death is always
senseless,

but sometimes
it outdoes
itself.

Eve's body

It was her mind
the Devil
desired most.
Really.

Lust had long ago
gone rigid
in his one track
mind.

But he could see
Adam's steady
attachment.
And lust's echo,
even attenuated,
accused his leaden
manhood.

So into the ear
of Eve's body—
at once columned
like a boy's or
a bare Greek
temple—

he whispered
the tallness
of knowing:
And lines once solid
foundered, undulating
into pale curves

& smooth surfaces
even a Devil's mind
could curse
for their
distraction.

Silent Prayer

At this moment
there are struggles

beyond these words
to write down,

images that scheme
or dream unable

to become wisdom
or even travail

in this mute present
where I endure truth's

anxious paradox.
Past this false self

I can never wholly claim.

Let my words be few,
renew the silence itself

that was not shattered,
nor enough.

Poems

NANCY THOMAS

A Psalm for High Places

Praise the Lord!
Praise him in his sanctuary,
Andean framed and cirrus vaulted.
    In the late afternoon light
    elongated shadows
    sway their gratitude,
    and every bush burns.
    The high plains blaze with praise.
    Wind whistles a litany
    in minor key
    and cuts its message through my coat,
    a piercing word and true.
    Young girls head herds
    toward home, walking into the sun.
    The flocks skip only in metaphor
and bleet their slow songs.
Praise the Lord!

Praise him with pinquillo, zampoña, quena.
Twang his worth on mandolin and churango.
In chorus chant -Yupaychanañ,
    Yupaychanañ.-
    Gnarled hands and creased brown faces
    reflect his image,
    receive his word.
    Adobe and prairie grass
    house his glory.
    Incense of prayer mingles with llama dung smoke,
    rises and pleases him.
    See! The Lord exalts the humble
    and bends his ear to the poor!
Praise him!

Praise him, creatures of the heights!
    Llama, vicuña, alpaca
    offer proud and swift praise.
    He alone fashioned the strength
    of legs, the proud arch of neck.
    They pound the earth with joy.
    Condors and hawks dip
    and swoop and rise again,

giving high praise,
cutting the wind to worship.
Small creatures--guinea pigs,
vizcacha, prairie snakes--
burrowing, know his secret name
and rejoice.
Praise the Lord!

Praise him, earth!
Clap before him!
Lay down your offerings!
    The fields bow low, rise, bend,
    feathering the air
    with their gentle harvest dance.
    Wheat and barley heads sway.
    Quinua purplely praises,
    and underground
    even potatoes know
    that the Lord of the Harvest
    is also Lord of the Dance.
Praise him!

Praise him in the yesterday rocks,
    the blue and silver stones,
    the silence of Tiahuanaco,
    for he was,
    and is
    and evermore will be.
    Bow quietly before him and
Praise!

Praise him in the heights!
    Bright Illampu, Hayna Potosí,
    Illimani, Mururata,
    white angels, guardians,
    praise him splendidly.
    "Lift up your eyes
    unto the hills,"
    is a commandment easily obeyed here.
Praise him!

Titicaca!
Praise him deeply, hilariously!

Light skips off the white caps
and a cold wind fills sails
with gladness.

Be joyful quickly, for the Lord has spoken!
From his words alone poured forth these waters!
Totora reeds bends low
before such magnificence,
and from deep down
frogs give comic obeisance
only he can hear.
Praise the Lord!

Praise him boisterously,
cacophony of thunder,
hail on tin roofs,
a dark wind that howls his might.
Fear him.
Tremble.
For the lightning destroys
and the darkness screams
the terrible names
of God.
Worship his awful ways.
Yes! Praise the Lord!

Praise him in the brash and bustle
of Chukiago, city of uncertain peace,
inverted ant hill,
pulsing with motion and noise.
Praise his energy,
his activity,
his ongoing creative life.
Praise the Lordl

Praise him in the cold wind
and the slanting light!
Praise him in the high thin air!
Let everything
that has breath
praise the Lord!
Yes! Praise him!
Praise the Lord!

Notes:

pinqullo, zampoña, quena—Andean wind instruments
churango—Andean stringed instrument
"Yupaychañan"—"We praise" in the Aymara language
llama, vicuña, alpaca—Andean animals of the camel family
vizcacha—small animal, similar to a rabbit
quinua—Andean grain
Tiahuanaco—ruins of an ancient Aymara civilization
Illampu, Hayna Potosí, Illimani, Mururata—peaks in the Andes
    Mountains
Chukiagu—ancient name for La Paz

I Love Tangents

I love them in all colors.
I love the orange ones that shock me
    with their brazen gestures and their teasing.
I love the lavender tangents, and the tangents
    that shift from blue to green; I love
    their innuendoes, their hisses,
    their strange and lovely lies.

1 love them in all shapes and sizes
    –the small round tangents, deceptively
    easy to handle, but once lost, impossible
    to retrieve;
    –the proper boxed tangents, predictable,
    safe, they serve as hobbies
    on application forms.

1 love the scent of tangents
    and how you can always know
    when one's coming by the slight pungency
    humming on the edges of the afternoon.

Once an unusually potent tangent
    let me go on it and we rode for miles,
    clear to Montana and back in less time
    than it takes to whistle the 1812 Overture.
    I still haven't recovered.

God at "The Penguin"

Outside "The Penguin"
on Citrus and Alosta,
the August evening hummed with traffic.
Sitting around a polar-white metallic table,
we spoke of silence and longing for God,
"as a deer pants for the water brooks."

Kids cruised the parking lot,
impressing with the volume of their stereos
and the screech of brakes.
My yogurt cone collapsed,
and Beth rescued me with a dozen napkins.
The store next door announced 25% off
on all clothes–while they lasted.
The cinema offered a choice: Tom & Jerry,
Terminator II, or I Married an Axe Murderer.

You asked, "Does he speak into the silence,
or is the silence itself his speech?"

We wondered, sitting there at the corner
of Citrus and Alosta on a warm August evening,
sharing the silence,
knowing the kingdom come.

Metaphors for Transformation

I like a quick miracle–
the slap-dash comedy
of a here's-mud-in-your-eye healing,
the hilarity of the lame man's leap,
the now-you-see-it-now-you-don't vanishing act
of the leper's sores,
the amazing multiplied bread.
I love to see him pull death
from his black forever hat,
and instantly change it to a pidgeon
or a sun-flower.
I wish all transformations were so quick,
so silver-slick and sudden.

The deeper changes move slowly.
The Maker nudges,
and root hairs grope in the dark,
grubbing the soil
for the words that bring life.
Sap swims slowly up the trunk,
heavy, thick, resisting the downward pull.
In a narrow path it feels its way,
searches all trajectories,
inches out to the tips of the smallest twigs.
As it goes it hums a subtle song,
a dim but certain gospel.
The tree hushes in anticipation,
waits for spring.

An Ecumenical Quaker Draws the Line

Can't say I'm not open.
I meditate with Mennonites,
chant with Catholics,
and belt out Baptist blues with the best of them.
1 cried at my daughter's marriage to a Nazarene,
and once I even rolled the aisle with a Pentecostal.
But with funerals I reach my limit.
When my time comes
I will insist on my own homespun,
tried and true Quaker version.
I just wouldn't feel dead
without it.

Poems

MICHAEL P. GRAVES

Pie in the Sky

It makes a great deal of difference
That the pie in the sky by and by
Is Aunt Jenny's homemade blueberry,
With still steaming crust and innards
That filled the house with promises,
That always set my mouth to watering.

I'll sit right down at that table
Across from Uncle Ned
With my mug of fresh-brewed coffee.
I'll bite into that ambrosia
And let the juice roll 'round my tongue
And down my chin and gather indelibly
In purple tokens on my button-down shirt
And paisley tie and puddle on my wing-tips.

I'll lean back, loosen the tie,
And take my time,
Savoring the heaven of those
New Hampshah wild blueberries,
Not the store-boughten kind.
I'll let the crust and juices
Explore my perfect teeth
And wash it all down with
A loud slurp of Java.

And I won't feel guilty
About the second piece.

The Iconoclast Has His Day

There is a bomb in Gilead;
Ticking away, hidden.
Inevitable.
Full of destruction.
All that is not timeless
Will explode.
On the Hill of Witness
The New is seconds away
And holding.
The device waits.

Tick. Tick. Tick.

Darkness at Noonday

RALPH BEEBE

P eter heaved a deep sigh and sat against a rock. The cave was cold and foreboding but a welcome refuge from the hostile world outside.

"It has been a difficult week, but victorious," he remarked. "A lot of new believers have been won." As he talked he idly inspected a long sword, one of several hundred weapons the believers had accumulated.

"Yes," Philip agreed. "And I think we have the Hellenist problem solved. The Lord has really been blessing our work."

"Stephen is certainly God's choice for the job of food distribution. He has deep spiritual insights and a real sense of justice," James added. "His zeal may get him in trouble, though."

"Yes—and all of us," noted Barnabas. "The authorities are cracking down. It is getting more and more dangerous to be a believer."

"The more the church grows, the more hostile the Pharisees get," Peter observed. "Everything we have worked for is in danger. If it hadn't been for Gamaliel they might have killed John and me. Now Stephen may be in real danger."

"I agree! We may have to fight soon," said Simon the Zealot. "I knew my revolutionary experience would be useful someday."

"But wouldn't fighting be terribly dangerous?" asked Thomas.

"Yes, of course. But against Christ's enemies we have to take risks. Besides, we really don't have a choice. Remember, they want to take away our right to worship God as we please. We have to show force or they will think that we are weak. Anyway, we'll move so fast they won't even know what hit them. How many of us are there?"

"Over five thousand, and even more women and children," Matthew estimated.

294 DARKNESS AT NOONDAY

"Great! What an army! When the time comes, most of us will fight with swords or daggers. The rest will carry rocks. I figure that if we kill a few hundred they won't cause us any more trouble."

"But what if they do?" Thomas doubted.

"Then we'll hit them again—over and over—and keep coming back to the caves. They'll never catch us. We can hold out forever. We'll teach them that aggression doesn't pay!"

Just then John came running up, out of breath. "The Pharisees are arguing with Stephen!" he panted. "I think they are going to kill him."

"Now is the time to act! Let's go!" Simon exclaimed.

As quickly as possible the weapons were distributed among some of the believers. After a brief prayer for God's blessing they left the caves and advanced toward the mob surrounding the pit. One hundred yards away they broke into a run toward the astonished Pharisees. A roar of defiance, a clash of swords, and the battle was joined!

Meanwhile, Stephen lay in the pit, already near death. He looked up into the hate-filled faces of the Pharisees. Then, contrasted beyond, he saw the tender face of Christ the Lord. Stephen's own face shone with compassion as he prayed, "Lord, do not hold this sin against them," and went to be with Jesus.

The believers quickly won the battle. Suffering only a few casualties themselves, they killed hundreds of the enemy. Although they failed to save Stephen, they proved that they would not submit meekly, like lambs. Peter, the Rock, fought valiantly, killing a dozen or more. Then he directed his rage against a young man who had been guarding the coats.

Saul of Tarsus was standing transfixed, nearly oblivious to the battle around him, his gaze on the radiant face of the man in the pit. Stephen's compassion moved him mightily, touching him like nothing in his experience. Then, suddenly, he saw an armed man lunging toward him. With a cry of fear, he grabbed a dagger and thrust it hilt-deep into Peter's belly. Instantly, Barnabas killed Saul with a great rock to the back of the head.

The believers carried Peter to the caves, where they mourned their losses but celebrated the victory. They vowed to fight whenever necessary to protect the church of Christ.

It was only noon when the battle ended, yet a deep darkness seemed to settle over the land. Peter, now near death, shivered in the cold darkness, mumbling that he heard a cock crowing in the twilight.

The strange gloom was so intense that observers many miles away said that there was no light at all on the road to Damascus.

The Public Arena

Abigail v. Harvey

Sibling Rivalry in the
Oregon Campaign for Woman Suffrage

LEE NASH

In the regular statewide election of June 4, 1900, Oregon's all-male electorate voted on the issue of woman suffrage for the second time. President Abigail Scott Duniway of the Oregon State Equal Suffrage
Association, completing 30 years of active leadership for women's rights,
stood at the height of her considerable powers. For three years she with her
cohorts had prepared with particular care for this election. They arranged a
systematic network of private correspondence that directed thousands of
timely letters to strategic destinations. They took pains to disassociate
themselves from the prohibition cause, perceived as an extraneous liability.
They worked closely with the Red Cross Society. They sought and received
endorsements from the Oregon Pioneer Association, the Oregon State
Grange, the local segment of the Grand Army of the Republic, and leading
male citizens. They courted the sympathy and support of several labor
unions and secret and fraternal orders. They prepared and distributed an
immense quantity of leaflets and varied papers. A four-page "Open Letter"
summing up their case was published in 220 of the 229 newspapers of the
state, and they enjoyed much editorial support.[1]

All this activity was kept as unobtrusive as possible—marches with tam-
bourines would have hurt the cause in conservative Oregon. Yet Mrs.
Duniway accompanied these effective, prudent promotions with an even

---

1. Abigail Scott Duniway, "History of Equal Suffrage in Oregon," *The Campain Leaflet* 1
(1900), 1-6.

more delicate, sub rosa campaign. She deeply coveted the support, or at least the quiet neutrality, of the most powerful opinion-maker in the region, her brother Harvey Scott, crusty editor of the Portland *Morning Oregonian*. For the sixteen months between the legislature's decision to submit a woman suffrage amendment to the people, and the 1900 election, her intimate correspondence regularly reports her anxieties about the fluctuating barometer of brotherly love. "The only thing we fear," she wrote her son Clyde in February, 1899, "is *Scott's pup*—Al. Holman, and Aunt Maggie [Scott's wife] has her pry under *him*. He's an *ass*."[2] The previous month, assistant editor Holman had lobbied in the legislature against the suffrage amendment, which occasioned one of the periodic tense Abigail-Harvey confrontations. As appears to have been usual in those interviews, the participants carried from it differing perceptions. "Your uncle and I have an understanding," she reported, "and the *Oregonian* will be held as [a] great reserve force till I say the word."[3] Yet four months later Scott was telling his sister that he would "*oppose* and *whip*" the amendment. She then took summer courage from *Oregonian* Publisher Henry L. Pittock's prediction that Scott would be all right on the suffrage question "when he goes to the hot springs and gets cured of rheumatism and dyspepsia." In July, also, there was a hopeful rumor that Holman would be fired.[4]

So it went month by anxious month through fall and winter, Abigail wary and worried privately, but cheerful in her relations with her brother, more careful than usual to avoid antagonism and cultivate harmony. In that amicable spirit Abigail and her four sisters came to dinner at the Scotts to do their brother honor on his 62nd birthday, February 1, 1900. Always subject to periods of deep depression and passionate outbursts, Harvey had one of his bad nights.[5] He vented his frustration in harsh verbal abuse of his sisters, especially Abigail. Hurt but unsubdued, two days later Mrs. Duniway went to see him about printing the address she was to deliver in two weeks before the National American Woman Suffrage Convention in Washington, D.C. "He made a most abject apology for what he said;" reported Wilkie Duniway to Clyde,

> told her he had been worried by a multitude of things Thursday and was almost beside himself; hoped that "sister, you will forgive me"; agreed to print the [paper]; furnished her a cut without charge, and unsolicited gave her transportation; besides, acknowledged he had been wrong to oppose

2. Abigail Scott Duniway to Clyde A. Duniway (February 19, 1899). Abigail Scott Duniway Papers, Special Collections, University of Oregon Library, Eugene. Subsequent Duniway letters cited are from this collection.

3. Ibid. (February ___, 1899). Day of month removed.

4. Ibid. (June 21, July 10, 31, 1899).

5. Ibid. (January 29, February 20, November 21, 1900). See T. W. Davenport to George Himes, October 26, 1910. Oregon Historical Society Library, Portland.

woman suffrage, and would not do so any more. So mother is happy that the incident occurred, as it probably removed the menace of opposition from the *Oregonian* in the coming election.[6]

This was a beautiful and unexpected boon indeed, and suffragist forces faced the spring weeks with buoyant hope. Abigail, to be sure, harbored a shred of doubt, knowing that her brother's photographic memory, stored with all twelve books of *Paradise Lost* and a myriad of detail, could sometimes draw a total blank when it came to conversational commitments between siblings.

Scott entrained east in early May to attend the quarterly meeting of the Associated Press Directors, leaving Holman in editorial command until just before the election.[7] "Command" is a relative term for an era of personal journalism, of course, when the paper was an extension of the editor's mind and personality whether he was in town or not. Particularly was this true when the surrogate was Alfred Holman, who had literally grown up in the *Oregonian* offices starting with deliveries in 1869, and to whom Scott fondly referred as the "well-beloved son of my professional life."[8] Thus when Holman began on May 15 a 20-day, 14-editorial pre-election barrage attacking woman suffrage from every angle, one could not think Scott was innocent of the proceedings. No doubt remained of the editor's involvement when he returned long enough before the June 4 election to write a devastating 1500-word editorial summation for the June 3 issue, the strongest and most comprehensive indictment he ever made of female suffrage.

Mrs. Duniway and the OESA increased efforts at the end to counter the long-feared attack—Abigail said it was "the busiest and most important week of my life"—and still hoped for the best.[9] The contest was so close that the result was in doubt for nearly three weeks after the election, but the final tally spelled defeat for the suffrage cause. There was a special concentration of negative votes in Multnomah County, in the *Oregonian's* greatest circulation perimeter. The work of 30 years had failed, and Abigail Scott Duniway was as bitter in defeat as her brother seemed vauntful in victory. Fortunately for the record, she wrote a running account of feelings and actions to her son Clyde, who as a history professor at Stanford constituted both a fully trusted correspondent and one who would preserve the sources. "Pray excuse my tardiness!" she wrote him on June 27,

6. Wilkie Duniway to Clyde A. Duniway (February 7, 1900). Abigail Scott Duniway, *Path Breaking: An Autobiographical History of the Equal Suffrage Movement in Pacific Coast States* (Portland, 1914), 163.

7. Leslie M. Scott, "Memoranda of the Files of the *Oregonian*." Typescript, n.d., Special Collections, University of Oregon Library, Eugene. *Oregonian* (May 17, 1900), 3.

8. Alfred Holman, "Harvey W. Scott, Editor—Review of His Half-Century Career and Estimate of His Work," *Quarterly of the Oregon Historical Society*, 14 (June, 1913), 87.

9. *Oregonian* (June 2, 1900), 5.

I have been overwhelmed with hard work, and the humiliation and shame of my brother's nefarious conduct. But I am rising above it and shall go right on. We would have won triumphantly if the *Oregonian* had not stirred up the slum and slime of the city's purlieus, causing them to throw his bilge water on his own family from the ballot boxes of White Chapel district. No, his fight was not reputable. It made every real friend he had ashamed of him and his paper. But we are not whipped. We are stronger than ever. We got over 48% of the vote. 21 counties gave us a majority. One lost by a tie and one by only one vote. Hubert gave the cheap old tyrant a raking that made him sick. Then, last Sunday, I had it out with him, but not till after he said he would whip us harder than ever next time. The sweetest thing I said was 'You have stood up naked before the world and you are not ashamed!' I talked for half an hour. It seemed that I was inspired. Then, Monday, I sent out through the Associated Press, this telegram signed by my own name and office:

"Defeated, but not beaten! Yes, 26,265; No, 28,402. Leaders are jubilant over the large vote. Going right ahead! Will win next time!"[10]

After that memorable confrontation Scott ordered his family to stop all social contacts with Mrs. Duniway. Relationships were renewed the following year,[11] but after that summer Abigail's resentment was never far beneath the surface. For months she released her bitterness in letters to Clyde, while putting on a family front to the public for the sake of the future cause. "I have no words to tell you," she wrote August 30, "how I despise him." The editor of the *Oregonian* was the "cheap boy," "no brother of mine," "your mad uncle," "the coward," and "my unnatural brother, whom I hate with perfect and justifiable hatred." "My work," she wrote in September,

is going quietly on, almost as if nothing had happened except that the estrangement with Harve has not healed, nor will it till he has brought forth fruits meet for repentance.[12]

Part of her work that fall was to prepare a chapter entitled "History of Equal Suffrage in Oregon" for Susan B. Anthony's and Ida Husted Harper's comprehensive history of the national movement. This she published locally as the November issue of *The Campaign Leaflet*, The OESA periodical. Her first draft, the printed proofs preserved by Clyde Duniway, included three pages portraying in villainous perspective Scott's role in the recent election defeat. "It is no fault of mine," read this highly personal recent history,

---

10. Abigail Scott Duniway to Clyde A. Duniway (June 27, 1900).
11. Wilkie Duniway to Clyde A. Duniway, (July 7, 1900); Abigail Scott Duniway to Clyde A. Duniway (February 14 and March 12, 1901).
12. Ibid. (August 30, June 9, July 4, 17, 28, and September 9, 1900).

that I must hand him down to history in these pages as the great editor who whipped his sister at the public whipping post when she was bound hand and foot before the laws which women were compelled to sustain as taxpayers, and to which they are held amenable, even to the extent of giving up their sons, the children of their peril, to lose their lives in the service of a country in the management of which they have no voice, but which holds them as perpetual aliens through fiat of sex, no matter what their endowment of brains, patriotism or patrimony.

Miss Anthony was spared the challenge of dealing with that heroic 108-word sentence, and the entire section, when Abigail permitted herself to be persuaded to remove it from the final draft. She did have the grim satisfaction of making sure that Scott received a copy of the original unexpurgated version.[13] And her seething resentment persisted. In 1903 she would rejoice at Scott's defeat in the Oregon legislature for a U.S. Senate seat. While she grieved at his death in 1910, six weeks later when his will was made public she complained that he excluded Scott relatives (though "we didn't expect it—knowing the man."), and declared "He left all his children immensely rich, and his wife a millionaire. Well! She earned it—living with *him*."[14]

* * *

This was one of those not-so-rare episodes in history when familial infelicity bore significantly on large public issues. Perhaps it is justifiable to invade the Scott-Duniway privacy long enough to gain perspective and insight into the course of the Oregon movement for women's rights. Perhaps, too, the tense drama attached to the familiar phenomenon of sibling conflict, here rendered larger than life in its societal dimensions, is worth telling for the human interest alone. Such ends require at least a brief summation of the adversaries' positions and interaction regarding woman suffrage both before and after the crucial 1900 election, followed by a modest attempt to suggest certain social and psychological dimensions of their relationship.

Converted early to the woman's movement, Abigail Scott Duniway was writing letters to the editor of the Oregon City *Argus* as a 24-year-old pioneer farm wife in 1858, declaring for the equality of the sexes. The next year she wrote an Oregon Trail novel, *Captain Gray's Company*, which showed keen sensitivity to women's disadvantages.[15] Then her husband Ben Duniway, without her involvement nor consent, lost their farm in the early 1860's by co-signing notes for a friend who defaulted. Soon after the family moved to town Ben suffered a handicapping accident, and Abigail become the pri-

13. Duniway, "History of Equal Suffrage in Oregon," 7. Proof sheets of the first draft, Duniway Papers. Abigail Scott Duniway to Clyde A. Duniway (November 21, 1900).

14. Ibid.(February 24, 1903; September 17, 1910).

mary breadwinner. First she found herself teaching school with her first class permit for half the pay of a man who had barely qualified for a third class certificate. She later took in boarders, and successfully operated a millinery shop. Business experiences confirmed her convictions and with Ben's influence brought her to conclude by the middle 1860's that the basic step toward redressing a host of economic and legal discriminations was to give women political identity with the vote.[16]

Doubtless stimulated both by her writing ambitions and by brother Harvey's notable success as editor of the *Oregonian* since 1865, she moved to Portland in 1871 and established a newspaper, *The New Northwest*. This high quality weekly added varied cultural features to its strong editorial promotions of women's rights, and paid its way until it was sold in 1887. Ben filled domestic roles and their five sons were active in the publication while Abigail traveled regularly throughout the region, speaking and organizing the movement, mailing back editorials, poems, and a dozen or more serialized novels, each with its feminist message. Probably no other equal suffrage paper survived so long on its own earnings, which result was directly due to Abigail's tireless creative energies and her family's considerable home efforts.

After graduation from Pacific University with the first B.A. degree awarded in the Pacific Northwest, Harvey Scott served a sort of editorial apprenticeship on the *Oregonian* from 1865 to 1872. Honing talents in writing and argumentation, he adhered faithfully to the Radical Republican line on political issues. On topics where he was permitted opinions of his own in those early years he tended to be progressive, and this included women's issues. He censured the universal practice of paying women one-third to one-half the salary men received for the same work, and he published comparative scales, by sex, for teachers' salaries across the land.[17]He welcomed Abigail's *New Northwest* in May, 1871, with an admiring editorial notice and an "extremely cordial" visit after her first issue. As Collector of Customs in Portland 1870-76, the appointment a lucrative reward for faithful party work, Scott hired Ben Duniway in 1873 as "Opener and Packer" in the customs office at $1,300 annually, a fine salary for those depressed times.[18]

In September, 1871, Mrs. Duniway sponsored Susan B. Anthony in a Northwest lecture tour, and women's issues, especially woman suffrage,

15. *Oregon Argus* (December 18, 1858; January 11, 1859). Mrs. Abigail J. Duniway, *Captain Gray's Company; or Crossing the Plains and Living in Oregon* (Portland, 1859). This is the first of over 200 adult and juvenile novels with overland trail settings. "Oregon Trail Fiction Plus California and Mormon Trail Titles: A Bibliography," unpublished manuscript prepared by the writer.

16. Duniway, *Path Breaking*, 13-40; Leslie McKay Roberts, "Suffragist of the New West: Abigail Scott Duniway and the Development of the Oregon Woman Suffrage Movement" (B. A. Thesis, Reed College, 1969), 32.

17. *Oregonian* (May 13, 1867), 2; (September 18, 1869), 2.

achieved new levels of prominence in the region. Of all Portland male editors, as historian Tom Edwards has shown, Scott discussed these issues at
greatest depth, and most sympathetically.[19] He felt the suffragists held unre-
alistically high hopes for the benefits the vote would bring them, argued
that citizenship did not necessarily insure the suffrage, and took a rigid
stand that "fixed laws of nature" would forever keep women in their domestic "sphere." But he answered some of the particularly chauvinistic jibes
against women made by his editorial rivals, and refrained from ridiculing
Miss Anthony where she made herself most vulnerable. "As an individual,"
he wrote, "we shall probably vote for woman suffrage when the question is
presented."[20] All told, it suggested the possibility of an effective Scott editorial alliance on women's rights, a hopeful first year for Abigail's public
career.

Scott was out of the *Oregonian* editorship from 1872 to 1877, returning
as part owner at 39, mature, studied, and more independent. From 1877
through 1883 he promoted his sister's lectures, contributed financially to
her cause, and gave woman suffrage occasional editorial support.[21] The
month of November, 1883, a crucial time with the suffrage issue before the
Washington territorial legislature, saw no less than three pro-suffrage editorials in the paper, and represents the apex of Harvey's early public alliance
with Abigail. The third of those essays, written after the measure had been
voted through in Olympia, took up in detail several objections to woman
suffrage raised by a Washington reader. All these were "considered and disposed of long ago," said Scott. They were the sort of questions

> invariably asked by persons who have but just begun to think on the sub-
> ject. After they have become familiar with it they no longer find the diffi-
> culties which at first seemed to them so great. Indeed the difficulties
> vanish, having no existence outside the imagination.

Is the anti-suffrage male, Scott asked rhetorically, really prepared to
assert that his wife, mother, and sisters are inferior to him in judgment, in

18. Ibid. (May 5, 1871), 2; Duniway, *Path Breaking*, 32; H. W. Scott to Hon. Secretary
William A. Richardson, (June 21, 1873; endorsed as approved July 11, 1873), Record Group
56, Customhouse Nominations Portland, Oregon, Department of the Treasury, the National
Archives, Washington, D. C.

19. G. Thomas Edwards, *Sowing Good Seeds: The Northwest Suffrage Campaigns of Susan B.
Anthony* (Portland, 1990), 19-82, 111-122. Professor Edwards' book covers Anthony's contacts
with Duniway from 1871 to 1905, providing rich setting and background for this essay.

20. *Oregonian* (September 16, 1871), 2; (September 19, 1871), 2; (December 6, 1871), 2;
(January 8, 1872), 2.

21. Ibid. (April 20, 1877), 2; Abigail Scott Duniway's Record Book of 1883 Contributions, Duniway Papers; *New Northwest* (May 1, 1879), 2. See *Oregonian* (October 25, 1912), 12,
for Mrs. Duniway's generally accurate summary of how Scott related to the suffrage question
from 1871 forward.

patriotism, in love of good government? They are not disqualified from voting because they don't "hold office, perform road work, do jury duty, pay poll taxes," or go to war, since half or more of voting males also avoid those things.The assumption that politics would degrade the ladies betrayed an unfortunately low view of public life, which should concern all moral men as well as women. "The whole sum of the matter," he concluded, is that woman is capable of exerting an influence in public affairs which the state needs, and this influence can be made effective only through the suffrage. Prejudice may for awhile prevent it, but no argument can stand for a moment in its way.[22]

It was a handsome endorsement of Abigail's cause, and of Washington Territory's decision to enfranchise women. She would treasure the clippings and the memories for 30 years, hoping for a sequel. By the next spring, however, Scott had cooled toward the issue to the point that the *Oregonian* did not support the woman suffrage amendment to the Oregon state constitution when it was before the voters for the first time on June 2, 1884. He was on a trip east for several weeks around election time, and S.B. Pettingill, his assistant, maintained a neutral stance on the woman's question, publishing both hostile and supportive correspondence.[23] The amendment lost decisively, 28,176 to 11,223.[24] By 1887 Harvey Scott was refuting some of the same arguments for woman suffrage that he had advanced four years before, and he lent his influence to the decision of the Washington State Constitutional Convention in 1888 to deny women the vote in the new state.[25]

Several factors moved Scott to reverse his position on the suffrage question in the 1880's. He seemed, first, to consider the lopsided Oregon defeat of 1884 an indication that the opposition was too great to combat practically. Washington's reversal of its earlier stand confirmed Scott's view that woman suffrage was a dying cause. He wrote repeatedly during those years that only a minority of women themselves wanted to vote, and those generally the discontented and the uneducated. With the redress of certain legal and economic grievances by legislative acts, woman suffrage was, moreover, less and less needed. He was concerned, too, about the strong alliance generally in Washington and elsewhere between prohibitionist and suffragist forces. If they had the vote, he feared, women would be betrayed by their sentimental nature to take similarly "unsound" positions on other issues, such as capital punishment.[26]

22. *Oregonian* (November 30, 1883), 2. See Ibid. (November 4, 1883), 4; and (November 26, 1883), 4.
23. Ibid. (June 1, 1884), 5; *New Northwest* (June 5, 1884), 4; (June 19, 1884), 4.
24. Charles Henry Carey, *History of Oregon* (Chicago and Portland, 1922), 826.
25. *Oregonian* (July 12, 1887), 4; (January 14, 1888), 4.

Faithful study of Edmund Burke and Herbert Spencer had equipped Scott with a variety of conservative convictions by the late 1870's, and in the next decade he came increasingly to recognize that philosophical, political, economic, and social conservatism was no natural ally to woman suffrage. In Washington the issue was "buried in the same grave with the single-tax proposition," and its successes in the 1890's in Kansas, Colorado, and Idaho "was but an outgrowth of the temporary socialistic spirit that prevails in those states."[27] Scott was confirmed in these conclusions when Mrs. Duniway opposed his long-standing fight against inflation in all its forms, culminating in the campaign for sound money and McKinley against William Jennings Bryan and free silver in the presidential election of 1896. Abigail also opposed his campaign against free high schools, and she enjoyed the patronage and friendship of his most hated political enemy, U.S. Senator John H. Mitchell.[28]

All such considerations led Scott periodically to inveigh against woman suffrage after the mid-1880's and prepared him for the major editorial capstone of his views on the subject, released the day before the crucial 1900 election. Aileen S. Kraditor has helpfully identified at least 30 antisuffragist ideas current between 1890 and 1920, and it is worth noting that Scott made use of about half of them.[29] Most of his arguments appear in some form in the 1900 essay, plus a theme or two that Kraditor overlooked. If it is unneedful to deal fully with each nuance of his views, it might yet be useful to sample his rhetoric and suggest what Abigail and her allies were up against. "There is far too little deliberation in the exercise of the suffrage now," Scott emphasized.

> Introduction of the feminine element would immensely increase this evil. For women as a rule are less deliberate than men. A due sense of the proportion of things; an adequate subordination of impulse to reason; an habitual regard to the ultimate and unexaggerated judgment, are elements which already are lamentably wanting in political life, and female suffrage certainly would not tend to increase them.

Men were "deplorably deficient" and "flighty" in understanding public affairs, but "all the evils that belong to indiscriminate male suffrage would

26. Ibid. (July 12, 1887), 4; (August 12, 1889), 4; (October 8, 1889), 4; (June 8, 1890, 6. See *New Northwest* (January 6, 1887), 1, Mrs. Duniway's final issue, where she takes a last dig at Scott, his sources, and his reasoning.

27. *Oregonian* (November 12, 1898), 4. On his Burkean conservatism see Ibid. (October 17, 1901), 10; (August 20, 1910), 6.

28. Abigail Scott Duniway to Clyde A. Duniway (January 15, 1894); (June 2, 1895); *New Northwest* (March 4, 1880), 2. She was also the friend of leftist attorney-poet C. E. S. Wood, another Scott *bete noire*. Duniway, *Path Breaking*, 12, 58, 59.

29. Aileen S. Kraditor, *The Ideas of the Woman Suffrage Movement, 1890-1920* (New York and London, 1965), 14-38.

be more than doubled by indiscriminate suffrage to women." One of the problems lay in the fact that "the conservative woman as a rule is probably feminine and likely to stay at home while the radical woman is pretty sure to go forth rejoicing to the fray." "Moreover," declared Scott, warming to his message and pursuing a seemingly original line of thought,

> with women, even more than with men, there is a strong disposition to overrate the curative powers of legislation, to attempt to mould the lives of all persons in their details by meddlesome or restraining laws, and the vast increase of female influence which the suffrage would give could hardly fail to increase that habit of excessive legislation which is one the great evils of the time.

Women themselves had no further legal nor economic wrongs to be redressed; the laws, in fact, now discriminated in favor of the wife in matters involving property and children. "Government," Scott continued,

> is a very practical business. It is very strenuous business. For government in its final analysis is always force; and if rash measures get the community into trouble, it is by men that it must be got out again. In the last resort, it is physical strength that rules the world, and it is in man, not in woman, that this last court of appeal resides.

All of this was not to imply that woman was inferior to man. In fact her special qualities in the "affections and graces" may be more important than man's practical qualities, but they did not equip her to govern. "Herein," the editor concluded,

> are the chief reasons why, as the *Oregonian* thinks, woman is as little fitted for political as man is for domestic life. Women suffrage, therefore, cannot be good for government and society, nor for woman herself; and womanly women see all this through their intuition as clearly as manly men apprehend it through their judgment and reason.[30]

For century's turn it was an impressive blend of bellicose realpolitik, anti-democratic elitism, Victorian decorum, and frontier male chauvinism. Its still-timely preachments fell on itching ears in the Oregon electorate, and Abigail was undone.

If the editorial of June 3, 1900 represented Scott's most effective effort on its subject, it may also be considered his antisuffragist valedictory. Never again in the decade remaining him was he to mount an editorial campaign against woman suffrage nor write a hostile leader on the subject. It is clear in retrospect that his 1900 victory over the suffragist forces was so decisive,

---

30. *Oregonian* (June 3, 1900), 6.

despite the narrow margin, that further campaigning would have been redundant. The momentum of 1900 greatly hurt later equal suffrage campaigns in 1906, 1908, and 1910, as did the declining energies and involvement of Mrs. Duniway. Scott maintained neutrality in the first two elections, and was three months in his grave at the third. But his views were known. "The *Oregonian* has not changed its mind," he wrote in response to several inquiries before the 1906 election, "but is tired of the contention."[31] Scott may have recognized that the suffrage amendment would lose without his current opposition, as indeed it did by increasing margins: 10,000 votes in 1906, 22,000 in 1908, nearly 24,000 in 1910. Two years after Scott's death the *Oregonian* actively supported the suffrage measure for the first time, and despite the dedicated efforts of Leslie Scott to use his father's negative influence from the grave, the women finally won, by 4,000 votes.[32] Abigail was there to savor victory, her spirit powerful still amid physical infirmities at 78. And she did savor it, but she never forgot that in all probability her triumph would have come twelve years sooner had the *Oregonian* been neutral in 1900, earlier still had her brother supported her cause.

* * *

That much told, the historian has fulfilled his journeyman responsibilities. The narrative is presented, the attitudes described, the ideas rationalized, the documentation recorded. Yet thoughtful practitioners have long known that there is more to intellectual history than the intellect. *Homo Sapiens*, including the intelligentsia of the species, are moved by ganglia and viscera as well as the cerebrum. Their range of styles in relating to others arises out of the complexities of early social environment. They live through identifiable stages in life that affect their thinking and judgments. Having combed, or rather brushed, some of what developmental psychologists unabashedly call their "literature," I would like to make some closing modest suggestions of extra-rational factors that may have been part of the historic Scott contention. This without serious psycho-historic pretensions, and with several common sense extrapolations.

---

31. Ibid. (June 2, 1906), 8.

32. Carey, *History of Oregon*, 904-905. Leslie Scott wired several of his father's early associates for their recollections of the editor's views on woman suffrage, hoping to use their replies just before the election. F. A. Carle to Leslie M. Scott (October 20, 1912); Alfred Holman to Leslie M. Scott (October 29, 1912); Ernest Bross to Leslie M. Scott (October 29, 1912); N. J. Levinson to Leslie M. Scott (October 31, 1912). Scott Family Papers, in possession of Leslie M. Scott family, Portland, Oregon. Margaret N. Scott, the editor's widow, joined son Leslie's campaign with an anti-suffragette letter to the *Oregonian*, which was reprinted and widely distributed, and answered effectively by Mrs. Duniway. *Oregonian* (October 11, 1912), 12; (October 25, 1912), 12.

Prominent among Abigail Jane Scott's earliest recollections was the severe disappointment of her parents at the fact that their first children to survive infancy were girls. As the second of those daughters, born October 22, 1834, Abigail recalled "my mother informed me on my tenth birthday that her sorrow over my sex was almost too grievous to be borne." At the birth of a later daughter the mother told Abigail, through her tears, "Poor baby! She'll be a woman someday! Poor baby! A woman's lot is so hard!"[33] The corollary of this traumatic early rejection by gender was the great joy and continuing affirmation that greeted the birth of the first surviving son, Harvey, on February 1, 1838, 39 months after Abigail's arrival. The frontier Illinois farm, and Oregon Country counterparts later, needed strong sons. Harvey's superior family standing and "value" relative to his six sisters was still further enhanced when his two younger brothers died early, one on the Oregon Trail in 1852 at three years, the other at 18 in 1862.[34]

Abigail's impressions from her mother, Ann Roelofson Scott, were driven home by the events of 1851 and 1852, when John Tucker Scott, the father, was preparing to migrate overland to Oregon. On September 8, 1851, a few weeks before her twenty-first wedding anniversary, Mrs. Scott gave birth to her twelfth child, another unwanted girl who died the same day. The mother was ill and weak all that winter, and quietly opposed, but in a patriarchal era would not veto, the projected trip to Oregon. On the last day of spring, 1852, having jostled along in the springless prairie schooner for 80 days, she died beside the Platte of the plains cholera, a worn-out invalid at 40 years of age. Thirteen months later, Abigail Jane followed her mother's path and the expectations of frontier society by herself becoming a hard-working farm wife, and in ten months a daughter arrived to begin the familiar pattern of biennial babies. There would be six of them.[35]

The frontier environment offered Harvey a variant set of experiences, also difficult but somehow co-operating more happily with his fulfillment than did his sister's drudgery with hers. Campaigns against rampaging Indians in the Yakima War at 17; hard outdoor work in clearing farmsites, building cabins, logging, and following the Boise basin gold rush—all such activities confirmed his aggressive, confident manhood, his expected role. He postponed marriage until he enjoyed a dependable income, as it was socially acceptable for a male to do. The thoughtful, well-read Scott clan even respected the atypical passion he felt to study Latin and Greek and get a college education. The greater range of his options than those of his sisters was readily apparent, and expanded yet further with his degree, as he served as Portland's first librarian, studied law, and finally became editor. At

33. Duniway, *Path Breaking*, 3, 8.
34. Harvey W. Scott, *History of the Oregon Country.* Compiled by Leslie M. Scott. (Cambridge, MA: 1924), I, 275.
35. Ibid., III, 239, 248-49, 272; Duniway, *Path Breaking*, 3-9.

the *Oregonian* helm Scott immediately conformed to the clearly understood "macho" norm of a fighting frontier editor.[36] Editors were *expected* publicly and visibly to be tough, combative, elemental, insensitive, uncompromising—in short, to demonstrate a sampling of the lesser proofs of virile masculinity. Scott fought a victorious street brawl with rival editor Jimmy O'Meara after a bitterly-contested election in 1866, during which he was obliged to disarm his pistol-packing opponent. He later took to carrying a firearm himself, and drew it in anger on at least one occasion.[37] All of this is intended to suggest the great gulf between socially-accepted sex roles for men and women in the 1860's. Abigail opposed powerful taboos when she launched the *New Northwest*. And Harvey faced massive barriers in trying to take her mission seriously, and to consider whether and how he should relate to that mission.

If those several factors would seem to strain brother-sister ties, they appear even more significant in the light of recent psychological research on children of various ages. Of all sibling relationships, these studies conclude, the most volatile, quarrelsome, and competitive are commonly between a girl and her younger brother. The sister tends to be jealous of her commonly less responsible and more heartily affirmed brother. She is also greatly stimulated by the relationship, scoring highest of all individuals studied in curiosity, creativity, tenacity, and ambition. The brother tends to be more withdrawn, depressive, exhibitionistic, selfish, and uncooperative, ranking low in friendliness, and is "highly quarrelsome at all ages."[38]

Everything we know of the Abigail-Harvey relationship, including her memories of physical beatings she sustained at his hand as a child, identifies them as a classic, intensified case of sister-younger brother sibling rivalry. When she started her newspaper she did not consult at all with Scott on details, and her opening editorial asserted, "if we had been a man, we'd have had an editor's position at a handsome salary at twenty-one." This gratuitous egoism was an obvious reference to brother Harvey, who had failed to attain such a position until the advanced age of 27. It is clear that Scott was always a more important and prominent factor in her social environment than she was in his, and that recognizing this fact she resented it. Disappointments impelled her repeatedly to consider what might have been. In her 1914 autobiography she expressed her belief that Scott would have supported her mission "if I had not been his sister."[39]

---

36. For a more extended, documented account of these themes, see Lee Nash, "Scott of the *Oregonian*: Literary Frontiersman," *Pacific Historical Review*, (August, 1976), 357-68.
37. Matthew P. Deady to James W. Nesmith (June 11, 1866). Deady Papers, Oregon Historical Society Library, Portland; *Oregonian* (March 12, 1868), 2; Scott Family Scrapbook, 90, Scott Family Papers.
38. Brian Sutton-Smith and B. G. Rosenberg, *The Sibling* (New York, 1970), 148-52.

Throughout the twelve years of public cordiality Scott and the *Oregonian* displayed toward Mrs. Duniway, 1871 through 1883, there were underlying tensions and private arguments. "The terror of my boyhood" in the 1870's, recalled Clyde Duniway half a century later, was to see family reunions destroyed as his mother and his uncle went at it hammer and tong at their father's home in Forest Grove.[40] The father, to be sure, himself a powerful personality, did all he could to exercise a moderating influence upon the more destructive intrafamily disputes, and to enlist Harvey's public support of his sister. "Jen [Abigail Jane was called "Jenny" in the family] lectured here last Friday night," John Tucker Scott typically wrote his son in early 1873.

> She acquitted herself *nobly* and earned the favor of all who heard her. The house was *full*.
> And now Harve let me say to you that it will be to the interest of the Republican party to remember her in the distribution of the federal offices. Give her...the Post Office.... . The fact is the *"Woman movement"* will hold the balance [*sic*] of power in all our coming elections, and we cannot ignore so powerful an ally as *Jen* with her *"New Northwest"* will be to the Republican party. I hope that her claims will be considered and *justice* done, and that *you* will aid her all that is in your power consistent with your duty as a *brother* and an influential public man.[41]

While Abigail Jane never got the Post Office, John Tucker Scott exercised a major restraining influence upon Harvey. The editor admiringly regarded his father as a "pioneer of pioneers" for his awesome physical strength, his "mighty and invincible nature," raw courage, and many exploits. Harvey was greatly affected by John Tucker Scott's death on September 1, 1880, which was followed the next February by another trauma, the death of his promising ten-year-old son, Kenneth.[42] These events shook the foundations of Scott's life at age 42, and removed the authority figure to whom he had always looked as a moral guide. He entered, during those hard months,

39. Abigail Scott Duniway to Clyde A. Duniway (June 21, 1899); *New Northwest* (May 5, 1871, 2: Duniway, *Path Breaking*, 31-32. Harvey's prominence in Abigail's consciousness is fictionally portrayed in the two youths in her two published novels, "Herbert" in *Captain Gray's Company* and "Harry" in *From the West to the West: Across the Plains to Oregon* (Chicago, 1905). The latter was the younger brother of the heroine, who was obviously a youthful Abigail. Herbert and Harry are both portrayed favorably as outspoken, impulsive, and mischievous.

40. Interviews with David C. Duniway (August 9, 1969; October 3, 1979).

41. John Tucker Scott to Harvey Scott (January 21, 1873), Scott Family Papers. Abigail was recognized as a highly effective public speaker and Harvey was awkward in delivery and demeanor on the platform, another probable source of jealous tension.

42. Harvey Scott to Margaret N. Scott, (September 4, 1880), Scott Family Papers; *Oregonian* (September 2, 1880), 2; Scott, *History of the Oregon Country*, I, 9. Scott's personal scrapbook holds several clippings and poems relating to both deaths on the same page, Scott Family Scrapbook, Scott Family Papers.

what Yale psychologist Daniel J. Levinson calls the "Mid-life Transition," the door to "middle adulthood." And as he sorted out his emotions and his options in the early 1880's, he achieved the new levels of "individuation" and take-charge independence first described by Carl Jung as the natural accompaniment of the start of the second half of life.[43] One of the noticeable results was for him to go public with his underlying convictions on woman suffrage.

When Harvey Scott entered his sixties in 1898, his crowning public triumph just behind him of "saving" Oregon for McKinley and sound money in 1896, he made some conscious transitions in interest and style. Vigorous fights remained, to be sure, especially with the new *Oregon Journal* after 1902, but his general tendency was to mellow and modify traditional hostilities, toward Senator Mitchell and free high schools, for two examples.[44] He became relatively less concerned for current contentions, and more for cultural projects such as the Oregon Historical Society and the Lewis and Clark Exposition, and for his own reputation and historic standing. He was greatly interested in topping off his career in the U. S. Senate, and worked hard behind the scenes to that end, though unsuccessfully.[45]

All of this made the late attack in 1900 on Abigail and woman suffrage untimely and unseemly, a sort of last battle against a particularly persistent foe, one with whom he had special emotional ties. After his victory and the year-long breach, he consistently tried to relate cordially to Abigail, recognizing belatedly the importance of family when one sought to appraise his life and shore up for old age. The most dramatic public expression of this effort to compensate for his failure to follow John Tucker Scott's early admonitions as to his brotherly duties occurred in August, 1906. "The Oregonian has not supported woman suffrage," wrote Scott in an untitled editorial note,

> but has opposed it; ... But it will say it has been an interested witness of the effort for it during the whole period of the agitation in Oregon, these forty years. It was begun by Mrs. Duniway, and has been carried on by her unceasingly; and whatever progress it has made is due to her more than to all other agencies together... . The progress it has made is an extraordinary tribute to one woman's energy. Richard Realf wrote of one who—

---

43. Daniel J. Levinson, *The Seasons of a Man's Life* (New York, 1978), 23-33.

44. George S. Turnbill, *History of Oregon Newspapers* (Portland, 1939), 131; Lee Nash, "Harvey Scott's 'Cure for Drones': An Oregon Alternative to Public Higher Schools," *Pacific Northwest Quarterly, 64 (April, 1973)*, 70, 78-79.

45. Lee M. Nash, "Scott of the *Oregonian*: The Editor as Historian," *Oregon Historical Quarterly*, 70 (September, 1969), 196-232; *Oregonian* (February 21, 1903), 1; Jonathan Bourne, Jr. to H. W. Scott (March 8, 1906), Jonathan Bourne, Jr. Papers, Special Collections, University of Oregon Library, Eugene.

Did not wait till Freedom had become
the easy shibboleth of the Courtier's lips.
But smote for her when God himself seemed dumb,
And all his arching skies were in eclipse.

If woman suffrage is a synonym for freedom, as its advocates claim, these lines are fit eulogy of Abigail Scott Duniway.[46]

It was not as pleasing to Abigail as that elusive alliance would have been, and it may not finally have absolved Harvey from lingering guilt. But it was more than he ever said for any other of his many vanquished enemies through the decades. And he said it here, obviously, because sibling rivalry held a different quality than his other contentions. Ties of blood asserted themselves in this last stage of the longtime love-hate relationship with sister Abigail, and his warmer impulses finally prevailed.

---

46. *Oregonian* (August 20, 1906), 6.

Herbert Hoover as an Enduring Model for American Leaders

A Personal Reflection *

SENATOR MARK O. HATFIELD

I would like to thank Professor Lee Nash for inviting me to speak to you today. I want also to thank George Fox College for creating a forum which might be considered revisionist. Today, too few appreciate the degree to which Herbert Hoover is an enduring model for American leaders.

Quite simply, I believe that Herbert Hoover was one of the greatest humanitarian leaders of this century. The qualities he exhibited while heading the Commission for Relief in Belgium, the American Relief Administration, the American Child Health Association, the Boys and Girls Clubs of America, the President's Famine Emergency Committee, and, of course, while serving as President of the United States were truly those of a compassionate leader. His legacy lives on in the organizations he co-founded, such as CARE and UNICEF, and in the hearts of the descendants of the millions of grateful people who he assisted across the globe. Even in the years before he was elected President, Herbert Hoover was one of the most prominent and best known Americans in the world.

Mr. Hoover not only provided food, he also delivered hope. He embodied the best that America has to offer and in the process inspired countless young people to join his endeavors, endeavors focused especially on the

---

* This was the luncheon address at Herbert Hoover Symposium X on the George Fox College campus, November 4, 1995

Four Horsemen of the Apocalypse—famine, pestilence, death and war—to which he often referred.

Few who have left such a legacy have been so maligned in our history; which makes our convening here today so important. As students and teachers of history, it is crucial for us to cut through imagery in order to fully understand and appreciate the facts in Herbert Hoover's life and career and to present this picture of him to future generations. As a true admirer of Herbert Hoover and as one who strives to follow his example as a leader and as a human being, it is an honor for me to participate in this symposium, to explore with you his legacy through the eyes and experiences of those who were so deeply inspired by him.

I am sorry that I cannot be here for each of your sessions, but l look forward to reading all of the papers in the future. You have chosen your subjects well. When we consider the people closest to Herbert Hoover, we invariably talk about Hugh Gibson, Christian Herter, James McLafferty, and many envoys and foreign service officers. There are many others, of course. Today I would like to first comment on two additional members of the "crew"—Maurice Pate and Admiral Lewis Strauss—and then to reflect on Mr. Hoover's impact on my own life in public service.

l include Pate and Strauss because both men have left us testimonials of the impact Herbert Hoover had on their lives and also because both men made enormous contributions to the betterment of humankind. I have no evidence that the two men knew each other well, yet they each shared a strong bond with Herbert Hoover. In fact, both Pate and Strauss, on learning of Mr. Hoover's death, compared him to their own fathers, referring to the great inspiration and constructive influence that Mr. Hoover had on their lives.

Maurice Pate joined the Hoover crew in April 1916, little more than a year after he had graduated from Princeton. He had been attracted to the Commission for Relief in Belgium as a way of making a contribution to the war effort. Through persistence, Pate won an overseas assignment to work with Mr. Hoover himself. It was a demanding and often frustrating job, but one with great spiritual rewards. "Remember whatever you do," Mr. Hoover wrote to Pate at a particularly difficult time, "I am one hundred percent behind you." That brief note of confidence buoyed Pate throughout his career. In fact, Pate would quote the comment more than 45 years later.

Pate had vivid memories of his service in Europe. "Any man working for Mr. Hoover immediately became three men because of the confidence the Chief inspired," he told a reporter from *The New Yorker* in 1961.[1] The two men continued to collaborate in the establishment and expansion of the United Nation's International Children's Emergency Fund, now known as

---

1. Quoted in Joseph Wechberg, "At the Heart of UNICEF," *The New Yorker* (December 2, 1961). 78.

UNICEF. Pate served as the first executive director of UNICEF from 1947 to 1964 and Mr. Hoover was his unofficial advisor.

There is no doubt that Hoover and Pate complemented each other well. In many ways, they were a masterful combination of a great humanitarian and his star pupil. Not one given to exaggeration, Herbert Hoover once referred to Pate as "the most efficient and dedicated human angel that I have ever known."[2] High praise, indeed. I doubt that Herbert Hoover ever referred to any other mortal as an "angel," with the possible exception of Mrs. Hoover!

And if Pate were an angel, he drew his inspiration from Mr. Hoover himself. "Year by year," Pate wrote to Mr. Hoover in 1954 about UNICEF, "your continuing moral support has been the single greatest factor of encouragement to me in this work."[3] In fact, Pate gave Mr. Hoover full credit for the idea and the framework of UNICEF. "No man in the world," wrote Pate in 1962, "has ever understood better the problems and the needs of children, and no man has ever done more in their behalf than Herbert Hoover."[4] That Herbert Hoover was an enduring model of leadership for Pate is without question, and Pate's contributions to the welfare of children around the world were extraordinary.

Like Pate, Lewis Strauss was drawn to Herbert Hoover at a young age. In fact, Mr. Hoover's humanitarianism so impressed the Strauss family that his picture had a place of prominence in their parlor. It is not surprising, therefore, that young Lewis Strauss would travel to Washington in May 1917 to offer his services to the new United States Food Administrator. "My idea," Strauss wrote at the time, "is to serve under Hoover if possible, and thus while serving my country, study this great man's methods.[5]

Strauss was more successful in his quest than he could ever dream. In a matter of weeks, his hard work had earned him an appointment as Mr. Hoover's private secretary, and from that vantage point, he absorbed Hoover's style of leadership. Many years later, Strauss referred to Mr. Hoover as a "man of decision," to be admired for his determination and his intellect, among other qualities.[6]

But for Strauss, as for Pate and many other members of the "crew," it was Herbert Hoover's human compassion that most impressed them. "He

2. "Remarks by Herbert Hoover at the Twenty-fifth Anniversary of the Waldorf-Astoria Hotel for the Benefit of the United Nations Children's Fund," September 28, 1956, Herbert Hoover Public Statement File, Hoover Presidential Library-Museum.

3. Pate to Hoover, November 1, 1954, Biographical File, Pate Papers, Hoover Library.

4. Pate as quoted in Herbert Hoover, The American Epic, (Chicago, 1960-1964), IV, 281-82.

5. Strauss oral history interview quoted in Richard Pfau, No Sacrifice Too Great: The Life of Lewis L. Strauss (Charlottesville, VA, 1984), 10.

6. Lewis L. Strauss, "A Man of Decision," Men and Decisions (Garden City, NY, 1962), 7-59.

felt for people who were suffering," Strauss recalled in one interview. But, as Strauss points out, Mr. Hoover's compassion was evidenced by deeds rather than words. Perhaps the somber Quaker household in Newberg where Mr. Hoover was reared, where emotions were often suppressed, influenced him even in later years. Whatever the case, his commitment to serving those in need was always clear. "This wasn't a mawkish feeling," Strauss said. "He didn't shed tears over the Belgian babies; he did something about it. Compassion led to action on his part, not to haggling.[7] Compassion and action underscored Strauss's lifelong admiration for Hoover as a leader. Strauss went on to an extraordinary career as an investment banker and later as chairman of the U.S. Atomic Energy Commission and as acting Secretary of Commerce. But at the core of his being, Strauss was a Hoover man. "We have found ourselves," Strauss wrote of himself and other members of the "crew," "somehow committed for life to good works under Hoover's leadership."[8] Pate and Strauss and all the members of the "crew" had a loyalty to Mr. Hoover that is hard to explain today in a world caught up in alliances of convenience. Even in the 1930's, few leaders had so devoted a following as did Herbert Hoover. Even Franklin Roosevelt had his defectors in Raymond Moley and James Farley among others.

What accounts for that extraordinary loyalty? Its roots lie not only in the personal character of Mr. Hoover, but also in his administrative style. From his earliest days as a manager of mines, Herbert Hoover placed a great deal of trust in his subordinates. He delegated responsibility freely, gave his assistants enough power and resources to do their jobs, and backed them to the limit. These subordinates responded to this administrative style with an unprecedented loyalty.

Yet it would be wrong to imply that Mr. Hoover's administrative style was idiosyncratic or subjective. Mr. Hoover made decisions based on facts, not emotions. He trusted his crew to assemble the experts on any issue and to develop alternate courses of action. Above all, Mr. Hoover wanted practical solutions to address the situation at hand. "The greatest catastrophe that could come to our country," Mr. Hoover told the Gridiron Club in 1929, "is that administration policies or legislation or voluntary movements shall be encouraged or enacted on the basis of emotion, not upon facts or reason."[9] Mr. Hoover's assistants knew that if they did their jobs well, the "chief" would back them all the way.

Like Maurice Pate and Lewis Strauss and may other members of the "crew", I cannot be dispassionate about Herbert Hoover's impact on my

---

7. Strauss oral history interview with Raymond Henle, Hoover Library, 14.

8. Quoted in Lewis L. Strauss, "A Birthday Letter to Herbert Hoover," *Reader's Digest* (September, 1961).

9. Herbert Hoover, "Address to the Gridiron Club, December 14, 1929," as printed in *Public Papers of the President: Herbert Hoover, 1929* (Washington. DC, 1974), 473.

own life and career. I first joined the "Hoover crew," as it were, at the age of ten when I took my wagon down to the local Republican headquarters and got a big box of "Re-elect Hoover" handbills to distribute around my neighborhood. I must also tell you that I was crushed that Mr. Hoover failed to carry either my neighborhood, the state of Oregon, or the nation in the election of 1932. It was my first taste of political defeat and I can still remember it.[10]

But this election loss did not reduce my deep affection for Herbert Hoover. Quite simply, I could identify with him. He was the son of a blacksmith, I was the son of a blacksmith. As a boy living in Salem, I could see the house where Herbert Hoover had lived. That was enough for me, at least at the age of ten. But my identification with Mr. Hoover ran deeper and I remained an unreconstructed Hoover man throughout my school years.

In fact, my appreciation and admiration for Mr. Hoover matured as I grew older. I went off to Stanford for graduate study in political science in part because of the Hoover Institution on War, Revolution, and Peace. Because of my longstanding interest in labor issues, it was logical that I turned to Herbert Hoover's leadership in establishing federal labor policy as the topic for my Master's thesis. I focused on his labor policies because his leadership in labor relations was largely unknown and unappreciated at that time. Few were aware, for example, of Hoover's active leadership as Secretary of Commerce to implement the eight-hour work day. Few knew of his long-standing support of workers in such matters as collective bargaining and sustaining strong trade unions. I had high hopes of rectifying the situation, and, like most graduate students would, I delved eagerly into the treasure trove of data centralized at Stanford. But unlike most graduate students, 1 was fortunate to have had the opportunity to discuss my work in detail with the very subject of my research.

I suppose it was impertinent of me to ask to meet with Mr. Hoover, but he graciously agreed to discuss my thesis with me in his office at Stanford. I still remember the excitement of entering that room more than 48 years ago, but I can't remember much of what I said. Perhaps the most important result of the meeting was twofold: he granted me permission to use all of his papers, including the Presidential ones and those that had not yet been open to accession, and he showed faith that this young graduate student would produce a useful study.

That meeting was the first of two or three sessions during which he answered my questions about his labor policies. He was as much of a tutor as any professor I had in my graduate study. I was also aided greatly by the archivists who worked with Mr. Hoover. Suda Bane, who had been Mr.

---

10. My own memories of these and other personal events are recorded in my oral history interview with Raymond Henle and in my correspondence within the post-Presidential files of the Hoover Papers in the Hoover Library.

Hoover's archivist for decades, knew where every piece of paper in the collection was located and was of tremendous help to me.

I stayed in touch with Mr. Hoover after I left Stanford and began teaching at Willamette University and increased our correspondence during my service in Oregon politics. When my travels took me to New York City, I would make an appointment to drop in and spend a few minutes in the Waldorf Towers with Mr. Hoover.

But the highpoint of my contact with him came when Mr. Hoover graciously invited me to be his guest at the Bohemian Grove encampment in the mid-1950's. There, I had an extensive amount of time to talk with him about politics and public service and all manner of subjects including the proper way to eat peaches!

Those days at "Camp Caveman" were important for me because I had the opportunity to see the Chief relate to the members of his "crew." Even at the age of 85, Herbert Hoover continued to teach, to inspire, to advise those around him. I am sure that the men who came back year after year to the Grove did so, in part, for the pleasure of Mr. Hoover's company.

I remember on my Saturday at the Grove, he spoke to the entire camp about his hope for this nation. These "lakeside addresses," as they were called, were Mr. Hoover's way of bringing the "crew" up to date on domestic and international problems and giving them his views. The address was not formal, but presented in warm, human terms that related to the past but foresaw trends that were moving us into the future. Everyone in attendance was inspired by those talks.

Mr. Hoover remained an inspiration to me throughout my career in public service. I continued to visit him at the Waldorf's suite 31A right up to his passing. His death was a great loss to the nation in general and to me personally.

Over the past thirty years, I have turned to Mr. Hoover's writings for guidance on leadership. Unlike many of his successors as President, Herbert Hoover wrote his own speeches and we can be sure that his plain-spoken prose reflected his deeply-held beliefs. Even if his speeches are not often quoted, they do have the ring of great truth and wisdom.

In looking back through his books, particularly *American Individualism, The Challenge to Liberty, The Problems of Lasting Peace*, and the many speeches gathered in the volumes of *Addresses Upon the American Road*, I found recurring commentary on the characteristics of good leadership, qualities that Herbert Hoover reflected throughout his own life.

Foremost among the qualities that Herbert Hoover thought necessary for good leadership was the pursuit of virtue. "We shall succeed," he told a Stanford audience on that day in 1928 when he accepted the Republican nomination for President, "through the faith, the loyalty, the self-sacrifice, and the devotion to eternal ideals which live today in every American."[11] A good leader inspires those who would follow by shining example.

In later years, Mr. Hoover added that anyone who aspires to lead others must be a person of honesty and integrity, a person with strong spiritual values and common sense; a person with enterprise and self-reliance; and a person open to change and creativity. Above all these virtues, Mr. Hoover told countless commencement classes, anyone who aspires to lead must have a firm belief in freedom, justice, and dignity of the individual.

Herbert Hoover's philosophy of leadership is perhaps best summarized in his essay on the "uncommon man," a message that he first delivered in 1948 to the graduates of Wilmington College in Ohio and repeated several times. "Let us remember," Herbert Hoover said, "that the great human advances have not been brought about by mediocre men and women. They were brought about by distinctly uncommon people with vital sparks of leadership. ... For the future of America rests not in mediocrity, but in the constant renewal of leadership in every phase of our national life."[12]

In Hoover's view, the guidance of our nation depended upon the transfer of leadership from one generation to the next. The older generation had both a moral and a civic obligation to share their wisdom with the younger generation. "Youth will demand a voice in its own destiny," Mr. Hoover told the Republican National Convention in June of 1944. "We, the older generation, who have learned something of the great forces in the world, can advise and counsel. The issues are not new and we can distill principles from the past."[13] This is sound advice, as relevant today as it was more than fifty years ago.

That Herbert Hoover served as a model for future leaders is evident in an invitation he received from John F. Kennedy less than two months after the new President's inauguration. "It gives me great pleasure to invite you to serve as honorary chairman of the national advisory committee to the Peace Corps," President Kennedy wrote. "Your acceptance of this position will rally millions of Americans and people all over the world who remember and respect your own pioneering leadership in this field of human assistance and constructive service."[14] Although Mr. Hoover felt that at the age of 86 years he could not take on any more responsibilities, he was greatly honored by the President's proposal.

---

11. Published in Herbert Hoover, *The New Day: Campaign Speeches of Herbert Hoover* (Stanford, 1928), 44.

12. Published in Herbert Hoover, *Addresses on the American Road, 1947-1948* (Stanford, 1948), 172.

13. Published in Herbert Hoover, *Addresses on the American Road, 1941-1945* (New York, 1946), 255.

14. John F. Kennedy to Herbert Hoover, March 2, 1961, Post-Presidential Files of Herbert Hoover, Hoover Presidential Library.

Young leaders are not born virtuous, of course, which is why Herbert Hoover repeatedly emphasized the central role of education in the leadership process. Great leaders are trained in the home, the church, and the school—the three great educational institutions in this nation. A failure of any one of these institutions to instill these virtues in young people would compromise the entire process. Though Hoover once affectionately defined a boy as "a piece of skin stretched over an appetite," he held children dear to his heart and never wavered in his attention to their welfare.[15] Herbert Hoover's deep concern for the next generation of leaders led him to call for a White House Conference on Child Health and Protection in 1929, only the second such conference in the nation's history (the first had been called by Teddy Roosevelt). On November 9, 1930, Hoover greeted conference participants in a speech combining whimsy and rare insight into the problems and possibilities of children everywhere. "We approach all problems of children with affection," said the President. "Theirs is the province of joy and good humor. ... We envy them the freshness of adventure and discovery of life; we mourn over the disappointments they will meet."[16] Hoover inspired the delegates to draw up a "Children's Charter" to dramatize the need for prompt legislative and administrative action which led to the passage of numerous laws on the state and local level.

His commitment to children did not end once he left office. In 1936, four years after he had left the White House, Herbert Hoover took over as Chairman of the Board of the Boys Clubs of America (now the Boys and Girls Clubs). This organization is dedicated to assisting young people, particularly those from disadvantaged backgrounds, to develop skills for employment as well as social and leadership skills. Under his direction, the organization grew rapidly and, in 1956, Congress chartered the Boys Clubs. Hoover remained the Chairman of the Board, its guiding force, until his death in 1964.

I have been asked on a number of occasions whether I think that Herbert Hoover is an enduring model of leadership for the current generation. I have no doubt that he is and I base my belief on the achievements of the tens of thousands of children who attend the sixty Herbert Hoover schools across this country or who visit the Herbert Hoover Presidential Library-Museum in West Branch and the Hoover-Minthorn home here in Newberg each year.

These young people have been inspired by leadership shown by Herbert Hoover in helping those in need. More importantly, they have translated that inspiration into practical action. Let me give you one exam-

---

15. Herbert Hoover, "What is a Boy?", Hoover Presidential Library.

16. Herbert Hoover, "Address to the White House Conference on Child Health and Protection, November 19, 1930," *Public Papers of the President: Herbert Hoover, 1930* (Washington, DC, 1974), 490.

ple. In the wake of the tragedy in Oklahoma City, students at Herbert Hoover School in Iowa City, Iowa mobilized a fund raising effort and turned over $160 to the Red Cross to be used for families of the blast victims. These same Hoover students had conducted earlier relief efforts for the earthquake victims in Japan, for the victims of Hurricane Andrew, and for impoverished people in Guatemala.[17]

The philosophy of these students was summed up best by young Molly Egan, a student at that Hoover school. "It's satisfying to get involved," Molly said. "When others see you doing things like this, it makes them want to help too. It's contagious."[18] Herbert Hoover could not have said it better.

The program at the Hoover School in Iowa City is being replicated across the nation. A new generation of young humanitarians will carry forward the message and the leadership of Herbert Hoover into the next century. When an American reaches out to help someone in need, the helpful spirit of Herbert Hoover is there. When we show compassion, we are all members of the Chief's "crew."

Just as Herbert Hoover first inspired me more than sixty years ago, he continues to inspire new generations of young people. Herbert Hoover showed us time and time again that each of us can make a difference in improving the world. We can ask for no more from a leader.

---

17. Steve Smith, "Hoover Students Reach Out." *Iowa City Press-Citizen* (May 3, 1995). I am grateful to the staff at the Hoover Presidential Library in West Branch for bringing this story to my attention.

18. *Ibid.*

Evangelical Quakers
and Public Policy

LON FENDALL

In Arthur Roberts' excellent volume reflecting on his life, *Drawn By The Light*, he briefly describes his involvement in state and local politics. He ran unsuccessfully for a position in the Oregon Legislature and later served a four–year term on the Yachats, Oregon, City Council. It was not easy for Arthur to bridge the gulf between the intellectual depth and erudite vocabulary of the scholar and the rough and tumble of state and local politics. But he felt that these political involvements had "quickened my appreciation for ordinary activity as the true vocation for the church."[1] Arthur took his city council work very seriously, devoting a great deal of time to preparing for the meetings. He also took seriously the opportunity to bear witness to his faith in Christ and had numerous opportunities to speak to others about that faith.

Arthur Roberts' service in public policy positions has been a relatively minor part of a life devoted primarily to teaching and scholarly work. But Arthur's interest in politics invites us to consider the complex issues surrounding Quaker convictions and activities in public policy. Others have discussed the ambivalence apparent in Friends' attitudes toward government and politics. In that discussion there has not been an effort made to examine the distinctive ways in which evangelical Friends have approached the question of political participation. Since Arthur Roberts is and always has been part of the evangelical segment of Quakerism, this discussion

---

1. Arthur O. Roberts, *Drawn By the Light: Autobiographical Reflections* (Newberg: Barclay Press, 1993), 214

seems to belong in a volume paying tribute to a person of great intellectual stature and a person whose words and life have impacted so many.

The term "evangelical" has been used so many different ways in this century, it needs to be defined in this discussion. Journalists often use the term "evangelical" interchangeably with the word "evangelistic." The latter term has to do with a commitment to evangelism, but there is more to being an evangelical than seeking to evangelize. As I use the term "evangelical" here and apply it to a segment of Quakerism, it means a person or group whose theology is conservative, i.e. who believes in the historic doctrines of early Christians—particularly the deity of Christ and the accuracy and authority of the Bible as a means of knowing God's truth.

The term "evangelical" as used here would not have been used the same way during much of the period being described in this article, but I am using the term with its present meaning. Evangelicals are sometimes inappropriately labeled "fundamentalist". The latter term as used today connotes an ultra–conservatism in political, social and theological issues, making the label inappropriate for most evangelicals. The term "fundamentalist" certainly does not fit an evangelical Friend like Arthur Roberts. To grossly simplify a complex issue, most evangelicals are moderates on many issues while fundamentalists are on the extreme, the "right" end of the spectrum.[2]

Four yearly meetings broke away from other yearly meetings or from broader groupings of yearly meetings in this century to form eventually what is now called Evangelical Friends International—North American Region. The majority of Friends in those yearly meetings would describe themselves as "evangelical", but there are many Quakers in the U.S. who are not connected with EFI who definitely belong within the definition of evangelical. The overwhelming majority of Friends outside the U.S. and Britain would also fit the definition of evangelical and their numbers are such that it is accurate to say that the majority of Friends today are evangelical. This is in keeping with the origins of the Quaker movement, as an effort to revive the doctrines and practices of New Testament Christianity.

As a part of the fiftieth anniversary of the Friends Committee on National Legislation, Wilmer Cooper prepared a brief, but helpful overview of Quaker involvement in politics. His essay is part of the FCNL anniversary volume, *Witness in Washington: Fifty Years of Friendly Persuasion.* Cooper drew on a number of the thoughts in a lecture given by Quaker historian Frederick Tolles. Quaker ambivalence about political participation was one of Tolles' major themes, as is evident in this statement: "If anything is clear from our quick historical survey, I think it must be this: that there is no one Quaker attitude towards politics. Historically, Quakers can be found

---

2. Lon Fendall, "We're Evangelicals, Not Fundamentalists," *Evangelical Friend*, 4.

practicing and preaching almost every possible position from full participation to complete withdrawal and abstention."[3]

Friends carried with them from England to the colonies an intense suspicion and aversion for governments. In England they had been persecuted not just because of major issues such as military service, but for such harmless offenses as refusing to take oaths and declining to remove their hats in the presence of officials. Founders of the first North American colonies brought with them a great deal of intolerance and bigotry and persecuted Quakers just as severely as had been done in England. But the founders of other colonies implemented greater tolerance for religious diversity, so Quakers became prominent in the governance not only of their "own" colony, Pennsylvania, but in Rhode Island, New Jersey and North Carolina. The pendulum swung very much in the other direction during the middle of the Eighteenth century, however, as Quakers ceased trying to make Quaker principles dominant in Pennsylvania, while in the other colonies they despaired of being able to resist the momentum toward using military means to obtain independence from England.

There was another shift, away from political withdrawal toward limited political participation, in the twentieth century. Philadelphia Yearly Meeting and Five Years Meeting approved minutes in 1927, 1945 and 1955, commending individual Friends who felt called into active participation in government.[4] But the entry of the United States into what became a global war, brought to the forefront one of the issues that had made Quakers an isolated and hated minority in the infancy of the movement in England. That issue was conscription, and the energy of Friends turned more toward establishing their right to exercise conscientious objection than toward influencing national policy more broadly. Moreover, individual Quakers faced the ultimate test of their devotion to individual principle versus the will of the majority, i.e., would they be part of a government completely absorbed in military mobilization? It is not an accident that this century's two "Quaker" presidents, Herbert Hoover and Richard Nixon, were Quakers primarily in terms of family heritage and not in the sense of a wholehearted support for historic Quaker convictions, including pacifism.

The concern to establish and protect the right of individual conscientious objection led directly to the formation of the primary vehicle for Quaker political expression in the U.S., the Friends Committee on National Legislation. FCNL was an outgrowth of a national Friends conference in 1940 opposing the draft, followed by the the formation of the Friends War Problems Committee. These efforts were set in motion too late for Friends

3. Quoted in Wilmer A. Cooper, "FCNL in Historical Perspective," in Tom Mullen, ed., *Witness in Washington: Fifty Years of Friendly Persuasion* (Richmond, IN: Friends United Press, 1994), 13.

4. Cooper, 12.

to have much opportunity to oppose the passage of conscription legislation later that year. Given the intensity of national mobilization, Quaker opposition would probably have had little effect. When Quakers formalized the creation of FCNL in mid–1943, they recognized the need to address broader issues than the draft, including such concerns as civil rights and international economic development.[5]

Wilmer Cooper, Raymond Wilson, Ed Snyder and others have told the FCNL story very well. The organization has made impressive contributions during its half–century of existence, providing for most Friends an attractive means of influencing government. Operating with a modest budget and limited staff, the diligence and effectiveness of such leaders as Raymond Wilson, Ed Snyder, Joe Volk have much to do with its success. The Quaker voice on national issues has been much stronger than their numbers would suggest.

In spite of the effectiveness of FCNL as a Quaker voice in Washington, evangelical Friends have been reluctant to give the organization their support. This has been puzzling to non–evangelical Friends, but it is not difficult to explain. Many of the founders of FCNL had been active in the American Friends Service Committee and for a time it even appeared that AFSC itself would become the vehicle for formulating and expressing Friends views on national issues. Because AFSC would have jeopardized its eligibility for receiving tax–deductible gifts if it had begun active lobbying and because AFSC lacked a strong tie to the Yearly Meetings, a separate organization, FCNL, was formed.

Those who cannot understand why certain yearly meetings have never appointed representatives to FCNL do not understand how profound the antipathy of evangelicals toward AFSC has been for most of the organization's history. Northwest Yearly Meeting, only a few years before Arthur Roberts grew up, decided to withdraw from Five Years Meeting responding to the perceived theological liberalism among mainstream Quakers. Similar efforts to stop the spread of "modernism and liberalism" occurred in many segments of Protestant Christianity. The concern of evangelicals Friends was aimed as much at the AFSC as against any other Quaker entity. Evangelicals were not opposed to providing humanitarian relief for the suffering related to global war, the principal reason for the birth of the AFSC. It was the fear that AFSC's focus on humanitarian service would leave evangelism in second place or neglected completely. At issue was the historic tension between faith and works, described in the New Testament book of James. Evangelicals were rejecting what they felt was an exclusive focus on works and in so doing, opted for almost exclusive attention to the faith side of the equation. Obviously not all supporters and staff of AFSC were theological

---

5. "Friends Committee on National Legislation," *Friends Intelligencer*, July 3, 1943, 439.

liberals, but some probably were. What started out as respectful debate turned into intense verbal battles and the result was a succession of withdrawals of yearly meetings from Five Years Meeting, providing the nucleus for what eventually became the Evangelical Friends Alliance (now Evangelical Friends International).

Another factor in the hesitancy among evangelical Friends regarding FCNL was the issue of militarism and the draft, central to the formation of FCNL. Members and attenders of evangelical Friends churches were not at all in agreement among themselves on the question of refusing military service on the one hand or accepting the "just war" argument for military service on the other. Most Christians in the U.S., many of whom had supported peace efforts after World War I, concluded that the evils of Naziism were so great that declining to support the war effort was morally unacceptable. A study of the number of conscientious objectors in Oregon Yearly Meeting (now Northwest Yearly Meeting) revealed that in 1945 about one-third of the young men in the yearly meeting were C.O.'s, while about two-thirds of that number had accepted noncombatant service in uniform.[6] There were significant numbers of conscientious objectors among other evangelical Friends but there were also large numbers who served in uniform and it would have been hard to generate strong support at the time for a group like FCNL, formed in part to influence national policy away from militarism.

Additionally, some evangelical Friends may have been nervous about the hazards of being misinterpreted when speaking out on national issues. The same year FCNL came into being, there was an embarrassing incident in the sessions of Indiana Yearly Meeting, which resulted in an unfortunate story in *Time* magazine. William C. Dennis, President of Earlham College, brought to the Yearly Meeting floor a resolution endorsing proposals by former President Herbert Hoover and others which favored "the creation of appropriate international machinery with power adequate to establish and to maintain a just and lasting peace among the nations of the world...."[7]

The word "power" in the Indiana Yearly Meeting resolution generated spirited discussion on the floor, the opponents of the wording fearing that the statement might suggest the legitimacy of military force. When agreement was not reached, a committee attempted to revise it in a way that all could accept, but the committee brought the resolution to the floor with the word "power" still in it and only three of the five members of the committee supported it. Discussion on the floor was limited because of other pressing

6. Ralph K. Beebe, *A Garden of the Lord: A History of Oregon Yearly Meeting of Friends Church* (Newberg: Barclay Press, 1968), p. 78.
7. "Indiana Yearly Meeting Resolutions: A Symposium," *The American Friend*, November 4, 1943, 436.

business and members approved the resolution over the stated objections of "a considerable number of Friends."[8]

The action in Indiana Yearly Meeting sessions would not have been expected to go further than the pages of *The American Friend*, but somehow word got to local reporters and articles appeared in the Richmond and Dayton papers, one of them with the headline, "Use of Force in Maintaining of Peace Approved by Friends." The stories characterized the resolution as a departure from the traditional Quaker peace stand. If that weren't bad enough, *Time* magazine picked up the story and ran a full column story which included the sentence: "Last week for the first time since George Fox founded the Religious Society of Friends in 1668, a group of Quakers endorsed the use of force by Quakers." Partially influencing the wording of the story was another resolution asking that Friends be supportive toward those who had chosen to participate in military service.[9]

Errol T. Elliott, editor of *The American Friend* at the time, wrote an editorial a few months after the fiasco in Indiana Yearly Meeting. The editorial, entitled "Let the Quakers be the Quakers," was cautiously worded and reflected the ambiguity characteristic of Friends' approaches to political involvement. On the one hand, Elliott expressed the hope that the media distortions of the yearly meeting action not prompt a withdrawal from political issues entirely. The fact that speaking out on political issues could lead to misunderstanding was "not a reason for dodging it. Certainly we cannot sit by smugly when the destiny of the next generation is being formed by legislative bodies. The question rather is the way by which we can make our testimony effective on the political front."[10]

Elliott warned Friends against becoming a "political pressure group," but at the same time acknowledged the recent creation of the Friends Committee on National Legislation, giving it what could safely be called "faint praise." He favored small scale efforts, such as encouraging individuals in local meetings who might feel called to work on "new world patterns" and modest efforts to serve in and study the "hot spots" of the world. He urged that future pronouncements "come out of *united* concern for an unswerving peace testimony," clearly referring to the hasty approval of a resolution around which there was not unity.[11]

Errol Elliott stopped short of endorsing the notion of individual Quakers becoming involved in elective office or in other ways serving in government. Interestingly, Friends in Britain moved much more dramati-

---

8. "Indiana Yearly Meeting Resolutions," 436.

9. *Time*, October 11, 1943, 46–47.

10. Errol T. Elliott, "Let the Quakers be the Quakers," *The American Friend*, December 2, 1943, 471.

11. Elliott, 472.

cally away from the Quietist pattern of non–involvement in public policy. In 1820 Thomas Shillitoe had advised:

> Friends, let us dare not meddle with political matters…Endeavour to keep that ear closed, which will be itching to hear the news of the day and what is going forward in the political circles…. Avoid reading political publications, and as much as possible, newspapers.[12]

But that attitude among British Friends changed in the Nineteenth Century, in part the result of the English Reform Bill of 1832, which permitted Friends elected to Parliament to substitute an affirmation for the usual oath of office. Many Quakers served in Parliament. London Yearly Meeting emphatically endorsed such participation in its 1911 Book of Discipline.

The shift away from caution or outright opposition to political involvement in Britain happened in the U.S. as well, but without the resulting widespread participation in elective office. After Quakers abandoned their "Holy Experiment" in Pennsylvania it took some time for the mood to shift, but minutes adopted in Philadelphia Yearly Meeting and Five Years Meeting in the first half of the Twentieth Century strongly supported individual Friends who might choose to get involved in government and politics. Why, then, would it be so difficult to come up with a list of Quakers who have served in Congress or in some other nationally prominent positions, corresponding to the impressive list of Quaker Members of Parliament in England?

Frederick Tolles in his lecture at Guilford in 1956 declared that Quakers more than others must choose between seriously compromising their ideals while in public office or remaining true to their ideals and accepting the reality that their impact would be nil. For Quakers, said Tolles, "compromise is under no circumstance allowable. If there comes a collision between allegiance to the ideal and the holding of public office, then the office must be deserted. If obedience to the soul's vision involves eye or hand, houses or lands or life, they must be immediately surrendered." The contrasting group of pragmatists, said Tolles, had concluded that "to get on one must submit to existing conditions; and where to achieve ultimate triumph one must risk his ideals to the tender mercies of a world not yet ripe for them."[13]

At the time Tolles spoke, a non–Quaker politician had begun what was to be a very long and successful political career. In the early Sixties Arthur Roberts invited the Governor of Oregon, Mark O. Hatfield, to speak in a convocation at George Fox College. Roberts was impressed with the

---

12. Cited in Cooper, 10.
13. Cited in Cooper, 13.

thoughtful, principled way this young governor spoke and responded to questions from a student panel. Hatfield's emphatic witness to a recent "born again" experience of personal faith in Christ put him clearly within the category of evangelical, but Hatfield did not accept many of the conservative political and social cliches of some evangelicals. Hatfield later served on the Board of Trustees at George Fox and returned with regularity to speak on campus.

Mark Hatfield is not a Quaker and has not called himself a pacifist, at least in the sense of an absolute refusal to serve in the military and absolute opposition to the use of military means in the international arena. But if Quakers were permitted to "adopt" an individual public figure whose political actions they might support most of the time, Mark Hatfield would probably be on the short list. It is revealing to look back through the annual issues of the FCNL newsletter in which the staff rate members of Congress on the compatibility of their votes on selected issues with the policy statements of FCNL. Senator Hatfield has often been ranked near the top in the FCNL rankings, surprisingly for a Senator who has remained loyal to the Republican Party.

If Mark Hatfield had been a Quaker and a conscientious objector, would he have been successful in his first campaign for the state legislator and his subsequent campaigns for statewide office, then the U.S. Senate? To answer "no" might be to accept Tolles' thesis that determined idealists like Quakers, particularly Quakers firmly committed to the peace stand have little future in politics. Another question might shed some light on the issue. What if Oregon voters had known when Mark Hatfield first campaigned for the Senate that he would become one of the most consistent voices and votes in favor of peace and against excessive militarism during his soon–to–be–concluded thirty years in that body? Actually, they wouldn't have needed a crystal ball to foresee his commitment to peace. Hatfield had spoken out against the Vietnam War as a governor, a stand which in some ways hurt him in his fairly close campaign for the Senate. And each campaign after that his "liberal" views on defense and foreign policy provided ammunition to his opponents. It would be hard to find among even the most liberal Democrats another member of Congress during those thirty years who voted so consistently against excessive military spending and who worked so hard for peace initiatives such as the U.S. Institute of Peace.

Some who are not very familiar with politics in Oregon assume Senator Hatfield's success is owing to a dominant progressive sentiment among Oregon voters. Actually, Oregon's liberal image is only deserved in limited ways. The stubborn conservatism of many Oregon voters in the early part of this century produced a strong following for the Ku Klux Klan, and this bedrock conservatism still is evident in many ways. It would be accurate to say that Senator Hatfield has been successful in his campaigns, not because of, but in spite of his liberal views and voting record. He has been an excellent communicator with Oregon voters and has earned the confidence of those who appreciate his decisiveness when others in office spend their time testing the wind and checking the polls. Those who don't agree with him on many issues praise him for his consistency and decisiveness. And some of those who can't accept his "Quakerly" voting record can at least tolerate it because of his attentiveness to the local needs of communities in Oregon and the individual needs of citizens frustrated with an unresponsive federal bureaucracy.

Republican politics in Oregon are very different in 1996 than in 1966 when Mark Hatfield was first elected to the Senate. As is true in many other states, a number of years ago conservatives set about to establish themselves in the Republican party and to get their friends elected to precinct committee positions, to the county central committees and then to elective offices at the city, county and state level. These party activists are zealots who have proven their determination to block the political careers of moderates and liberals.

Mark Hatfield has always developed his own campaign organizations independent of the Republican party. But his heroes have been the Republicans Abraham Lincoln and Herbert Hoover. Nevertheless, his respect for Republican heroes and principles would not be enough to overcome the antipathy of the Republican right wing if he were starting from scratch in 1996. He could pass the "litmus test" of opposition to abortion on demand, but his consistent efforts for peace and against militarism would make it very hard for him to win conservative support today.

Likewise, evangelical Friends choosing to run for elective office today, who firmly embraced Quaker convictions about peace and justice would have a hard time in the Republican Party. Even attempting to function in the Democratic Party might be difficult at a time when there are still millions of Americans who are confident that such U.S. military action as has been undertaken in Bosnia is both legitimate and desirable.

In conclusion, as we celebrate the life and work of Arthur Roberts, it is appropriate to issue a call for greater clarity about the response of evangelical Friends to government and politics. Among the challenges and opportunities are these:

1. *Clarifying our Convictions:* Some unresolved questions are embedded in the uncertainties some Quakers feel about political involvement. Anabaptists have typically held a dim view of governments, but Quakers from the days of William Penn have had a very different view of the redeemability of governments. Friends have considered government to be a suitable instrument of God for meeting the needs of humanity. But evangelical Friends have often absorbed strongly anti–government views from their evangelical environments. Some would come close to embracing libertarian views, feel-

ing that less government is always better. But these evangelicals, who read their Bibles carefully, don't find that view in the Scripture. Running through the New Testament is the narrative of God working in and through government to achieve justice and compassion. That would not support the notion that the least government is the best government, but rather that the best government is one that is patterned after biblical righteousness and justice. If Christian people join in the anti–government rhetoric of the day, they lose their chance to be voices for constructive change. It may be time for evangelical Friends to convene a national dialogue or gathering to clarify their convictions about political involvement.

2. *Lobbying*: Amidst their uncertainties about getting directly involved in politics, Friends in general in the last half–century have settled on lobbying as one of the most useful and acceptable channels of action. But several yearly meetings still do not appoint representatives to the Friends Committee on National Legislation, apparently still associating it with the liberalism they attribute to the American Friends Service Committee. Evangelical Friends need to take a close look at the governing process of FCNL and to discover that the development of policy statements in the annual meetings is an open process and all representatives have a voice. There would be ample opportunity for evangelical Friends to influence the policy statements guiding staff actions. If one alternative is to form a corresponding evangelical Friends lobbying group, that is not at all practical. If the other choice is be represented only by groups such as the National Association of Evangelicals or Focus on the Family, where there is very little opportunity to influence policies, how does that allow Friends to be faithful to their particular concerns and distinctive?

3. *Serving in Office*: If one searched, they could find some Quakers who have served in significant public policy positions, but few names come readily to mind. It would seem that Quakers have shied away from major elective offices and have served in various appointive positions, particularly with international development entities and other arms of the executive branch. It is time for some dialogue about the possibilities for Friends in elective office. Was Frederick Tolles right that such service requires such major compromises that this is not a good choice for Quakers? Could it not be that persons with the moral courage and charisma of a Mark Hatfield might be found among Quakers and encouraged to pursue political service? Will that happen on its own, or do we not need to begin to nurture and seek out such potential leadership and begin to point such individuals toward elective office? Conservative Republicans have been very skillful in getting "their people" in office. Couldn't Quakers do the same?

Arthur Roberts has had an enormous influence on me personally and on many others who enrolled in his classes and did their best to understand him. Arthur was a do–er, not just a teacher. When he found that he could write excellent poetry and produce beautiful art, he did just that. When there was farm work to be done, he rolled up his sleeves and did it. He had thought a great deal about civic virtue and the concepts of justice and morality. When the way opened for him to be a do–er, not just a thinker in the public arena, he acted on his convictions. For that example of thoughtfulness and conviction flowing into action I will always be grateful to Arthur Roberts.

A Basis for Civility

PHILIP D. SMITH

G ive attention, if you will, to the virtue of civility. In this essay I
want to define civility, then give a bit of its history, continue by
predicting something of its future, and conclude by explaining
civility's true ground, at least as I understand it.

We are not here interested in politeness or courtesy, though those
meanings of "civility" may be ancillary to our topic. We are thinking instead
about the political realm, and we are aware that many voices have been
raised to decry the mean-spirited and vicious nature of politics, both in
attaining and using public office. Wise people warn us that democratic governance depends on a kind of self-control, by which the participants in the
process guard it against internal meltdown. We ought to give careful attention to civility, for democracy may depend on it.

Readers may find much to which they object in this essay, but they will
agree that it marks off an interesting topic for discussion. Suggested correc-
tions, at any point, are welcome. The most important thing comes last, for I
hope readers will approve of what I say about the ground of civility even if
they disagree with my account of what it is, what its history has been, or
what its future may be.

A Definition of Civility

Civility has to do with treating political opponents well.

We set the stage by first defining "politics." Politics is the art or science
of making decisions for groups of people. Note that by this definition, many
activities count as political. Besides the politics of various kinds of governments, this definition includes office politics, church politics, family politics,

and university politics. "Politics" has a negative connotation in many minds, but this need not be. Whenever groups of people need to make decisions, there will be political decision-making. Sometimes political decisions are made badly (unjustly, stupidly, or whatever), but sometimes they are made well. Some political systems tend to produce more bad decisions than others—but that is the stuff of political theory, not the topic of this essay.

With this broad definition of politics in mind, we can ask interesting questions about morality and politics. For instance, people often distinguish political allies from political enemies, and we treat them very differently. I am particularly interested in how we treat—more precisely, how we should treat—our political enemies.[1] The answer, I think, is that we should treat our political opponents well.

What does it mean to treat one's political opponents well? For starters, here are some prohibitions. We should not lie about our political opponents; we should not attack their positions with "straw man" arguments, *ad hominem* arguments, or other fallacious arguments; we should not break our agreements with them; and we should not unnecessarily impute evil motives to them. Positively, we should negotiate in good faith with our political enemies; we should debate issues honestly with them; and we should respect them.

More could be added, but this gives some idea of what I mean by treating political opponents well. Provisionally, I define "civility" to be a virtue, that is, it is *a properly grounded character trait (or combination of traits) which moves individuals or groups to treat political opponents well.* Later, I will suggest some modification of this definition, but it gives us enough to go on for now.

Notice the qualification "properly grounded" in the definition. It is possible for someone to be motivated to treat his political opponents well for wrong reasons. Perhaps, like Aristotle's ignorant soldier, he does not understand the cost of virtue; he blithely assumes that everything will turn out fine. Just as we would not say that a soldier who fails to comprehend danger is truly brave, we would not say that a politician who had no idea that treating his political opponents well might bring political defeat is truly civil. Or, like Aristotle's professional soldier, someone might exhibit a merely instrumental pseudo-virtue. If we treat political opponents well because we calculate that such behavior is the best way to win, we are not truly civil, just calculating.

True civility is the trait or traits of character that move one to treat one's political opponents well for the right reasons. Further on, I will suggest what I think those reasons should be. But first we should look at the reasons that have been traditionally given as grounds for civility.

---

1. I think there are also interesting issues surrounding the way we treat political allies, but those matters are not the topic of this paper.

A Modernist Virtue

In October, 1555, Hugh Latimer was executed during the reign of England's "Bloody" Mary. He was burned at the stake with a fellow protestant, Nicholas Ridley. As recorded in the martyrology, *Acts and Monuments*, by John Foxe, Latimer cried out when the fire was laid to the fuel: "Be of good comfort, Mr. Ridley, and play the man! We shall this day light such a candle, by God's grace, in England, as I trust never shall be put out."[2]

Latimer's courage when faced with death, and his good fortune to have his death recorded in a popular martyrology, made him into a hero/saint of the English reformation. What generations of readers of protestant history didn't read, however, was that some years before his own execution, Latimer presided over a "'jolly muster,' as a traditional-minded friar, John Forest, was roasted alive over a fire made of a wooden statue of a saint hauled out of a pilgrimmage church."[3]

Latimer's life and death is only one, though fairly gruesome, reminder that Christians have not always treated their political enemies well. Medieval and Reformation histories are replete with imprisonments, tortures, executions, and treacheries. Undoubtedly, many motivations and circumstances lie behind such behaviors. People acted out of greed, fear, superstition, hatred—the whole catalogue of human sinfulness. But part of the reason for some of this incivility, particularly in a case like Latimer's, was philosophical.

All sides in reformation disputes assumed that there was such a thing as true doctrine. If someone rejected true doctrine, he earned God's judgment of eternal death, so if torture could bring about repentance, it was actually good for the offender. Further, the heretic was a public blasphemer who deserved death. Finally, innocent people might be corrupted if they listened to the heretic's ideas. Matters of truth, especially of religious truth, were regarded as having highest importance—literally infinite importance. These factors produced a logic of intolerance. Those with positions of influence or power, such as Queen Mary, or Latimer himself when he presided over Forest's death, felt they had a duty to do all they could to eliminate heresy.

We should remember all this, because the ideological cold war between Protestants and Catholics formed much of the background to the emergence of modern philosophy.[4] Louis Dupré has argued recently that we

2. "A Tale of Two Martyrs" *Christian History* (Vol. XIV, No. 4), 18-19.

3. Martin, Dennis. "Catholic Counterpoint: What was it like to be on the losing side of England's Reformation?" *Christian History* (Vol. XIV, No. 4), 30.

4. I owe to George Marsden the likening of the Protestant/Catholic conflict of the sixteenth and seventeenth centuries to the anti-Marxist/Marxist conflict of the twentieth. Both cold wars were protracted struggles, they were interrupted by "hot" wars, and they mixed nationalism with ideology. Cf. Marsden, George. *Religion and American Culture* (Fort Worth, TX: Harcourt Brace College Publishers, 1990), 12-13.

should be wary of oversimplifying our accounts of the emergence of the modern worldview, and he is probably right; significant changes in European intellectual history going back to the thirteenth century are part of the story of the development of modernity.[5] Nevertheless, there is also merit in the traditional identification of the seventeenth and eighteenth centuries as the beginning of the modern era. Dupré describes the Enlightenment as a canonizing of options which had first been opened by the first phase of the passage to modernity.[6] One of those options, which the Enlightenment canonized as a settled principle, was a turn from authority to rationality as ground for knowledge.

During the Catholic/Protestant cold war, both sides appealed to authority—of scripture or of church—to certify truth. Early modern philosophers from Descartes and Leibniz to Hume and Kant appealed rather to reason. Many saw this not only as intellectually better, since appeal to authority was akin to superstition while appeal to reason was akin to science, but also practically better, since religious appeals to authority played so easily into the hand of warmakers. It was the Europe of 1648 and after, tired out by a hundred years of religious wars, that accepted a new worldview. To be sure, the cold war continued, but it played a gradually decreasing role in international politics, and to an ever-increasing degree Europe's intellectuals looked to reason rather than authority.[7]

It is hard to generalize about such things, but we probably owe the emergence of the virtue of civility to Enlightenment modernism. With philosophers like Hume, and especially Kant, the modern worldview changed the way Europeans thought about political enemies. If reasonable people can differ, and if a person's dignity is founded on his or her reason, then even people who disagree with each other ought to be able to respect and tolerate each other. It is not a remarkable coincidence that while Kant was explaining that the categorical imperative, which was the product of reason alone, required that we treat all people as ends and not merely means, Thomas Jefferson and other American reformers were enshrining religious freedom and toleration as fundamental principles of government. It was a fundamental assumption of the Enlightenment, which Kant only made

---

5. See Dupré, Louis. *Passage to Modernity* (New Haven, CT: Yale University Press, 1993), To oversimplify, Dupré's thesis is that the Enlightenment, which is usually thought of as the beginning of the modern era, was the second of two important revolutions in thought that transformed the Medieval world into the modern world. His book charts the first, largely thirteenth century, revolution.

6. Dupré, 253.

7. It's easy to overstate and oversimplify. Medieval philosophers and theologians did not denigrate reason. But, like Aquinas, they sought to bring their theorizing under the authority of church, creed, and scripture. I take it that one mark of a modern philosopher is that he or she will not submit the products of philosophical investigation to external authority.

more explicit than most of his contemporaries, that Reason was the same for all people. Universal rationality was the modernist basis for civility.

Postmodern Prospects for Civility

We live, as the culture watchers constantly din into our ears, in a post-modern world. If Dupré is right, in one sense this is simply not true. Our culture is still working out the implications of the breakup of the ancient and medieval worldviews; in that sense we are still moderns. What the culture watchers have right is that we no longer accept some of the principles of the Enlightenment.

To illustrate: The modernist (whether of the fourteenth century, the eighteenth century or the twentieth century) believes that the *now* is a significantly new thing.[8] All modernists believe that the contingencies of time produce *fundamental* reshapings of knowledge and reality. (Ancient and medieval worldviews denied that true knowledge or reality could undergo fundamental change.) Some modernists, Enlightenment modernists, believed that changes over time exhibited progress. Some contemporary modernists, who call themselves post-modernists because they define modernism by the Enlightenment, have come to disbelieve in progress. They worry: If the human race is not progressing morally, is it really good that we are gaining more technological power? So, while all modernists (in Dupré's sense) believe that time has produced basic change, some of them have given up thinking that change is progress.

Something significant happens when our contemporaries reject principles of the Enlightenment, even if "post-modernism" may be an inappropriate description of that rejection. Now, one of the most widely proclaimed post-modernist (or anti-Enlightenment) assumptions is the rejection of universal rationality. The standards of reason, especially the standards of practical reason, which Enlightenment philosophers like Kant assumed to be universal, are labeled partial and parochial by post-modernists. Some people, who accept certain assumptions about individualism, objectivism, and self-interested rationality—that is, people with Enlightenment worldviews—will approach problems of practical reason in ways that Kant or Hume or Hobbes would recognize as rational. But other people do not think that way. So "rationality" means different things to different peoples, say the post-modernists.

This post-modern rejection of universal reason is surely right. Alasdair MacIntyre, in *Whose Justice? Which Rationality?*, persuades me that even in the West we have several different traditions of practical reason, competing for our allegiance.[9] Autonomous reason, a capitalized "Reason" that stands

---

8. Cf. Dupré, 145.

alone independent of historically conditioned reasoners, does not exist unless in the mind of God.

So the Enlightenment assumption of universal rationality is undermined. Post-modernists find they no longer believe in it. What happens to civility in these conditions?

For an Enlightenment modernist, a political opponent can be assumed to be a reasonable person. The political opponent can be appealed to on grounds of good evidence or clear reasoning. The political opponent, a reasonable person, is worthy of respect, even if disagreements persist between competing parties. The implications of Kant's categorical imperative are quite clear: We can work to defeat our political opponents—in a sense, they are obstacles to be overcome, means to our ends—but we may never treat political opponents as *merely* obstacles. We must always treat them as ends in themselves. Even further, since our worst political opponents are rational seekers of truth, they are actually our allies. Through vigorous debate, seekers pursue the truth together.

But post-modernists need not believe this. The post-modernist does not assume that all people are "reasonable." Rather, some people are reasonable in one way, while others are reasonable in another way, and still others are reasonable in still other ways—and the various kinds of rationality may be incommensurable and irreconcilable. There is no way to appeal to all political enemies on the grounds of evidence (they may not see the evidence as relevant) or good reasons (they may reject the assumptions behind the reasons). Therefore there is no compelling need to treat political enemies with respect. After all, some political enemies are most easily dealt with summarily: we see them just as obstacles. There is no independent standard of rationality which would require us to treat them as more than obstacles.

Some post-modernists, like Richard Rorty, still urge civility and other liberal values. But he does not urge this on the basis of some truth about the universe or ourselves. Rather, this is just the way liberal people happen to feel.[10]

I suspect—this is where I pull out my crystal ball and predict—that we shall soon hear from post-modern voices that do not urge civility. Like Nietzsche, they will call us to a bracing acceptance of our "thisness": "I am this, and I want that. My political enemy is that which stands between me and the fulfillment of my desire." From a subjectivist point of view, the enemy is and can be nothing more than an obstacle. And there is no objective point of view (objectivity is another Enlightenment concept deconstructed by post-modernists) to correct the subjectivist's point of view.

---

9. MacIntyre, Alasdair. *Whose Justice? Which Rationality?* (Notre Dame, IN: University of Notre Dame Press, 1988), Cf. pp. 1-11 for an initial statement of his position, which is argued at length throughout the book.

In short, I predict dark days ahead for civility. As we know it, civility is largely the gift of Enlightenment assumptions that we no longer make. Those who feel like it, or whose historically contingent way of exercising practical reason recommends it, will continue to treat their political opponents well and train themselves in the virtues that motivate such behavior. But as people come to recognize their feelings in this regard and the ways they have learned to think about this matter as pure historical accidents, they will have little defense against the temptations of incivility.

Solid Ground for Civility

All of this suggests an historical irony, given the history of civility outlined above. Though Christians of the modern era have learned to regard civility as a virtue through the influence of Enlightenment modernism, it is Christian doctrine, not modernist philosophy, which provides a sufficient foundation for civility.

This may seem surprising. After all, according to my brief account of reformation disputes, it was the Christian assumption that true doctrine had great importance that lay behind a logic of intolerance. "Since we have the truth, the heretic must be made to see that it is the truth." Right?

Wrong. The assumption that truth exists is not the problem. We need further assumptions to create the logic of intolerance. First, we need to think that we have the right formulation of the truth. Second, we assume that we gain our right formulation of the truth independently of the thought of those who disagree with us. Third, we believe that the truth is itself compatible with intolerance. A "fallibilist" rejects the first two of these assumptions; that is, a fallibilist will always keep alive in her mind the possibility that she is wrong, and she will believe that opposing views are useful in the pursuit of truth. Some philosophers have suggested that fallibilism is, or is part of, the cure for intolerance.[11] It may be that we should be fallibilists about our political positions and many other beliefs we hold. However, rather than dipping into that debate, I want to take issue with the third assumption just mentioned.

---

10. Rorty, Richard. *Contingency, Irony and Solidarity* (Cambridge: Cambridge University Press, 1989), Cf. p. 189: "...a belief can still regulate action, can still be thought worth dying for, among people who are quite aware that this belief is caused by nothing deeper than contingent historical circumstance." And pp. 197-98: "There is no *neutral*, noncircular way to defend the liberal's claim that cruelty is the worst thing we do, any more than there is a neutral way to back up Nietzsche's assertion that this claim expressed a resentful, slavish attitude. ... We cannot look back behind the processes of socialization which convinced us twentieth-century liberals of the validity of this claim and appeal to something which is more "real" or less ephemeral that the historical contingencies which brought those processes into existence. *We have to start from where we are... .*"

Most parties to reformation disputes, and many political groups in the generations since, have assumed that truth is compatible with the forcible suppression of error. They have thought that truth is so important that error must be suppressed. But what if the content of truth was itself incompatible with incivility? If that were the case, it would be possible for a person to hold a truth with absolute certainty, and believe that opposing views are useless in the pursuit of truth, and still have good reasons for being civil.[12]

My belief is that truth is incompatible with intolerance or incivility. The proper grounds for civility are not to be found in fallibilism, but in the truth itself. It is not because I am uncertain of the doctrines I espouse that I listen attentively to those who disagree with me, but because of the content of those doctrines.

What truth or doctrines could I be referring to? Just this, the heart of Christianity: Jesus Christ died for sinners, that is, for his enemies.

Christian dogma teaches us that we, who made ourselves God's enemies, are the objects of his love. His love overcame that emnity and made us his friends, through the cross. Jesus' words, expressed on the cross about the particular soldiers who crucified him, express his attitude toward all his enemies: "Father, forgive them, for they don't know what they're doing" (Luke 23:34).

Christian truth requires civility in at least three ways. 1. Because God, in Christ, loved his enemies, Christians have no option but to try to love their enemies. Christ is our example. 2. Further, Jesus explicitly told his followers to love their enemies. Christ is our lawgiver. 3. Further still, as the light of the world, Jesus is the light in every person. We should look for the light of Christ in everyone, including our enemies. Christ is our *logos* of civility.[13]

---

11. Cf. Quinn, Philip L. "Political Liberalisms and Their Exclusions of the Religious," the Presidential Address delivered at the 93rd Annual Central Division Meeting of the American Philosophical Association, in *Proceedings and Addresses of the American Philosophical Association*, Vol. 69, No. 2, 47. Quinn agrees with other writers who think that fallibilism ought not to be a requirement of discourse in the public square, since such a requirement would exclude certain religious traditions, which explicitly reject fallibilism, from joining in political debate.

In this regard it is helpful to remember the form of fallibilism of the dissenting puritans in the Westminster Assembly, who helped move English society from the religious wars of the sixteenth century to the *Act of Toleration* in 1689. Although the Dissenters did not carry the day during the Westminster Assembly, they argued that differences of opinion among Christians were due to the weakness of human apprehension of the truth, and that differences of opinion could lead to fuller apprehension of the truth. Thus, the Dissenters' position anticipated that of fallibilists. Cf. Koivisto, Rex. *One Lord, One Faith: A Theology for Cross-Denominational Renewal* (Wheaton, IL: Victor Books/SP Publications, Inc. 1993), 98-101.

12. These comments should not be construed as meaning that I reject fallibilism. The point is that one need not be a fallibilist to have good grounds for civility. We don't have to convert people to fallibilism to convert them to civility.

Part of the irony, of course, is that though Christians have always had perfectly good reasons to treat their enemies well, they failed to do so and had to learn civility from Enlightenment philosophers. This was not just because Christians failed to live up to their understanding of the gospel, but because they partly failed to understand the gospel. Part of the Quaker mission in history, it seems to me, has been to help correct that misunderstanding. Quakers, who understand that the light of Christ is present in others, even enemies, can help other Christians to see that civility is a virtue.

If my earlier prediction comes true, we will hear Nietzsche-like postmodern voices that forthrightly reject civility. I hope my prediction does not come true; it would be better to live in a culture that honors civility than to be an accurate forecaster. But even if some around us find that they no longer have reasons to be civil, Christians should not be deterred from training themselves in this virtue. We want to be like Christ; we want to obey his commands; and we want to recognize Christ in all people, including our political opponents.

In conclusion, a small correction to my definition of civility should be made. I defined civility as a character trait (or traits) which moves one to treat enemies well. As it stands, that definition is act oriented, as if right actions were of first importance and virtues consisted in propensities to carry out right actions. I don't think that is the way we should understand the relationship of actions and virtues, but it is hard to express the intertwined nature of doing and being without extending this essay far too much. Perhaps it is enough to say that Christians ought to strive to *be* civil as much as they ought to act civilly.[14]

---

13. Readers might compare this idea—that Christ is the *logos* of our civility—to Arthur Roberts' paper, "Good and Evil in a World Threatened by Nuclear Omnicide: A Proposed Epistemological Paradigm." The paradigm he proposes posits rational, sensory, and intuitive modes of apprehending truth, modes which different individuals combine in varying ways. Such a model reinforces for us the need to listen to others. Other people, even political opponents, can teach us something of the *logos*, the center toward which we must move if we want to progress morally, intellectually or esthetically.

14. Thanks to Paul Anderson for his helpful comments on an earlier version of this paper.

Arthur O. Roberts: A Select Bibliography

Books and Monographs:

An Appeal for Concurrent Action. Richmond, IN: Indiana Yearly Meeting, 1969.

The Association of Evangelical Friends: A Story of Quaker Renewal in the Twentieth Century. Newberg, OR: Barclay Press, 1975.

Back to Square One. Newberg, OR: Barclay Press, 1990.

Drawn By the Light: Autobiographical Reflections. Newberg, OR: Barclay Press, 1993.

Early Quaker Writings, 1650-1700, edited with Hugh Barbour. Grand Rapids: Eerdmans, 1973.

George Fox's Concept of the Church. Boston University Graduate School Ph.D. dissertation, 1954.

The Intellectual Substance of the Educated Christian: Some Contributions of Philosophy to its Prophetic Function. St. Paul, MN: Christian College Consortium, 1984. (Consortium Monograph)

Listen to the Lord: A Collection of Poems. Newberg, OR: Barclay Press, 1974.

The Message of Friends for "Such a Time as This": The Story of the Second American Conference of Evangelical Friends held June 21-25, 1950. Wichita, KS: University Friends Church, 1950.

Messengers of God: The Sensuous Side of Spirituality. Newberg, OR: Barclay Press, 1996.

Move Over Elijah: Sermons in Poetry and Prose. Newberg, OR: Barclay Press, 1967.

The People Called Quakers. Portland, OR: Barclay Press, 1959.

Sunrise and Shadow: A Collection of Poems. Newberg, OR: Barclay Press, 1985.

Through Flaming Sword: A Spiritual Biography of George Fox. Portland, OR: Barclay Press, 1959.

Tomorrow is Growing Old: Stories of the Quakers in Alaska. Newberg, OR: Barclay Press, 1978.

Weeds Among the Wheat: A Quaker Approach to Christian Relevance. Indianapolis: John Woolman Press, 1965. (Shrewsbury Lecture series, 1965)

Contributions to Books:

"Foreword" in Dean Freiday, *Speaking as a Friend,* Newberg, OR: Barclay Press, 1995.

"Jesus is Lord: Reflections on a Theology of Righteousness," and "Toward the Third Millenium (Keep Quaker Vision Alive)" in *Practiced in the Presence.* D. Neil Snarr and Daniel L. Smith-Christopher, eds. Richmond, IN: Friends United Press, 1994, pp. 133-146, 207-213.

"Introduction" in *J. Walter Malone: The Autobiography of an Evangelical Quaker,* John W. Oliver, ed. University Press, 1993.

"Foreword" in *The Sense of the Meeting: The Editorial Writings of Jack L. Willcuts,* Susan Willcuts Kendall, ed. Newberg, OR: Barclay Press, 1992.

"John Frederick Hanson," in *The Lamb's War: Quaker Essays to Honor Hugh Barbour.* Michael L. Birkel and John W. Newman, eds. Richmond, IN: Earlham College Press, 1992, pp. 143-172, 292-297.

"The Hope That Inspires" in *The Day of the Lord.* Dean Freiday, ed. FWCC, 1981, pp. 22-29.

"Foreword" in Donald McNichols, *Portrait of a Quaker: Levi T. Pennington,* Newberg, OR: Barclay Press, 1980.

"Spring Storm," "A Prayer at Tree-Planting," "Touch," "Somewhere in Montana," "Master of Ceremonies," and "The Age of Metal," in *On the Edge of Truth: A Small Anthology of Poetry by Northwest Quakers.* Nancy Thomas, ed. Newberg, OR: Barclay Press, 1980, pp. 77-90.

"Evangelical Friends Alliance," in *American Quakers Today.* Edwin B. Bronner, ed. FWCC, 1966; revised as *Friends in the Americas.* Francis B. Hall, ed. Philadelphia: Friends World Committee, Section of the Americas, 1976, pp. 43-52.

"Can Wars Be Just?" in *New Call to Peacemaking: A Challenge to All Friends.* Norval Hadley, ed.; Ralph Beebe, Robert J. Rumsey, assoc. eds. Philadelphia & Plainfield, IN: The Faith and Life Movement, 1976, pp. 23-33.

Other Works to Which Contributions Were Made:

Beacon Dictionary of Theology, R. Taylor, ed. Beacon Hill, 1983.

Great Christian Leaders. Woodbridge, ed. Moody. 1987.

Handbook of Church History, Tim Downey, ed. Lion & Eerdmans, 1977/1990. (Also Fortress Press, 1995.)

Evangelical Dictionary of Theology. Walter A. Elwell, ed. Grand Rapids: Baker Book House, 1984.

Quaker Understanding of Christ and of Authority. Jones, T. Canby, ed. Philadelphia: The Faith and Life Movement, 1972.

Fruit of the Vine. Many devotional articles, varied dates.

Journal and Magazine Contributions:

"Apples of Gold," *Evangelical Friend* July/August 1994, pp. 6-7.

"Review of 'New Light on George Fox and Early Quakerism: The Making and Un-
making of a God' by Richard Bailey," *Quaker Religious Thought* 26:2, pp. 57-
59.

"Poems of Christmas Hope," *Evangelical Friend* Nov./Dec. 1991, pp. 14-15.

"Comments on 'George Fox and the Children of Light' by Jonathan Fryer, and
'George Fox and the Quakers' by Cecil W. Sharman," *Quaker Religious
Thought* 25:2, pp. 67-69.

"Christ the Key to Mystery," *Evangelical Friend* March/April 1990, pp. 13-16.

"A Cherished Sentinel," *Evangelical Friend* July/Aug. 1990, p. 17.

"On Becoming a Christian," *Evangelical Friend* Sept./Oct. 1990, pp. 16-17.

"Jesus is Lord: Reflections on a Theology of Righteousness," *Evangelical Friend* Nov./
Dec. 1990, pp. 2-3, 17-19.

"A Response: Mark Hatfield on the Christian and Politics," *Quaker Religious Thought*
24:3 (Summer 1990), pp. 31-36.

"A Tribute to Our Friend Jack," *Evangelical Friend* Nov./Dec. 1989, pp. 2-3, 16.

"Paths Toward a Quaker Future," *Evangelical Friend* Nov. 1986, pp. 13-16. (Appeared
conjointly in *Quaker Life*, Oct. 1986 and in *Friends Journal*, Feb. 1987.)

"Spiritual Disciplines: Confession," *Evangelical Friend* April 1985, pp. 6-7.

"Queries for the Quaker Campus," *Evangelical Friend* Nov. 1984, p. 4.

"Argument Over the Ram," (poem) *Sojourners* 12 No. 10:30 (N 1983).

"Thoughts on Ministry," *Evangelical Friend* March 1982, p. 2-4, 27.

"A Visit to China," *Evangelical Friend* Dec. 1981, p. 6-8.

"Chasing After Naaman," (poem) *Evangelical Friend* March 1980, p. 10.

"On Being a Yearly Meeting Representative," *Evangelical Friend* April 1979, p. 9.

"The Prospering of Truth," *Evangelical Friend* May 1979, pp. 2-4, 28.

"Comments on 'Early Quaker Ecclesiology,'" *Quaker Religious Thought* 18:1 (Autumn
1978), pp. 39-42.

"Triennial Meeting of FWCC," *Evangelical Friend* 10:3 (November 1976), p. 10.

"Holding Fast To What is Good," *Evangelical Friend* 9:6 (February 1976), pp. 10-13.

"Follow Peace," *Evangelical Friend* 1:6 (Feb. 1968), pp. 6-7.

"Holiness and Christian Renewal," *Quaker Religious Thought* 9:1 (Spring 1967), pp. 4-
20.

"Comments on 'Christ as Servant as Motivation to Quaker Service,'" *Quaker Religious
Thought* 5:2 (Autumn 1963), pp. 40-44.

"Early Friends and the Work of Christ," *Quaker Religious Thought* 3:1 (Spring 1961),
pp. 10-20.

Other Journals to Which Contributions Were Made:

Almanar (Arabic Journal)

The Banner

Canadian Journal of Northern Studies

Christianity Today

Christian Scholars Review

Eternity

Faculty Dialogue

Fides et Historia

Friends Journal

Friends Quarterly (London)

Kwekeren (Norway)

Quaker History

Quaker Life

Lectures, Sermons, Speeches, and Other Presentations:

"Friends and the Broader Christian Movement." Quaker Theological Discussion Group, George Fox College, Newberg, OR, 1996.

"Recovering the Church." Wilmington Yearly Meeting, 1995, and Berkeley Friends Church, 1996.

"Use of Media in Restoration England." Quaker Historians and Archivists, Guilford College, 1994.

"Education as an Adventure in Hope." Friends Association of Higher Education, Earlham College, 1993.

"To Give You a Hope and a Future," a Centennial Sermon, Reedwood Friends Church, Portland, OR, 1993.

"A New Call to Holiness." Malone College, 1991.

"Toward the Third Millennium." George Fox College Baccalaureate address, 1991.

"Back to Square One: Turning Losses into Spiritual Gain." Sermons presented at Friends Adult Fellowship Camp, Twin Rocks, OR, 1989.

"Right Standing." Carey Memorial Lecture, Baltimore Yearly Meeting, 1988.

"The Automobile as Icon: Autobiographical Reflections." George Fox College Faculty Lecture, Fall 1986.

"Good and Evil in a Nuclear Age." International Philosophers for the Prevention of Nuclear Omnicide. Moscow, USSR, 1986.

"The Poet as Ombudsman for the Universal." International Philosophers for the Prevention of Nuclear Omnicide. St. Louis, 1986.

"Quaker Poets" (videorecording). Newberg, OR: George Fox College Television Center, 1983.

"The Christian and the State." A forum held at George Fox College with Governor Mark O. Hatfield, moderated by Professor Arthur O. Roberts, 1963.

"Judgment and the Meaning of History." George Fox College Faculty Lecture, Fall, 1956.

Other Groups and Institutions to Which Presentations Were Made:

American Academy of Religion, regional meetings

The Christian College Consortium

Earlham School of Religion

Fuller Theological Seminary

George Fox College: Chapel Addresses; Curriculum for Management of Human Resources

Malone College

Quaker Theological Discussion Group

Quaker Groups and Yearly Meetings: Alaska, Australia, Baltimore, Denmark, Finland, Friends World Committee for Consultation, Indiana, Iowa, Mid-America, New York, New Zealand, North Carolina, North Pacific, Northwest, Norway, Rocky Mountain, Southwest, Spain, Sweden

Southern Oregon University

Warner Pacific College

Whittier College

William Penn College

Woodbrooke (England)

XIV Congress History of Religions (Winnipeg, 1980)

Musicals:

Roberts, Arthur O. and David Howard. "Emmaus Road." 1994.

Roberts, Arthur O. and Dave Miller. "Jonah ben Amittai." 1986.

Roberts, Arthur O. and Dave Miller. "Children of the Light: A Christian Musical." (Newberg, OR: A. Roberts, 1983).

Editorial Service:

Quaker Religious Thought, editor, 1989-Present.

Faith and Practice, Northwest Yearly Meeting, 1987 edition.

Alaska Quaker Documents, (microfilm) 1977.

John Frederick Hanson Papers, (microfilm).

Concern, a publication of the Association of Evangelical Friends, editor 1959-67.

Pacifica Theologica, co-editor with Jack Willcuts, 1944-47.

The Crescent, student newspaper of George Fox College, editor, 1942-43.

Contributors

Paul N. Anderson, Associate Professor of Biblical and Quaker Studies, George Fox University; Associate Editor of *Quaker Religious Thought* and former editor of *Evangelical Friend*

> "Arthur Roberts has been a deeply significant mentor and encourager to me over the last two decades. I first met him in Canton, Ohio, while in college, and upon my describing my sense of call to Christian service he said, 'Make your contribution among Friends, Paul; you're needed there.' Later, I read his works on Quakerism and have come to labor alongside him as a teacher, writer and editor—but his formative influence on my life continues."

Rebecca Thomas Ankeny, Professor of Writing and Literature, George Fox University

> "I first encountered Arthur Roberts as the minister who performed my sister's wedding. He surprised my father by having a McCarthy for President sticker on his car. As an undergraduate, I took Introduction to Philosophy, History and Doctrine of Friends, and Contemporary Religious Thought from him. He exemplified the teacher/scholar to me. ... I studied Christian feminists under his guidance and made the acquaintance of Stephen Grellet through his journal. He broadened my mind without destroying my faith. Arthur Roberts always emphasized substance over showmanship, and some of what I learned from/through/because of him has permanently changed the way I think."

Hugh Barbour, Professor of Church History at Earlham College and School of Religion, 1953-91

> "Arthur and I collaborated in editing *Early Quaker Writings* (1973), first asked for by Oxford University Press. When their series was cancelled, Arthur arranged for our book's publication by William B. Eerdmans. To many of us Eastern Friends he speaks for the warmth and integrity of Evangelical Quakerism."

Gayle Beebe, Associate Professor of Pastoral Theology; Director, Friends Center, Azusa Pacific University

> "It was through Arthur that the whole philosophical and theological worlds were opened up to me. Many of the ideas and concerns initially encountered while studying with Dr. Roberts (1977-1981) continue to occupy my academic interests today. He was and is a splendid teacher, thinker, mentor and friend."

Ralph Beebe, Professor of History, George Fox University

> "Arthur was my teacher in 1953-54, his first as a GFC prof, my last as a GFC student, in History of Christianity. Since then he has been a good friend and mentor, and was a great encouragement in my decision to prepare for and return to GFC."

Irv A. Brendlinger, Professor of Church History and Theology, George Fox University

> "Arthur and I served together at Reedwood Friends Church as 'pastoral team resource persons,' preaching and working with the team. We also worked together in the Center for Christian Studies (CCS) at Reedwood, both in teaching and in directing the program. I have greatly appreciated Arthur's deeply spiritual and thoughtfully Quaker influence in the church and the academy and personally in my own life."

Edwin B. Bronner, Professor of History and Curator of Quaker Collection, emeritus, Haverford College

> "Arthur Roberts and I became acquainted through our mutual involvement in Friends Association of Higher Education and Friends World Committee for Consultation. He reached out to the wider Quaker community, and I have admired him for this and have responded to him. When I edited *American Quakers Today* in 1966, for the 1967 Friends World Conference, I turned to Arthur to write the chapter about the Evangelical Friends Alliance."

Gary K. Fawver, Associate Professor of Outdoor Ministries, George Fox University; founding director of Tilikum: Center for Retreats and Outdoor Ministries, 1971-1990

> "In the mid-1970s Arthur and I shared leadership at Tilikum of several week-long courses in Contemporary Religious Thought. These were experiments in community living/learning. What first drew me to this erudite philosophy professor was my sense of his connectedness with the earth, garnered as we walked around the lake, split firewood, and picked and prepared fruit for the drier. From his wool wardrobe, his hand-crafted wood treasures, his love of the ocean, to his recently completed book on the senses, Arthur remains a friend who models love for God's creations."

Lon Fendall, Vice President of Academic Affairs, Tabor College (Hillsboro, Kansas)

> "Arthur was my advisor at George Fox College. Arthur and Fern have continued to be great encouragers and role models to Raelene and me."

Dean Freiday, Member, Manasquan (New Jersey) Friends Meeting (New York Yearly Meeting); editor of *Barclay's Apology in Modern English* (1967); author of *Speaking as a Friend* (Barclay Press, 1995)

> "Everett Cattell in 1963 and Arthur O. Roberts in 1965 gave the annual Shrewsbury (NJ) Meeting Lectures. Edmund Goerke designed this pioneer series to open dialogue among the Quaker varieties. However, it was not until the ten years when Arthur and I both served on the Faith and Life Panel established after the 1970 St. Louis Conference that we became fast friends. It was a special bonus when he agreed to relieve me as editor of *Quaker Religious Thought*."

Michael P. Graves, Chair, School of Communication Studies, Regent University (Virginia Beach, Virginia)

> "Arthur is my former dean and colleague at George Fox College, and perpetual mentor and friend. Habitually, I stand on his shoulders in order to catch a better glimpse of both the fleeting and permanent."

Mark O. Hatfield, Senior Senator from Oregon, United States Senate

> "I have known Arthur Roberts since the 1960s, largely through his work at George Fox College. I have come to appreciate his leadership there, the creativity and thoughtfulness of his writing, and his active interest in public affairs."

Tom Head, Associate Professor of Economics, George Fox University

> "Arthur has been my colleague at George Fox College since 1971 and, on or off-campus, a mentor and friend. Inspired and instructed by Arthur's work and counsel, I have been involved with Friends broadly, including active roles in the Friends Association for Higher Education, the American Friends Service Committee and the Quaker United Nations Office. I am currently involved in a writing project on the economics of John Woolman, whom Arthur first introduced to me."

Ed Higgins, Quaker poet; Professor of English, George Fox University

> "From Arthur I long ago learned the stewardship mandate of planting at least one tree a year. And I have learned many more things about the journey from him."

T. Canby Jones, Professor of Religion and Philosophy (emeritus), Wilmington College (Ohio)

> "I first met Arthur and Fern Roberts on a visit to Everett, Washington Friends Church in 1948, when Arthur was pastor there. When working on his Ph.D. at Boston University and I on mine at Yale, Arthur came to visit. We have been brothers in the Spirit ever since. He has twice invited me to speak at George Fox College, and we have worked together in the Quaker Theological Discussion Group. He became my close friend in more ways than one as my roommate on a three-week Quaker study tour of the Philippines and the People's Republic of China in 1981."

James D. LeShana, Associate Pastor, Rose Drive Friends Church (Yorba Linda, California); Ph.D. Candidate in History at the University of California, Riverside

> "I have known of Arthur since I was a young boy when my family first moved to Newberg. When I was in high school, Arthur accepted graciously my invitation to speak to Jr. Highers at Twin Rocks Friends Camp. He made an impression on me by demonstrating a love and enthusiasm for his topic (the history of Quakerism) as well as for the young Friends with whom he spoke. I still remember his first lecture my freshman year at George Fox College. Arthur's example and commitment to the Friends Church, evangelicalism, and scholarship have greatly influenced my life."

Howard R. Macy, Professor of Religion and Biblical Studies, George Fox University

> "As his student at George Fox College (1962-1966), Arthur's integrity, perceptiveness, creativity, and range shaped me deeply. His silence often taught me as much as his speaking. In the years since, Arthur has continued to be a faithful mentor and friend, especially in offering, under concern, timely words of guidance and encouragement."

Charles Mylander, General Superintendent of Friends Church, Southwest Yearly Meeting

> "I was a student of Dr. Roberts at George Fox College, 1962-1964."

Lee Nash, Herbert Hoover Professor of History, George Fox University

> "Asked to join the George Fox College ministry twenty-some years ago, I did an advance colleague quality check by reading some faculty books. The prophetic creativity of Arthur's *Through Flaming Sword: A Spiritual Biography of George Fox* beckoned me hither. Then came the best part of this bibliophilic decision—friendship with the author."

T. Vail Palmer, Jr., Clerk, Center for Christian Studies Board, Reedwood Friends Church (Portland, Oregon). Retired; formerly taught at Kentucky Wesleyan College and Rio Grande College (Ohio); edited *Quaker Religious Thought*

> "Arthur has been a long-time colleague in the Quaker Theological Discussion Group. More recently we worked together in guiding Reedwood's Center for Christian Studies."

John Punshon, Professor of Quaker Studies, Earlham College and Earlham School of Religion

> "I have learned much from Arthur, both through his writings and through personal contact. I stayed with him and Fern on my very first trip to the United States and I have treasured his friendship ever since."

Philip D. Smith, Assistant Professor of Philosophy, George Fox University

> "Arthur Roberts was my first college philosophy teacher. I think of him as my wisest philosophy teacher, perhaps because I also took Bible, Church History and Religion courses from him. Later, Arthur encouraged me to pursue college teaching and helped open the door for an adjunct instructor who was just

returning to graduate school. For wisdom and encouragement, both shared generously, I thank him."

Daniel L. Smith-Christopher, Associate Professor of Theology (Old Testament), Loyola Marymount University

"I have discovered to my delight that one is never a *former* student of Arthur Roberts. His wisdom, so often spiced with provocative insight and a subtle wit, continues to guide us toward a renewed future for Friends. I am very pleased to be a part of honoring the intellectual and spiritual guidance of Arthur Roberts in my own life and in the lives of many others. Thank you, Professor!"

Nancy Thomas, Friends missionary and writer, currently a graduate student at Fuller Theological Seminary

"Since I first sat under Arthur Roberts' teaching as a sophomore at George Fox College (1964), he has greatly influenced my life. Arthur has been to me mentor, encourager, fellow-poet, advocate, colleague, and friend."